Tradition and Change

The Development of Conservative Judaism

EDITED BY

RABBI MORDECAI WAXMAN

THE RABBINICAL ASSEMBLY

THE UNITED SYNAGOGUE OF CONSERVATIVE JUDAISM

©1958, by

RABBINICAL ASSEMBLY OF AMERICA

——

Library of Congress Catalogue Card Number: 54-8409

ISBN: 0-8381-3116-6

Paperback Printing 1994

PRINTED IN THE UNITED STATES OF AMERICA

CONTENTS

Contents

Contents

Contents

PREFACE

The principles of Conservative Judaism set forth in the first edition of this book continue to dominate the Conservative Movement thirty-five years later, but the context in which they function has changed sufficiently so that it would be desirable to examine how these principles should be applied today and in the future.

One change of context is that both American Orthodoxy and American Reform have been affected by Conservative Judaism. Thus, Orthodoxy, with the exception of the recently arrived Hasidic right wing, has become Americanized, employing conservative patterns in language, in communication, in organization, and markedly in accepting the role and program of the synagogue as a Jewish center. Reform has embraced patterns and principles which it had eschewed, including Zionism, the Hebrew language, and *Bar* and *Bat Mitzvah*, and has even opened the door to the acceptance of *kashrut* as a Jewish value.

The result of this movement towards the center by Reform and Orthodoxy might have been to develop the "*Minhag* America" (a distinctive American Judaism) which had been sought in the nineteenth century. Thirty-five years ago, Jewish religious pluralism was both recognized and seemed acceptable. This possibility has been thwarted by the introduction of new factors which promote separation rather than unification.

In essence, these factors reflect a heightened sense of partisanship in the various Jewish religious movements, born out of the tendency of both Orthodox and Reform Judaism to adopt extreme positions. American Orthodoxy, profoundly affected by the arrival on these shores of Hasidic groups and of elements of the Lithuanian Yeshivah outlook, has become more fundamentalist and increasingly rejects a pluralistic approach. Reform Judaism has sought to cope with the increasing and very high rate of intermarriage by adopting ever more permissive positions. Thus, almost fifty percent of the Reform rabbinate officiate at intermarriages; conversion, without halakhic process is normative; and, finally, the idea that Jewish identity may be derived from either father or mother, rather than the mother alone, is now accepted policy in the Reform Movement. Since both Orthodox and Conservative Judaism reject these Reform practices, the question of "who is a Jew" is likely to loom larger as time goes on and the separation between movements is likely to increase. The situation has been further exacerbated by the rigorous attitude of the Israel Orthodox rabbinate, which enjoys a monopolistic role in the Jewish state, and by the recurrent attempt of the religious parties to legislate the "who is a Jew" issue.

Preface

Despite these developments, the Conservative Movement has clung strongly to the principle that it is the interest of *K'lal Yisrael* ("Catholic Israel") which must be served and that the things which unite Jews, rather than the things which separate them, must be emphasized. It has often done so at the expense of its own interests and it has frequently been unsuccessful. It may well be that this central principle of Conservative Judaism must be reexamined in the light of the developments of the past thirty-five years. There may be an equal need to examine the question of whether Conservative Judaism is really operating as a united movement rather that as a group of organizations loosely united by a common ideology.

One notable change which is already taking place is the shift in emphasis within Conservative Judaism from sociology to theology. This is mandated by the fact that the major peoplehood cause which claimed our attention and concern through most of the twentieth century has been largely achieved. The establishment and security of Israel, the rescue of repressed Jewries, the combatting of anti-Semitism are battles which have been waged and are, essentially, won. The increasing rate of intermarriage has made it clear that dedication to these causes is not enough to retain the loyalty of a new generation of Jews, many of whom are converts or children of converts. The questions of the meaning of Judaism as a faith, a culture and a way of life are now the central issues which we have to confront and, so, Conservative Judaism and the other movements are all engaged in theological speculation to an unprecedented degree.

The foundations of Conservative Judaism are set forth in this volume. They are, essentially, still the music to which we march because they represent a distillation of the principles of Judaism developed over long centuries and because they reflect a conscious and conscientious attempt to cope with changing circumstances. But the tradition is called upon to face a world in which change is a constant factor. Our generation has experienced an unprecedented and unexpected revolution in Jewish life and experience and expectation. Thus the tension between "Tradition and Change" requires reexamination and restatement and pointing of new directions periodically. This will be the subject of another volume. But, if the challenge is great, the need and the opportunity to establish Conservative Judaism as the dominant force in modern Jewish life is greater still.

Rabbi Mordecai Waxman
5754/1994

FOREWORD

A collection of writings on Conservative Judaism has long been needed. Unfortunately, such writings have been few and fragmentary and have been inaccessible to most people interested in the subject. This volume is intended to make some of the relevant statements on the subject available.

The first problem that had to be faced in assembling this collection was the nature of the material. The Conservative movement has issued few formal statements; there are very few books which purport to state the philosophy and attitudes of the movement. The Conservative movement seems rather to have relied largely on its synagogues and institutions to represent its point of view by their actions and their programs. Over the course of the years, however, a considerable number of articles and speeches on Conservative Judaism have been published. These are, inevitably, fragmentary and overlapping. However, they represent the form in which the ideas of Conservative Judaism have been presented to the Jewish public. I, therefore, elected to extract these articles and statements from their nesting places in periodicals and in the publications of the Conservative movement and present them in their original form. Speeches are thus rendered as speeches and articles as articles.

The second problem involved in assembling this material was a principle of selection. I acted upon the principle of including statements by men who are recognized as representative figures in the Conservative movement or pronouncements by bodies, such as the Law Committee of the Rabbinical Assembly, which are entitled to speak for the movement. I sought, also, to reflect the major divergences of opinion within the movement.

There is a considerable body of excellent writing on Jewish

themes by leading figures in the Conservative movement and by distinguished scholars of the Seminary. Most of this work, however, does not, in my opinion, reflect the viewpoint of Conservative Judaism and I have, therefore, omitted it from this volume. I have also acted upon the assumption that the real history of the Conservative movement was acted out upon the American scene, beginning with the end of the nineteenth century and, as a consequence, I have been content to represent German Jewish thought through one article by Zacharias Frankel and earlier American developments through some statements of Isaac Leeser.

Most of the selections in this volume are drawn from publications which bear the copyright of the Rabbinical Assembly, the United Synagogue of America and the Jewish Theological Seminary. For permission to use the selections by Milton Steinberg and Robert Gordis, I am indebted respectively to Bobbs-Merrill Publishing Co. and Behrman House. Some of the selections appeared originally in the pages of *The American Hebrew* and in pamphlet form.

The problem of transliteration of Hebrew words and titles was a major one. Different patterns of transliteration were in vogue, for example in the 1880's, from those which prevail today. Several different patterns, with varying claims to technical accuracy, are being currently employed. Certain terms, titles and names enjoy a conventional transliteration which does not accord with the technical forms. Very frequently, writers varied their transliteration of the same words from sentence to sentence. In view of these complications, I have acted on the assumption that the transliteration in the body of an article should largely be left alone, so long as it is not too difficult for the modern eye and ear to make out its intent. I have, however, attempted to make the transliterations within any given article consistent with one another.

In preparing this volume I have been acting for the Rabbinical Assembly. I am deeply indebted to Dr. Ira Eisenstein who, as president of the Rabbinical Assembly, suggested the project and appointed me to execute it. I am grateful as well to Rabbi Wolfe Kelman, Executive Vice-President of the Rabbinical Assembly, for his consideration, to my wife, Ruth Waxman, for her aid and advice, and to Dr. Maurice Jacobs, for his unending patience and for his great competence.

M. W.

Introduction

Conservative Judaism—A Survey

CONSERVATIVE JUDAISM—A SURVEY

By Rabbi Mordecai Waxman

Conservative Judaism is perhaps the most misunderstood term in current Jewish life. The movement which it represents commands a considerable following among the Jews of America, but it has not succeeded in achieving a universally accepted definition. At the moment it us under attack by the Orthodox as a deviation from "true" Judaism, is regarded by many Reform Jews as indistinguishable from Orthodoxy and is being subjected, from within its own ranks, to a demand for clarification and definition of its position. Outside the United States and Canada it is virtually unknown and, where known, misunderstood. The average Jew in Israel or the British Empire, for example, either has never heard of it or identifies it very vaguely with Reform Judaism.

This combination of vagueness of definition and non-acceptance outside the United States and Canada, has led to the characterization of the Conservative movement as a body of sentiment occupying a position somewhere between the Orthodox and Reform movements and as a product of the American scene not suitable for export. It has led some to study the Conservative movement in almost exclusively sociological terms and has led others to deny that it is a movement or has any ideology. All these contentions have partial merit but they are far from the whole truth and they do little justice to the inner dynamism which has animated the Conservative movement since its beginning. It is the contention of this article that there is a clearly defined Conservative movement, that it has an ideology, and that it is considerably more than the product of American sociological forces. To make these points it will be necessary to examine the Conservative movement in terms of the background against which it has operated and against which it continues to impinge, the principles which dominate it, the organizational structure which it has evolved, the internal politics which shape it and the effect that it has had upon Jewish life.

I. THE BACKGROUND OF THE CONSERVATIVE MOVEMENT

The scene against which Conservative Judaism has acted out its role in Jewish life consists both of background and foreground. In the background is Judaism itself, as it flowered through the ages with and without its adjectives. It is a truism that each generation stands on the shoulders of its predecessors. Equally in the background are the thinking and researches of the German Jewish School of Jewish historical research and, perhaps, as some have contended, the national cultural thinking of Aḥad Ha'am. In this same background is the general tone of American life with its highly pragmatic and practical philosophy.

The foreground, and more immediate factors, are the religious divisions in the American Jewish community at the turn of the century and the character of the American Jewish population at that time and in the intervening years up to the present. While it would be incorrect to characterize Conservative Judaism as an American philosophy, these last two factors are nevertheless intimately related to it and must be considered in their turn.

A. *Religious Divisions*

At the turn of the century, American Jewry was divided into parts. There was a Reform movement which had begun to grow about the middle of the nineteenth century under the joint influence of the German movement and the exigencies of the American scene. By the latter part of the century it had its rabbinical school, its congregational organization, its rabbinical organization and a clearly articulated body of principles. By the turn of the century it had departed far from Jewish practice, the Hebrew language, the national sentiment and even the Jewish calendar. Many Reform congregations held their services only on Sunday, almost all observed one day of the holidays, and such Jewish practices as the dietary laws had been contemptuously characterized by Isaac Mayer Wise as "Kitchen Judaism." The emphasis was placed upon a non-legalistic ethical Judaism to the virtual exclusion and derogation of any of its other aspects. While the traditional Jewish emphases were thus minimized, the imitation of Protestant forms of worship and organization were maximized. By the beginning of the twentieth century, Reform Judaism was the best organized Jewish religious body in the United States and was endowed with a Protestant flavor.

The other major Jewish religious grouping was Eastern-European Orthodoxy. It comprised the largest group of Jews — and an observant group — and its growth paralleled their arrival en masse upon the American scene, beginning with the 1880's. It was numerous and poorly organized on the national scene, albeit over-organized or subdivided locally. Its characteristic flavor was not only Jewish, but East-European Jewish and its characteristic language was Yiddish, to the virtual exclusion of English. Indeed, it represented an attempt to transplant the East-European community entire to the streets of New York and Chicago.

Attention should also be called to a numerous but non-religious segment of American Jewry. By 1900 it consisted of organized secular groups including the Yiddishists, the workers' groups and the like which were devoted to certain aspects of Jewish culture or to Jewish social ideals, but looked with hostility upon Jewish religion and institutions. It was this group in this period that produced the Yom Kippur Eve balls and the open flouting of Jewish religious patterns which even Lincoln Steffens and other non-Jewish observers have noted.

The smallest group of all were those synagogues which had several generations of tradition on the American scene behind them, and were thus as old or older than the Reform congregations in the American environment, but had rejected the Reform movement. They continued to pursue their way, conscious of their rooting in the American scene, and thus differentiated from East-European Orthodoxy, but equally conscious of the traditional patterns of Judaism, and thus distinguished from Reform.

At the turn of the century several things were clear. East European Orthodoxy was numerically superior but the organized Reform movement was in a position to sweep the boards. As East-European immigrants began to be Americanized, they moved out of their spiritual environment. The only paths open to them were an extreme Reform movement and a secularism either with or without a Jewish viewpoint. While little could be done by religious leaders to combat the rising secularism, a great deal could be done to fill the yawning center which existed between the East-European Orthodoxy and the extreme Reform and thus to provide a spiritual haven for the increasing number of Jews who were at home in neither.

Into this vacuum stepped the leaders of the older American congregations which had retained a traditional bent. It must be confessed that they backed onto the stage, rather than bounding, hero-like, to front and center. There had been too many fits and starts during which these leaders and congregations had attempted to deal with the nascent Reform movement in the '60's and '70's and '80's and had sought to moderate its tendencies. The congregations of Marcus Jastrow and Frederick De Sola Mendes had been part of the Reform Union of American Hebrew Congregations and had then withdrawn. Sabato Morais had been one of the examiners for Hebrew Union College. Benjamin Szold was a moderate reformer. However, by the 1880's it was obvious that the Reform movement was proceeding to even more extreme steps and that it was prepared to repudiate many of the long traditions of Judaism. The final jolt was provided by the Reform Pittsburgh Platform of 1885 in which Jewish law, save for its moral elements, was rejected and it was held that "we consider ourselves no longer a nation but a religious community and therefore expect neither a return to Palestine . . . . nor the restoration of any of the laws concerning a Jewish state."

The Reform position could readily have been anticipated. It was an extension of theories and declarations which had been clearly articulated in Germany and of the thinking of Isaac Mayer Wise and others who had raised their voices to call for a Minhag Amerika (American Rite). It could be combatted with good grace and without hesitation by the new East-European Orthodox group who saw it as totally out of consonance with the conditions of life which had prevailed in their native heath and which they had sought to transplant to America. The leaders of the older American traditional congregations, however, were caught in a dilemma. The members of their own congregations exhibited a steadily declining knowledge of Hebrew, a lessening amount of observance, had western conceptions of decorum and aesthetics and were profoundly influenced by the ideals and behavior of general American society. Some of these congregations had already adjusted to the environment by issuing special editions of the prayerbook with English translations, by introducing sermons and prayers in English, and even by seating men and women together and introducing the organ into the service. They needed a theory of their own which would harmonize tradition and change.

They found this theory in the ideas of the Historical School, articulated by Zacharias Frankel and his contemporaries in Germany, that Judaism was a changing and developing entity which through the ages had recognized the temper of the times and changing conditions and had adjusted to them without sacrificing its own integrity. In Isaac Leeser, Sabato Morais, Alexander Kohut and others this doctrine had found its spokesmen on the American scene. Although they did little to elaborate the theory, they pointed out that Judaism historically was both mobile and static, that it must in measure adjust to the spirit of the time and in measure resist it, and that a conclusive factor in all judgements must be a sensibility to the history, needs and unity of the Jewish people.

Armed with a theory which had been explored in polemics over more than a decade, dedicated to a traditional view of Judaism and goaded by the Pittsburgh Platform, the leaders of traditional congregations at length moved to action. In 1887 they organized the Jewish Theological Seminary of America in New York to give expression to their idea.

The constitution of the Seminary Association set forth their moderate goals.

"The purpose of this Association being the preservation in America of the knowledge and practice of historical Judaism, as ordained in the law of Moses and expounded by the Prophets and Sages of Israel in Biblical and Talmudical writings, it proposes, in furtherance of its general aim, the following specific objects:

1. The establishment and maintenance of a Jewish Theological Seminary for the training of Rabbis and teachers.

2. The attainment of such cognate purposes as may upon occasion be deemed appropriate."

In this action and in this institution Conservative Judaism found its formal expression. The goal, however, it may be observed, was not to found a new party in Judaism. On the contrary, Morais who presided over the Seminary, and H. Pereira Mendes and Alexander Kohut who taught there and the laymen who cooperated with them had severely limited objectives. They were out to counter Reform in the name of tradition. They had no quarrel with Orthodoxy. Indeed, Morais had suggested that the institution be called the Orthodox Seminary. Mendes, in his turn, sought to align the avowedly Orthodox element with it by taking the lead in organizing a union of Orthodox congregations. While these efforts proved fruitless and Orthodoxy rejected the Seminary and went on to organize the Rabbi Isaac Elchanan Yeshiva in 1896, the institution and its protagonists continued to regard themselves as representatives of traditional Judaism. Both the early leaders and the subsequent presidents of the Seminary, Solomon Schechter and Cyrus Adler, avowed again and again that they were not seeking to create a new wing in Judaism but rather to provide a rallying point for traditional Judaism. Even when Schechter organized the United Synagogue in 1913 to join together the congregations affiliated with the Seminary, he insisted that he was merely providing a medium for uniting American Jewry.

The object of the Seminary was thus not to found a new party, but to train certain types of men for the rabbinate and for the teaching profession. It was in consonance with the old proverb that "if you want a crop in a year, plant corn; in ten years, plant trees; in one hundred years, plant men." The founders of the Seminary obviously felt that an institution which stood for traditional Judaism would be a counter-balance to the only other rabbinical seminary, the Hebrew Union College of the Reform movement. And they felt, too, that its American trained and oriented students would, once they had entered into the rabbinate, halt the tendency to the Reform movement.

This aspiration proved to be correct. The movement towards

Reform Judaism was halted. However, contrary to the expectations and wishes of the founders and leaders of the Seminary, this success was achieved, not by uniting American Israel under one banner but by creating a new party in religious Judaism, the Conservative movement. In some measure this unanticipated result was due to a second major background factor, the character of the American Jewish population.

B. *The Character of the American Jewish Population*

The late Professor Alexander Marx used to characterize Jewish history since 1800 as current events. In the sense that many of the problems which came to the fore in Jewish life with the advent of modern times have continued to remain on the agenda and to be unresolved, and that cause and effect in these areas have continued to exist side by side, this is an accurate appraisal. It is nowhere better illustrated than in the relation between the patterns of the Jewish community and the Jewish religion.

The modern era confronted Jewry and Judaism with a series of challenges which they had not met in the same measure in their earlier history. Scientific thought, the nineteenth century doctrine of progress, the intensification of nationalism, the emergence of the Jew from ghettos, the prospect of civil, political and social equality, the availability and the need for general education changed the character of Jewish life. Shmaryah Levin, the Zionist leader, pointed this up by an anecdote. He had approached Jacob Schiff to seek to interest him in the Zionist cause. He appealed to him as a Jew. Schiff responded. "Dr. Levin, I am three men in one. I am an American, a German and a Jew." Levin's reply had philosophical overtones. "Mr. Schiff, which way are you divided, horizontally or vertically?"

The anecdote makes clear that the modern era turned people who used to be wholly Jewish in thought, action and emotion into divided men. This, in turn, had the effect of making Judaism more self-conscious than it had ever been since the middle ages. In that period, Maimonides had undertaken to meet the intellectual threat posed by Aristotelianism to Judaism by harmonizing the two. Jehudah ha-Levi had undertaken a defense and glorification of his faith as against Christianity and Islam. Jews had often been forced into polemics on the relative merits of Judaism and Christianity. Challenge had led to response. In the intervening centuries the challenges had been few and Judaism had not really needed to re-examine itself. In the modern period, the challenges grew to gigantic proportions. The conventional Jewish pattern was called into question and a self-conscious re-evaluation was necessary. This came earlier to the Jews of Western Europe; it came later to the Jews of Eastern Europe; it came to many only after they had migrated to America or England. But it came at length to all of them. And the point must be made that it does not belong to the past. It is current events. It continues to impinge upon them.

The three movements in modern Jewish religion are all products of this self-conscious Judaism which was compelled to re-assess itself to meet the needs of the divided Jew. This is obviously true of Reform and Conservative Judaism. But it is equally true of the western brand of Orthodoxy which called itself Neo-Orthodoxy in Germany and calls itself Modern Orthodox or Traditional in America. Here too self-examination, justification, rationalization, the confrontation of scientific thought and the acceptance of the divided Jew as a fact were evidenced in the writings of Samson Raphael Hirsch and others.

The impact of the challenges of the modern era was even greater for the several million Jews who had assembled in the United States by the early years of the twentieth century. In addition to the challenges already enumerated, they had to deal with a new environment, a new language, with economic stringency and with the great pressure to "Americanize" themselves. It was, under these circumstances, almost inevitable that Jewish education should become secondary, that the Sabbath, the dietary laws and many other observances should begin to lapse and that Jews should correlate the Americanization they coveted with de-Judaization.

This was largely true for the Jews who constituted the laity of the Reform movement in America and the Jewish religious pattern they developed — more extreme than German Reform — reflected it. In strict logic, it should have been equally true of the mass of Eastern European Jews who came to America in the late nineteenth and early twentieth centuries. The Reform Temple was the most American of Jewish religious institutions and it condoned the way of life of American Jews by asserting that the practices they were discarding were superfluous and irrelevant. However, history belies logic. It did not become universally true of Eastern European Jewish immigrants and their descendants because another factor played a role. The Reform movement came into being when American Jewry numbered perhaps 100,000 scattered Jews. The Eastern European immigration involved hundreds of thousands, mounting into several millions. It involved a mass which settled in closely packed communities. It thus offered an opportunity for the *tradition of life* which had prevailed in Eastern Europe to transfer itself to these shores. It is thanks to this *tradition of life* that Conservative Judaism found a field for operation and that Orthodoxy was enabled to continue.

Someone has observed of Jews that "they can change their noses, but they can't change their Moses." The life tradition would not be denied, even by logic. People who labored on the Sabbath could not bring themselves to discard their hats in the synagogue. Men and women who stayed away from the synagogue throughout the year wanted the *shul* they stayed away from to be a *shul* where people *davvened*. People who came to services only on the High Holidays wanted to feel a sense of warmth and belonging and to hear the cadences of Hebrew liturgy which they rarely understood, but which rang in their ears from their early youth. Men who rode on the Sabbath and had discarded the dietary laws wanted to belong to a synagogue which said that these things were important, and to have their rabbis observe them. When they faced the death of a father or mother, these same people wanted to observe mourning in a traditional way and then to gather with a *minyan* to recite the *kaddish*. With total inconsistency, people who violated the dietary laws the year around desired to be sumptuously observant on Passover. When a son was born, they wanted the services of a *mohel*, rather than a doctor, a modern up-to-date *mohel*, it is true, but a *mohel*. When their son attained the age of thirteen, they wanted him to chant a *haftorah* in a synagogue on the Sabbath, even if he had to cram it down at the last moment by rote. When marriage came, at length, to their children, they wanted the ceremony performed under a *hupah* even if it consisted only of flowers, and to stand by its side.

All these things have been stated in the past tense. They might equally well be put in the present tense. They are as true of members of Conservative congregations in 1958 as they were in 1910. None of them, analyzed individually, makes logical sense in view of the non-observance or casual observance of many Conservative Jews. But, collectively, they constitute a tradition of life, the impregnable rock upon which the movement to Reform in the early decades of the century was broken. *"A minhag brecht a din"* is an oft quoted Yiddish proverb. Custom is stronger than law, and life is stronger than logic.

The two elements of the background of the Conservative movement — the religious division in American Jewry at the turn of the century and the character of the American Jewish population help to explain the rise of Conservative Judaism. But they do not comprehend it. Its ideology and then its organization must now be examined to bring it into clearer focus.

THE IDEOLOGY OF THE CONSERVATIVE MOVEMENT

The ideology of Conservative Judaism is more a matter of emphasis than of a radically new doctrine. The religious developments and the American Jewish character, described in the preceding section, did not, in the view of the founders and later leaders of Conservative Judaism, call for more than a shift in emphasis. Reform responded to the modern era by revolutionizing Judaism and Neo-Orthodoxy, in the persons of Samson Raphael Hirsch and other less articulate defenders, called for a resistance to the spirit of the times. The Conservative leaders, more traditional than the Reform and less obdurate than the Orthodox, were disposed to heed the admonition of the sages "be as pliant as the reed and not as unyielding as the cedar." The pliancy led to new emphases. But it should be recognized that underlying them there were two firm principles.

1. The founders of Conservative Judaism had no intention of starting a new wing or denomination or party in Judaism. They did not even pretend to be modern Judaism. Their purpose and their philosophy were clearly expressed in the name they applied to themselves. They were conservative and their object was to conserve the Jewish traditions. Morais, Mendes, Kohut and their successors in official leadership, Solomon Schechter, Louis Ginzberg and Cyrus Adler, were all scrupulous in asserting that

they represented a tendency and not a party. They conceived of their role as that of presenting an organized and meaningful alternative to the Reform movement and to Hebrew Union College. When Morais suggested that the Seminary be called "The Ortho-dox Seminary" and when Mendes sought to organize the Orthodox forces and to rally them behind the Seminary, they were not playing politics. They believed that they represented traditional Judaism. And so did Schechter who, in organizing the United Synagogue in 1913, asserted that he was providing a medium for all of traditional Judaism.

The Conservative movement has always clung to the position that it is not a denomination in the Jewish fold. It holds that it *is* Judaism. It is the Jewish tradition continuing along its path in time and space with its characteristic dynamism. It is true that there are other variants of Judaism, Orthodoxy and Reform. But, then, there have always been movements to the left and right of normative Judaism. Mishnaic times resounded to the clash be-tween the Pharisees, the Sadducees, the Essenes and the early Chris-tians. Eight centuries later Jewry was reft by the conflict between Rabbinites and Karaites. Ultimately, the Pharisees and their spiritual descendants, the Rabbinites, prevailed and gave a specific tone to Judaism. Conservative Judaism sees itself as being in this tradition — a sort of twentieth century Pharisee tradition. While it recognizes that Orthodoxy and Reform play a significant role in Jewish life, it feels that Reform is a revolutionary deviation from Jewish tradition and that Orthodoxy, in stultifying the inner dynamism of Judaism, has taken itself on to a side path of Jewish life. To itself it assigns the role of being the staunch upholder of the Jewish tradition and of its inherent dynamism.

2. In making the conservation of the Jewish tradition their objective, the founders and leaders of Conservative Judaism were not blind to the pressures created by the American Jewish scene and by the modern world. They recognized that the survival of Judaism was imperilled by non-observance, by ignorance and by intellectual confusion. But they were not prepared to make these factors the determinants of what Judaism is and should be. The Conservative movement has not really been a mass phenomenon even though it has attracted the loyalty of a great number of Jews. It has sought to shape the community rather than allow the com-

munity to shape it. Its thinking and goals have been derived from the Jewish tradition rather than from doctrinaire or sociological forces. It feels that the Jewish community is malleable, that it is reclaimable and that it is, potentially at least, devoted to Judaism. The problem, as it sees it, is to state Judaism in meaningful terms, to focus attention on its essentials and to communicate these things to the Jewish public.

Starting from these underlying principles, — that the Jewish tradition must be preserved and conserved, and that American Jewry must be moulded to that end, Conservative Judaism evolved not a doctrine, but a technique. The technique consisted of emphasizing the following aspects of the Jewish tradition.

A. *Catholic Israel*

The phrase "Catholic Israel" is in its English form a nimble paradox born in the fruitful mind of Solomon Schechter. But it derives from the solid and meaningful phrase *Klal Yisrael*: — the totality of Israel. Jewish tradition has always maintained a sort of theological equation of its own whose best statement is found in the words of the medieval sage — "God, Torah and Israel are one." This formulation asserted the close relationship between faith in God and His primacy in life and history; the Torah as the means of coming close to God and His will by thought and action; and the Jewish people and its history through which the faith and the action are carried. To make the equation workable it was always necessary to recognize not only the demands of God and Torah but the needs, the ability and the situation of the Jewish people. Apparently this harmony was maintained rather successfully in Jewish history. In the modern era, however, it came to grief.

Reform Judaism in the early 20th century virtually eliminated the Torah as it had developed through the Jewish ages. It rejected many of the legal elements of the Five Books of Moses and it denied the relevance and validity of Talmudic law and thought and the codes which stemmed from it. Samuel Adler, one of the leaders of American Reform, put the matter quite clearly when, in a Passover sermon, he said "We are like the Israelites at the Red

Sea. Let us strike the sea of Talmudism with the staff of reason and, splitting it, pass through to the other side." Even as it rejected Talmudism, so did Reform spurn the Jewish people, the national element of the equation. It denied that a national senti-ment existed, it extirpated the hope for a return to Zion from its prayer-book. It thus reduced the equation to one element — God and an ethical religion.

Orthodoxy distorted the formula in its own way. God and the Torah remained primary in its equation. The Torah, indeed, was accepted in all its jots and tittles as it had been developed in inter-pretation through the years and as it was formulated in the 16th century code of Joseph Karo and in the 16th century commentary of Moses Isserles. The Jewish people, however, received shorter shrift. Some elements of Orthodoxy were bitterly opposed to Zionism and some minor groups still remain so, despite the exist-ence of the State of Israel. The real distortion, however, appeared in the refusal to recognize the needs, the history and the sociological condition of the Jewish people as a factor to be reckoned with. Orthodoxy upheld the claims of the Torah irrespective of the needs of "Catholic Israel."

The Conservative position has been that the balance in the equation must be restored. It eagerly accepts God and Torah as the fundamentals of Judaism. But it asserts that the national sentiment which is part of Judaism must be acknowledged and so, Conservative Judaism has gone hand in hand with Zionism since its inception. It equally asserts that the needs and the state of the Jewish people must be taken into account and so it has been con-cerned to face the current facts in Jewish life. English readings in the service, for example, is not a principle of Conservative Judaism but rather a realistic recognition that most Jews do not under-stand Hebrew and many do not read it. The retention of Hebrew in the service and the concentration upon it in the Conservative religious school, on the other hand, come out of the recognition that the Hebrew language is a cardinal binding force in Jewish life and a major element in Jewish history. Thus the Jewish need is at once recognized and the national principle and historical outlook are maintained.

B. *Positive-Historical Judaism*

The natural complement to concern with Catholic Israel is attention to the historical past of Israel. The Conservative movement has recognized the fact that every generation is "an omnibus in whom all . . . (its) ancestors ride." And so it has sought enlightenment for the perplexities of its day in the historical experience of Israel. Three attitudes have emerged from this emphasis.

A study of Jewish history has first of all made clear that each generation has builded on the past. No generation starts *de novo.* Judaism has been a historical growth which has sustained the Jewish people and has been sustained by it. It was because Reform Judaism was deficient in this sense of history, as applied to the Hebrew language, that Zacharias Frankel abandoned its Frankfort conference in 1845. In abandoning it he proclaimed the doctrine of positive historical Judaism. Still later it received elaboration at the hands of others, including Zunz, Graetz and Schechter.

As a cardinal emphasis of Conservative Judaism it means respect for the Jewish past and a discernment of its guiding principles. Chief among them is that, as Saadyah long ago pointed out, "Israel is a nation only by virtue of the Torah." Respect for the historical character of Judaism, therefore, means respect for the religious-legal system which has been developed as the means of preserving and effectuating Judaism.

However, historical Judaism means something more. It involves a recognition of the fact that Judaism has changed through the ages and with this it involves an understanding of why and how it has changed.

Conservative Judaism calls attention to the fact that Judaism through the ages has manifested an inner dynamism. It has proved able to adapt itself to changing conditions — to move from a faith and a way of life based upon a physical fatherland to one which found its home in a "portable fatherland" (the Torah); to move from land to land, from age to age and to remain contemporaneous. This is the fact of change. The reason is to be found in the internal dynamism of Judaism interacting with the external circumstances. The masters of Judaism did not and could not ignore the winds of circumstances and doctrines which swirled about them. When

Judah the Patriarch found that his contemporaries were not observing the interdiction on the "oil of gentiles," he caused it to be
revoked. When Maimonides found that philosophic doctrine constituted a threat to Judaism, he composed his "Guide for the
Perplexed." The Jewish world reflected this propensity for change
in accord with circumstances in other ways. While the essential
forms remained the same, many customs of the Oriental Jews
differed from those of the East European Jewry and many of the
prescriptions of the codes are accompanied by the statement "In
this we follow the custom prevailing in our land."

Conservative Judaism, being historically aware, thus confronts
the need for combining reverence of the past with the fact that
Judaism has changed. The third element that rises out of historical
awareness is the manner in which change has been effected in
Jewish life. And here it becomes quite obvious that the tradition
has changed not by revolution but by evolution. It has itself
provided the mechanism for legal change and interpretation and
so has grown in the face of the exigencies of life even as the common
law or American Constitution has grown. A notable example of
this is afforded by the Talmud, which is, as a whole, the cardinal
example of the Jewish tradition being interpreted and expanded.
The dispersion of the Jewish people inevitably led to the problem
of what status to accord Jewish civil and criminal law when they
were in conflict with the law of the land in which Jews resided.
The problem is resolved in the Talmudic formula "the law of the
land is law." Thus Talmudic law showed its capacity for modifying
itself, even to the point of self-limitations, within the framework
of the law.

These three elements taken together constitute the historical
approach to Judaism which the Conservative movement has
adopted. It holds that the religious legal tradition must be held in
reverence, but that the need for changes and adjustments must be
recognized when they become pressing, and it believes that the
legal tradition of Judaism itself provides the remedy if we allow
it to be implemented. An example of the application of these
principles was recently afforded by the modified marriage contract
(*ketubah*) adopted by the Rabbinical Assembly. The Assembly
confronted the fact that it was often difficult for women who

desired a Jewish divorce to secure one. The difficulty arose out of the refusal of the divorced or divorcing husband to grant the divorce as Jewish law requires. The Reform approach, which is to assert that there is no need for a Jewish divorce, is untraditional. The Orthodox stand that the matter should be left unresolved makes Judaism unlivable. The Conservative approach was to examine the alternatives available in Jewish law. The simplest remedy — to empower a court to grant the divorce when the husband declined — was held to be out of consonance with the structure of Jewish law. The alternative which was adopted was to make an addition to the marriage contract in which both bride and groom agreed to hold themselves bound in the event of divorce by the decisions of a court which was set up by the Assembly. This action was taken by the Rabbinical Assembly joined together with the faculty of the Seminary. Thus a felt need was recognized, the tradition was approached reverentially and a solution in harmony with the spirit of the tradition was worked out.

C. *Vertical Democracy*

A third emphasis in Conservative Judaism and complementary to the ideas of Catholic Israel and Historical Judaism, is the idea of vertical democracy in Jewish life and thought. The underlying notion has not been formulated in this phrase, but it is implicit in the outlook of the movement. Horizontal democracy implies majority rule and looks for its majority to those who vote or are represented at any given time. It operates upon the principle that no system is enforceable or viable unless it receives the consent of at least the majority of the participants. To some extent the Reform movement has been guided in its thinking by this concept. In point of fact, this is questionable doctrine whether applied to a nation or a religion. Even democratic nations are not guided in their fundamental policies by the whims of the moment. Behind the democracy of Great Britain stand the English tradition and a mass of custom and the loose but powerful English constitution; American democracy must inevitably confront the constitution of the United States and answer the question of how would Lincoln or Washington have reacted to this proposal. Religious communities are even less susceptible to the majority rule of the moment.

They start with presuppositions which cannot be debated or rejected. The existence of God and His relation to man does not depend upon a majority vote. The festivals, the holy days and much of the service are beyond the reach of majority voting at any given time since they represent the accumulation of the centuries.

The Conservative movement has tacitly recognized that even in an age which desires democracy in its institutions, the concept of democracy must be refined. Vertical democracy is a recognition that it is not only the present generation which has a voice in ongoing institutions. The past and the future must be allowed an equal vote. Thus, in evaluating Judaism in the present, we are constrained to let all the weight of past decisions play upon our own thinking and we are impelled so to treat Judaism that it will live on for future generations.

This frame of mind which would carefully balance the past and future with the present, has led the Conservative movement to be scrupulous in seeking to maintain the traditional patterns of Judaism, to be cautious in appraising the need for change, to be meticulous in making necessary changes and to seek to create institutions and a frame of mind from which a stronger Judaism might grow. Thus, the Conservative synagogue initially offered the Sunday school pattern as an alternative to the several times a week Hebrew school. But, being aware that inadequate Jewish education was creating too great a gulf from the Jewish past and was incapable of developing a knowledgeable and traditionally rooted Judaism in the future, it has called for the discontinuation of the Sunday School and concentration upon the Hebrew School.

D. *Modern Thought*

In according a voice to the past and in making its center of gravity the traditional pattern of Judaism, the Conservative movement is by no means prepared to ignore modern thinking. On the contrary, one of its principle emphases is that Judaism must be able to confront modern thought and research and assimilate it or harmonize it with itself, or disprove it. This has meant in practice that Biblical criticism, archeological and historical studies, the scientific emphasis of the modern age, the changing political and economic philosophies and the various philosophies of the twentieth century, ranging from pragmatism to existentialism and to neo-mysticism, have all found a receptive ear in the Conservative movement. It has, of course, not issued any formal statement which harmonizes these patterns of thought with Judaism. There is rather a general mood of awareness that the developments of modern thought must be taken into consideration. In many respects this is achieved operationally by the individual rabbi. In some areas, individuals like Mordecai Kaplan and Abraham Heschel have presented their views in books which receive an attentive hearing, though not necessarily acceptance, in the Conservative movement. In some fields, the Seminary, through its Institute of Social and Religious Studies and its publications, has brought Jewish and general thought to bear upon specific problems.

The emphasis is all important in this area. In the Conservative movement it is felt that Judaism should be enriched but not dissipated by modern thought.

E. *Authority and Interpretation*

The emphases described above are all meaningless unless they are accompanied by a further development, and that is a willingness to recognize that the principles of authority and interpretation which have secured to Judaism its inner dynamism apply to our own day. Reform has asserted the right of interpretation but it has rejected the authority of the legal tradition. Orthodoxy has clung fast to the principle of authority, but has in our own and recent generations rejected the right to any but minor interpretations. The Conservative view is that both are necessary for a living Judaism. Accordingly, Conservative Judaism holds itself bound by the Jewish legal tradition, but asserts the right of its rabbinical body, acting as a whole, to interpret and to apply Jewish law.

While this principle has, for most of the life of the Conservative movement, been honored more in theory than in practice, it remains a fundamental outlook and in the last few years it has begun to be implemented. The most notable instance of it is the recently adopted modification in the marriage contract (*ketubah*). But many minor examples may be adduced from the decisions of the Law Committee of the Rabbinical Assembly.

F. *Controlled Experimentation*

The bent for interpretation of Jewish law and practice has also manifested itself in another way. Certain practices have grown up in Conservative congregations which are not the product of formal decisions, but rather the outgrowth of practice. Thus, men and women are seated together at services, prayers in English are included in worship, the High Holiday ritual has been somewhat abridged, the priestly benediction by laymen has been eliminated. These are all products of the philosophy that within tacitly recognized, but undefined limits, Conservative congregations may experiment in finding more effective forms for presenting Judaism. Some of these experiments have succeeded and have been generally adopted. Others have been attempted and abandoned. In this category the Sunday school as the alternative to the mid-week Hebrew school deserves further notice. It was adopted as a response to the time pressures of American life. It was recognized as inadequate and it has already been rejected by the movement as a whole and by the majority of its congregations.

Such experimentation could readily get out of hand. The element of control lies in the fact that there is an undefined but generally sensed set of standards in the Conservative movement and its congregations. The guarantee that these standards will be maintained is that discretion in these matters lies in the hands of the rabbi, and the rabbi, in turn, is a member of a limited group of some six to seven hundred, most of whom are graduates of one institution and all of whom are members of the Rabbinical Assembly. In so small a group which is organized to maintain its own standard of behavior and attitude, it is possible to create a general feeling of what is done and what is not done and to enforce it.

G. *The Theory of Leadership*

The final question in any outlook or movement is what is it supposed to achieve in practical terms and how is it going to do so. All outlooks must have a theoretical foundation. This is equally true in the realms of science or religion. But the theory is of interest only to the professional or interested layman. It achieves meaning for the mass of people only when it is applied.

In the case of Conservative Judaism, this application involves its goal and the means that it takes to secure it. The means is the organizational structure which it has developed and which will be discussed in the next section. The goal is, very simply, to win the Jewish population to Judaism.

The goal is not as self-evident as it appears. In twentieth century America, two meaningful approaches to Judaism are possible. One is to make the attitudes and the behavior of the Jewish community the basis of thinking. The other is to start with the Jewish tradition, distinguish between its essential and peripheral elements, modify the peripheral, if necessary, and attempt to persuade the community to accept the result. This, of course, presupposes an elite group which will select and communicate.

Conservative Judaism has adopted the second alternative. It has already been suggested that it is not a mass movement despite its numbers. Its one million members have not made or basically affected the thinking or the emphases of the movement. They are, rather, a response to the ideas proposed and implemented by the rabbinic leaders of the movement over the last fifty years. The aims and the intellectual orientation of Conservative Judaism have been provided by a kind of elite which sought to mold the community without itself being molded.

This is not merely fortuitous. It is a basic policy which is much in consonance with the traditional theory of authority in Jewish life. It stems out of a belief that the form and character of Judaism are properly the concern of those who are both learned and interested. This has meant, in practice, in Conservative Judaism, that laymen have been discouraged and debarred from dealing with the ideology and basic policies. It has also involved a particularly high concentration of influence and policy determination in the Seminary and its scholars as against congregational rabbis. It has made it possible for the more traditional elements in the individual congregations to exercise a greater control over synagogue patterns than they would be entitled to by their numbers. It has made it possible to debate policies in a partial vacuum, ignoring the behavior and attitudes of the laity of the Conservative movement. This may seem an unrealistic pattern, but it is actually psychologically sound. In the area of religion, people do not expect to set beliefs and patterns; they rather expect to be guided in them. The Conservative movement has successfully operated on the assumption that if guidance were forthcoming and if it were properly communicated in an idiom that people understand, it would be accepted.

The means by which it has sought to achieve these ends are the subject of the next section.

THE ORGANIZATIONAL STRUCTURE OF THE CONSERVATIVE MOVEMENT

Conservative Judaism started as a tendency among a small group of men and congregations who believed that their desire to preserve traditional Judaism was shared by many other Jews. The very act of clarifying the tendency produced a series of emphases which collectively made up an ideology. The inevitable third step was an organizational structure to communicate the outlook.

No idea which finds an organizational housing can remain unaffected. At some point the claims of the organization and the power structure built up within it begin to impinge upon the idea. This is equally true in secular and religious organizations, in political parties and in religious bodies; in the British Labor party, for example, coming to governmental power and in the Catholic Church. It has been equally true in Conservative Judaism. The demonstration of it is to be found in terminology itself. Until well on into the 1930's the leaders of Conservative Judaism continued to characterize it as a tendency. In more recent years it has been increasingly referred to as a movement. As a result, it will be necessary to consider the organizational structure of Conservative Judaism in two phases, its earlier form and its current form.

The first organization produced by Conservative Judaism was the Seminary. Organized in 1887, it had a rather stumbling existence for fifteen years and was then reorganized and redirected. Solomon Schechter was called from England to head it and a group of eminent Jews, many of them from Reform congregations, undertook to provide for its support.

The Seminary was organized for the training of rabbis and teachers in pursuit of the aim of the founding association to preserve traditional Judaism. Morais, Schechter and Cyrus Adler, the successive presidents of the Seminary until the late 1930's, continued to avow this policy. They saw the salvation of traditional Judaism as dependent upon rabbis and teachers grounded in, and sympathetic to, the tradition, and capable, at the same time, of communicating with the American Jew. Their most notable contributions were the creation of a specific type of rabbinic personality and the furtherance of the movement for modern Hebrew education.

The educational approach with which the Seminary and its offshoot, the Teachers Institute, cooperated, or which they produced, had far reaching significance. It led to the organization of Bureaus of Jewish Education, and of Hebrew schools with a modern approach and a Hebrew and Zionist emphasis. While many of the schools fostered by the Bureaus were community schools rather than branches of the Conservative congregations, they were in approach and emphasis close to the Conservative outlook. Out of them came many of the members of Conservative congregations, some Conservative rabbis and teachers and a goodly number of people who have a positive approach to Jewish education. Other schools, of course, grew up under the aegis of Conservative congregations and, naturally, shared their outlook.

The most necessary function of the Seminary, however, was the creation of a type of rabbi who could organize the community to adherence to Conservative Judaism. The problem was complicated by the fact that such a rabbi must appeal equally to first, second and third generations of Jews of East-European origins. Solomon Schechter has been reported as observing, in a private conversation, that a rabbi henceforth would have to understand and play baseball in order to function effectively in an American congregation. Actually, the Conservative rabbi had to be a sort of ecclesiastical department store. He was expected to be young and baseball minded in order to appeal to the youth, to be a hail-fellow-well-met so that he might appeal to the middle-aged, learned and at home in traditional modes so that he might satisfy the older and more orthodox groups. He was expected to be an administrator handling a broad program, to double as a teacher or principal, to preach in English but with a Jewish flavor, to create and experiment with new patterns of communication, to figure in the community and to be a pastor. He was to be approachable, but to maintain his dignity, to be tolerant of his congregation's failure to observe Jewish law and practice, but to reprimand them light-handedly and himself remain personally observant. On the face of it a rabbinical chameleon was demanded. But in reality, granted that a rabbi received extensive Jewish and general training before he entered the Seminary, granted the program at the Seminary, and granted that a man was capable of learning from experience, the necessary rabbinical type could be produced and, for the last fifty years or so, it has been produced.

The second organization to emerge in Conservative Judaism was a natural outgrowth of the first. Once rabbis were graduated, they formed an alumni association which was known as the Rabbinical Assembly. While at first it was confined to graduates of the Seminary it came, in time, to include other rabbis, some Reform, some Orthodox, some from abroad, who associated themselves with the aims of Conservative Judaism. In its early stages, the Rabbinical Assembly was an alumni association in character and action. But as its membership increased, it began to acquire an independent character, based upon the problems its members encountered and upon the necessity for clarifying and propagating their outlook. In consequence law committees, prayer-book committees and the like were formed. And in consequence, too, the aims and outlook, the approach and the experiments of Conservative Judaism began to be debated. As membership increased and as experience mounted, differences of viewpoint began to manifest themselves and to appear more frequently in the proceedings of the Assembly.

In 1913 the United Synagogue was called into being by Solomon Schechter. It was conceived as a means of rallying all American congregations into a common association. This was an aim which the Reform Union of American Hebrew Congregations had espoused some decades earlier. Like the Reform Union, the United Synagogue failed to achieve this objective and emerged instead as an organization of congregations identified with Conservative Judaism. While its aims were high, its organization was weak and its budget was small. In its early years it undertook to publish some prayer-books and did little else. Its effective power was limited, so that the anomaly was developed whereby some congregations with Orthodox rabbis were affiliated with the United Synagogue and other congregations with Conservative rabbis were not affiliated, and many congregations which were affiliated did not pay the rather nominal dues of the parent organization.

However, within the United Synagogue framework a different type of synagogue conception found housing. That type has become so universal today in all branches of Judaism that it is difficult to realize that it was an innovation of a sort. The Conservative synagogue set out to be a religious community center. In this it went further than most Reform temples and far beyond the Orthodox synagogue. Within its walls not only the synagogue organizations were to gather, but the secular bodies in the Jewish community, as well. Here the school was to meet and, even more important, the Jewish youth of the community was to find a home. Somehow, it was assumed that the youth, meeting even on a casual social basis within synagogue walls, was to be saved for Judaism by some process of osmosis. At the very least, it would be dissuaded from intermarriage by being projected into a Jewish atmosphere and Jewish contacts. Some synagogues introduced center facilities — a gymnasium and a swimming pool. Most synagogues could not afford such lavish expenditures, but they clung to the "center" notion and regarded the synagogue as more than a place of worship. Indeed the "center" was a name often applied to Conservative congregations, in distinction from "the temple" of the Reform and "the *shul*" of the Orthodox

The organizational structure developed by Conservative Judaism, it may thus be seen, was a rather loose one. Nevertheless, and in the belief of some, precisely because of its looseness, Conservative Judaism grew apace. The Seminary continued to produce rabbis and teachers, more and more congregations and rabbis identified themselves as Conservative. And both the Rabbinical Assembly and the United Synagogue continued to grow in numbers and in potential capacity. By 1940, the situation was ripe for a radical change in the character of Conservative Judaism and its organizational structure.

The change has been very marked in the Seminary which has moved increasingly from a passive to a dynamic role in Conservative Judaism and the American scene. In part this was due to a different conception of the Seminary's role which was introduced and fostered by its new president, Dr. Louis Finkelstein; in part it was due to the Seminary's need for funds; and in part it was due to the changing intellectual and spiritual climate.

The Seminary was, at that point, one of the leading institutions of Jewish learning in the world and Conservative Judaism was numerically a major force on the American Jewish scene. As the thirties passed and the forties of the century progressed, it became evident that the Jewish community of Europe and its institutions had been destroyed. Inevitably, American Jewry became the major Jewry in the world and the Seminary, gifted with an outstanding faculty and library, became the outstanding Jewish theological institution in existence.

The situation was ripe for the conception of the Seminary which Dr. Finkelstein entertained to be promulgated. He saw the Seminary as an institution capable of having a strong Judaizing influence upon the Jewish community and of making a spiritual impact upon the general American community. He accordingly moved to convert the Seminary from an institution for the training of rabbis and teachers alone, into a force. Such things as an "Eternal Light" radio program and, later, a television program emerged. They were designed to bring the Jewish teachings to a much larger audience — Jewish and non-Jewish — than the synagogues themselves could reach. The rather limited museum collection housed at the Seminary was greatly expanded in conception and materials and set up in separate quarters to secure the same result. An approach to the general intellectual community and the shaping of opinion was achieved through the Institute of Social Religious Studies and its publications and through the Conference on Religion, Science and Philosophy. The schools of the Seminary were expanded and this involved an increase in faculty personnel. It also raised the question of where future students were to be secured and this in turn led to the development of ventures in training selected youth throughout the country, in setting up summer camps and in setting up pre-theological training departments. The expanded conception of the Seminary also led to the notion of decentralization. A substantial Jewish community had grown up on the West Coast and was still in an inchoate state. An opportunity for shaping its character and orientation seemed to be available and led to the organization of a Seminary branch in Los Angeles which was called the University of Judaism.

All these projects in expansion required money. It was required, in any event, because the endowments which had hitherto maintained the Seminary had been depleted during the depression. A different approach to the problem of maintaining the Seminary was now projected. Campaigns were initiated in the congregations to secure maintenance funds annually. These have led, over the last decade, to the development of a substantial campaign staff and to the need for more and more organization of the congregations and the communities for fund-raising purposes. United Synagogue regions, staffed by directors, were set up and the unification of congregational efforts on a regional basis was inaugurated; committees proliferated. More and more laymen from the Conservative movement were drawn into regional and national activity. The composition of the Seminary Board of Trustees began to include more laymen from Conservative congregations than it had in the past and the Board of Overseers involved even more. While the United Synagogue and the Rabbinical Assembly became minor partners in the campaign proceeds, the emphasis in the campaigns was primarily on the Seminary. The Seminary was projected more and more to the fore as the major factor in Conservative Judaism, as the foremost Jewish institution in the world and as a dynamic force in American life. While all the above has been put in the past tense, it is a process that is being described rather than a past event. All these elements have been created and all these factors have come into play. The results will unquestionably be more far-reaching than they are now. What is significant is that the Seminary has achieved a new status as a dynamic force in Conservative Judaism, in the Jewish community and in the American community as a whole. Its future activities are likely to be determined by this conception of its role.

Meanwhile, the Rabbinical Assembly had been undergoing changes, as well. As membership increased, the necessity for better organization also increased. The war and the need for chaplains and for maintaining the positions of absent rabbis precipitated a situation in which the Assembly began to exercise greater control over the membership. Inexorably, this led to an executive secretary and a placement committee which began to control the availability of Rabbinical Assembly members for positions and to exert some discipline over rabbis and congregations. The process, having been initiated, is continuing, with the result that the Assembly, through its officers and committees, is moving in the direction of greater centralization and control over its members and their behavior. This process of forming a loosely knit federation into an organization has been facilitated by the availability of greater funds to the Assembly, from increased dues from the joint Seminary-United-Synagogue-Rabbinical Assembly campaign and from the proceeds of the prayer-book issued by the Assembly. It was further facilitated by the marked increase in membership in the Assembly in the last few years and by the increase of member congregations in the United Synagogue. Both new groups were predisposed to accept the idea that they were associated with a disciplined and organized body.

The most noteworthy development in the Assembly, however, has been the increasing preoccupation with Conservative ideology and with the means of clarifying it. Points of view which hitherto had been politely advanced but not pushed in accordance with the view of Lord Balfour that "A gentleman is a man who does not insist that two and two make four", now received sharper statement. Calls for implementing Conservative thinking began to be sounded and *ad hoc* blocs to push specific matters were organized and dissolved as issues arose and were dealt with. In short, ideological politics of a sort developed to supplement the personal politics which always prevail in an organization.

These internal diversities of viewpoint which had been inherent in the Conservative movement from its beginning became both clear and articulate with the publication, in 1934, of Dr. Mordecai Kaplan's book *Judaism as a Civilization*. Professor Kaplan, who was one of the early graduates of the Seminary and a force in the Rabbinical Assembly, had been Dean of the Teachers Institute of the Seminary and Professor of Homiletics and Midrash in the Rabbinical Department since 1913. He had, thus, directly influenced generations of rabbis, teachers and social workers. The viewpoint expressed in his book was formulated over the course of years and had long been foreshadowed in his articles, in his pulpit addresses in important New York synagogues, in the tone he had given to the congregations which he led, as well as in his teaching and lecturing. It was shared in full by a significant number of rabbis and laymen, and in part by a considerably larger number. With their aid, in 1935, he began to publish a magazine, *The Reconstructionist*, devoted to his point of view, and proceeded further to organize the Reconstructionist Foundation.

Dr. Kaplan's approach to the problems of Jewish life in America and to the question of Conservative Judaism was markedly pragmatic. He realistically faced the fact that there were many affirmative approaches to Jewish life in America, not all of them religious, and that there was a vast indifference and negativeness, too, which was particularly evident in the 1930's. He appraised the discrepancy between actual Jewish life and theoretical Jewish law, analytically characterized the various currents in the Conservative movement, as well as in Orthodoxy and Reform, and proposed a program of his own which he labeled Reconstructionism. This program characterized Judaism as "a dynamic religious civilization" and proceeded to define the means for implementing this conception. It was strong in logic, highly sociologically oriented, even in its theology, and rather weak in emotion.

There is no need to define the Reconstructionist position here. That is done in several of the papers in this volume. What is noteworthy from the point of view of the development of a Conservative ideology is that the efforts of Dr. Kaplan and his disciples plunged the Conservative movement into a debate on aims and means which still goes on. The effect of his books, his teachings and of the magazine was to bring the Conservative ideology under sharp examination. Simultaneously, it split the Rabbinical Assembly into ideological groups.

In the last twenty years, the Assembly has conceded that it consists of three different groups: a left, represented by the Reconstructionist group, which is relatively small but articulate and active; a right, which is smaller still, but is presumed to have the support of the Seminary faculty and so to command strong backing in matters relating to such vital questions as Jewish law; and a center group to which the overwhelming majority of the members of the Rabbinical Assembly adhere. This is a neat enough classification, but it by no means describes the actual state of affairs. The left actually commands more support than its formal numbers would lead one to suppose, and it has been responsible for a great percentage of the writing on problems confronting American Jewry and the Conservative movement. The majority of the center is in many ways a standing army waiting for a direction in which to march, and, so, on many issues it can be mustered to support a program of the left group. Furthermore, it is doubtful that there is really an effective right group. If it ever existed it has been dissolved by time. There are now a few right-wing individuals, but no group, and they exercise the role of restraining extreme action and modifying it, but have no power to initiate or control the course of action in the Assembly. Thus a picture emerges in which the left, after goading to action for a long time, finally sees action undertaken by the center, has it modified slightly by right-wing thinking, and finally sees it emerge as considerably less than it wants, but as somewhat more than the quiescent center would have been prepared to initiate itself.

Three factors have operated to create this situation.

The first and most significant is that the highly articulate Reconstructionist position has failed to create a party. The Reconstructionist group has never been sure whether it is a movement or a school of thought. In terms of a movement it is too small. In terms of a school of thought it has been markedly successful, but not under its own name. Many of the ideas which it has promulgated have been accepted by most of the members of the Rabbinical Assembly as part of their standard intellectual equipment but are not labelled Reconstructionist. Dr. Kaplan has been in an enviable position to make his outlook known to, and accepted by, the members of the Rabbinical Assembly. All of them have read his works, most of them have been his students, and almost all of them acknowledge that for many years he was almost the only member of the Seminary who was willing to confront the realities of the American scene. In a sense then, most of them are semi-Reconstructionists. But, by and large, they reject the means which the Reconstructionist group has taken to implement its outlook, such as its prayer-books, its partial de-emphasis of Jewish law and its tampering with certain rituals, practices and ceremonials.

An equally significant factor in shaping the alignments within the Rabbinical Assembly and the Conservative movement is the preeminent place now taken by Dr. Louis Finkelstein and the Seminary which he heads. This position of preeminence, so far as it affects the Rabbinical Assembly, has been buttressed by the fact that Dr. Finkelstein and several men associated with him in the active direction of the Seminary are drawn from the ranks of the Assembly in which they enjoy positions of eminence. This group might be characterized as an ideological bloc, which is at least a counterpoise to, and probably outweighs the left-wing group in the Rabbinical Assembly. Probably, by virtue of its own temperament, this group is a part of the center of the Assembly. Moreover, events have conjoined to make it inevitably centrist. Under the presidency of Dr. Finkelstein, the expanded Seminary has needed considerably greater support. It has sought it through the congregations affiliated with the Conservative movement and through the mediacy of the rabbis. The leaders of the Seminary are thus impelled, by circumstance, to occupy a position in the center of the movement from which they can legitimately and with grace appeal to all wings of the body.

A third significant factor in the shaping of ideologies within the Rabbinical Assembly is the conflict within the individual members. Many of the rabbis are willing to assent to a proposition intellectually without being able to give it emotional endorsement. Thus, at recent conventions, there has been discussion of such questions as revision of marriage and divorce laws, changes in the form and length of the services and calling women to the Torah. Strong arguments have been advanced for action in these fields, and such action would be quite in consonance with the proposition which every one in the movement accepts — that Conservative Judaism believes in change within the framework of the Jewish law. Nonetheless, a great many men have taken the position that they can say "yes" with their heads but not with their hearts, and, in a movement of this sort, consensus rather than a majority is necessary to achieve a line of action. Meanwhile, however, several techniques have been developed for dealing with legal problems. The Rabbinical Assembly has always had a Law Committee whose duty it was to pass on legal problems. In 1948 this committee was reorganized and expanded. It now includes men representing all the shades of opinion in the Rabbinical Assembly. The committee now not only passes on specific questions, but it also presents responsa to the Rabbinical Assembly on broader issues as, for example, the question of riding on the Sabbath, the use of electricity on the Sabbath, the question of calling women to the Torah. The responsa which appear before the convention of the Rabbinical Assembly frequently involve majority and minority reports. There is an understanding that where the Law Committee is not unanimous in its recommendation, the Assembly does not vote on the matter and no definitive ruling is made. Another technique for legal action is represented by the Joint Law Conference which was established some years ago. This body involves both the members of the Rabbinical Assembly and the members of the Seminary faculty and it was set up to deal with questions relating to marriage and the family. This collective body has asserted the power to make *takkanot* (enactments) in the area of marriage and family law. The first result of its efforts was the revised *ketubah* (marriage contract). Further action was left in the hands of a Joint Steering Committee. Thus there now exist two media through which the legal opinions existing in the Assembly can be translated into action. Their usefulness is limited only by the willingness or reluctance of the membership to use them.

It has been argued by those who have analyzed Conservative Judaism from the outside that the debates over law and the ideological divisions are inconsequential. They have been characterized as role-playing by the rabbis. While it is true that these debates have not notably affected the laymen in Conservative ranks, they have impinged upon the character and potentialities of the Rabbinical Assembly. In Conservative Judaism, which from its inception has been ideologically a rabbinically dominated philosophy, this can be very significant. Moreover, now that a technique has been created for the problem of law, there seems to be a disposition to recognize the legal program, not as an end but as an instrumentality. Attention is now being focused on over-all goals and a comprehensive outlook for Conservative Judaism. Furthermore, the developments described in the Rabbinical Assembly, when considered together with what has transpired in the Seminary and the United Synagogue, have led to a basic result which will be discussed below.

In the last fifteen or twenty years, the United Synagogue has also undergone radical transformation. Its membership approaches the 700 mark, its organizational apparatus and departments have expanded considerably, and its financial structure has been greatly enhanced. More important, it now commands the active participation and loyalty of a greater number of men than ever before and its creation of a regional structure and a group of regional directors has enabled it both to involve more people and to play a larger role in the activities of affiliated congregations. In short, its organizational structure and efficiency are hardening. However, it still lags considerably behind the Seminary and the Rabbinical Assembly in its capacity for independent action and for initiating events.

The result of all these organizational developments in recent years has been to change the character of Conservative Judaism. In the view of its founders, Conservative Judaism was a tendency which was designed to offer an acceptable alternative to Reform Judaism. It was hoped that it would give renewed vitality to traditional Judaism and ultimately capture the American Jewish public. For years its leaders denied that it was a party or a denomination within Judaism and sought to avoid becoming one. However, the very development of an increasingly complex organizational structure, the debates on ideology and the increasing projection of a Conservative viewpoint, have converted Conservative Judaism from a tendency into a *movement*. It is not only referred to as a movement, but it thinks and acts as a movement. Thus, the Rabbinical Assembly is now prepared to take independent action in the field of law; the Seminary relies primarily on the support of its member congregations instead of turning to the community as a whole as it once did; the United Synagogue is self-consciously an organization of Conservative congregations and has standards and theoretically, at least, exercises sanction. And at the 1957 convention of the United Synagogue a world union of Conservative congregations was organized.

This development, of course, is not due to the internal dynamics of the Conservative group alone. In the last few decades the organizational structure of Reform Judaism has continued to harden and Orthodox Judaism has become increasingly organized and increasingly inclined to characterize any group which is not of them, as against them. Perforce, Conservative Judaism has been impelled to increasing self-awareness as a movement.

THE EFFECT OF THE CONSERVATIVE MOVEMENT UPON ORTHODOXY AND REFORM

Although Conservative Judaism has, contrary to its original intention, became a movement, it has succeeded in partially achieving its original objective of conserving traditional Judaism. It may even be on the way to winning its goal of a dynamic traditional Judaism in the United States.

Conservative Judaism in its ideology and practice has long stood to the left of Orthodoxy and to the right of Reform. It is, thus, in the center of the Jewish religious triad and in this position it has prospered. Reform and Orthodoxy have meanwhile been impelled by force of circumstances to reconsider their own positions.

Reform, in its classical formulation at the turn of the century, has, to some extent, failed. In the first place, it was not completely successful in retaining the children of its members in its fold. Secondly, by the late 1930's, it had reached a stasis and had ceased to expand. Thirdly, developments in the Jewish world, such as the increasing need for a Zionist solution to the problems of European Jewry, made its anti-Zionism out of date. Moreover, its rabbinate was increasingly being recruited from traditional, East-European-originating sources.

Impelled by these circumstances, Reform began to change and proceeded, in 1937, to the stage of modifying its Pittsburgh Platform of 1885. It began to endorse Zionist activity, to reintroduce Hebrew into its schools, to reintroduce some of the ceremonials and rituals and, in general, to become more traditional. However, in the period since 1940, as the Jewish population began to shift to the suburbs, it found itself confronted with an opportunity to increase its membership. However, it had to compete for the new suburban population with the Conservative and Orthodox groups. Here it found itself face to face with an unavoidable fact. The bulk of this population, whether it had previously been affiliated or unaffiliated, came from traditional homes and had a nostalgia for many traditional forms. To capture them, Reform had to represent itself as more traditional than it had ever been. Henry IV of France, reared as a Protestant, had, when Catholic adherence was made a pre-condition of his accession to the throne of France, resolved his doubts by concluding that "Paris is worth a mass." Reform Judaism has recently, particularly on the Eastern Seaboard, often concluded that a new congregation is worth a *tallis*, *yarmulke* and Bar-Mitzvah. Once this new population was assimilated into the Reform structure, it acted as a continuing pressure group for more traditional norms. Since this tendency conformed to the thinking of many of the traditionally minded Reform rabbis, it has had a notable success. We even encounter the plea by many Reform rabbis to draw up a *Shulḥan Arukh* for the movement.

The result is that the Reform movement is today moving back to a more traditional orientation. It lacks the lucidity and clarity of its classical days. The diversity of practice within its synagogues is greater than that which exists in Conservative synagogues, and the temper, behavior and attitudes of its members are not always distinguishable from those of the members of Conservative congregations. There are few ideological Reform Jews in its ranks and even some Reform rabbis have been known to assert that their synagogue is just as traditional as a Conservative synagogue.

While this state of affairs is partly due to internal factors in the Reform movement, it is partly due, too, to the very existence of the Conservative group. By its success, the Conservative movement afforded Reform an example of the successful combination of tradition with the American scene and created a strong center in the community to which men could repair. Its very existence as an alternative compelled Reform to change in order to survive.

But a changed Reform Judaism is, after all, very close to Conservatism. The American Council for Judaism was organized to protest this and to maintain the pattern of traditional Reform. In repudiating it, the Reform movement has confirmed that it is consciously embarked upon a new direction — and that that direction is to the right, towards the Conservative position. It is unlikely, with the organizational hardening which has taken place, that Reform and Conservative can merge. But it is undeniable that the Reform Judaism of the future will be couched increasingly in the Conservative vein. Thus, so far as Reform is concerned, the founders of Conservative Judaism have succeeded in halting and reversing its bent.

Orthodoxy has gone through a similar revolution. With the virtual cessation of European immigration, it has had to recruit its membership from an American-born population and its rabbinate from men born and reared in this country. Inevitably, it has had to alter its patterns to conform to the American scene. It has begun to distinguish the American Orthodox congregations by calling them "Modern Orthodox" or "Traditional" synagogues. But these synagogues are virtually indistinguishable from the Conservative congregations and many of them share the distinguishing attributes of the Conservative synagogue, — mixed seating and English readings combined with the Hebrew, and the center conception of the synagogue.

Here, as in the case of the Reform and Conservative movements, there has been a hardening of organizational lines and, so, there is no concession that in essence the "Traditional" synagogues are Conservative. Indeed, because there is now a recognition that the very existence of a Conservative movement is a major threat to the Orthodox organizational structure, there has been in recent years a tendency to attack Conservative Judaism with violence. However, it is incontestable that the American Orthodox synagogue is moving increasingly towards the center.

While Conservative Judaism itself has become a movement rather than an all-embracing form of Judaism, the aims of its founders seem to be on the way to realization. Even if Conservative Judaism may not achieve the unity of American Israel under its own banner, the American scene seems destined to body forth a type of synagogue and a Jewish religious approach which is in substantial accord with the ideology of the founders of the movement.

Part I

The Origins of Conservative Judaism

Section 1 — The History of an Idea

A NOTE ON THE HISTORY OF AN IDEA

"Every man," said Oliver Wendell Holmes "is an omnibus in whom all of his ancestors ride." The same thing may be said of any idea. A whole history of ideas and shreds of ideas are embodied in any new conception. The real genesis of any outlook, cannot, therefore, be accurately traced and an attempt to present one must involve stringent and often arbitrary selection.

Conservative Judaism as an idea obviously stands on the shoulders of the millennial Jewish tradition. Passages could very readily have been adduced from the Talmudic writings, from Responsa and from medieval Jewish literature which agree with many of the emphases of Conservative Judaism. Selection from several of the writers of the Galician and Russian Haskalah movements might have seemed even more cogent, since they are closer to us in time, circumstances and form. The thinking of Krochmal, Zunz, Rapaport, Graetz and several other leading figures of the "Historical Judaism" school quite obviously had an effect upon the emergence of the idea of Conservative Judaism, and Ahad Ha'am may well have had a major effect, as some writers have contended, upon Conservative thought.

The approach employed here, however, has been to assume that the major role in the birth of the Conservative idea was played by those actually on the American scene. They, themselves, were frequently the communicators of ideas rather than their inventors. But the ideas, having been distilled through their personalities and through the American environment, were more applicable and acceptable than the general formulations made, for example, in Germany. Accordingly, the selections included here are taken from the writings and speeches of men who played a role, at some point in their lives, in the American Jewish community. The sole excep-

tion to this policy is Zacharias Frankel. He is generally regarded as
the intellectual progenitor of Conservative Judaism and he is
clearly the source of many of the ideas and some of the phrases
which played a significant role in the birth of the Conservative
idea and movement.

Some of the writings are undistinguished, some are unformed.
But ideas, like rivers, have many sources both great and small and
it seemed realistic to let an anthology reflect the varied types of
statements which were influential in creating the Conservative idea.

ON CHANGES IN JUDAISM

By RABBI ZACHARIAS FRANKEL

Zacharias Frankel (1801–1875), who is generally regarded as the ideological founder of the Conservative movement in Judaism, was one of the chief figures in Jewish historical-legal research in 19th century Germany. He served as rabbi in Dresden and later in Berlin and then for twenty-two years was head of the newly founded Rabbinical Seminary in Breslau. There he instructed a generation of rabbis in his own view of Judaism, which combined an emphasis upon tradition with a recognition that Judaism was facing a series of problems in his time. He looked for succor to diligent research into Jewish sources and to a recognition of the historical-growth character of Judaism. While he participated in the Frankfort Rabbinical Conference of 1845 which was summoned by the growing Reform movement, he was a vigorous opponent of Reform and contested some of its extravagances at this conference. In 1844 he initiated a monthly publication called Zeitschrift für jüdische religiöse Interessen *which continued for three years and which, in frequently polemic fashion, gave expression to his views on Judaism. The article printed below is a translation, in condensed form, of the lead article in the second volume of the* Zeitschrift *which was published in 1845, and reflects both Frankel's involved style and the tenor of his thinking.*

The purpose of the *Zeitschrift* is the reconciliation of belief and life, the assurance of progress within our faith, and the refining and regenerating of Judaism from and through itself. This is the circle in which our effort must move. Anything outside this circle ceases to be Judaism. Those to whom even this circle seems to be extensive, incline to stagnation and oppose the demands of life and its activity. For centuries Judaism has engaged in a successful struggle with the world. Through the ages Judaism has shed its

light abroad and illumined the way of many nations who even today, whether consciously or unconsciously, make use of its enlightenment. Not in vain did Judaism oppose paganism, materialism,
sensuality, and the striving after earthly things. Through many
generations Judaism sustained and guarded the sparks of divine
spirit, and in helping them to develop, developed itself. Shall we
assume that its power is now exhausted and consumed, that its
living high spirit has lost its force? Does the spirit of the age really
rise against it with might and strength?

Maintaining the integrity of Judaism simultaneously with
progress, this is the essential problem of the present. Can we
deny the difficulty of a satisfactory solution? Where is the point
where the two apparent contraries can meet? What ought to be
our point of departure in the attempt to reconcile essential Judaism and progress and what type of opposition may we expect
to encounter? How can we assure rest for the soul so that it shall
not be torn apart or be numbed by severe doubts while searching
for the warm ray of faith, and yet allot to reason its right, and
enable it to lend strength and lucidity to the religious feeling
which springs from the emotions. The opposing elements which
so seldom are in balance must be united and this is our task.

In order to find the way for uniting them, we must consider
both the starting point and the aim of the movement which seeks
this reconciliation. Even in advocating social and political change
one must think of the starting point and the goal. Usually the
former is the situation as it is, while the latter is the situation as
it should be. The aim can be arrived at by reflection and definition,
but the starting point is rooted in life relations. Both elements
must be properly understood and valued in order to determine
the chain of activity and thought which will lead from "what is"
to "what ought to be." In religious matters there is in addition
to the starting point also an inner force which must be reckoned
with and added to the mere statement of "what is." To be understood, religion must be lived and deeply felt. And if we want to
determine the measure for a discreet progress and change, we
must first of all have a clear conception of the point of departure,
namely Judaism itself. Judaism is a great historical truth and its
role in world history cannot be minimized either through mistaken
dialectical interpretation or through prejudiced polemic.

Judaism contains, at its core, the highest teachings about God, His attributes, and doctrines, about the existence of man, his goal in life and the nature of his activity. To the Jew his God is a personal and an extra-mundane Being, and yet One who is within the world; nay more, even One who lives within his heart, for whom the right name is "Father." The beautiful expression of the Bible: "You are children of your eternal God" (Deut. 14:1) was conceived by Judaism in a warm and profound sense. The loving relation between father and children became the essence of the whole complex of its faith and formed the corner and the capstone of its spiritual structure. To this fundamental thought embodied in the Scriptures in brief dry sentences, there is added an oral tradition which breathes warmth and gentleness about the relation between the Jew and his God. This tradition is filled with the awareness of God and in consequence embodies a truth the value of which cannot in any way be lessened or be made light of.

Judaism ties its teachings to divine revelation, which is an expression of the highest will of God. The eternal truths regarding the Godhead and morality flow from this source, and around these there are grouped other laws which are saturated with the same spirit, and in which the high ideas of the nobility of man and his closeness to God find expression. These revealed laws are the guardians of Judaism, the never-slumbering watchman of the holiest elements within it. They are designed to protect the highest truths and they have faithfully carried out this mission to the present day. These laws have one of two purposes. Some have the purpose within themselves, though it may not always be clearly evident in each particular law. Thus the dietary laws aim at cultivating restraint of appetite; the sexual laws at inculcating chastity and purity of morals. Other laws which mirror the power of God as the creator have another function — to remind man of God. Through their practice man is enabled to bind himself to the divine and enable the spiritual and the heavenly within him to gain victory over the earthly and the beastly in his character. It is clear that man can apprehend the highest ideas meaningfully, only by means of sense data. Ideas are not always presented or apprehended with clarity. Men cannot rise to lofty complicated ideas at will, and frequently, in the whirl of life, these ideas are entirely lost to the mass of men. Abstraction and mere contemplation are not enough. The soul must have experience of sensation and reverence; the idea must clothe itself in a body, else it is lost to man. To prevent this loss is one of the aims of the precepts. They express recognition of, and reverence for, the divine will; they themselves become spiritualized and carriers of spiritual impulses.

Again, Judaism is a religion which has a direct influence on life's activity. It is a religion of action, demanding the performance of precepts which either directly aim at ennobling man or, by reminding man of the divine, strengthen his feelings of dependence on God. And because of this trait neither pure abstract contemplation nor dark mysticism could ever strike root in Judaism. This, in turn, guaranteed that the lofty religious ideas were maintained in their purity, with the result that even today the divine light shines in Judaism.

By emphasizing religious activity, Judaism is completely tied to life and becomes the property of every individual Jew. A religion of pure ideas belongs primarily to the theologians; the masses who are not adapted to such conceptions concern themselves little with the particulars of such religions because they have little relationship to life. On the other hand, a religion of action is always present, demanding practice in activity and an expression of will, and its demands are reflected in the manifold life of the individual, with the result that the faith becomes the common property of every follower.

Thus we have reached the starting point for the consideration of the current parties in Judaism. The viewpoint of the Orthodox party is clear. It has grown up in pious activity; to it the performance of precepts is inseparable from faith, for to it, the two are closely and inwardly connected. Were it to tear itself away from observance and give up the precepts, then it would find itself estranged from its own self and feel as though plunged into an abyss. Given this viewpoint, the direction and emphasis of the Orthodox party is clear. Where else, save in the combination of faith and meticulous observance of the precepts, can it find that complete satisfaction which it has enjoyed in the heritage of the fathers? When it will reject that which it has so long kept holy and inviolable? No — that is unthinkable.

Against this party there has arisen of late another one (Reform) which finds its aim in the opposite direction. This party sees salvation in overcoming the past, in carrying progress to the limit, in rejecting religious forms and returning merely to the simple original ideas. In fact, we can hardly call it a party in Judaism, though its adherents still bear the name Jew, and are considered as such in social and political life, and do not belong to another faith. They do not, however, belong wholly to Judaism, for by limiting Judaism to some principles of faith, they place themselves partly outside the limits of Judaism.

We will now turn to a third party which has arisen from the first party, and not only stands within the bound of Judaism, but is also filled with real zeal for its preservation and endeavors to hand it over to its descendants and make it the common good of all times.

This party bases itself upon rational faith and recognizes that the task of Judaism is religious action, but it demands that this action shall not be empty of spirit and that it shall not become merely mechanical, expressing itself mainly in the form. It has also reached the view that religious activity, itself, must be brought up to a higher level through giving weight to the many meanings with which it should be endowed. Furthermore, it holds that we must omit certain unimportant actions which are not inherently connected either with the high ideas or with the religious forms delineated by the revealed laws. We must, it feels, take into consideration the opposition between faith and conditions of the time. True faith, due to its divine nature, is above time, and just as the nobler part of man is not subjected to time, so does faith rise above all time, and the word which issued from the mouth of God is rooted in eternity. But time has a force and might which must be taken account of. There is then created a dualism in which faith and time face each other, and man chooses either to live beyond time or to be subjected to it. It is in this situation that the Jew finds himself today; he cannot escape the influence of the conditions of the time and yet when the demands of faith bring him to opposition with the spirit of the time, it is hoped that he will heed its call — find the power to resist the blandishments of the times. This third party, then, declares that Judaism must be saved for all time. It affirms both the divine value and historical basis of Judaism and, therefore, believes that by introducing some changes it may achieve some agreement with the concepts and conditions of the time.

In order to have a conception of what changes should and can be introduced, we must ask ourselves the question — does Judaism allow any changes in any of its religious forms? Does it consider all of them immutable, or can they be altered? Without entering into the citation of authorities pro and con, we may point out that Judaism does indeed allow changes. The early teachers, by interpretation, changed the literal meaning of the Scriptures; later scholars that of the Mishnah, and the post-Talmudic scholars that of the Talmud. All these interpretations were not intended as idle speculation. They addressed themselves to life activities and imparted different forms to the practice of certain precepts. Thanks to such studies, Judaism achieved stabilization and avoided estrangement from the conditions of the time in various periods. Not in vain was the day declared a festival when the Pharisees overcame the Sadducees and ruled that the Biblical statement "An eye for an eye, a hand for a hand" was not to be taken literally, but was designed merely to indicate that the proper compensation should be imposed for such injury (*Megillat Taanit*, Ch. 4). This was a triumph not because of the humanitarian interpretation that it proposed, but, mainly, because it led to the establishment of the principle that the letter of the law is not decisive, but rather that the spirit must animate the law and raise it to a divine status worthy to become a norm to man who is himself endowed with spirit. The teachers of the oral law supported such interpretations in a number of cases. But on the other hand, they established a rule which was intended as a guardian and protector against undue changes. It reads as follows: That which was adopted by the entire community of Israel and was accepted by the people and became a part of its life, can not be changed by any authority (*Abodah Zarah*, 36).

In this fundamental statement there lies a living truth. Through it there speaks a profound view of Judaism which can serve for all times as a formula for needed changes and can be employed both against destructive reform and against stagnation.

This fundamental statement helps to make clear to us what changes in Judaism are justified and how they can be realized.

True, Judaism demands religious activity, but the people is not altogether mere clay to be molded by the will of theologians and scholars. In religious activities, as in those of ordinary life, it decides for itself. This right was conceded by Judaism to the people. At such times as an earlier religious ordinance was not accepted by the entire community of Israel, it was given up. Consequently, when a new ordinance was about to be enacted it was necessary to see whether it would find acceptance by the people. When the people allows certain practices to fall into disuse, then the practices cease to exist. There is in such cases no danger for faith. A people used to activity will not hurt itself and will not destroy its practices. Its own sense of religiosity warns against it. Only those practices from which it is entirely estranged and which yield it no satisfaction will be abandoned and will thus die of themselves. On the whole there is always a great fund of faith and religious activity to afford security against negation and destruction.

We have, then, reached a decisive point in regard to moderate changes, namely, that they must come from the people and that the will of the entire community must decide. Still, this rule alone may accomplish little. The whole community is a heavy unharmonious body and its will is difficult to recognize. It comes to expression only after many years. We must find a way to carry on such changes in the proper manner, and this can be done by the help of the scholars. Judaism has no priests as representatives of faith nor does it require special spiritual sanctimoniousness in its spokesmen. The power to represent it is not the share of any one family, nor does it pass from father to son. Knowledge and mastery of the law supply the sanctity, and these can be attained by everybody. In Jewish life, spiritual and intellectual ability ultimately took the place of the former priesthood which, even in early times, was limited in its function primarily to the sacrificial cult. Even in early days, Judaism recognized the will of the people as a great force and because of this recognition a great religious activity came into being. But this activity, in turn, was translated into a living force by the teachers of the people through the use of original ordinances and through interpretation of the Scriptures. At times these actions of the sages lightened the amount of observance; at times they increased it. That the results of the studies and research of the teachers found acceptance among the people proves, on the one hand, that the teachers knew the character of their time, and, on the other hand, that the people had confidence in them and that they considered them true representatives of their faith.

Should Jewish theologians and scholars of our time succeed in acquiring such a confidence, then they will attain influence with the introduction of whatever changes may be necessary. The will of the community of Israel will then find its representatives and knowledge will be its proper exercise.

The scholars thus have an important duty in order to make their work effective. It is to guard the sense of piety of the people and to raise their spirit to the height of the great ideas. For this they need the confidence of the people. Opposition to the views of the people, such as some reformers display, is unholy and fruitless. The teacher thereby loses the power to make the essence of faith effective, for in place of that confidence which is the basis in correct relations between teacher and community there comes mistrust and an unwillingness to follow. The truths of faith must be brought nearer to the people so that they may learn to understand the divine content within them and thus come to understand the spiritual nature and inner worth of the forms which embody these truths. Once the people are saturated with an awareness of the essential truths and the forms which embody them, a firm ground will have been established for adhering to Jewish practices. And if the people then cease to practice some unimportant customs and forms of observances it will not be a matter of great concern. And it will not, as recent changes have, lead some Jews into shock and hopelessness. They will no longer see all such changes as leading to the disappearance of our faith and spelling, as their pusillanimity leads them to believe, the end of the existence of Judaism.

EXCERPTS FROM THE ADDRESSES
OF RABBI ISAAC LEESER

Isaac Leeser (1806–1868) was the most vigorous and able defender of traditional Judaism in the United States in the period when the Reform movement was coming into being. Indeed, he might be described as a movement in himself. Endowed with vigorous energy, he was at once rabbi, author, translator, editor and publisher, the pioneer of the Jewish pulpit in the United States, the founder of the Jewish press in America, and a vigorous battler for congregational unions, Jewish day schools and a college devoted to Jewish studies (the short-lived Maimonides college). Born in Prussia, he came to America at the age of seventeen and worked in his uncle's counting-house. In his early twenties, he began to write on Jewish subjects and in consequence was invited, in 1828, to stand for the position of Hazzan at Congregation Mikveh Israel in Philadelphia. He protested his own lack of qualifications, but was realistic in realizing that in the America of that time, when the Jewish community numbered some 15,000, there were few or none who were suitable to the work. He speedily recognized the fact that there were no Jewish textbooks, so he proceeded to write them. Finding no Jewish version of the Bible in English, he proceeded to prepare one. In 1843, he founded The Occident, *a monthly magazine which continued to appear until 1869. In it, the major issues confronting American Jewry received a thorough, though often highly partisan, airing.*

Leeser may be regarded as a foremost spokesman for the American-based and American-oriented traditional synagogue out of which, in due course, the Conservative movement developed. He introduced the English sermon in 1830 and realistically confronted the fact that a new land presented Judaism with new problems. Withal, he was an ardent traditionalist and a vigorous controversialist. Some of his sermons in which he attacks the new bent to Reform Judaism are tremendously emotional and highly vituperative.

The two selections printed here are excerpts from two of his lengthy Collected Discourses *(10 vols., 1867). They show Leeser at his constructive best in dealing with problems presented by the nascent Reform movement. They equally make it clear, however, that he had no great gift for ideological formulation or intellectual*

51

synthesis. His great contribution to the later Conservative movement lay in the fact that he was a leading figure, articulate on platform and in print, a vigorous battler, an able organizer and a willing devotee to even elementary tasks.

ON CHANGES IN THE SYNAGOGUE

Mere mechanical praying, to utter words without thought or feeling, is not what Orthodoxy will sanction, not what Jewish religion requires. Do not, therefore, believe that we, who uphold the ancient order of things, are opposed to all improvement, or that we oppose Reformers merely for the sake of party spirit: not so; we dread their inroads on the principles of faith and practice, or their leading people away from the true object of religion by dwelling so much on externals, as though the synagogue were the sum total of Judaism. Synagogue-going is certainly a duty; our wise men teach us that whoever attends not the house of God in his city is to be called a "bad neighbour": all this is true; but it is only a means to an end, not the end itself. Good reforms may therefore be regarded as authorized, and consequently admissible; but those which are not, can never be legalized, though they might tend to fill the synagogue to overflowing, while under the ancient order it should stand empty and forsaken. If you accordingly want mere improvement, no Orthodox will oppose you. For instance, the sale of the *mitzvot* in your congregation is an abuse; the reciting of money offerings on Sabbath is a thing which should not exist: abolish both, and the sooner they are abolished the better; every day they exist is to continue so much longer an intolerable evil; and the loss to the revenue ought not to be considered of the least importance, as all they bring ought to be obtained by some other mode of finance. In this reform, I pledge you my word that all leaders of Orthodoxy will go hand in hand with you, and applaud your abridging the service by the removal of such extraneous matters, which never had any business there. If you merely desire to leave out some useless poetical pieces, the *piyyutim*, which are in some respects unintelligible even to good Hebrew scholars; if you only require that the phraseology in some pieces should be altered to suit the altered state of the times; in short, if the intention is only to revise some portions of the prayerbook which are in themselves non-essential: ask, and I think that I can promise you, in the name of the principal teachers of the Orthodox section, that your demands will be taken respectfully into consideration, and everything will be conceded which it is lawful to concede. Orthodoxy is not that unbending, unyielding, bigoted opposition to improvement which our opponents represent it; it understands perfectly well what the spirit of the age requires; but it can yield nothing to public clamour, nor to the demands which seekers of innovations may make to render Judaism a thing to accommodate itself to every phase of history. Such a religion would be none at all, as its ground would be constantly shifting; but to progress with the age, to adopt all the improvements which have been proved lawful, is perfectly within the limits of Orthodoxy, and will therefore meet with no opposition from those who really love our religion.

But the Reformers are not satisfied with this; "the prophets who wish to impose upon you the deceit of their own heart" will not improve merely; they wish to change, to revolutionize, to alter. They aver that Judaism is a very sick man, very sick indeed, and that this man must perish unless they come to his aid, with their medicines, with their university-purchased learning, drawn from sources which are un-Jewish in their nature and tendency. For my part, I do not think our religion is as sick as they represent it, consequently their aid is not needed. There are defects in practice; there is irreligion which stares us in the face; but this should be amended by our returning to first principles, not, however, by organic changes. Thus you teach your children to kiss the *Sepher* as it is carried from and to the ark; all this is well enough; but you ought to do more, you ought to impress them with the sacredness of the law, to teach them by a good example how to honour its precepts, and thus will you succeed in restoring among us a strict conformity of the old and young to the dictates of God, and remove the public disregard of the main duties even, which stamp us as Jews. But as for our modern doctors, we need them not, I boldly assert; if Judaism be sick now, as they maintain, it will perish, if they can slay it; if it have a little life, a small portion of vitality left, it will die outright, if their remedies be applied. No, no; our religion will not die; it is instinct with life, with undying strength, and it will resume its empire, notwithstanding the many doctors which now attempt its cure. But in very truth they are more likely to do mischief than good; they have done so whenever they have essayed their skill, and may the Guardian of Israel defend us against such physicians, against those who, if their advice be followed, will slay both the body and soul of our people.

ON THE IMPORTANCE OF THE HEBREW LANGUAGE

BRETHREN!

To the man whose eyes are opened by a knowledge of the way of righteousness; to the soul that adores her God and Creator; to the mind filled with love for mankind, it must be a matter of surprise and grief to observe, among the multifarious and varied classes that constitute the mass of mankind, so little perception of the utility and necessity of a religious education for their children, or of the duty every one is under to make himself familiar with the behests of revelation. What pains are not taken to teach our children the tongues of various nations; how much labour is not spent in the pursuit of worldly sciences; what stress is not laid upon the acquisition of mere accomplishment even; — but only touch the subject of religion and branches therewith connected, and you are at once told, that is quite useless to learn Hebrew, a language no more spoken, consequently of no practical use; and as for religious knowledge — that can be obtained by reading the sacred writings; and morality can be gotten very easily by going to churches of the various sects amongst whom we live; practical knowledge of political sciences is promulgated in worldly schools; and consequently there can be no necessity for spending years, and months, and days in the obtainment of religious information, properly so termed. That such reasoning prevails, cannot be denied, and that it is very fallacious and very pernicious, must be evident from the first view a candid man takes of the subject. Still so many are misled, and so many have become irreligious, immoral, and I fear infidel, that I beg you, my brethren, to bear with me whilst I endeavour to show the necessity of a particular religious education for our children, and the obligation which rests upon parents to qualify themselves for the holy task incumbent on them, as fathers and mothers, of bringing up the pledges of conjugal love, the trust confided to them by God, in the way which best comports with the love and duty which the creature owes to the Creator, and which secures in the best possible manner individual and general happiness. I have alluded to a knowledge of the Hebrew as in some manner connected with religion; and since all our forms of worship and our sacred records are in that language: it may not be out of place to offer a few observations to prove the necessity of retaining it in our worship, and to deprecate a substitution of any other in its stead. A national tongue binds together the people speaking it in one bond, and cements a union hardly otherwise attainable. Such a thing may be, as nations or tribes speaking different languages being governed by the same law; but where is that fellow-feeling, that brotherly attachment which people of the same speech feel? Not to go farther than a neighbouring country,* which was conquered now about eighty years ago, where the people have never been molested, as far as I know, in their laws, privileges, and even mere prejudices; add to which that the benefits of an extension of wholesome laws, of freedom from public burdens, of a wide-spreading commerce have been conferred: and still the difference of language between the rulers and the ruled has been the constant cause of heart-burning and contention, and a united effort for the public good is hardly thought of. Let us apply this single fact, which can be strengthened by a thousand others, from ancient and modern story, to our own case. In the land of the East, where first were cradled the germs of civilization and knowledge, our nation sprung up like a tender sprout, like a feeble shoot, from amidst the multitudes of nations. Abraham wandered out of his father's idolatrous home and went forth over the fair regions of the South, the harbinger of peace wherever he came. He spoke the language of Shem his ancestor, a language forcible and clear, full of elegant imagery and true to nature in its figures and sublime conceptions. With the growth of the people the language also grew into a national dialect, and even in the midst of the powerful and polished state of Egypt the Israelites still retained the language of Heber. Think you, it was a close bond during their dreadful sufferings? Most undoubtedly; and what better could have been found to make their hearts glow with rapturous hope, when the father bondman told to the child, whose prospect too was slavery and bondage, of the wonders which God had displayed unto their simple shepherd-ancestors, and how He had promised (using the sacred words of the holy Jacob) והיה אלהים עמכם והשיב אתכם אל

---

* Canada, where the French is the vernacular of the eastern portion.

ארץ אבותיכם "And God will be with you, and bring you back to
the land of your fathers"? Think you that hope could have fled
at words like these? Think you that the language too did not fall
on the ear like sweet music which bids the mourning soul rejoice? — Anon the law was given, and in words clear and distinct
the Most High announced His will. — The words spoken we have
read this day, and the language again was the language of Abraham. Israel conquered the land of promise, and dwelt in their
inheritance in security. And nobly too did the language do its
work, and there arose a Deborah to sing the song; there was a
David, who attuned his harp to inimitable and undying praise;
there was a Solomon, whose wisdom yet teaches the world; an
Isaiah, whose eloquence yet rouses the heart; a Jeremiah, who yet
bids the tears to flow at the downfall of the populous city, — and
a host of others, whose genius and whose piety must in all ages
command admiration. And when Israel fell, because they had
become sinful, and when the language was supplanted by the
speech of various nations: it found restorers in Ezra, Nehemiah,
Zechariah, and Malachi, besides many more who assisted them in
the holy task. And although the Hebrew has been banished by our
dispersion from being our every-day language: it yet holds, I
may freely say, a higher place, it embraces all that remains of the
wisdom of our ancestors; nay more, it contains all the commands
which God revealed to mankind for their guidance! This is the
Hebrew, and this is briefly its history. Despite now of our dispersion — despite of our being, alas! known as Americans, English-
men, Frenchmen, Germans, Poles, Grecians, Tartars, and by
numerous other names: still the Hebrew has always maintained its
position in the love and the heart of all true Israelites, and has also
constituted the bond which has kept united the captivity of Jacob
in all parts of the world! And here comes one from the burning
plains of Africa; there another from the icy fields of the Arctic
regions; yonder pilgrim calls the highlands of Middle Asia his
home; and this one is an exile from Spain's blood-stained sierras.
And listen! as the *messenger* addresses the throne of Grace, how a
simultaneous Amen bursts from all their lips! the language they
hear is not to them the language of the stranger, the sounds,
though ancient sounds, are to their ears familiar as the first breathing of childhood's years, and in the land of their exile, where they

all meet but as strangers, the holy tongue is their bond, and by it they do meet as a band of brothers, and all thus unite to call with one voice upon their God, who is truly the Preserver of Israel. — Does it then comport with reason to retain the knowledge of so great a gift? or shall we idly throw it off as a thing whose value is lost; forsake it as a spring whose waters are dried up? Never may this be! The blessing which this inheritance has always bestowed is of yet daily recurrence, and who would madly neglect what is of vital importance to him? Thus you have presented to you, brethren, an illustration; an argument would require more time, of the object and advantage of the Hebrew to us, as Jews. It is, namely, our national, our vernacular tongue; it is one of the links in that great chain which has ever firmly bound Israel together as one people. I take it for granted, that there are but few who wish its knowledge altogether extirpated; but still there are also an immense number, especially in this country, and I grieve to say in this city, perhaps among those who now hear me, that think but lightly of the importance of its acquisition by a careful study. But as the acquaintance with an instrument so valuable must be in the same proportion useful, it is certainly a matter of surprise that no more is done to further the means of its attainment. As a mere matter of curiosity much is studied; more things again receive attention solely because they are elegant; and therefore it is inconceivable, how a Jew can rest satisfied with an entire ignorance of his sacred language, when the opportunity for the removal of such unpardonable ignorance is within his reach. Even if means were not readily at hand, I should still think it the duty of every Israelite, no matter of what sex, station, or capacity, to endeavour to remedy the defect with regard to teaching, or in other words, schools should be established wherein the instruction of the Hebrew should be one of the principal objects of education. If this were done, if the acknowledged defect were to be encountered by a united effort, it is impossible but that the blessing of God would attend the undertaking; and even in this western world, almost at the opposite extreme whence civilization commenced her course, even here I say, men honouring their brethren by their splendid acquirements in the learning of our ancients, and in a correct knowledge of Biblical criticism, would crown the effort so piously undertaken and so happily accomplished.

CAN WE CHANGE THE RITUAL?

By Rabbi Sabato Morais

As one of the founders and as the first president of the Jewish Theological Seminary of America, Sabato Morais (1823–1897) may be designated as the founder of the Conservative movement in the United States. While he pursued his studies in his native Italy, the bulk of his active life was spent as Hazzan of Congregation Mikveh Israel in Philadelphia. From that vantage point, he participated actively and with ever growing prestige in every phase of American Jewish life. At the beginning he participated in the plans for a union of congregations organized by Isaac Mayer Wise and later served on the examining board of Hebrew Union College. Nonetheless, he remained one of the most articulate and effective spokesmen of traditional Judaism, and stood strongly opposed to changes in the ritual, as the article below makes clear.

Like Leeser, Morais was not the propounder of a new ideology, nor even a particularly incisive expounder of the German historical school. He was, however, endowed with character and conviction, he ministered to a congregation rooted in the American scene, he was a product of Western training and he managed to expound a viewpoint vigorously without evoking enmity. Moreover, in a decisive period of American Jewish history, he enjoyed a distinguished position and he used these facts to good advantage.

Morais' contribution to the rise of the Conservative movement was partly organizational and partly an oral Torah. This latter was reflected in his sermons which are represented by the talk printed below. It was delivered to Congregation Mikveh Israel in 1885.

"Why do you stand still, when all are moving on?" This question is put to me by men and women of Israel, who have a right to an answer, for they form part of the congregation for whose special benefit my services were engaged. Now, had I less respect for querists, and an opinion less exalted of my calling, I might reply in a manner precluding discussion. I would simply point to the constitution of the *Kahal Kadosh Mikvé Israel,** in which it is stated that "the fixed prayers, the Torah and the Haftarah shall *always* be read in the original Hebrew language, according to the custom of the Portuguese Jews." I would also disclose to view the written contract into which I entered for the faithful performance of my official duties, wherein the same identical rule has been laid down. But I am anxious to reason with my brethren, to show cause for my opposition to changes in the service of the Synagogue. The obstacle presented by the documents to which I have just alluded, might be honorably overcome. I might urge an alteration of the organic laws made by the founders of this religious body, and possibly bring it to pass. But the principal impediment would yet remain. My conscience would rise to the defense of sacred ground. The still small voice within would speak and rebuke the presumption of encroaching upon that which the wise and the upright have established. For, you ought to know, my fellow-believers, that the authors of a number of our prayers are the prophets and sages of old. Not to speak of the Psalms and of detached fragments of the Bible interspersed through the ritual, we offer daily to God entreaties, praises, and benedictions which Ezra the priest, conjointly with Zachariah, Malachi, Nehemiah, and their pious associates, composed and set in order. I will not assert that nothing was ever added to what that august Synod framed. I acknowledge that certain passages bear internal evidences of a later origin. So, for example, it cannot be supposed that our fathers, after their return from the Babylonish exile, petitioned God for the reconstruction of our nationality, and the restoration of the Temple service. But, admitting all this, I nevertheless trace in the general uniformity existing among the various *minhagim*, or rituals, the same ancient source. For, regarding the main prayers, to which reference is made in the Mishna, no essential difference can be discovered between the liturgy of the Sephardic and the Ashkenaz, the Italian and the Oriental. It is an error shared by many, to believe that — as it happens with the creeds of gentilism — the formulas of one body of Jews are entirely distinct from those of another.

Not until the Synagogue was transformed into a novel insti-

---

*Congregation Hope of Israel.

tution — a servile imitation of the Nazarene Church — did such
an anomaly appear in Israel. Before the misapplied name of
"Reform" came in vogue, all the remnants of Judah repeated
almost literally the national invocations and orisons stamped with
the seal of high antiquity. True, in the course of time, rhythmical
and prosaic writings, very dissimilar in style and purport, swelled
up the ritual. But, without entering into the respective merits of
those productions, chiefly of the Middle Ages, I maintain that they
never superseded the more ancient compositions emanating from
and arranged by Ezra and the one hundred and twenty men
traditionally styled "Members of the Great Assembly." Those
devotional effusions being read in the language sanctified by the
sound of the words heard at Sinai, opened among all the adherents
of the Mosaic code a current of spiritual magnetism — if I may
employ the term — reaching from one end of the world to the
opposite end. However circumstances may have affected the Jew
socially or politically, he felt on entering a Synagogue, that he was
still bound in faith, in hope, and destiny to the whole household
of Jacob.

Now that "minor sanctuary" is undergoing such changes, that
Hebrew hailing from a foreign land will scarcely recognize it.
And I am asked to help in disfiguring what our fathers thought
it wise to make. To this I might again briefly reply, that when
I put on the ministerial robe, I enlisted in the service not only of
a small body of brethren, but of the entire Jewish Church. And
that I could no more trespass against the orders of my superiors,
the Rabbis, than the sentinel desert his military post.

But the demands of our rising generation are pictured to me.
The absolute necessity of yielding, to prevent a further estrangement from Judaism, is advanced as an argument against my per-
sisting in the same course. That appeal does indeed affect me
deeply; and happy would I consider myself if I could reach out
the hand, which will prevent the youth of my people from leaping
over the boundaries of our holy religion. Happy, I say, if I could
honestly, consistently resort to some contrivance by which to keep
my straying flock within the pale of the Synagogue. But what,
if whilst engaged in saving a few, I expose the many to danger?
If I cause a whole congregation gradually to lapse into gentilism,
by too close an approximation to its rites and practices?

Anxious to strengthen Judaism in America, without loosening in the least the ties of our national bond, I suggested, some years ago, a plan conducive to harmony. I sought, through the press, and "Board of Delegates of American Israelites," the co-operation of all my colleagues to the compilation of a uniform ritual. The differences between the Portuguese and Germans, between the so-called progressive and the conservative — fruitful always of prejudice — should be sunk, and every one worshipping Israel's God in this country of United States should unitedly offer unto Him supplications and thanksgivings. Whatever the Talmud records as the teaching of tradition was to have been scrupulously retained, and whatever lacked the support of that authority was to have been submitted to the mature judgment of a general conference of the pious and the erudite, and adopted, rejected or modified. Then the objection raised to the length of our prayers, and some repetitions, would have been met in a legal manner, and with due circumspection removed. The ritual abridged, but still containing the elements of our faith, the declaration of divine truths, and the expression of national hopes, would have been recited in the sacred tongue throughout the land of our adoption, and ample time would have been reserved for communicating those lessons, which the pulpit must necessarily impart in the vernacular. But my call did not awaken a response. Reform became daily more rampant; each minister of a congregation — forgetful of his duty to Judaism at large — arrogating to himself the power to abolish what had been held in reverence; curtailing in one instance, deforming in another, substituting his own words for those of our inspired leaders, supplanting the accepted ideas of the past to pander to the extravagant notions of the present. Nothing was left for me singly to do, but to endeavor to interest the young in the worship, by the occasional introduction of new melodies, by more frequent preaching, and by the delivery, at times, of a benediction at the conclusion of the service. That those means have failed to accomplish the end, I confess with exceeding humiliation. But the cause should be ascribed not to my inactivity — for no task would I consider too onerous, that profiting my congregation, might benefit my people. — It should rather be attributed to the increasing defection of your teachers, O American Israelites; and to your sinful negligence, O Jewish parents! Your teachers, who ought to have fostered the knowledge of the Hebrew tongue, proved palpably by their actions that they neither attach to it any sanctity, nor desire to see it perpetuated. By admitting into the Synagogue, as songsters and songstresses, the believers in the Trinity,— men and women who know not and care naught for what they say, uttering for *pay* unintelligible sentences, on the true Sabbath, intended as a devotional offering to the One God, and praying for *choice* on the first day of the week to the deified man of Nazareth; your teachers — oblivious of their sworn allegiance to tradition — by reducing the ancient ritual to a shadow of its former self, displacing it to make room for operatic strains, have encouraged a distaste for the language of the Bible, and a prurient curiosity to hear the warbling of the strangers. And you, parents, have aggravated the evil. You are, undesignedly perhaps, aiding to sunder apart a strong link which binds together the dispersed of Judah. For you do not regret the sums expended to train your children in all the accomplishments of the age, but you rest satisfied if your son can, at best, learn by rote a portion of the Pentateuch, when he attains his religious majority; if your daughter can memorize a verse or two in Deuteronomy, containing the *Shema*. Nowhere is their ignorance of the Hebrew so general, as in our midst, and, therefore, nowhere is pseudo-reform so successful. Your offspring, estranged from the house of worship which resounds with the outpourings of David, throng that in which every vestige of Jewish ceremonies and customs is being erased. But . . . . can you not foresee the end? Why, it stares us in the face! The next generation will not be recognized as the disciples of Moses and the Prophets: so complete will be the transformation wrought by the changelings. I may be unable to prevent it, but I shall not deliberately hasten the disruption of our brotherhood.

Dear hearers! For very nigh a century this congregation has stood as the exponent of traditional Judaism. When the thought of rearing the magnificent fanes now so attractive, would have been derided as a wild dream, the descendant of Abraham, visiting Philadelphia, rejoiced to find a dwelling of prayer, awakening the delightful memories of childhood, of parents and home. That dwelling of prayer was ours. I will not carry to the grave the sin of having perverted the object of its establishment. Lamenting most sincerely the absence of any among my flock, I shall still continue to perform the service, according to the Sephardic ritual, neither adding to, nor diminishing from it, until I may authoritatively propose alterations; I mean until a synod of learned and God-fearing ministers shall have met and decided. Meanwhile to familiarize with the prayers the attendants of this Synagogue, and also to secure more harmony in our popular chanting, I will devote one evening each week to the rehearsal of the same. On that occasion any of my brothers and sisters may feel at liberty to propound questions pertaining to the subject in which we shall be engaged, or suggest what may be deemed of utility. Let us, beloved friends! co-operate to further the exaltation of the house of our God. Let us labor zealously together for the spiritual weal of our posterity, for the preservation of the Lord's eternal truths, for the perpetuation of our race in this blessed land of freedom. Let us labor steadfastly, indefatigably, that the *Mikvé Israel*, the "Hope of Israel," be fulfilled through this congregation, as it is written, "When thy children shall be taught of the Lord, great will be the peace of thy children." They vying with each other to rebuild by their knowledge what has been faithlessly pulled down; to restore to Judaism that of which it has been robbed; thus becoming the support of their old faith; and earning for themselves abundance of peace and happiness.

WHICH IS RIGHT?

A Talmudical Disputation

By RABBI ALEXANDER KOHUT

Alexander Kohut (1842–1894) was one of the key figures in bringing to a head the Conservative movement of the mid 1880's. He came from Hungary where he had enjoyed great prestige as the scholar who had already published part of the monumental Aruch Completum *on the Talmud, as the representative of Jews in the Hungarian Parliament and as an outstanding orator. His acceptance of the pulpit of Congregation Ahavath Chesed in New York created a considerable stir and his arrival there in 1885 provided the traditional forces in American Judaism with an eloquent and vigorous spokesman. Kohut almost immediately plunged into debate on the religious issues confronting American Jewry, a debate in which he found a vigorous opponent in Kauffmann Kohler. He found a ready forum for his views in the pages of the* American Hebrew, *in which the* Talmudic Disquisition *printed below appeared (in June and July, 1885). While his style in controversy was frequently over-coy and rather heavy, his conception of historical Judaism was clearly formulated, his resources of learning were rich and his willingness to stand and battle for his viewpoint was quite clear. Moreover, he had a sense for the American scene. He was willing to reckon with the need for modification in Jewish religious life and quite prepared to concede that issues must be debated. He sought to eschew the party and the parochial and thus, in the face of Morais' suggestion that the Seminary be called the Orthodox Seminary, he successfully held out for the more inclusive name, the Jewish Theological Seminary. Once that institution was organized, he served it as Professor of Talmudic Methodology until his death.*

The following passage at arms, between a Reformer of what may be called the "Declaration of Independence" school, and a Conservative, took place within the four walls of a room whose sole hangings were shelves and whose ornaments were books. The seconds in this intellectual duel were the formidable folio volumes of the Talmud.

Conservative: " 'Welcome, my teacher and pupil! My teacher in the truth, my pupil in obedience.'[1] I as a second Gamaliel, apostrophize you as another Joshua, and mean herewith neither to concede defeat, nor predict victory; I trust that you have come imbued with the same feelings towards me."

Reformer: "Certainly, else I would not have appeared at all. Of course, unlike Joshua, I have not come with staff and purse. Not with my staff, as our contest is to be conducted with the weapons of reason. Not with my purse as I have nothing to save therein. Still, unlike Joshua, I cannot even secure a livelihood by the making of needles; though I have felt the needle pricks of fortune, whose latest was the machinations of a Conservative congregation who would not permit me to make them happy with my Reform ideas. My independence was more to me than my livelihood. It is from this feeling of Independence and love of truth that I call to you with Joshua: 'You do not know the pangs that must be suffered by one learned in the Talmud. You do not know what can serve as spiritual food for him, and what nourishment the people desire.'[2] To be sure, I mean in this country, which is not only the new world in an historical sense, but also in spiritual development, higher progress toward culture, refinement of religious conceptions, and freedom from prejudice."

Conservative: "Pray, let us have no empty phrases or false hypotheses. 'Religious refinement' and 'freedom from prejudice' are terms altogether too vague and elastic to serve as precise, determinate conceptions. If refining in religion is to have unbridled sway, the most important fundamental attributes of religion are in danger of being swept away, or transformed into the symbols of Philo, into impalpable notions, or bare and empty ideas. Only when these ideas are embodied in deeds that are imbued with, and harmonize with those ideas, are they characteristic of Judaism. That the practical execution of this is impeded by manifold obstacles, and causes considerable personal inconvenience, I readily concede."

---

[1] R. Hash. 25a.
[2] Berach. 28a.

Reformer: "You are very condescending to make the concession. But I would have the Judaism which I find in my consciousness emancipated from the patronizing condescension of Legalism, and would therefore earnestly strive to urge the view that religion should not be hampered by any inconvenience, that instead of its being a burthensome lip-service and ceremonial worship, it should be a Religion full of life and enjoying life. How otherwise should it be? Even the ancient sages have said, 'the teaching of Moses was not given to the angels.' We belong to the earth, and must place ourselves in harmony with the world. And too, in religion we must be in accord with the spirit of the times, even if by so doing we must surrender much that was formerly considered important. Here the saying holds good, 'The Commandments were given only for the purpose of elevating man.'[3] But we must draw the necessary conclusion from this ethical view, that when our conceptions in any particular are refined and elevated in comparison with the limited views previously prevailing, it is impossible for us to return to our narrower views on that subject. Would it not be absurd to cling to a Mosaic command, to say nothing of a Talmudic law, if its elevating influence, its moral force had long since flown? Must we not rather exclaim, with R. Jochanan: 'Let the dead wrap itself in its shroud' ?"

Conservative: "Yes, indeed, I accept your position as a broad generalization. You are right, that which is dead can by no manner of skill be galvanized into life. But is everything that is so glibly declared to be dead and lifeless, really so? Or have we entirely infallible tests for judging what is really bereft of life; what is but seemingly dead, and finally, what is falsely declared to be dead? The contemporaries of Ezekiel also exclaimed: 'Our bones are dried up, and our hope is lost; we are cut off.' And R. Jeremiah correctly expounds the passage 'Those were they from whom the life of God's commands had departed.'[4] They but became dead to Judaism, and thought that Judaism had died. I do not, indeed, belong to the class that would make Judaism burthensome; I rather vindicate the Talmudical axiom 'higher than the power of adding to the burthen of the Law, is that of alleviating its rigor.'[5]

---

[3] Gen. Rabb. c. 44; Levit. Rabb. c. 13.
[4] Sanh. 92b.
[5] Beza 2b.

In our times there are many directions in which the principles urged particularly by Isserles, cannot be applied, viz: 'There where all have accepted the principles of making the Law more difficult there it must be followed; there where the additional burthens have, from the beginning, not been accepted, there they may in the future also be rejected.' Naturally this can only be applied to Talmudical ordinances, and not to the Mosaic Commands of whose validity there is no question."

Reformer: "That is by far not so natural nor as self-evident. See what violence the men of the Talmud did to the letter of the Biblical Law. Like a potter they molded from it as they deemed advisable for their times, such images as they wished, but such as have nothing in common with the spirit of our age. With all their wonderful force we cannot but look with reproof at their superlative conception of their own work and worth, as for instance in the phrase: 'The decisions of the Soferim are of higher validity than those of the Bible.'[6] Is not that arrogance?"

Conservative: "No, for it is expressly declared that by means of the traditional explanations of the Soferim, the Biblical Law is to be more firmly established by being more clearly understood. You dare not, like Eisenmenger, who makes the same charge as you do, confine yourself to the passage which you quote and refrain from giving the sound and truthful explanation which the context affords."

Reformer: "But what if the explanation is not satisfactory? If placing the Law upon such a foundation is not permissible, or is false in principle? It must be false in principle, since it often occurs that one interpretation will be found confronted by another diametrically opposed to it. How can there be truth, when one permits, another forbids, a certain action? The same thing cannot at the same time be right and wrong. Or is such ambiguity a specialty of Talmudic dialectic?"

Conservative: "Not at all. There is but one Truth. But do not forget in speaking in regard to what is true, that is, what is traditionally established, that there is never, as Maimonides has shown, any evidence of difference of opinion. Only in the establishment of a tradition, in the deduction of a decision from the

---

[6] Sanh. 87b.

Bible, do opinions vary in that one authority cites one, another a different passage to support his view. Even in differences as to matters of fact, such as the disputes between the Hillelites and the Shamaites, the controversies always bore the academical stamp. Life and conduct were seldom affected by these differences, as the vote of the majority decided the *halacha* for the practical affairs of life. At the same time individual opinion was respected, because freedom to learn and liberty to teach were always held in honor in Judaism."

Reformer: "And should not the freedom to learn and liberty to teach be accepted as a heritage for our times as well as deemed an ornament for our ancestors! What shall hinder us from claiming the present validity of the proposition laid down already in the Talmud: 'Only such decisions can and should be determined upon as can be borne by a majority of the people.'[7] Does it not follow from this with mathematical exactitude, that the people shall be relieved from the over-burthensome legal requirements? Surely we have the same right that our ancestors claimed, to relieve the people of our times from some of the intolerable burthens of the Law. Bear in mind that the people in the midst of the vehement struggle for existence have lost much of their religiosity, and are not as zealous as formerly in the study of the *Torah.* But surely you would not seriously confront me with the famous phrase 'If former generations were angels, we are only human beings; if they were human, we are but senseless creatures.' "

Conservative: "No, it is not quite as bad as that! But I am inclined to think that it is unreasonable and a wrongful use of power to settle religious matters on a basis of merely personal accomodation and convenience. But let us confine ourselves for the nonce to the alleged Talmudic axiom which you have cited, to the effect that in arriving at legal decisions the wishes of a majority of the people should be decisive. But you could read on the same page of the Talmud 'When a prohibitory ordinance has become prevalent among a majority of the people, it cannot be altered.' That which has secured for itself vitality among the body of the people, has passed into their lives as a vital factor: cannot be repealed by any authority, as Maimonides has codified the proposition.[8] The prin-

---

[7] Ab. Zara 36a.
[8] Hilch. Mamrim II 2, 3.

ciple that the will of the people is decisive, is an unambiguous testimony that with the ancient spirit of Judaism there was ever the tendency towards legitimate reform. Just because Judaism possesses the capacity for development, and is preserved against the danger of immovable quiescence by the Talmudical methods of interpretation, just therefore the arrogant individualism which says: *Sic volo sic jubeo*, 'Thus I will it, so I command,' must not be permitted to contend against the will of the people, but should in all modesty subject itself thereto. The self-will of the individual dare not nullify the voice of the community. 'Go forth into the world, and observe the customs which are observed by the people.'[9] That message should guide reform. That which still has a hold upon the hearts of men and women, which still retains vitality should be preserved as sacred; attempting to destroy it is equivalent to Temple sacrilege. Instead of positive Judaism, such a process would give a negative religion, and is not any longer a historically developed Judaism — at most but a diluted Christianity."

Reformer: "Let me joyfully exclaim *Eureka*! I too would set my lever at this point. If reform is to spring from the people, then have we already the ripe fruit. The people in their sovereignty have declared their will; they by their categorical imperative have given the impulse to the Reform movement. Only he who is afflicted with spiritual blindness does not see that the Judaism of the nineteenth century is no more that of even the eighteenth century, let alone that of the Talmudical epoch. Even the most pious Jew does not observe the minute ordinances of the Talmud in their scrupulous detail, be they never so excellently codified in the *Shulchan Aruch* by the worthy and learned Rabbi Joseph Caro, and it is well known that the credo of the pious is not the Talmud, not the Bible, but the *Shulchan Aruch*. A wit once proved thus: he asked, (so he said) a strict Talmudist why the eighth commandment is so frequently broken by Jews, notwithstanding that the Talmud has enlarged upon the Biblical prohibition against stealing. 'Do you not know?' he was answered, 'that is the fault of Rabbi Moses Isserles? If he had embodied in his marginal notes to the *Shulchan Aruch* a phrase like the following, "It is the *minhag*, not to steal," no Israelite would have dared to infringe on such a codified ordinance;

_____
[9] Berach. 45a.

but as it is only in the Decalogue — that is another thing.' But
aside from that, conceding for the sake of argument, but not as a
matter of fact, that the Jews of the old world are more pious, because pinning more faith to the letter than those of the new world,
shall that circumstance have any weight with us, who live in a
different hemisphere and atmosphere, with different views, needs
and hopes. The voice of the people which comes to us from the old
world cannot and should not be permitted to lead us astray; we set
up against it another voice of the people, which issues from the
heart of Young Israel on the soil of free America. We have reached
the heights of unprejudiced religious conceptions; those on the
other side are still in the slough of narrow-minded views. Because
they say: 'We cannot or will not ascend to your exalted standpoint,'
shall we descend to their depths, down from an elevated position,
where we are surrounded by a balsamic atmosphere and enjoying
a wide and extensive prospect of the religion of the future? No, we
cannot, we would not. Here we hold with the Talmud, 'Ascension,
not delusion, in things sacred.' "[10]

Conservative: "Truly, a beautiful ethical expression, which however is proof for me, and not for you; for Conservatism, not for
Radical Reform. Surely that cannot lay claim to be characterized
as sacred which stands in open and confessed contradiction with
the use and custom of centuries. On the same page of the Talmud
which you have just cited you may also read: 'That which secludes
itself, does so from the majority.' In Judaism, however, the decision
of the majority has been expressed in life and conduct. Much
clamor may be raised in religious matters, but majorities cannot
be distilled by the magic of a voice. That which may have some
propriety in a certain sense, for one individual, is senseless when
opposed by the emphatic voice of the common usage, which says
that Judaism has a base broad enough to accomodate the most
divergent views without danger to the community, but that no
vote of any fraction can ever be esteemed as possessing any validity,
nor can the subjective views of any individual be of any binding
force upon the community, for here Lessing's expressive aphorism
finds application: 'Do you conceive how much easier by far it is to
be imbued with pious enthusiasm, than to do good?' But as Juda-

---

[10] Berach. 28a.

ism is a religion of deed and not of emotional vaporing nor of any individual philosophical speculation, so the people, accustomed to the fulfilment of religious duties, does not with self-destructive haste cast off the customs and observances made sacred by centuries of usage; but clings to the traditional so long as it possesses moral force and spiritual power, and if there are some religious observances to be given up, the remaining customs assure a wealth of positive religion to be secure against negation and destruction. Here may especially be applied the historic truth: 'All these commands for whose fulfilment Israel has suffered martyrdom are observed with like sacredness.'[11] In these commands are included not only pure monotheism but also the Abrahamic covenant. Has there been infringement of this principle, and has Historic Truth been outraged, then we may say also 'The fools who withstand will be called to account before the tribunal of God and the History of Israel.' "

Reformer: "I accept the principle that you lay down, and recognize its validity. I too would appeal to the people to act as judge concerning what is permitted and what is prohibited. This judge has however already rendered a decision concerning the interpretation of which there is no ambiguity, insofar as regards the religious affairs of the people. The laxity which is prevalent in the observance of even the Biblical laws, could not possibly be more widespread nor more profound, and it would require a veritable miracle to produce a change in this respect among the people. I say however in the words of the Talmud 'We who have not the spirit of the martyrs, cannot any more be dependent upon miracles.'[12] The fact of martyrdom, however, I admit, and the dauntless, earnest Reformers accept martyrdom when they strive to reach their goal without respect to the favor or disfavor of the people; when on the ruins of a faith dictated by authority they plant the will of the people; when they uproot blind credulity and place in its stead untrammelled science, and the people have ever bowed in reverence before the results of learning when produced by worthy teachers in accordance with the Talmudical proverb: 'Jephthah in his time is as worthy as Samuel in his;' and

---

[11] Shabb. 130a.
[12] Berach. 20a.

in accordance with the rule of the Talmud: 'You must be governed by the decision of the judge of your times; his judgment must be your authority.' "[13]

Conservative: "Very true! But that judgment can only be rendered on the existing stratum of Law; in the spirit and not antagonistic to the spirit of the Law upon which the decision is based. It is true that decisions have often been rendered according to the precedent set by R. Jehuda Hanassi, that in order to support the Law, the operation of some portion might be temporarily suspended, the religious conscience being consoled with the thought: 'The suspension of a command of the Torah is often the means of more firmly establishing its observance.'[14] But these cases were never in relation to anything vitally essential, nor were they anything other than temporary in character and caused by the exigencies of transitional stages in important turning-points of religious or national history. They were, however, always governed by the limitations of the seed and root and growth whence the religion has developed. So should it be with the Reformers; . . . the sphere of Reform must be limited, and nothing must be admitted whose results and conclusion can not be foreseen, for the law must always be firmly established and irrevocable so far as concerns the revealed Law and Religion, according to its etymological derivation from *religio*, involving always the idea of being bound. The true idea of Liberty excludes the idea of License. Development does not mean destruction. Recasting is a very different process from casting aside. Because the circumstances of life render it difficult to observe one or another positive command of the Law, does not by any manner or means constitute a good and sufficient reason for annulling the Law or suspending its operation. Accommodating pliancy is, from this point of view, a crime committed against the revealed fundamental principles of Judaism; more than a wrong, it is a fatal error which in the course of time will bear its maleficent fruit. It cripples the reverential attitude in relation to the divinity of the Divine Laws, which lose their essential and forceful power when conceived of as variable human contrivances. It results in tightening to strangulation the arteries of Judaism, and ultimately evolves suicide — and suicide is not Reform, said Zunz.

---

[13] R. Hash. 25b.
[14] Menach. 99b.

"Progress can only be effected within the limits of revealed law, always in harmonious connection with the entire community and ever true to historical continuity. No single individual is empowered to speak authoritatively for the community as a whole in relation to any project for leaving a path which leads from ancient law and custom. Only the community speaking through the medium of its representatives, capable leaders whom they themselves have chosen, has the right to develop new forms from the spirit of the old for the rejuvenation of the present. They who are imbued with the historic spirit of the eternally new and fresh and living Judaism, must be sponsors for these new forms, that they be bone and flesh from the bone and flesh of Judaism. If it should please the community, or rather if it should arise as a burning question, to undertake thorough-going transformations, the stress of the times will be succumbed to, and the right men will be found in the right time to interpret and pronounce the will of the people. Until that time the words of the Midrash are as applicable in this as in political affairs: 'Do not awaken the love of the people, until it stirs of itself.' To prepare for this time in peaceful intellectual labors, hand in hand, shoulder to shoulder, in closed phalanx, with hearts warmed by faith and nurtured by knowledge, in freedom, with piety, conscious of and striving for the fulfilment of our great mission, this should be the united task of the teachers in Israel."

———————

Thus the duel was ended. The two contestants clasped hands, and the Reformer said, echoing the words with which the Conservative had greeted him: "Peace be with you, my teacher and my scholar. You taught me something that was worth the learning. You learned from me something of truth. Our silent but learned and wise seconds, the volumes of the Talmud, reserve their decision as to which of us can perch the wreath of victory upon his banner."

But you, dear readers, shall each decide for himself: Which is right?

THE PROBLEM OF JUDAISM
IN AMERICA

By Rabbi Israel Friedlander

The essay printed below belongs in an anthology of Conservative Judaism by virtue of its central outlook rather than because of its specific terminology. Friedlander here confronts the American Jewish scene and sees in it both challenge and opportunity. Cognizant of the problems involved in living in a double civilization, he is nevertheless sanguine that the inherent vitality of the Jewish tradition is sufficient to create a great Jewish community in America. The realistic confrontation of the challenge of a new situation, the emphasis upon religion and upon learning, the call for a conception of a total community, the rich resort to historical material and the firm belief that American and Jewish ideals can be harmonized, combine to make a splendid presentation of the point of view of Conservative Judaism, even if the term itself is not employed.

Israel Friedlander (1876–1920), the author of this essay, was born and educated in Poland and subsequently went to Germany to study. In 1903 he was appointed Professor of Biblical Literature at the Seminary. In the ensuing years he served as chairman of the new Bureau of Jewish Education and as the first president of Young Judea. He was a devoted Zionist of the Aḥad Haʿam school and, consequently, a firm believer in a vital Diaspora.

This essay was first delivered as an address to a synagogue group in 1907 and subsequently included in a collection of essays entitled Past and Present.

In considering the problem of Judaism I am probably expected to set out with an exact definition of what I understand by the term "Judaism." But if I allow myself to be entangled in the snares of definitions, which are, after all, only a decent way of begging the question, I am afraid I shall never be able to return to the subject of this lecture. If definitions are irksome in general, because they represent the delicate attempt to reduce the phenomena of living, palpitating reality to a dead, stationary formula, and doubly irksome when applied to phenomena which bear the stamp of spirituality on their "ism," they are almost unattainable in the case of an historical organism like Judaism, which, during the whole unparalleled length of its history, has been undergoing uninterrupted, though imperceptible, changes, which in the course of its career has encountered innumerable influences of every origin and description, and, in consequence, presents in almost every age and country a modified appearance. It will, however, suffice for our immediate purposes, if I say, vaguely perhaps, but briefly, that Judaism represents the sum total of those inner characteristics, as instincts, sentiments, convictions and ideals, which are to a lesser or larger degree common to the individuals of the aggregate known as the Jewish people. If the Jews, or Jewry, represent the ethnological or physical appearance of the Jewish people, Judaism may be said to represent its spiritual or psychological make-up; in other words, Jewry constitutes the body, Judaism the spirit, or the soul, of the Jewish people. As the soul of the individual, so the soul of a nation is in itself invisible. It finds its visible expression in a certain manner of life, as customs, habits and ceremonies, and in a certain spiritual production, as literature, art and the like; in short, in the two spheres, which, taken together, form what we call the culture of a nation. Judaism would thus, more exactly, represent the Jewish soul or spirit and its outward manifestation in Jewish culture. Jewry without Judaism is no more than a body without a spirit, a dead inanimate mechanism, which may, by sheer mechanical force, move on for a little while, but must in the end come to a complete standstill. The problem of Judaism would then consist in the fact that the soul or spirit of the Jewish people as manifested in its culture has in modern times shown symptoms of decay of so alarming a nature as to make us fear for its utter extinction. The beginning of this decay is obviously coincident with the beginning of Jewish emancipation; that is to say, with the moment when the Jews left the Ghetto to join the life and the culture of the nations around them.

* * * * * *

Wherever we turn our gaze we witness the spectacle, the decomposition of Judaism, of Jewish living and Jewish thinking, under the influence of freedom. No amount of high-sounding phraseology can deceive us as to the meaning of this terrible truth. Judaism that was able to subsist and even to develop in the narrowness and darkness of the Ghetto is cut off in its very strength when brought out into the airy breadth of modern life. Judaism that stood out like a rock amidst the billows of hatred and storms of persecution is melting away like wax under the mild rays of freedom. It may be painful to realize it and far more painful to express it. But if the correct diagnosis of a malady is indispensable for the remedy, then it is the sacred duty of every Jew who loves his people and thinks of its future fearlessly to perceive and fearlessly to proclaim the critical condition of modern Judaism and the terrible dangers that beset it.

This apparent incompatibility of Judaism with modern life and culture is the most depressing and the most humiliating experience which can torment the soul of the Jew who still has a particle of Jewish pride in his heart. It is a tragedy far more stirring and heartrending than all the material sufferings of our people. Yet there are few in our midst who are sensible of this terrible problem. The problem of the Jews, of the physical sufferings of our nation, engages the heart and the hand of every Jew with a spark of Jewish consciousness or Jewish sentiment in him. Powerful organizations grapple energetically, though not always successfully, with this problem. But most of us utterly ignore the problem of our spiritual misery. Most of us still swear by the panacea of Jewish emancipation, and pin all our hope and faith on the political, economic and social advancement of the Jews. Their policy can be summed up in the words of the Prophet: "When thou wilt deal thy bread to the hungry and bring the poor that are cast out to thy house, when thou wilt see the naked that thou wilt cover him, and thou wilt not hide thyself from thine own flesh, then shall thy light break forth as the dawn and thy cure shall spring forth speedily." They are blind to the fact that the dawn of the Jews is the dusk of Judaism; that the nearer the problem of Jewry reaches its solution, the more complicated and the more dangerous becomes the problem of Judaism; that the more emancipated, the more prosperous, the more successful the Jews become, the more impoverished, the more defenseless and the more threatened becomes Judaism, the only reason and the only foundation of their existence. And while our heart is aroused over the martyrs that fell by the hands of violent mobs, we witness with indifference the disappearance of that for which they became martyrs. And while we bewail the few leaves that were plucked off our trees by brutal hands, we coolly observe how large sections of our foliage wither and fall off, because the growing forces of the tree are too weak to hold them. Of what use is it, then, to boast of the achievements of Jewish emancipation and to point to the mental, economic and social advance of the Jewish people if purchased at the expense of the Jewish soul, without which Jewry is but an empty, and not always attractive, shell? Of what avail is all the material prosperity of our nation when bought at the price of our spiritual death, which must unavoidably lead to the entire annihilation of our community?

Having stated the nature of the problem we must now try to search for a solution; but none seems to be forthcoming. We are on the horns of a dilemma: either return to the Ghetto, or complete absorption. *Tertium non datur*! But of the two openings, the one is impossible, the other unacceptable. For we may recognize as clearly as possible the preserving influence of the Ghetto; we may, when made to shiver in a cold, large world, affectionately dream of its lowly roof, its narrow walls, its cheering fireside, its peaceful atmosphere; but there are thousands among us — in itself the surest symptom of our decay — who coolly or even longingly look forward to complete absorption. But those of us who still feel the stream of Jewish life rolling through their veins, who are dominated and actuated by Jewish sentiment and Jewish thought, to whom Judaism is the breath of their nostrils and the fountain of their life, are struck with a terror that no words can express at the mere possibility of their spiritual death, and every fibre of their being cries out aloud against a solution which strikes at our life of lives.

But is there really no escape from this frightful dilemma? Is there no hope for the Jews to participate in the life and culture around them and yet remain Jewish? Is Judaism actually like a gas, which can only be kept by the grip of iron and evaporates when allowed to escape from its prison? Were it proved by the facts of our history, with its unparalleled store of experience, that union between Judaism and freedom is impossible, then our fate would be sealed, and all our protests and agonies would be of no avail. All that we should have to do would be to lie down in our shame, to wrap ourselves in our ignominy and to wait with deathly stupor the verdict of nature. But happily enough, our history does not prove it impossible. To be sure, the period in Jewish history preceding the era of emancipation was one of isolation, but this period was in its turn preceded by another, which was one of freedom. The great and glorious Jewish-Arabic period deals a death blow to the dilemma besetting the problem of Judaism, and is in itself an overwhelming proof and shining example of the compatibility of an active participation of the Jews in the life and culture of the nations around them, with a strong, vigorous, genuine development of Judaism. The amount of freedom enjoyed by the Jews of that epoch was in no way inferior to that of our own. The Jews took an honorable and energetic part in the economic, social and political development of the Eastern, as well as the Western, Califate. We encounter among the Jews of that period men of affairs wielding a powerful influence in the public life of the country. We find Jewish merchants, Jewish financiers, Jewish dignitaries of high standing; and Jewish viziers and ministers of state are more frequently to be met with than in our own times. The association with the culture and spiritual influences of the age was just as close and intimate. The Jews made themselves the possessors of all the intellectual achievements of Arabic civilization with an eagerness and rapidity which remind us vividly of our own days, and which found a curious echo in the outcry of a fanatic of the early part of that period, which sounds quite familiar to our own ears. "Every day," thus runs this lamentation — which, characteristically enough, has a Karaite for its author and is written in Arabic, the language of the new culture — "every day we commit a number of sins and make ourselves guilty of a great many transgressions. We mix with the Gentiles around us and imitate their doings. Our chief aim is the study of the Arabic language and its philology, for which we leave aside the knowledge of the Holy Tongue and the meditation in the commandments of the Lord." The intimate acquaintance of the Jews with the religion of Islam and its highly developed theology can be inferred from the fact that the religious terminology of the Jewish thinkers is largely that of the Mohammedan dogmatists, and that Moses is often designated by the same

titles which were otherwise applied to Mohammed. The close relation of Judaism with the philosophy of the age, which, rooting in
Greek thought, was far from favorable to a positive religion, is illustrated by the fact that Aristotle was to the Jews of that period
"the Philosopher" and was put on a level scarcely inferior to that
of the Jewish Lawgiver. Yet the very same age saw a development
of the Jewish spirit and Jewish culture, so many-sided, so fascinating and so rich in results as never before or after in the lands of
the exile. No department in the spiritual treasury of our people
remained untouched by the loving care of its sons. Bible, Talmud,
Hebrew literature, Hebrew poetry and philology, Jewish philosophy and everything that constitutes the pride of the Jew found
their greatest and most brilliant representatives in that period, and
the profound attachment to Judaism went hand in hand with a
noble enthusiasm for everything noble outside of Judaism. Hisdai
ibn Shaprut, the powerful diplomat of Cordova, was not only a
generous supporter of every manifestation of Jewish learning, but
took, himself, a most profound and stimulating interest in the rise
of Hebrew philology in Spain. Samuel ibn Nagdela, the prime
minister of Granada, conducted not only the affairs of the State,
but also the affairs of the Beth Hamidrash, where he lectured on the
Talmud, and he is celebrated both as a Talmudic scholar and
Hebrew poet. Solomon ibn Gabirol, who summed up the philosophy of the age in an Arabic work which profoundly influenced
mediaeval Christian philosophy, is one of the greatest poets of our
nation in its sacred tongue. Moses Maimonides, who is a living
expression of the whole Arabic culture of the age, is at the same
time the greatest scholar and thinker of post-Biblical Judaism, and
while in his philosophical standard work, written in Arabic, he
guides the perplexed of his time in the paths of Aristotelian philosophy, he leads in his religious code the large mass of his people
"with a strong hand" to the sources of Judaism. Everywhere we
witness harmony and beauty, a full, luxuriant growth of Judaism
under the benign rays of freedom and culture.

Thus the great Jewish-Arabic period irrefutably shows that
Judaism is compatible with freedom and that a full participation
in the life of the nations can very well be reconciled with a deep
attachment to Judaism and a vigorous activity in its behalf. The
same holds true of our own age. There is nothing in modern life or

culture which is more opposed and more dangerous to Judaism than were the conditions of that era. Modern Christianity possesses no more attraction for the adherents of Judaism than did the highly developed Islam of that age, and modern thought is no more irreconcilable with the Judaism of the twentieth century than were the philosophies of Aristotle with the Judaism of the twelfth. But in confronting Judaism with the culture of the surrounding nations we must present it as it is, in its true shape and size, and not as a caricature. It was the fatal mistake of the Jews of emancipation, which is the real source of all the subsequent disasters in modern Jewish life, that, in order to facilitate their fight for political equality they introduced Judaism not as a culture, as the full expression of the inner life of the Jewish people, but as a creed, as a summary of a few abstract articles of faith, similar in its character to the religion of the surrounding nations. I said before that Judaism represents the inner characteristics of the Jewish people as manifested in its culture, in its mode of living and in its intellectual productivity. We only need recall the truism — almost too trivial to be repeated — that there is no "exact equivalent for the term religion" in Hebrew, or point to the well-known fact that, despite the aptitude of the Jewish mind for theological intricacies, Judaism carefully refrained from formulating a creed, to realize that Judaism is far more than a religion, and that it is essentially different in its origin and structure from Christianity and similar religions. Forced on the Procrustes' couch of a religious denomination, and stripped of all those elements that bore special relation to the people that produced it, Judaism was crippled in its vital functions and rendered unfit to meet and to resist the new conditions. Jewish living had to be sacrificed for the sake of emancipation. The beliefs of Judaism had to be refashioned so as to purge them of their intimate connection with the Jewish national aspirations. The progress of Judaism was no more an organic development from within, but a mere series of mechanic changes dictated by considerations from without. The whole structure of Judaism was thus turned top to bottom. Judaism became a church, the rabbis became priests and the Jews became a flock, not quite as tractable perhaps, though quite as ignorant, as other flocks. The Jewish education of the children which formed the corner-stone of Biblical and Talmudic Judaism, dwindled down to Sunday-school experiments, and the children of Israel often enough know of Judaism and their people no more than what they are told by Israel's enemies. Jewish scholarship, which, to an unequalled extent, was the possession of the rank and file of our nation, gave place to widespread ignorance, and the name *am-haaretz*, which in olden times disqualified the Jew for the humblest social aspiration, almost became a title of honor. All the intellectual activities of Judaism which could not be pressed into the mould of theology, though being of enormous value for the development of Jewish consciousness, which produced the "Song of Songs" and, in the Middle Ages, gave birth to a highly developed literature and poetry, were thrown out of Jewish life, or in the best case, confined to the cabinets of a few scholars. Thus the modern Jew, while partaking of the fullness of modern culture, was made to starve within the precincts of Judaism. He satisfied his highest tastes and desires outside the Jewish camp, while in Judaism he only perceived a few colorless doctrines, which could be had elsewhere, and a few cold liturgical ceremonies which did not always appeal to him. He was often forced to ask himself, "Why am I a Jew?" — a question which implies a negation and which was and still is heard from official representatives of Judaism in the pulpit.

To be sure, the picture I have just drawn applies only to a certain section of our people. "Israel is not yet forsaken, nor is Judah bereft of his God, though their land be filled with sin against the Holy One of Israel." Large numbers of our people still cling to Judaism with all their heart, their soul and their substance, and see in it the consummation of their lives. But we are no doubt on a slanting plane, and, unless we check ourselves in time and retrace our steps to the top, we shall roll down the precipice whence there is no return.

If, therefore, Judaism is to be preserved amidst the new conditions; if, lacking, as it does, all outward support, it is still to withstand the pressure of the surrounding influences, it must again break the narrow frame of a creed and resume its original function as a culture, as the expression of the Jewish spirit and the whole life of the Jews. It will not confine itself to a few metaphysical doctrines, which affect the head and not the heart, and a few official ceremonies, which affect neither the head nor the heart, but will encircle the whole life of the Jew and give content and color to its highest functions and activities.

Perhaps two illustrations, derived from historical facts, the one belonging to the Jewish-Arabic period, the other to our own age, will bring out more clearly than can any abstract exposition the different results of these two different conceptions of Judaism.

There is scarcely any civilization in which poetry, the rhythmic sentence and the rhymed word, occupies so prominent a place as in Arabic civilization and those dependent on it. All classes and occupations worshipped with equal devotion at its shrine. The starving nomad of the desert, the prince on the throne, the frivolous comedian and the grave scholar, all loved and practiced the art of rhyme. It was the label of fashion, the touchstone of genius, a source of income, and a fountain of delight. When the Jews came in contact with Arabic culture the only poetry they created outside the Bible was the so-called *piyyut*, a more or less uncouth form of poetry which merely served liturgical purposes. But the Judaism of that period, which embraced all that had any connection with Jewish life, soon took cognizance of the new factor. It introduced the form and spirit of Arabic poetry into the Hebrew language, and the mediaeval Hebrew poetry, the richest after the Biblical, sprang up, singing not only of God, His land and His people, but also of matters far less divine — of wine, woman, and all the moods and passions of the human heart. Moses Maimonides, who from his high metaphysical observatory looked down upon poetry as a meaningless waste of time, indignantly protested against the use, or abuse, of the sacred tongue for contents of so frivolous a nature. But there can be no doubt that the secular Hebrew poetry, however slight its connection with Jewish religion, had as much share in attracting and attaching to Judaism the *beaux esprits* of the period as had Maimonides' metaphysics in keeping within the precincts of Judaism the philosophical sceptics of the age.

And now for our own time. There is scarcely anything in modern life which is so characteristic an expression of the soul of a people and so apt to arouse the emotions of its members as its music. The language of the angels, as it has been styled, has now become a means of expression of the whole of humanity. There is no nation, whether standing on the lowest or the highest rung of the ladder of civilization, which does not enshrine its joy and sorrow, its memories and hopes, in song and tune. The Jews have been blessed with an exceptional gift for this divine art. They have as composers and performers enriched the musical repertoire of almost every nation. Dozens of Jewish musicians, though keeping their Judaism in strict incognito, arrive every season in this country. But modern Judaism, which has curtailed its functions down to those of a creed, has no room for the talents of its children. And while even the hapless Ghetto has been able to breathe forth its woe in strains peculiar to it, modern Judaism, with its freedom and prosperity, is deprived of this sweetest of arts, and even in its places of worship has to depend on the talents of non-Jews.

Such a Judaism of freedom and culture as advocated above will not be a mere reproduction of the Judaism of the Ghetto. It will have to take in and digest the elements of other cultures, and will seek and meet new conditions and interests. This modern Judaism will evolve from the Judaism preceding it, as did Talmudic Judaism from Biblical, philosophical Judaism from Talmudism, mysticism from Jewish philosophy, Chassidism from Rabbinism. It will develop and be modified along the lines of its history, prompted by inner necessity, not by dictation from without. While the Judaism of isolation accentuated the ceremonial side of Jewish life and crystalized itself by a natural process into an *Orach Chaim*, a "Mode of Living" (as the ceremonial part of the *Shulchan Aruch* is entitled), the modern phase of Judaism will probably tend to emphasize more strongly its cultural aspects. While it will endeavor to preserve all those features of Jewish practice which give shape and color and vigor to Judaism, it will develop and call forth all those powers of the Jewish spirit which will be apt to supplement or counteract the influences of modern life. It will give full scope to our religious genius, but will also foster all other departments of the Jewish intellect. It will develop our literature, create or preserve Jewish art in all its functions, stimulate and further Jewish scholarship, so as to make it a powerful factor of Jewish consciousness. It will reorganize and put on a firmer basis the Jewish education of our children, who are the pledge of our future, and thus create the basis and sounding-board for all other Jewish activities. It will regulate our spiritual demand and supply, and will make Judaism a living, flourishing, impregnable organism that deserves to be loved, to be respected, to be lived for.

If such a Judaism, presenting a harmonious union between the culture of the Jewish people and that of the other nations is possible in the dispersion — and that it is possible is convincingly shown by our history — the only place where it has a chance of realization is America. For America, this even the Zionist, who works and hopes for the establishment of a center of Jewish culture in its native land, will fully and readily admit, America is fast becoming the center of the Jewish people of the Diaspora. Jewish history teaches us that, despite the centrifugal forces of the dispersion, Judaism was seldom without a center, and that this center, following the wanderings of Jewry, moved from place to place. The Jewish center shifted from Palestine to Babylon, from Babylon to Spain, from Spain to Poland and Russia. It is now shifting before our very eyes to this country. America is already the center of the Jews. As regards the number of its Jewish population, it is second to none but Russia, which is in a state of dissolution, and every steamship that anchors in our harbors increases our prospects for becoming first instead of second. But America has every chance of also becoming the center of Judaism, of the spiritual life of the Jewish people in the dispersion. Those who are on the spot may, with the self-criticism so characteristic of our race, be slow or even reluctant to recognize it. People who stand in front of a painting and see mere blotches of greasy color are seldom able to realize the purport of the painting as a whole. But there is no thinking Jew outside of America whose eyes are not turned towards this country as the center of Judaism in the nearest future. America presents a happy combination of such manifold and favorable circumstances as have been seldom equalled in the history of the Diaspora. It has the numbers which are necessary for the creation of a cultural center. It possesses the economic prosperity indispensable to a successful spiritual development. The freedom enjoyed by the Jews is not the outcome of emancipation, purchased at the cost of national suicide, but the natural product of American civilization. The idea of liberty as evolved by the Anglo-Saxon mind does not merely mean the privilege of selling new clothes instead of old, as it often does in Europe, but signifies liberty of conscience, the full, untrammeled development of the soul as well as the body. The true American spirit understands and respects the traditions and associations of other nationalities, and on its vast area numerous races live peaceably together, equally devoted to the interests of the land. The influx of Jewish immigrants in the past and present brought and brings to these shores the enormous resources of the Ghetto, and presents American Jewry with a variety of Jewish types which will be of far-reaching significance in its further development. In short, this country has at its disposal all the materials necessary for the upbuilding of a large, powerful center of Judaism, and it only depends on the American Jews whether these potentialities will ever become realities.

But it is to be hoped that the American Jews will not be so forgetful of the task, as gigantic as it is honorable, that lies before them. He who feels the pulse of American Jewry can detect, amidst numerous indications to the contrary, the beginnings of a Jewish renaissance, the budding forth of a new spirit. The Jews of America, as represented in their noblest and best, display larger Jewish sympathies, a broader outlook on Jewish life, a deeper understanding of the spiritual interests of Judaism than most of their brethren of Mosaic persuasion in the lands of assimilation and emancipation. The type of the modern American Jew who is both modern and Jewish, who combines American energy and success with that manliness and self-assertion, which is imbibed with American freedom, is becoming a species, while in other countries the same characteristics are to be met with in but a few exceptional individuals. The American Jews are fully alive to the future of their country as a center of Jewish culture. They build not only hospitals and infirmaries, but also schools and colleges; they welcome not only immigrants, but also libraries; not only tradesmen and laborers, but also scholars and writers. Everywhere we perceive the evidence of a new life. To be sure, we are only at the beginning. Gigantic and complicated tasks confront us in the future. The enormous stores of latent Jewish energy that are formlessly piled up in this country will have to be transformed into a living power. The dead capital which we constantly draw from the Ghetto will have to be made a working capital to produce new values. We first of all have to lay our foundation; to rescue the Jewish education of our future generation from the chaos in which it is now entangled. But we are on the right road. The American Jews will take to heart the lesson afforded by modern Jewish history in Europe. They will not bury Judaism in synagogues and temples, nor imprison it in charitable institutions. They will work and live for a Judaism which will compass all phases of Jewish life and thought; which will not be a faint sickly hothouse plant, but as it was in the days of old, "a tree of life for those who hold it fast, bestowing happiness on those who cling to it."

But will a Judaism that does not confine itself to synagogues and hospitals, but endeavors to embrace the breadth and depth of modern life, leave sufficient room in the heart of the Jew for the interests and demands of his country, or, to put it into the mould of a current formula, is Judaism, and a Judaism of the kind advocated above, compatible with Americanism? The people who thus anxiously inquire betray a poor conception of human psychology. They seem to think that the souls of men are like those cheap musical slot-machines which can only play a single tune. The human soul is characterized not by uniformity, but by variety. The higher a human type, the more multifarious its interests, the more manifold its activities, the more varied its affections. That a full and successful participation in all phases of American life is reconcilable with a deep attachment to Judaism in all its aspects is sufficiently warranted by the historical precedent of the Jewish-Arabic period. To be sure, in blending Judaism with Americanism the edges and corners will, on both sides, have to be levelled. Compromises will be unavoidable. But the happiest of marriages is a series of mutual compromises. These compromises may not be exactly identical with those of the Jewish-Arabic era. Perhaps not all our Jewish dignitaries will be immersed in the niceties of Hebrew philology, like Hisdai ibn Shaprut, and not all our ministers of state will be Talmudic lecturers and writers, like Samuel ibn Nagdela — and why should we demand this from our ministers of state, when our ministers of religion occasionally fail in these departments? But these compromises will never be such as to obliterate or mutilate the character of either. Judaism and Americanism will not be intersecting, but concentric circles. In the great palace of American civilization we shall occupy our own corner, which we will decorate and beautify to the best of our taste and ability, and make not only a center of attraction for the members of our family, but also an object of admiration for all the dwellers of the palace.

There is an old rabbinic saying that after the destruction of the Temple the gift of prophecy passed over to children and fools. I am not young enough to claim the privilege of a child, nor am I modest enough to use the pretext of a fool. True, prophecy without inspiration, which predicts the future as a matter of fact, is childish and foolish, because no human eye can perceive and no human mind can calculate the innumerable and imponderable effects of the concatenation of human events. But prophecy as a matter of hope, the prediction of the future not as it will be, but as it ought to be, is indispensable for all who have, or desire to have, a clear conception of their duties toward the coming generations. And when we thus try to penetrate the mist that encircles the horizon of the present, a vision unfolds itself before our mind's eye, presenting a picture of the future American Israel. We perceive a community great in numbers, mighty in power, enjoying life, liberty and the pursuit of happiness — true life, not mere breathing space; full liberty, not mere elbow room; real happiness, not that of pasture beasts — actively participating in the civic, social and economic progress of the country, fully sharing and increasing its spiritual possessions and acquisitions, doubling its joys, halving its sorrows; yet deeply rooted in the soil of Judaism, clinging to its past, working for its future, true to its traditions, faithful to its aspirations, one in sentiment with their brethren wherever they are, attached to the land of their fathers as the cradle and resting place of the Jewish spirit; men with straight backs and raised heads, with big hearts and strong minds, with no conviction crippled, with no emotion stifled, with souls harmoniously developed, self-centered and self-reliant; receiving and resisting, not yielding like wax to every impress from the outside, but blending the best they possess with the best they encounter; not a horde of individuals, but a set of individualities, adding a new note to the richness of American life, leading a new current into the stream of American civilization; not a formless crowd of taxpayers and voters, but a sharply marked community, distinct and distinguished, trusted for its loyalty, respected for its dignity, esteemed for its traditions, valued for its virtues, a community as the Prophet of the Exile saw it in his vision: "And marked will be their seed among the nations, and their offspring among the peoples. Everyone that will see them will point to them as being a community blessed by the Lord."

HISTORICAL JUDAISM*

By Rabbi Solomon Schechter

The Jewish Theological Seminary is still known in many circles as "Schechter's Seminary." This popularly applied title is a tribute to the fact that under Schechter's eadership, which began in 1902 and continued until his death in 1915, the ailing Seminary was reorganized and revitalized. Because he was the dynamic leader of the Seminary and because he later organized the United Synagogue and because he impressed the stamp of his own thinking and personality upon both institutions, he is regarded as historically the most important figure in Conservative Judaism. However, it is wise to note that he nowhere set forth a coherent statement of doctrine and position. Indeed, he repeatedly asserted that he was not creating a new party, but reviving a very old one — traditional Judaism, and he generally referred to a Conservative tendency rather than to a Conservative movement.

Schechter's tendency to "halt between two opinions" is reflected in the selections below. He describes the "Historical School," in the first selection, and seems to approve it intellectually, while confessing, at the end, that he cannot quite stomach it, emotionally. The selections from his very eloquent addresses are those fragments from much longer speeches in which he affirms the historical outlook and the conservative spirit. They are fragments by necessity. There is no complete essay or speech in which he undertakes to define the role and function of a Conservative movement.

Solomon Schechter (1847–1915) studied in European Seminaries and Universities and subsequently taught at Cambridge University. He achieved world-wide renown by virtue of his discovery of the Cairo Genizah and by his extremely felicitous writings on Jewish subjects. To the Conservative movement of future years he bequeathed a seminal phrase — "Catholic Israel" — by which he meant that Judaism has an inner unity which is manifested in the generally accepted sentiment of devoted

---

* Excerpted from the Introduction to *First Studies in Judaism*, Philadelphia, 1896.

Jews. He left it, too, the legacy of a strong Seminary, with a remarkable group of scholars, and the United Synagogue. One of his more remarkable achievements was that, by dint of his personality, his outlook, and his prestige he interposed a counterweight to the Reform movement in the early years of the century and served as a rallying point for Jews of a Conservative tendency.

In reading the proofs (of this volume) I have been struck by the fact that there is assumed in them a certain conception of the Synagogue which, familiar though it be to the Jewish student, may appear obscure and even strange to the general English reader. For brevity's sake I will call it the High Synagogue, though it does not correspond in all details to what one is accustomed to understand under the term of High Church. The High Synagogue has a history which is not altogether without its points of interest.

Some years ago when the waves of the Higher Criticism of the Old Testament reached the shores of this country (England), and such questions as the heterogeneous composition of the Pentateuch, the comparatively late date of the Levitical Legislation, and the post-exilic origin of certain Prophecies as well as of the Psalms began to be freely discussed by the press and even in the pulpit, the invidious remark was often made: What will now become of Judaism when its last stronghold, the Law, is being shaken to its very foundations?

Such a remark shows a very superficial acquaintance with the nature of an old historical religion like Judaism, and the richness of the resources it has to fall back upon in cases of emergency.

As a fact, the emergency did not quite surprise Judaism. The alarm signal was given some 150 years ago by an Italian Rabbi, Abiad Sar Shalom Basilea, in his pamphlet *The Faith of the Sages.* The pamphlet is, as the title indicates, of a polemical character, reviewing the work of the Jewish rationalistic schools; and after warming up in his attacks against their heterodox views, Basilea exclaims: "Nature and simple meaning, they are our misfortune." By "nature and simple meaning" Basilea, who wrote in Hebrew, understood what we would call Natural Science and Philology. With the right instinct of faith, Basilea hit on the real sore points. For though he mostly argues against the philosophical systems of Aristotle and his commentators, he felt that it is not speculation that will ever seriously endanger religion. There is hardly any metaphysical system, old or new, which has not in course of time been adapted by able dialecticians to the creed which they happened to hold. In our own time we have seen the glorious, though not entirely novel spectacle, of Agnosticism itself becoming the rightful handmaid of Queen Theology. The real danger lies in "nature" (or Natural Science) with its stern demand of law and regularity in all phenomena, and in the "simple meaning" (or Philology) with its inconsiderate insistence on truth. Of the two, the "simple meaning" is the more objectionable. Not only is it very often at variance with Tradition, which has its own code of interpretation, but it is constantly increasing the difficulties raised by science. For if words could only have more than one meaning, there would be no objection to reading the first words of Genesis, "In *a* beginning God *evolved*." The difficulties of science would then be disposed of easily enough. Maimonides, who was as bold an interpreter as he was a deep metaphysician, hinted plainly enough that were he as convinced of the eternity of matter as he was satisfied of the impossibility of any corporeal quality in the Deity, he would feel as little compunction in explaining (figuratively) the contents of the first chapter of Genesis as he did in allegorising the anthropomorphic passages of the Bible. Thus in the end all the difficulties resolve themselves into the one great difficulty of the "simple meaning." The best way to meet this difficulty was found to be to shift the centre of gravity in Judaism and to place it in the secondary meaning, thus making religion independent of philology and all its dangerous consequences.

This shifting work was chiefly done, perhaps not quite consciously, by the historical school which followed upon that of Mendelssohn and his first successors. The historical school, which is still in the ascendant, comprises many of the best Jewish writers who either by their learning or by their ecclesiastical profession as Rabbis and preachers in great communities have acquired some important position among their brethren. The men who have inaugurated this movement were Krochmal (1785–1841), Rapoport (1790–1867), and Zunz (1794–1886).

It is not a mere coincidence that the first representatives of the historical school were also the first Jewish scholars who proved themselves more or less ready to join the modern school of Bible Criticism, and even to contribute their share to it. The first two,

Krochmal and Rapoport, early in the second quarter of this century accepted and defended the modern view about a second Isaiah, the post-exilic origin of many Psalms, and the late date of Ecclesiastes; whilst Zunz, who began (in 1832) with denying the authenticity of Ezekiel, concluded his literary career (1873) with a study on the Bible (*Gesammelte Schriften*, i. pp. 217–290), in which he expressed his view "that the Book of Leviticus dates from a later period than the Book of Deuteronomy, later even than Ezekiel, having been composed during the age of the Second Temple, when there already existed a well-established priesthood which super-intended the sacrificial worship." But when Revelation or the Written Word is reduced to the level of history, there is no diffi-culty in elevating history in its aspect of Tradition to the rank of Scripture, for both have then the same human or divine origin (according to the student's predilection for the one or the other adjective), and emanate from the same authority. Tradition becomes thus the means whereby the modern divine seeks to compensate himself for the loss of the Bible, and the theological balance is to the satisfaction of all parties happily readjusted.

Jewish Tradition, or, as it is commonly called, the Oral Law, or, as we may term it (in consideration of its claims to represent an interpretation of the Bible), the Secondary Meaning of the Scrip-tures, is mainly embodied in the works of the Rabbis and their subsequent followers during the Middle Ages. Hence the zeal and energy with which the historical school applied itself to the Jewish post-biblical literature, not only elucidating its texts by means of new critical editions, dictionaries, and commentaries, but also trying to trace its origins and to pursue its history through its gradual development. To the work of Krochmal in this direction a special essay is devoted in this volume. The labours of Rapoport are more of a biographical and bibliographical nature, being occupied mostly with the minor details in the lives and writings of various famous Jewish Rabbis in the Middle Ages; thus they offer but little opportunity for general theological comment. Of more importance in this respect are the hints thrown out in his various works by Zunz, who was just as emphatic in asserting the claims of Tradition as he was advanced in his views on Bible criticism. Zunz's greatest work is *Die Gottesdienstliche Vorträge* — an awkward title, which in fact means "The History of the Interpretation of the

Scriptures as Forming a Part of the Divine Service." Now if a work displaying such wide learning and critical acumen, and written in such an impartial spirit can be said to have a bias, it was towards bridging over the seemingly wide gap between the Written Word (the Scriptures) and the Spoken Word (the Oral Law or Tradition), which was the more deeply felt, as most of Zunz's older contemporaries were men, grown up in the habits of thought of the eighteenth century — a century distinguished both for its ignorance of, and its power of ignoring, the teachings of history. Indeed it would seem that ages employed in making history have no time for studying it.

Zunz accomplished the task he set himself, by showing, as already indicated, the late date of certain portions of the Bible, which by setting the early history of Israel in an ideal light betray the moralising tendency of their authors, and are, in fact, little more than a traditional interpretation of older portions of Scripture, adapted to the religious needs of the time. Placing thus the origin of Tradition in the Bible itself, it was a comparatively easy matter for Zunz to prove its further continuity. Prophecy and Interpretation are with him the natural expressions of the religious life of the nation; and though by the loss of Israel's political independence the voice of the prophets gradually died away, the voice of God was still heard. Israel continues to consult God through the medium of the Scriptures, and He answers His people by the mouth of the Scribes, the Sages, the Interpreters of the Law; whilst the liturgy of the Synagogue, springing up at the time when Psalms were still being composed, expands in its later stages through the work of the Poets of the Synagogue into such a rich luxuriance "that it forms in itself a treasure of history, poetry, philosophy; and prophecy and psalms are again revived in the hymnology of the Middle Ages." This is in brief the lesson to be learned from Zunz's *Gottesdienstliche Vorträge* as far as it deals with the significance of Tradition; and it is in the introduction to this work that Zunz expresses himself to the following effect: Indispensable is the free Spoken Word. Mankind has acquired all its ideal treasures only by Word of Mouth; an education continuing through all stages of life. In Israel, too, the Word of Instruction transmitted from mouth to mouth was never silenced.

The historical school has never, to my knowledge, offered to the

world a theological programme of its own. By the nature of its
task, its labours are mostly conducted in the field of philology and
archaeology, and it pays but little attention to pure dogmatic
questions. On the whole, its attitude towards religion may be
defined as an enlightened Scepticism combined with a staunch
conservatism which is not even wholly devoid of a certain mystical
touch. As far as we may gather from vague remarks and hints
thrown out now and then, its theological position may perhaps be
thus defined: — It is not the mere revealed Bible that is of first
importance to the Jew, but the Bible as it repeats itself in history,
in other words, as it is interpreted by Tradition. The Talmud, that
wonderful mine of religious ideas from which it would be just as
easy to draw up a manual for the most orthodox as to extract a
vade-mecum for the most sceptical, lends some countenance to this
view by certain controversial passages — not to be taken seriously
— in which "the words of the scribes" are placed almost above the
words of the Torah. Since then the interpretation of Scripture or
the Secondary Meaning is mainly a product of changing historical
influences, it follows that the centre of authority is actually removed from the Bible and placed in some *living body*, which, by
reason of its being in touch with the ideal aspirations and the
religious needs of the age, is best able to determine the nature of the
Secondary Meaning. This living body, however, is not represented
by any section of the nation, or any corporate priesthood, or Rabbihood, but by the collective conscience of Catholic Israel as embodied in the Universal Synagogue. The Synagogue "with its
long, continuous cry after God for more than twenty-three centuries," with its unremittent activity in teaching and developing
the word of God, with its uninterrupted succession of Prophets,
Psalmists, Scribes, Assideans, Rabbis, Patriarchs, Interpreters,
Elucidators, Eminences, and Teachers, with its glorious record of
saints, martyrs, sages, philosophers, scholars, and mystics; this
Synagogue, the only true witness to the past, and forming in all
ages the sublimest expression of Israel's religious life, must also
retain its authority as the sole true guide for the present and the
future. And being in communion with this Synagogue, we may also
look hopefully for a safe and rational solution of our present theological troubles. For was it not the Synagogue which even in
antiquity determined the fate of Scripture? On the one hand, for

example, books like Ezekiel, the Song of Songs, and Ecclesiastes, were only declared to be Holy Writ in virtue of the interpretation put upon them by the Rabbis: and, on the other hand, it was the veto of the Rabbis which excluded from the canon the works that now pass under the name of Apocrypha. We may, therefore, safely trust that the Synagogue will again assert its divine right in passing judgment upon the Bible when it feels called upon to exercise that holy office. It is "God who has chosen the Torah, and Moses His servant, and Israel His people." But indeed God's choice invariably coincides with the wishes of Israel; He "performeth all things" upon which the councils of Israel, meeting under promise of the Divine presence and communion, have previously agreed. As the Talmud somewhere expresses itself with regard to the Book of Esther, "They have confirmed above what Israel has accepted below."

Another consequence of this conception of Tradition is that it is neither Scripture nor primitive Judaism, but general custom which forms the real rule of practice. Holy Writ as well as history, Zunz tells us, teaches that the law of Moses was never fully and absolutely put in practice. Liberty was always given to the great teachers of every generation to make modifications and innovations in harmony with the spirit of existing institutions. Hence a return to Mosaism would be illegal, pernicious, and indeed impossible. The norm as well as the sanction of Judaism is the practice actually in vogue. Its consecration is the consecration of general use, — or, in other words, of Catholic Israel. It was probably with a view to this communion that the later mystics introduced a short prayer to be said before the performance of any religious ceremony, in which, among other things, the speaker professes his readiness to act "in the name of all Israel."

It would be out of place in an introductory essay to pursue any further this interesting subject with its far-reaching consequences upon Jewish life and Jewish thought. But the foregoing remarks may suffice to show that Judaism did not remain quite inactive at the approach of the great religious crisis which our generation has witnessed. Like so many other religious communities, it reviewed its forces, entrenched itself on the field of history, and what it lost of its old devotion to the Bible, it has sought to make up by a renewed reverence for institutions.

In this connection, a mere mention may suffice of the ultra-Orthodox party, led by the late Dr. S. R. Hirsch of Frankfort (1808–1889) whose defiance of reason and criticism even a Ward might have envied, and whose saintliness and sublimity even a Keble might have admired. And, to take an example from the opposite school, we must at least record the name of that devout Jew, Osias Schorr (1816–1895), in whom we have profound learning combined with an uncompromising disposition of mind productive of a typical champion of Radicalism in things religious. These men are, however, representative of two extremes, and their followers constitute mere minorities; the majority is with the historical school.

How long the position of this school will prove tenable is another question. Being brought up in the old Low Synagogue, where, with all attachment to tradition, the Bible was looked upon as the crown and the climax of Judaism, the old Adam still asserts itself in me, and in unguarded moments makes me rebel against this new rival of revelation in the shape of history. At times this now fashionable exaltation of Tradition at the expense of Scripture even impresses me as a sort of religious bimetallism in which bold speculators in theology try to keep up the market value of an inferior currency by denouncing loudly the bright shining gold which, they would have us believe, is less fitted to circulate in the vulgar use of daily life than the small cash of historical interpretation. Nor can I quite reconcile myself to this alliance of religion with history, which seems to me both unworthy and unnatural. The Jew, some writer aptly remarked, was the first and the fiercest Nonconformist of the East, and so Judaism was always a protesting religion. To break the idols, whether of the past or of the present, has always been a sacred mission of Judaism, and has indeed been esteemed by it as a necessary preliminary to the advent of the kingdom of God on earth. One of its daily prayers was and still is: "We therefore hope in Thee, O Lord our God, that we may speedily behold the glory of Thy might, when . . . the idols will be cut off, when the world will be perfected under the kingdom of the Almighty." It bowed before truth, but it had never made a covenant with facts only because they were facts. History had to be re-made and to sanctify itself before it found its way into its sacred annals. Nor did Judaism make a virtue of swallowing down institutions. Such institutions as crept into it in course of time had, when the Synagogue was conscious of their claims to form part of religion, to submit to the laborious process of a thorough adaptation to prophetic notions before they were formally sanctioned. But when this process was deemed impossible or impracticable, Judaism boldly denounced the past in such fierce language as the prophets used and as still finds its echo in such passages of the liturgy as "First our ancestors were worshippers of idols and now God has brought us near to His service"; or "But of a truth, we and our ancestors have sinned."

However, it would be unfair to argue any further against a theological system which, as already said, was never avowed distinctly by the historical school — a school, moreover, with which speculation is a matter of minor importance. The main strength of this school lies in its scientific work, for which Judaism will always be under a sense of deep gratitude. And living as we do in an age in which history reigns supreme in all departments of human thought, we may hope that even its theology, as far as it goes, will "do" for us, though I neither hope nor believe that it will do for those who come after us.

EXCERPTS FROM THE SEMINARY ADDRESSES OF SOLOMON SCHECHTER

from THE PREFACE (1915)

Generally speaking, the burden of these Addresses, mostly delivered on Commencement and other fête days of the Seminary, may be described as a plea for traditional Judaism, which it is the mission of the Seminary to teach and preach in this country. They protest against the "shock-tactics" of Higher Bible criticism; they plead for a better appreciation of Israel's past and a closer connection between this past and the present and the future; they demand a more thorough study of Jewish thought and Jewish life as deposited in our great literature; they insist on the development of Jewish science which would enable us to compete with other institutions of higher learning; they also advocate a deeper devotion to the laws distinctly characteristic of the Jewish conception of holiness, leading to a more strict observance of the precepts of the Torah, and endeavor to make us sensible of the danger of incessant innovations which must in the end touch the very vital organism of Judaism.

At the same time, however, these Addresses often revert to the desirability of adopting in our studies all the methods which distinguish modern research from the mere erudition of olden times. They also set forth the necessity of the future Rabbi's receiving a proper training in secular subjects, as guaranteed by the degree of B. A. obtained in some College of standing, before wholly devoting himself to Jewish learning. The greater part of a rather

lengthy lecture is devoted to proving that not only was the application of scientific methods to Jewish studies not incompatible with
the spirit of conservative Judaism, but that it was largely conservative Jews, or at least, men indifferent to Reform tendencies,
who availed themselves of the scientific method and became subsequently the most prominent representatives of the scientific
movement, both by their zeal and their productions. . . .

As indicated above, the papers constituting this volume are an
expression of the conservative position occupied by the Seminary.
This conservative spirit, I need hardly say, permeates the whole
Institution. It is taught by the Professors in the classroom; it is
expounded in the pulpit by the majority of our alumni; and is
propagated by its friends both in writing and by word of mouth
on every occasion. . . .

The third paper in this book is the one headed: "Zionism,
A Statement," published in December, 1906, in which I explain
the reasons for my allegiance to Zionism. But I should like it to be
distinctly understood that this allegiance cannot be predicated of
the Institution over which I have the honor to preside, and which
has never committed itself to the Movement, leaving this to the
individual inclination of the students and Faculty, composed of
Zionists, anti-Zionists, and indifferentists. Speaking for myself,
Zionism was, and still is, the most cherished dream I was worthy
of having. It was beautiful to behold the rise of this mighty bulwark
against the incessantly assailing forces of assimilation, which became the more dangerous, as we have now among us a party
permeated by Christianizing tendencies, the prominent leaders of
which are even clamoring for a recognition of Paul, the apostle to
the heathen — not to the Jews. These tendencies which it must be
said in justice, would have been strenuously opposed by the
founders of the Reform school, are now thrust upon us on every
occasion, and Heaven knows where they might have landed us,
but for the Zionist Movement which again brought forth the
national aspect in Jewish thought.

But this dream is not without its nightmare. For in their struggle
to revive the National Sentiment, some of the Zionist spokesmen
calling themselves by preference Nationalists, manifested such a
strong tendency to detach the movement from all religion as can

only end in spiritual disaster. There is such a thing as the assimilation of Judaism even as there is such a thing as the assimilation of the Jew, and the former is bound to happen when religion is looked upon as a negligible quantity. When Judaism is once assimilated the Jew will surely follow its wake, and the Jew and Judaism will perish together. All this is a consequence of preaching an aspect of Nationalism more in harmony with Roman and similar modern models than with Jewish ideas and ideals. However, nightmares are fleeting and evanescent — the vision as a whole still remains glorious. The aberrations will, let us hope, be swept away quickly enough as soon as their destructive nature is realized by the majority of the Zionists whose central ideas should and will remain, God and His people, Israel. . . .

In conclusion, I should only like to remark that when reading these proofs it gave me special satisfaction to see that the conciliatory note is not absent from this volume. Standing as the Seminary does for the healthy development of traditional Judaism in the midst of many movements and vagaries none of which are without excesses, and against which we are constantly struggling, it was not possible that the controversial feature should be entirely eliminated from the volume. Yet it will be found that the ultimate goal at which we are aiming is union and peace in American Israel. The union of which I am thinking is not one of mere organization. Organization is useful in the way of an auxiliary, but its saving virtues cannot be always relied upon. Whatever its effects may be for good, they are more than counterbalanced by its tendency towards materialization, resulting as history teaches in the desecration, if not profanation of things holy. The union we are in need of, is one on principle and the recognition of vital facts, decisive in our past and indispensable for our safety in the future, by which alone Israel can hope for a "name and remainder upon the earth." Such a recognition, however, can only be brought about by a thorough knowledge of our great literature, in which alone the Jewish soul found shelter and expression for untold generations, joined to broad sympathy and loving understanding for all the aspirations and cravings and longings and hopes recorded in this very literature. This is the mission of colleges and Jewish learned societies. The longer I live in this country, the more

I am convinced that it is only such a thorough and hearty union which will enable us to deal with the great problems, spiritual and otherwise, confronting us. Parties come and parties go, but the word of our God shall stand forever. And so shall Israel.

from THE CHARTER OF THE SEMINARY (1902)

Let me say a few words about the general religious tendency this Seminary will follow. I am not unaware that this is a very delicate point, and prudence would dictate silence or evasion. But life would hardly be worth living without occasional blundering, "the only relief from dull correctness." Besides, if there be in American history one fact more clearly proved than any other it is that "know-nothing-ism" was an absolute and miserable failure. I must not fall into the same error. And thus, sincerely asking forgiveness of all my dearest friends and dearest enemies with whom it may be my misfortune to differ, I declare, in all humility, but most emphatically, that I do know something. And this is that the religion in which the Jewish ministry should be trained must be specifically and purely Jewish, without any alloy or adulteration Judaism must stand or fall by that which distinguishes it from other religions as well as by that which it has in common with them. Judaism is not a religion which does not oppose itself to anything in particular. Judaism is opposed to any number of things, and says distinctly "thou shalt not." It permeates the whole of your life. It demands control over all your actions, and interferes even with your menu. It sanctifies the seasons, and regulates your history, both in the past and in the future. Above all, it teaches that disobedience is the strength of sin. It insists upon the observance both of the spirit and of the letter; spirit without letter belongs to the species known to the mystics as "nude souls" נשמות ערטילאות wandering about in the universe without balance and without consistency, the play of all possible currents and changes in the atmosphere. In a word, Judaism is absolutely incompatible with the abandonment of the Torah. Nay, the very prophet or seer must bring his imprimatur from the Torah. The assertion that the destruction of the Law is its fulfillment is a mere paradox, and recalls strongly the doctrines of Sir Boyle Roche, "the inimitable maker of Irish bulls." He declared emphatically that he "would give up a part, and, if necessary, the whole of the constitution, to preserve the remainder!"

President Abraham Lincoln, the wisest and greatest of rulers, addressed Congress on some occasion of great emergency with the words: "Fellow citizens, we cannot escape history." Nor can we, my friends. The past, with its long chain of events, with its woes and joys, with its tragedies and romances, with its customs and usages, and above all, with its bequest of the Torah, the great entail of the children of Israel, has become an integral and in-alienable part of ourselves, bone of our bone and flesh of our flesh. We must make an end to these constant amputations if we do not wish to see the body of "Israel" bleed to death before our very eyes. We must leave off talking about Occidentalizing our religion — as if the Occident has ever shown the least genius for religion — or freeing the conscience by abolishing various laws. These, and similar platitudes and stock phrases borrowed from Christian apologetics, must be abandoned entirely if we do not want to drift slowly but surely into Paulinism, which entered the world as the deadliest enemy of Judaism, pursued it through all its course and is still finding its abettors among us, working for their own destruction. Lord, forgive them, for they know nothing. Those who are entrusted with carrying out the purpose of this institution, which, as you have seen, aims at the perpetuation of the tenets of the Jewish religion, both pupils and masters, must faithfully and manfully maintain their loyalty to the Torah. There is no other Jewish religion but that taught by the Torah and confirmed by history and tradition, and sunk into the conscience of Catholic Israel.

I have just hinted at the desirability of masters and pupils working for one common end. You must not think that our intention is to convert this school of learning into a drill ground where young men will be forced into a certain groove of thinking, or, rather, not thinking; and after being equipped with a few devotional texts, and supplied with certain catchwords, will be let loose upon an unsuspecting public to proclaim their own virtues and the infallibility of their masters. Nothing is further from our thoughts. I once heard a friend of mine exclaim angrily to a pupil: "Sir, how dare you always agree with me?" I do not even profess to agree with myself always, and I would consider my work, to which, with the help of God, I am going to devote the rest of my life, a complete failure if this institution would not in the future produce such extremes as on the one side a raving mystic who would denounce me as a sober Philistine; on the other side, an advanced critic, who would rail at me as a narrow-minded fanatic, while a third devotee of strict orthodoxy would raise protest against any critical views I may entertain. "We take," says Montaigne, "other men's knowledge on trust, which is idle and superficial learning. We must make it our own." The Rabbis express the same thought with allusion to Ps. 1:2 which they explain to mean that what is first — at the initiation of man into the Law — God's Torah, becomes, after a sufficient study, man's own Torah. Nay, God even deigns to descend to man's own level so as not to interfere with his individuality and powers of conception. I reproduce in paraphrase a passage from a Midrash: "Behold now how the voice of Sinai goes forth to all in Israel attuned to the capacity of each; appealing to the sages according to their wisdom: to the virile according to their strength; to the young according to their aspiring youthfulness, and to the children and babes according to their innocence; aye, even to the women according to their motherhood." All that I plead for is that the voice should come from Sinai, not from Golgotha; that it should be the voice of Jacob, not of Esau. The Torah gave spiritual accomodation for thousands of years to all sorts and conditions of men, sages, philosophers, scholars, mystics, casuists, schoolmen and skeptics; and it should also prove broad enough to harbor the different minds of the present century. Any attempt to place the centre of gravity outside of the Torah must end in disaster. We must not flatter ourselves that we shall be allowed to land somewhere midway, say in some Omar Khayyam cult or in some Positivists' society or in some other agnostic makeshift. No, my friends, there are laws of gravitation in the spiritual as there are in the physical world; we cannot create halting places at will. We must either remain faithful to history or go the way of all flesh, and join the great majority. The teaching in the Seminary will be in keeping with this spirit, and thus largely confined to the exposition and elucidation of historical Judaism in its various manifestations.

from THE SEMINARY AS A WITNESS (1903)

A condition for producing greatness is that the teaching in our seminaries should be wide and comprehensive, containing within itself the elements of eternity and catholicity. I will explain myself: Among the various legends attaching to the account of the revelation on Mount Sinai there is one to the effect that this glorious act was not only witnessed by the master of the prophets and his contemporaries, but also by those who departed from these regions long since and who came to life again for that blissful moment, as well as by the souls of those who were still to be born. "For," the Rabbis proceed to say, "was it not said by Moses, 'Neither with you only do I make this covenant and this oath, but with him that standeth here with us this day before the Lord our God, and also with him that is not here and with us this day.' " The underlying idea is that a religious manifestation, to be truly great and inspiring, must also have regard for those who are not there. It must include both an appeal to the past, to which it should give back life and continuity, and hold out a good message to the future, which would, in its turn, endow it with immortality. It is true that it is the present and its needs which have the first claims upon our attention, and I would be sorry indeed to see the Jewish ministry proof against the demands of our own time. What attracted me many years ago to Krochmal's famous work was the title, "The Guide of the Perplexed of the Times," thereby showing that every time has its own perplexities and therefore is in need of its own guidance; but it is also from this immortal work and other kindred works from which I have learned that unless it is a present which forms a link between two eternities, representing an answer of Amen to the past and an Opening Prayer to the future, it will be a very petty present indeed, while its so-called needs will often turn out to be mere a caprice of the mob, or a whim of fashion, or the hobby of some wilful individual sure to disappear when viewed "sub specie aeternitatis."

Perhaps I may be permitted to read here with relation to such needs the following passage from a book existing only in proof.*

---

* The passage later appeared in Schechter's *Some Aspects of Rabbinic Theology*, New York, 1910.

After showing that Judaism has the same powers of adaptability as any other religion, the author proceeds to say:

"It must, however, be remarked that this satisfying the needs of anybody and everybody, of every moment and every fleeting season, is not the highest ideal which Judaism set before itself. Altogether I venture to think," our author says, "that the now fashionable test of determining the worth of religion by its capability to supply the various demands of the great market of believers has something low and mercenary about it. Nothing less than a good old honest heathen Pantheon, with beautiful gods, jovial gods, lusty gods, ailing gods, fighting gods, intoxicated gods, male gods and female gods — nothing less than this would satisfy the crazes and imaginary cravings of our pampered humanity, with its pagan reminiscences, its metaphysical confusion of languages, its aesthetic pretensions, and its theological idiosyncracies. No! True religion is above all these silly demands. It is not a jack-of-all-trades, meaning Monotheism to the philosopher, Pluralism to the crowd, some mysterious Nothing to the agnostic, Pantheism to the poet, and Service of Man to the Hero worshipper. Its mission is just as much to teach the world that there are false gods and false ideals as to bring it nearer to the true one. It means to convert the world, not to convert itself. It disdains a victory by defeating itself, in giving up its essential doctrines, its most sacred symbols, its most precious traditions and its most vital teaching. It has confidence in the world; it hopes and prays and waits patiently for the Great Day when the world will be ripe for its acceptance. . . ."

The teaching in the Seminary must not be overmuch burdened with the considerations of locality. The Directors of this institution, by terming it the "Jewish Theological Seminary of America," have distinctly shown their intention of avoiding sectarianism; for it is an especial American feature that no preference is given to any denomination or sect or theological "Richtung." They are all alike welcome, each working out its salvation in its own fashion. Again, if there is a feature in American religious life more prominent than any other, it is its conservative tendency. The history of the United States does not begin with the Red Indian, and the genesis of its spiritual life is not to be traced back to the vagaries of some peculiar sects. This country is, as everybody knows, a creation of the Bible, particularly the Old Testament, and the Bible is still holding its own, exercising enormous influence as a real spiritual power, in spite of all the destructive tendencies, mostly of foreign make. Nay, it is this very excess of zeal and the over-realization of the presence of Biblical times which unfortunately enabled quacks to create new Tabernacles here, with new Zions and Jerusalems, and to proclaim themselves as second or first Moseses, and even to profit their followers with caricature revelations. But these are only the excesses. The large bulk of the real American people have, in matters of religion, retained their sobriety and loyal adherence to the Scriptures, as their Puritan forefathers did. America thus stands both for wideness of scope and for conservatism. But be this as it may, forget not that this is a "Jewish Theological Seminary", having the mission to teach the doctrines and the literature of the religion which is as old as history itself and as wide as the world. Any attempt to confine its activity to the borders of a single country, even be it as large as America, will only make its teachings provincial, narrow and unprofitable. Israel, and Israel alone, must be the end for which synagogues and seminaries are erected, even in this country. Thus teaches the Book of Maccabees: "God did not choose His people (Israel) for the sake of the place (that is, His Temple), but the place for the sake of the people."

I am not an opponent of state rights, and much less of the rights of a whole continent, and I readily concede that the Seminary should always give due consideration to the religious needs of this country. For instance, I am of opinion that we should in this country, with its peculiar theological atmosphere, pay more attention to Bible and theology than we did in Europe. I am further of opinion that in a democratic country like this, everything should be avoided in the teaching of theological institutions which is calculated to emphasize the difference between layman and Rabbi. I am also inclined to think that any attempt towards the centralization of the spiritual power into the hands of a man or a body of men will only prove injurious to this country, with its free and broad spirit. But these, and many other questions like these, of a disciplinary nature, are of minor importance. The great body of Jewish doctrine and Jewish law as taught by Catholic Israel has nothing in it to collide with the American spirit, and the Seminary to be really great will have to be catholic, and of a uniting nature.

There is an old Jewish prayer reading thus: "Oh, God, protect me against the day when one part (of my body) will become a burden to the other." Unfortunately, there are symptoms that this day is not far. There is even a tendency noticeable not only to hasten this day, but at last to drop the burden and to give up all notion of solidarity and of mutual responsibility. There is no other way to save us from such a calamity but to strengthen our loyalty to the Torah and to devote ourselves to its study.

Lord John Morley, in his essay on Emerson, relates that while the New England mystic was lecturing, one of the audience asked his neighbor: "Can you tell me what connection there is between that last sentence and the one that went before, and what connection it all has with Plato?" "None, my friend, save in God!" If I were asked what connection is there, say, in order to except present company, between Rabbi Moses ben Maimon of Cordova (known as Maimonides), and Solomon ben Isaac, of Troyes (known as Rashi), I would say, "None, save in God and His Torah." The one lived under a Mohammedan government; the other under a Christian government. The one spoke Arabic; the other French. The one had all the advantage of an Eastern civilization, the other lived in the barbaric West. The one was a merchant, afterwards a famous physician in the great capitals of Cordova and Cairo; the other was a Rabbi, without salary, in an unimportant provincial city. The one was a "persona grata" for many years of his life at the court of Saladin, "the most enlightened despot who ever sat on a throne;" the other probably never had the good or rather the bad fortune, of ever speaking even to the chief constable of his place. The one was a thorough Aristotelian and possessed of all the culture of his day; the other was an exclusively Rabbinic scholar and hardly knew the name of Aristotle. The one was all system and method, writing everything in a smooth, elegant style; the other belonged to the great inarticulates, and wrote very little beyond commentaries and "occasional notes." But as they both observed the same fasts and feasts; as they both revered the same sacred symbols, though they put different interpretations on them; as they both prayed in the same language — Hebrew; as they both were devoted students of the same Torah, though they often differed in its explanation; as they both looked back to Israel's past with admiration and reverence, though Maimonides' conception of the

Revelation, for instance, largely varied from that of Rashi; as their ultimate hopes centered in the same redemption — in one word, as they studied the Torah and lived in accordance with its laws, and both made the hopes of the Jewish nation their own, the bonds of unity were strong enough even to survive the misunderstandings between their respective followers. And they both became the rocks and pillars of Judaism; and a Leopold Zunz, or an Isaac Hirsch Weiss, of Vienna, were able to appreciate both Rashi and Maimonides, and to fall in love with both of them. It is only by strengthening these bonds of unity, by appreciating everything Jewish and falling in love with it, that this great monument presented to us and to Judaism by our noble donor, whom one dares not thank but in oblique sentences, will become a blessing and a prayer, and, like the trans-Jordanic altar of the Book of Joshua, it will stand not only for unity and brotherhood, but like that, it will also be called witness, "for it shall be a witness between us that the Lord is God!"

CATHOLIC ISRAEL*

By HENRIETTA SZOLD

While Henrietta Szold (1860–1945) is most closely identified with Hadassah and with Zionist work, she had a distinguished career before she embarked upon these enterprises. From 1892 to 1916 she served as secretary of the Literary Committee of the Jewish Publication Committee. During that period she translated some notable volumes, including Ginzberg's Legends of the Jews, *and prepared them for publication. She also edited several volumes of the* American Jewish Year Book.

In 1902 Miss Szold enrolled as a student at the Jewish Theological Seminary. Her contact with Dr. Schechter and the other leaders of the Conservative movement are reflected in the selection printed below. Miss Szold is not presented here as an architect of Conservative Judaism, but rather as an interpreter of one of its ideas. The phrase "Catholic Israel" was a catchword and a watchword employed by Dr. Schechter. He never fully elaborated it, but it nonetheless made a powerful impact upon the Jewish community. The selection printed below is designed to indicate how this phrase was elaborated and interpreted and conveyed to the Jewish community. It also calls attention to the question of an American Jewish Synod which was widely debated as a solution to religious problems — and so presented a problem to Conservative Judaism — at the beginning of the century. The selection was originally prepared as a speech and was delivered before the New York Council of Jewish Women. It was subsequently printed in The American Hebrew *in 1913.*

In characterizing what he calls the historical school of Judaism, at present in the ascendant, Dr. Schechter uses the term "Catholic Israel" to designate the "living body" which it constitutes the final authority for the interpretation of the Scriptures and the fixing of custom. Presuming upon his generosity, I abstract, for my own purposes, a happy term of his coinage, together with his elaboration of its meaning as "the collective conscience . . . em-

---

* Delivered before the New York Council of Jewish Women.

111

bodied in the Universal Synagogue . . . . 'with its long, continuous cry after God for more than twenty-three centuries,' with its unremittent activity in teaching and developing the word of God, with its uninterrupted succession of Prophets, Psalmists, Scribes, Assideans, Rabbis, Patriarchs, Interpreters, Elucidators, Eminences, and Teachers, with its glorious record of saints, martyrs, sages, philosophers, scholars, and mystics, . . . the only true witness to the past, and forming in all ages the sublimest expression of Israel's religious life." (*Studies in Judaism* — Introduction.)

With your permission I shall speak to you of our relations and obligations towards this broad, universal, Catholic Israel; Israel at once a race, a nation, a religious brotherhood; Israel past and present; Israel scattered from East to West; whose subtle, yet none the less real, standard is explicitly laid down in no one book, expressed with finality in no one age, illustrated completely in no one synagogue, monopolized by no one community. The Chassidim of Galicia and the Bene Israel community at Bombay alike may contribute to the spirit informing Catholic Israel. On the other hand, the American Jew, liberal and cosmopolitan, may fail to grasp it in its breadth. Consciousness of Catholic Israel hallows the ritual, a fixed form of prayer, apparently so contradictory in the spontaneity that should characterize the outpouring of the heart. Public divine service itself, the gathering on predetermined days at definite places, would sink to the level of a dead ceremonial without the implied allegiance due to Catholic Israel.

The supremacy of Catholic Israel differs from and is more than the solidarity of the Jews. Solidarity means that each Jew stands ready to suffer with every other Jew, to succor him with the superabundance of prosperity, defend him against the aspersions of prejudice, espouse his cause when he is maligned — outward loyalty far from ignoble in view of the widespread misery and the frequent calumniation of the Jew.

Allegiance to Catholic Israel requires such sacrifices, such lessons got by heart, such emotions translated into effective action — and it requires far more. The duty of the Jew tingling with the consciousness of Catholic Israel extends beyond his outcast brother to the prosperous. He is, not patron, but fellow aspirant. He seeks to understand mental conditions as well as physical needs. For him neither "bigot" nor creature of darkness exists. His obligation

grows out of whole-souled belief in a mission waiting to be performed by Israel — Israel scattered or Israel nationalized. His
conviction is that the Jew who has blessed the human race with
a God, has not yet finished teaching true worship of Him and the
true love of man involved in acceptance of Him. He keenly feels
his responsibilities towards mankind. If the Jew deserts the watch-
tower, injustice and pagan recklessness may undermine the strong-
holds of culture. He may not lull himself into security with the
fond thought that the college professor studies and expounds the
textbook of religion. What if he should feel inclined to drop the
Bible, and turn to more lucrative pursuits! Has the college professor
an hereditary obligation to cherish the Bible, under which, if he
has a conscience, the Jew should stagger? Is he descended from a
race of prophets, scribes, sages, Gaons, Rabbis? The tasks set by
such a mission are gigantic. The co-operation is needed of every
owner of a half-shekel, be it of mind, heart, or muscle. We cannot
afford to let a single son of Israel fall out of line; no one can afford
to let himself drop out of line.

The Jew permeated with these views knows Catholic Israel
without a definition. Himself a part of it, he in turn creates Catholic
Israel. Solidarity is the bold, if need be, aggressive front that we
turn to the enemy upon the warpath; Catholic Israel is our fireside,
at which we sit discussing, arguing, taking counsel, confessing
longings, nursing hopes and aspirations, and, in intimate moments,
not shrinking from the betrayal of God-intoxicated feelings.

In 1881 the Jews of America were taught to support the arms
and grasp the hand of the outcast Russian Jew. We learned how
to pity effectively. We learned more. With a shock we realized
that some Jews are unlike ourselves. "Bigots," superstitious
fanatics, "creatures of darkness," we called the others. Simultaneously with the realization, that latter-day product, American
Judaism became self-conscious. Pity fed our pride. We found ourselves liberal, creatures of light, sweetly reasonable Jews. As such,
in 1885, at Pittsburgh, we formulated a program, our declaration of American Jewish independence. Thereafter little of noble
dissatisfaction with ourselves manifested itself. If, occasionally,
it occurred to us to question, investigate the extent of our liberality, determine whether or not it trenched upon the domain
of indifference, the result was apt to be increase of pity for

the others, increase of pride in ourselves. We commiserated the immigrant more on account of his intellectual limitations, as we saw fit to characterize his religious attitude, than on account of the shortness of his purse. In due proportion we extolled our own penetration and ability in having had immigrant forefathers sagacious enough to take the first step towards becoming American Jews a generation earlier, enough time, according to one of their proud descendants, to transform "the creeping, cringing peddler into an upright, polished gentleman." (Papers of the Jewish Women's Congress, p. 29.)

When our immigration problem defined its huge dimensions, we continued to learn. Amazed and delighted — for thus we knew them flesh of our flesh in spite of all differences — we beheld that a brief respite enabled the Russian Jew to hang up his sign on Broadway. Equally amazed, with perhaps an abatement of delight, we faced the imminent danger of seeing him occupy a Fifth-Avenue mansion and not seriously disgrace it by unconvention ality in speech, manners, and dress. A suspicion began to dawn upon us that to the outside world a Jew is a Jew. And, indeed, before long we had to acknowledge the Russian Jew bone of our very bone, for upon the field of American Judaism, our own peculiar province, he out-Americanized the American Jew. In respect to indifference, irreligion, recklessness, drifting, yielding to existing conditions from choice or compulsion, or, let us say, out of deference to our predilections, in respect to advanced views and liberality, the Russian Jew has proved himself forever an indispensable ingredient in our home-brewed Judaism. The ease with which he overtook us in the race after negations should have given us pause half a generation ago. It might, upon reflection, have suggested the possibility that American Judaism is not wholly the product of earnest thought, not wholly of Jewish thought. The fear might have been aroused that Occidental Judaism may contribute, not to the solution of Jewish questions, but to the dissolution of the Jewish race.

The lessons of the Russian exodus are not exhausted. When the Jew peddlers fleeing from Slavonic mobs regained breath they opened their mouths and spoke, and we stood dumb. They told of their intellectual activity, their writers, their poets, their exegetes — of their Isaac Baer Levinsohns, their Smolenskins, their Judah

Loeb Gordons, their Reifmanns, not one of them down upon the
pages of our old stand-bys, Graetz and Karpeles. We were abashed.
The circumstance that we were non-Russians was our salvation.
The negative earned for us the right to summon to our rescue, if
not from Jewish literature, at least from the pages of a history of
Jewish literature, every Galician, Hungarian, German, French
and Roumanian scholar. With the labor of European, exclusive of
Slavonic, Judaism, American Judaism justified itself, at all events
in its own sight. Or, if there lurked a wee doubt concerning our
originality and philosophic consistency, and honestly refused to be
muzzled by subterfuges, diluting pride with chagrin, we drowned
it in a boisterous proclamation of American Judaism for American
Jews, insisting upon its beauty and holiness, its only saving power,
its spirituality. Spirituality — that was our trump card. Intellectualism, we held, had emaciated Slavonic Judaism. It was exanimate,
nothing but dead bones, awaiting the breath of American-Jewish
enthusiasm to resuscitate them. To this day, in the bout between
Oriental and American Judaism, intellectualism plays the role of
the old charges, legalism and Phariseeism, the stock in trade of
Christian controversialists.

Yet I venture to say that the opponents of Zionism will grant
that the one great spiritual current rejuvenating the Jewish world
of our day flows, not from American Temples, à la Pittsburgh, but
from Talmudists' back rooms in Polish and Russian Jew streets.

One of the Jew peddlers fleeing from Slavonic mobs met me
at New Year's time. In extending the greeting appropriate to the
season, he emphasized the wish for life. "Life, life, that is the main
thing," he ruminated. "So long as man lives he can do something
for his *neshamah*. He goes to Shul morning and evening; he learns
a bit of *Mishnayot*; he does a *tova* to a fellow poorer than himself" — a trilogy of the life spiritual, exactly corresponding in the
concrete to the abstract props of the universe — Law, Worship,
and Charity — erected by Simon the Just, the magnificent Elder
of the Synagogue.

Though examples like these of spiritual thinking and living be
multiplied as they might be; though demonstration be made of the
truth that intellect and emotion are not mutually exclusive concepts; the power of spiritual living being raised to the highest
degree in the intellectual; though our search for an American-

Jewish author of commanding stature be vain; yet, doubtless, we shall go on prating of our esoteric spirituality, and in our reliance upon it shall go on shutting ourselves wantonly into an American-Jewish Ghetto, gates unlocked to Christian and barred to cosmopolitan Jewish thought. In our new spiritual Ghetto, entered with open eyes and of our own volition, we shall imitate Karaism, exclude light and progress, stagnate in our barrenness, our conceit, our lawlessness, our sullen rejection of the sympathy, spiritual and intellectual, of Catholic Israel.

We shall stagnate, I say, unless we pay heed to the warning voices raised against our consequential folly. They have spoken in no uncertain tones. Neither Judge Sulzberger in describing the origin of Reform in this country, nor Dr. Kohler in noting the recurrence of the phenomenon in various circles during the last two generations, glories in the existing state of affairs. They agree in deprecating the lawlessness rampant in American Israel. They lament that each congregation is a law unto itself; that "the thing that hath been is again;" that again "every man does that which is right in his own eyes." Their remedy? The one proposes a synod with the reservation that the suggestion must long remain an academic question to be debated, modified, adapted to crystallizing conditions; the other accepts it enthusiastically, apparently refusing to consider difficulties in the way of instant realization, and confident that an American-Jewish Synod will expand into a Pan-Jewish body. The suggestion has been received not without approbation; some who shrugged their shoulders, and called it a theoretic solution impossible of practical application, when it appeared in the *Sabbath Sheni* form, now declare a Synod feasible and necessary.

The voices of the synodists are not the only ones crying in the wilderness. Other lovers of Israel gathered in council, primarily to discuss measures of relief for the physical misery of the Jews the world over, could not avoid taking note of the spiritual degradation following in the wake of unremitting sordid care. That other time, long ago, when "every man did that which was right in his own eyes," the reason alleged for the prevalence of disintegrating individualism was that "in those days there was no king in Israel." A central power was lacking, the national bonds were loosed, the people were wretched and lawless. The Zionist holds that the whirligig of time has brought back the same state of affairs, and proposes, in effect, the same remedy, a central power, figuratively speaking, a king in Jerusalem, as the synodist proposes, a central organization, a Synod, for the American Zion. Themselves, perhaps, ignorant of the force impelling them, the leaders of Zionism are working through the spirit from which, by reason of training and associations, they believed themselves completely estranged. Yet, if the leaders of the ecclesiastic movement, with, I am sure, equal unconsciousness of the purpose I am attributing to them, are endeavoring to counteract racial features of Zionism, asserting themselves to the detriment of Judaism, partisan though I be, I do to the extent of this crusade welcome their efforts.

Zionism I believe to be in consonance with allegiance to Catholic Israel as race and faith alike; its tendency is centripetal, not centrifugal; towards unification, not towards disruption. But I am now not concerned with it. As for the Synod, inasmuch as its organization would, in my opinion, be ruinous to the catholicity of Israel, the maintenance of which I hold indispensable to the performance of our mission, I venture to express one of my objections to it.

At first sight it might seem that allegiance to Catholic Israel embracing, as it does, not only present-day Israel scattered the world over, but the Israel of all the ages as well, would compel acceptance of a solution of our difficulties conceived in an historical spirit, and sanctioned by the Deuteronomic recommendation to "come unto the judge that shall be in those days." As such, a Synod would rightly be considered. Disregarding for the present the insinuation that loyalty to Catholic Israel requires obedience to every mandate it issues, I pass to the important question, whether a Synod, though composed of ideal delegates, would actually be in a line of spiritual descent from the old Sanhedrin. The ancient body existed only so long as the Jews formed a State governed supposedly by the Mosaic law and its development. Religious life and civil life were co-terminous. The synagogue coincided with the polity and literature reflected and shaped both. Life was a unit. If there was talk in those days of bringing religion into harmony with the demands of the time, the process was not like our way of doing or letting be done. Religious regulations were not the only ones to suffer clipping and curtailment. Civil conditions likewise had to endure modification and pay tribute. There was no "stemming of the tide" of indifference and unbelief, but a deepening and widening of the bed of the rivers of life, that the waters transgress not their legitimate bounds, as they sweep steadily and calmly into the sea that is never full.

The classic example of Sanhedrin legislation is the *prosbul* enactment. The following account of it, taken from Graetz, illustrates my point: "In the Sabbatical year all debts were by law cancelled. At the time when the State was a republic based upon moral laws, this was a wise measure for equalizing property; but, at a later period, when capital became a power in itself, the rich were not willing to relieve their less wealthy neighbors from their difficulties by giving them loans. On this account Hillel, without entirely abrogating the law which already existed, ruled that the creditor should give over the debt in writing to the court, so that the court might collect it, and the creditor be relieved from the necessity of violating the law. This timely statute, equally advantageous to debtor and creditor, was called by the Greek word *prosbul*, because the debt was given over to the Council of Elders." (Vol. II, p. 100).

Here we have a thoroughly modern instance. Economic conditions threatened to reduce a law upon the religious statute book to a dead letter or the poorer classes to serfdom. But the ancient legislators enjoyed an advantage beyond the most sanguine expectations of the modern synodists. Within the Jewish State and under the Jewish law the baleful conditions had arisen; within the Jewish State and under the Jewish law they were met and counteracted. Hillel's "legal fiction" fairly transformed the law to suit the new circumstances, yet its spirit was preserved, the Council of Elders being vested with the power to enforce it. Will our Synod control the Stock Exchange? Will it have representation in the Executive Board of Trusts and Syndicates and Combines; in Parliament, in Congress, in the Reichsrath? Unless it does, we shall have to resign ourselves to seeing its province limited to the repeal of statute after statute, letter and spirit both victims to the Moloch of economic and industrial conditions, which will be as unappeasable despots towards the Synod as they have been towards the individual Jew. Decidedly, the advocate of the Synod, who cares to resume our religious life where it was cut through by Vespasian's

legions, will have to pray and work for the success of the Zionist
cause. Let Zionism establish a realm governed by Jewish principles, and a Synod in the historical sense may come within the
range of possibility.

There is another difficulty. Our dilemma occurs, not like that
disposed of by Hillel once in seven years, but once in seven days.
The enemy has long had possession of the outworks; he is now
standing within the Holy of Holies. The proposers of the Synod
and the rest of us, we all admit that our disease has attacked a
vital organ. Our trouble is connected with the observance of the
Sabbath. This is the kernel of the whole modern question, and the
distressing circumstance is that it is at the same time the kernel of
the whole of Judaism, as the Sabbatical year never was even
approximately. The importance of the Sabbath in the system of
Judaism is not derived from its present peril nor augmented by it.
What, now, can a Synod do about it? Invent a legal fiction which
shall prove that it is all a mistake about the Sabbath we have been
celebrating these three thousand years; that there is a miscalcula-
tion in the calendar; that, at bottom, according to the latest
scientific hocus-pocus, it is an Assyrian institution, and that we
therefore are right to abrogate it and choose a genuinely Jewish
day, one that will inconvenience neither ourselves nor the Tyrian
fishdealers? Or should we resort to the Synod in the spirit of the
passage in Deuteronomy (xvii, 8). "If there arise a matter too
hard for thee in judgment . . . . come unto the judge that shall be
in those days?" Is the Sabbath ordinance a matter too hard for
us in judgment? Do we require the sentence of judgment to be
shown to us? Is it not rather very nigh unto us, in our mouth, and
in our heart, that we may do it?

Far be it from me to dismiss the Sabbath difficulty lightly.
The quality of mercy were indeed strained if we insisted that any
who will can keep the Sabbath. Stress of circumstances does not
mean choice of circumstances. But I do maintain that Judaism
is powerless in the matter. To abrogate a practice that is the vital
fluid of Judaism is a crime; moreover, a useless crime. So long as
injustice is not perpetrated, a cause that will outlast and benefit
generations must be set above individuals. An eternal statute is
abolished that it may cease to be true that, as Judge Sulzberger
said, "the weak point in the whole structure is the teaching that

Saturday is the only Sabbath of the Lord with the uniform and continuous avowal by act that it is not" ("A Jewish Synod", *American Hebrew*, Jan. 13, 1899). I ask, are the defenses strengthened by the declaration that the Sabbath of men is the Sabbath of the Lord? Concessions are made for the sake of those who either will not or cannot, in any event, do not, observe the Sabbath, and are therefore elapsing into irreligion. Will concessions save them from their fate? We emasculate a religion in their behalf; we shear it of its essential elements of stability and eternity; is what remains a religion or a cracked reed? Are its devotees religious or are they irreligious self-deceivers? Stability, eternity, universality are the marks of a true religion; willingness to make sacrifices for one's convictions, the mark of true religiousness. An individual decides that certain duties are of paramount importance, more important than the commands enjoined by the religion of his fathers, with which besides they conflict. So be it. It is either his misfortune or his fault. In either case, he must bear it alone. It is not removable by an untruth, by the perjured statement that black is white; by the illusion that the first day is the seventh . . . Hard as life's terms are, they never dictate untruth, dishonor, unrighteousness. Judaism surely has arrived at the stage of resignation to the fate of being the religion of a minority. It stands ready to hear each one's decision without flinching, itself prepared not to yield a principle. It holds that, like intermarriage, the observance of the Sabbath is a purely personal question.

For my part, one good reason for not being frantic about making concessions is that I have no difficulty in imagining some of those whom we are called upon to pity as victims of modern conditions as satisfactorily religious from their own point of view as some of the strict Sabbath observers. There are, indeed, two points, of view, legitimate and religious, though only one of them Jewish. The seventh-day Sabbath is not the indispensable condition of a religious life. Non-Jews, Christians and agnostics can and do reach the highest dignity of manhood. They do justice, they love kindness, they walk humbly with their God or through their ideal. Into this category I am prepared to put the "Israelites without guile" who believe that the time has come to abandon a distinctive creed and unite with the majority to attempt the formation of that tiresome brotherhood of man manifesting itself not in justice and charity, but in uniformity of thought — an impossible, mistaken and stupid ideal. All these may rest and worship on any day with perfect truthfulness. But the Jew who believes that mankind stands not yet upon Sinai's height, demands of them a guarantee for the future, else each generation will have to begin the work of civilization anew. Of the Jew with a conscious mission it must be known as of Abraham, "that he will command his children and his household after him, that they shall keep the way of the Lord, to do righteousness and justice." For this the historic Sabbath — and, I may add parenthetically, a number of other Jewish forms so-called, — with its freight of Jewish teaching, sentiment, and association marked "not transferable," is an indispensable condition. Jews without the Sabbath may have a religious spirit, but they are not useful Jews. Their ceremonial laxness incapacitates them for the task of spreading the mission of Judaism. If we should tamper with the Sabbath ordinance for their sake, they would not be benefited religiously, and Judaism would be past benefiting, for without the Sabbath its mission dies.

These are the two legitimate points of view, the non-Jewish and the Jewish. Opposed to them is the irreligious attitude of the Orthodox or un-Orthodox Jew who admits the sanctity and binding character of the seventh-day Sabbath, yet entreats a "power not himself," but hardly "making for righteousness," to absolve him from inconvenient Sabbath keeping, wipe out the discrepancy between his teaching and practice, and create for him a new standard to sin against it, haply it becomes convenient so to do. He demands that Judaism be cut and trimmed to fit his unsymmetric heart. Having fallen from grace, he wishes to associate others with himself in wrong-doing — the most execrable of sins according to the rabbis. The truth which his irreligious spirit has not conceived vividly is that the worst heterodoxy is offense against one's own orthodoxy.

In the course of historical evolution, what has taken the place of the Sanhedrin? When Palestine lost its independence, the Sanhedrin was merged into academies, where they fore-gathered, "the judges of those days," of whom the perplexed might inquire, and who were ready to show the people the "sentence of judgment." Though the dispersion of Israel was wide, Palestine was still the center towards which all Jews turned, and wherever possible they obtained from benevolent rulers the authorization to constitute themselves in some respects a State within the State, with jurisdiction over its members. The polity in the early days of the diaspora, then, was not wholly dissociated from religion. Soon, however, Palestine lost, besides independence its natural and religious supremacy. The center of Judaism shifted to the banks of the Euphrates. In Babylonia the civic-religious organization of the Jews was all but complete, with its political head, the Exilarch, a veritable prince, and a religious head, the Gaon. To the Babylonian authorities as to the "judges of those days," the Jews in the dispersion looked for guidance. The Mohammedan conquest changed little. Among the Arabs, a related race, Jews found the conditions of life malleable. After seven centuries, Babylonia forfeited its Jewish importance, and at last the dispersion was complete. Thereafter the "judges of the day" were the great scholars, living in isolation here and there. The vast literature of "Questions and Answers" originating in Gaonic times developed to an amazing degree. Customs became differentiated, decision numerous. The need for manuals easy of reference and definite in statement made itself keenly felt. As far back as the eighth century the labor of abstracting and summarizing had begun, and historians trace a continuous line from Judah the Blind (759–762) through Simon of Cairo (900), Alfassi (1013–1103), and Maimonides' *Mishneh Torah* (1135–1204) to the two great codes, *Arba Turim* (1280–1340) and the *Shulchan Aruch* (1488–1575). What gave the last vogue and seeming finality, and thus made it the butt of scorners Jewish and anti-Jewish, is the simple fact that it appeared after the invention of printing. More accessible, it was more widely scattered, more widely used than its predecessors. If printing stereotyped it, it did not stereotype Judaism, as so often has been asserted. Catholic Israel is at least as well served by Guttenberg's art as the *Shulchan Aruch*. In point of fact, scarcely had the *Shulchan Aruch* appeared, before the death of its compiler, when a commentary upon it was written, so important that many Jews rank it with the text it explains. With means of communication developed as they are today men need not meet and see each other face to face to understand each other. Catholic Israel, the judge of these days, can readily make its mandates known to all who care to read and to heed.

If Catholic Israel is the judge of these days, why not resolve it into a Pan-Jewish Synod, whose "sentences of judgment" will be distinctly formulated and clearly expressed as well as widely published? Obligation to Catholic Israel would certainly invest the decisions of such a body with the highest authority, with sanctity! The very clearness, precision, and definiteness of its sentences would be objectionable. A Synod would count votes instead of weighing opinions; it would have to resort to inquisitorial methods to formulate an official Judaism, to which, in the end, some of us would be able to pay nothing more than "soulless conformity." In time Judaism would lose one of its fountains of strength, the benefit of the thought, feeling and stimulating presence of the Protestants who stamp their feet and exclaim: "And still it moves!" They would be outside instead of inside the fold. Not that the bugaboo of heresy trials need scare us; we may safely assume that their day is past even among non-Jews. But the cause of religion is served as little by cathechetical finality as by interdict and excommunication. The subtlety, the aroma, the poetry, which are essential principles of religion, would volatilize and escape in the process of systematizing them. The desire and necessity to satisfy the demands, not only of the times, but of all regions at a given time, would lead to an evening up and leveling down process, to endless compromising and temporizing. The great motto of the Synod would be: "Yield part of the ground to save the rest" (Dr. Kohler), until there were no rest to save, and with Judaism the religious spirit itself would suffer annihilation. That a Pan-Jewish Synod is an alluring project is undeniable. Life seems gracious with doubts resolved, beliefs defined and prescribed, inconveniences removed. But is it life or the similitude of life? What if doubting should cease entirely, beliefs become stereotyped, Judaism no longer cause discomfort, because stagnation and authorized indifference have supervened; because we think and are encouraged to think that religion is the business of accredited delegates, official directors of consciences? As things are, the reproach is more or less true that we are inclined to leave religious concerns, if we are Jews of the male sex, to Jews of the female sex, especially to the Council of Jewish Women; if we are parents, to the teachers and children of the Sabbath schools; if we are of the laity, to those whom we are pleased to regard as professional religionists, and to blame them for all difficulties and shortcomings. Under existing conditions, however, such a view is at least frowned down. With official Judaism as the obverse of the coin, legalized and justified indifference would be the reverse.

Perhaps religion in the abstract has less to fear from an American-Jewish Synod; least if, as has been suggested, each of the two parties in American Judaism, has its separate body. There would be less occasion for compromises upon a subject the nature of which abhors compromise; less need for "stemming the tide." The Reform Synod would legalize the religious laxity of the past — catch up to itself, as it were; the Orthodox Synod would authorize intended laxity and absolve Orthodox consciences. But where would be the gain? Carried to its logical conclusion, the system would demand a central organization for every shade of opinion that may spring up, and lawlessness tantamount to individualism would ensue. Maintained upon the lines of our two existing divisions, the Synods would change what we now shrink from calling sects into schism. An American Judaism would be officially constituted, completely cut loose and alienated, in fact and in spirit, beyond hope of restoration from the communion of Catholic Israel.

In recognizing the existence of lawlessness, I virtually admitted the inability of Catholic Israel to secure obedience to its decrees. If, in truth, it be the judge of these days, it cannot execute its judgments. How, then, can it help us out of our dilemma? Catholic Israel does, indeed, fail us if we seek a nostrum. There is none. Catholic Israel acknowledges that things are at sixes and sevens in its household, and maintains that they can be set to rights only by the exertions of each individual member. Its appeal is personal. Thou art the man, it says, who stands at the very centre of the Jewish universe. All depends upon thee. I ask not so much that thou shalt do something as that thou shalt be something. Be a Jew, conscious of thy mission, of thy part and duty as God's witness.

Catholic Israel cautions us against hampering ourselves by accepting external, practical makeshifts that do not measure us to ideal standards. It warns us not to impoverish Judaism for the sake of maintaining numbers intact; not to give it so ironclad a form that useful missionaries are forced from its ranks. It admonishes us to reflect that in our present fluid state we are intellectually untrammeled. Far-reaching as our disintegration, superinduced by industrialism, may be, we still rejoice in a body of accepted truths definite enough to serve thinking men beyond the catechism stage as a basis for old-established religious practices — a tangible possession transmissible to posterity. Perhaps our descendants will enjoy the golden opportunity of living them out fully here or in our own Holy Land, or all over the world, if Zionistic hopes and aims are realized. Catholic Israel repudiates the idea that allegiance to itself requires obedience to every utterance in any age or country. Sanity unresolvable by logical analysis enables Catholic Israel, in a mysterious, subtle way, to elaborate, from a chaotic mass of opinion and facts, what is final and permanent. In the interim every member of Catholic Israel, by means of temperament, studies, and meditation, selects what is orthodox for him, the most important thing being that he honestly live up to it, the next important thing being that he refrain from forcing it upon the world as the whole of Judaism, or as its only true essential element. It has been said that so many commandments were enjoined that every one may have the opportunity of fulfilling at least a part of the Law, and among 613 every human being will assuredly find what is suitable for the development and full expression of his individuality. Catholic Israel has no specific practical measures to suggest — not public Seders, not reinvesting Succoth and Hanukah with modern meaning, not the lighting of Sabbath lamps. It has faith in neither symposiums, nor synods. It has faith only in you. It asks you not to drift. It entreats you to let your actions be result of thought, and your thought be as Jewish as possible. Catholic Israel is individualism at its thoughtful best, and its exhortation is directed to the best in man — to his heart.

But alas! our hearts are uncircumcised. The ideal is denied entrance to them; they must first be converted. At this point Catholic Israel becomes definite and practical, though not very startling in its suggestions. It proposes a solution, a conversion to which there is no royal road — education it was formerly called, intellectualism it is now nicknamed. The remedy has at least the quality of universal applicability to recommend it. It may be adopted by Zionists, and need not be scorned by Synod partisans.

The Jewish doctrine has always been, not as usually stated,

that we have no priests, but that we have no laity. "A nation of priests" we are. Paradoxical as it may seem, the greatest effect of the anti-intellectual current has been a division of our people into the laity and a priesthood. We are, in fact, closer to having a hierarchy than ever before in our history, not because the priests are too learned, which can never be a fault in a whole class of people, but because the laity are too ignorant. The good old times cannot be extolled unreservedly; many of our diseases are inherited from them. Yet it must be conceded that in the past the Jewish education of the people formed the substantiation upon which the learning of the rabbis rested. The people were intelligent enough to question intelligently. The difference between them and their leaders was one in degree, not in kind. The people understood the rabbis, the rabbis could readily appeal to the people. They stood upon common ground. At present a gulf yawns between the people and the pastors they have forced their rabbis willy-nilly to become, and the separation exists whether the rabbis be learned or unlearned. Instead of being expected to serve as enlightened inter- preters of the literature, history, and genius of Catholic Israel unto the eager questioners who seek the fount to quench their thirst, they are required to be pastors who are to seek the indifferent and probe and save their souls. An old Jew's soul was his very own to keep and make, or to keep and mar. The modern Jew sells his birthright of individuality and dignity, and pays a man of clay like himself to take care of his soul and act as his scapegoat. Thus a new thing is being made in Judaism. Not qualification for a position bestows influence, but the ordination conferred by election to the rabbinate of a congregation — an esoteric, mysterious something, often an esoteric, mysterious nothing. Members of congregations quote the opinions of their rabbis upon philosophy, literature, politics and Judaism alike. To my ears "the Doctor says" sounds perilously like "my father-confessor says." But not even the degenerate Jew will long endure the priestcraft he has fostered. Those who even now were loudest in their deprecation of rabbis crammed with learning and their demand for men as Occidental as themselves, are censuring certain leaders, created in their own image, for keeping their ears to the ground and doing the bidding of their constituents. Instinctively they know that special prepara- tion for a high calling argues at least steadiness of purpose, the sign-manual of character, and that, on the other hand, the man who accepts a post without having used every effort to equip himself for it is certainly not of the most exalted character, be he ever so modern in perception and ever so up-to-date in practical devices. If we persist in our demand for pastors we must inevitably take the retrograde step from rabbi — that is, teacher-hood, to priesthood. The doom can be averted, I maintain, not by beginning at the top, with the training of rabbis, but by educating the people. With the people truly educated even the Synod idea is robbed of some of its terrors.

The remedy is efficacious and universal, but not easy. Discussion helps little, enthusiasm alone is abortive. Every man and woman of us must stop talking and buckle down to steady work. It again resolves itself into the impressive home-thrust: "Thou art the man." Upon thee everything depends. Thou canst create a world, thou canst destroy it. The alternatives are set before thee: in the Ghetto of American Judaism, death and evil; in openhearted, intelligent communion with Israel, past and present, life and good. Choose thou life everlasting.

OUR STANDPOINT

An Address to the United Synagogue of America

By Rabbi Louis Ginzberg

The Conservative movement has always regarded the findings of Jewish legal and historical scholarship as fundamental to its thought. This stress gave Louis Ginzberg (1873–1953) a central position in the development of the Conservative Jewish ideology. He was universally regarded as the outstanding Talmudist and the leading Jewish scholar of his generation. Since he approached his material in the spirit of the school of "Historical Judaism" he would under any circumstances have had a profound effect upon Conservative thought. His influence, however, was considerably enhanced by the fact that for fifty years he was Professor of Talmud at the Seminary. Almost every man who entered the Conservative rabbinate was his student and was guided by his thinking.

Most of Professor Ginzberg's writings were scholarly in nature. Few of his works bore directly upon the problems of the Conservative movement. But the general tone of these works, his approach to Jewish legal problems and his lectures and private conversations had a wide and continuing effect upon the standard bearers of the Conservative movement. Moreover, for a period in the early years of organization, he played an active role not only in shaping the Seminary, but in organizing the United Synagogue.

The selection printed below is from his Presidential address to the United Synagogue Convention in 1918. It is one of the few public statements in which he articulated his view of Conservative Judaism and its potentialities.

There seems to prevail an erroneous idea as to the origin of conventions. The modern man is inclined to take them to be a product of our age. Now, while it cannot be disputed, that no previous age had as many conventional laws as ours, we must not forget that the one, but last commandment of the Torah is, "the law of convention." This law, observed by the Jews until the very end of the second commonwealth, prescribes that at the end of every seven years all the people, men and women, shall assemble at the holy place to listen to the reading of the Torah, that they may hear and that they may learn. I am far from recommending a servile imitation of the past, but "such a reproduction of it as is really new, while it is old."

A convention at the end of every seven years, would, in our times, hardly be a success. The spirit animating our annual convention, however, should be the one prescribed in the Torah: "To hear and to learn." You came to hear the reports on the various activities of the United Synagogue. Important as the activities of an organization may be, one must not forget that of every institution a certain idea is the vital principle on losing which it ceases to be; hence, to learn to understand the idea forming the vital principle of an institution is more important than to become acquainted with its activities. "Unqualified activity of whatever kind," a great poet and thinker remarked, "leads at last to bankruptcy."

The United Synagogue, while following the principle that intelligent silence is preferable to loquacious ignorance, insists nevertheless, that the ideas which it embodies and the ideals for which it stands, should become clear and intelligible to all who want to listen. But it is a well-known fact that the truer doctrines are, the more liable they are to be perverted, and we must therefore from time to time restate our principles, that they may not be misunderstood by ignorance or perverted by malice. Of course, I shall not engage in apologetics or polemics. A bad cause is in need of apologetics, and a bad taste produces polemics. The United Synagogue stands for a noble cause, and possesses a good taste so that it can dispense with polemics and apologetics.

Let me at the outset repeat the words of Dr. Schechter, the founder of our organization, "We do not intend to create a new party." Indeed, I would rather say, that our policy is to destroy parties by building up a United Israel. We are opposed to all separatist movements in Israel, and are prepared to fight sects and still more so, sectarians without sects. It would be a comparatively simple process to affix the regulation labels of theology to our organization. But labels are devices for saving talkative persons the trouble of thinking. Nothing is easier, but nothing is more dangerous than definitions; I shall attempt a description, in the hope that my words may confirm you in your own convictions and possibly make clear the reasons for these convictions.

Our organization bears the name, the United Synagogue of America, and it would pay the trouble to examine carefully the meaning of that name. The opening line of the Sabbath afternoon prayer reads, "Thou art one and Thy name is one, and who is like Thy people of Israel, one nation on the earth." In these few words the most characteristic feature of the mental make-up of the Jew is expressed with precision and thoroughness. A striving for unity in all realms of the human mind describes the Jew best. In monotheism the religious aspect of this striving is expressed in the doctrine of equality of man, the ethical and in the strong feeling of solidarity, the national. We Jews of America pride ourselves, and justly so, on our solidarity; and to the honor of American Jewry be it said that in these times of distress and sorrow, American Israel does not know parties or classes. Yet we have to admit that an internal principle of union is wanting, and, to quote the words of a great religious leader of the last century, "when this is wanting, the principle of life is wanting, and all is outward show." Societies and institutions, however well organized and energetic, will avail nothing without a living principle. Unity without is a result of unity within, but when there is nothing real within, what appears is as little real and substantive as a shadow. Lacking unity, we today live partly on the shadow of the past, and one shudders at the thought that those who will come after us will have to live on the shadow of a shadow.

The internal principle for a united Israel as expressed in the preamble of the constitution of our organization, is: "loyalty to the Torah and its historical interpretation," in other words, the United Synagogue stands for historical Judaism. Now let us understand the exact meaning of the expression historical Judaism. It does not intend to give you the content of Judaism while you are standing on one foot. All attempts made in the last two thousand years to create an acrobatic Judaism had to fail; one cannot go on forever standing on one foot. Looking at Judaism from an historical point of view we become convinced that there is no one aspect deep enough to exhaust the content of such a complex phenomenon as Judaism, no one term or proposition which will serve to define it. Judaism is national and universal, individual and social, legal and mystic, dogmatic and practical at once, yet it has a unity and individuality "just as a mathematical curve has its own laws and expression." By insisting upon historical Judaism, we express further our conviction that for us Judaism is no theory of the study or school, no matter of private opinion or deduction, but a fact. Only what happens, do we understand, not what might have happened. Accordingly, a Torah-less Judaism, if such a being could exist at all, would be a thing entirely new, and not the continuation of something given. If we look upon Jewish history in its integrity as a simple and uniform power, though marked in portions by temporary casual parenthetical interruptions, we find that it was the Torah which stood forth throughout the history of Israel as the guiding star of its civilization.

In their morning prayers our young children are made to recite the Biblical verse: "Moses commanded us the Torah as the inheritance of Israel." We thus teach them the deep truth that the Torah is law to the Jewish consciousnesss and Jewish consciousness becomes law to the Torah. God's Torah, when revealed, became the Torah of Israel, his inheritance. We cannot go back to the fountain head and simply ignore the thousands of years of Jewish development. It is true the essence of Judaism need not be distilled for us out of its whole history; the key is given in its source, but there is nevertheless great vitality and value in the later courses of the stream. It is a well-established fact that a variation from a type which in its origin is accidental, may become a source of a new type promising advantages which enable it to survive and prevail and reach a higher life of efficiency than the original type possessed. The development of Talmudical Judaism from Biblical Judaism while preserving the unity of type, characteristic as it is of faithful developments, became only possible by means of variation. Biblical Judaism was limited to one small country, and to a time of cultural homogenity of the Jewish people. Talmudism made Judaism suited to all time and places, to every state of society, to every stage of civilization, and accordingly Talmudism could not but vary in its relation and dealing towards the world around it. Historical Judaism therefore does not rest exclusively on the Bible, but also on tradition. Or, as our preamble expresses it, "loyalty to the Torah and its historical interpretation." If one be weary of the past, let him remember that he cannot shake himself clear of the past. One is in his character and spiritual life as much a child of thousands of generations behind him as he is in mind and body. The part one contributes to his own making, bodily or spiritually, is infinitesimal. The greater part of what we are is due to heredity and the atmosphere of the time and place into which we are born. Our historic conscience as embodied in tradition, tells us, do what I tell you, for I represent the collective experience and wisdom of myriads of holy men for thousands of years. Conscience is not infallible but still it is the safest guide and best teacher. Like all good teachers, conscience teaches us to reason out things for ourselves, and to see that tradition has indeed brought with it from the past much that is good and true and eternal, but also things that were good and true and temporal.

For a constructive criticism of the contents of tradition however, the first requirement is sympathy. Where there is no love there is no understanding. There is such a thing as learned ignorance, a stir and curiosity of the shadows and trifles. Hence, the attempts of those, otherwise learned men, who without love for historical Judaism tried to reform it, were doomed to failure. One does not break with history without darkening it. Reform, that is shaping of new forms for old truths was turned into radicalism, that is, the uprooting of old truths. But all progess is a deeper penetration into the meaning of old truth, and a larger appropriation of it.

Originality in physics is not man's creation of new forces but the discovery of forces that were never seen before, or the bringing to light of relations between them that were never before suspected. In the domain of religion to be absolutely new — original, is equivalent to being false or groundless, namely, totally detached from the old and everlasting foundations, without connection therewith and consequently isolated and arbitrary. In this sense the Jewish dogma of the immutability of the Torah must be understood. Yet, immutability must not be confounded with immobility; it is not stereotyped sameness, but impossibility of deviating from its own course. Any student of calculus will tell us that the idea of continuity is very important in the study of functions. "A function is said to be continuous in an interval of values of the argument if it is continuous at all points of the interval."

An often quoted and nearly as often misunderstood saying of the rabbis reads: "God sent Israel into Exile solely for the purpose of making converts to Judaism." For the last two thousand years the number of converts to Judaism was so small that it certainly could not be looked upon as a compensation for Israel's great suffering in the Exile. But while the Jews made few converts of men, Judaism converted many ideas, redeemed and purified them for the glory of God and the salvation of Israel.

The problem of the day is, how to convert the world of the Jew into a Jewish world. There are many among us Jews who have to say something about this problem, but very few who have something to say. We have Jewish Bourbons who have learnt nothing and forgotten nothing, while there are many things to learn and not a few to forget. To them Judaism seems to be a tottering structure which a too bold word will overthrow, and who are not aware of the fact that truth of what kind soever is by no kind of truth gainsaid. They show not only intellectual weakness, but also a religious egotism, and of all forms of egotism there is none so repellent as the religious kind. These are the people who in their mistaken zeal for their own salvation would cling with tenacity to all the forms and customs of the past, but would not care if their rigidity drives their children out of the synagogue. There is such a thing as a healthy mental disturbance, for mental peace and placidity are often only precursors of spiritual slumber. The policy of drifting must have no countenance from us. We must be aware of the profound crisis in the midst of which we are living. The religious and moral dissolutions in progress about us, and the enormous perils of sailing blind-fold and haphazard without rudder and compass or chart, must become fully visible to us.

A novel product of recent development in American Jewry is what one is inclined to describe as vicarious Orthodoxy. America was declared by a clever man to be the land of great possibilities, which really means of great impossiblities. Ours is a country where the impossible becomes possible. The conflict between authority and private judgment as old as religion itself has been finally abolished by the spokesmen of vicarious Orthodoxy. Their formula is: There is no other guide for you but blind authority; as for us, we are modern men and are guided by our private judgment exclusively. The Prophet Jeremiah, a Jewish legend narrates, succeeded by means of mystic combinations of the Hebrew alphabet in creating a golem. But no sooner was the golem created, when he took a knife and scratched out the word "truth" engraved on his forehead. He went out of existence when this word disappeared. By miraculous or only clever combinations of the Hebrew letters, or of any letters, one may be able to create phantoms, but they will disappear without leaving the slightest trace; the faint imprint of truth on the forehead cannot withstand the slightest touch.

Another shibboleth of the day is: "Practical Judaism." We are told we are living in a practical age; what we want is practice not theory; we are after results, how they came, or how their coming may be philosophically explained. But few minds can remain at ease without some sort of rational grounds for their religious belief. Practical, if it means anything, means capable of achieving a useful end, but of what value is the adjective useful in defining the word practical if there is no such thing as an end. As a matter of fact, our age is far from being practical, as proclaimed by those who know only their own time. They cannot distinguish between the characteristics that are transient and those that are permanent. One is certainly more entitled to speak of our age, as an age of reason. What antiquity imagined, the middle ages felt and modern times reason.

The great task before us is to promote intelligent thought on the great problem of Jewish religion. It is easy to perform the old ceremonies, but it is not easy to give them a real meaning for the world as we view it now. You cannot have two or more watertight compartments and place in one an agnostic or materialistic conception of the world, and in the other the old Jewish ideal of life. Israel went into exile, to repeat the saying of the Sages, "that he may make converts of ideas." The new knowledge must serve the old Jewish teachings, the Jewish message must be stated that it can be understood by the modern man. The religion of the Jew must have its roots in the past, and yet nourish him in the present world. It must have the power to take up and assimilate new ideas, all the while retaining a real continuity with the past from which is has sprung. Historical Judaism, I remarked on some other occasion, does not want to live on residues, nor on substitutes, but attempts to create new equivalents for old values. If we are told that life is the power of adaptability to environment, and accordingly, Judaism must, if it should continue to live, adapt itself to its surroundings, we reply, a life perfectly adapted to its surroundings is a life without mentality. A person lacking individuality is no person at all, but a thing. It is true the current of the age cannot be stopped, but it may be directed. We know now that the nature and structure of the organism are far from being controlled by the surrounding conditions, though they are doubtless affected by them. Judaism was always an *ecclesia militans* in the real sense of the word; it had to combat hostile surroundings, and yet it survived. Judaism in its long course of history showed its strength of life in its power of assimilating without being assimilated. The outside conditions do limit the form and nature of an organism, but the driving power is given within. Our slogan must be, to adapt our surroundings to us but not to adapt ourselves to them. We must assimilate the good we find among our neighbors, which will only enhance the good we already possess.

Our organization is called the United Synagogue of America, by which name the fact is emphasized that, while we see in the synagogue the bond of union of dispersed Israel we nevertheless want it to be in our country, a Synagogue of America. The English sermon must be an integral part of our synagogue. It is one of the most effective instruments for the work we are called upon to do, the salvation of the generation now growing up. Order and decorum in the synagogue, though not identical with devotion and religious enthusiasm, as some are apt to forget, are very important and we cannot dispense with them, if we are not prepared to have our children despise and hate the House of Worship, and with it Judaism. We must have our religious schools conducted in accordance with modern conceptions of education. If the school is to fulfill its mission we must not take the Lublin *cheder* of the sixteenth century as our model. It is wise counsel to beware of the method which is popular, but we ought to beware still more of results which are not popular.

Variety, a famous writer remarks, is a great source of beauty and richness in the system both of nature and religion, provided the true foundation is preserved throughout. Judaism always abhors the identity of the narrow absolute formal kind. Alexandrian

Judaism differed from Palestinian during the second common-wealth, and so did Spanish Judaism differ from Franco-German Judaism in the twelfth century. Nothing illustrates better the liking of the Jew for variation than the history of the prayer book. Within the brotherhood of the Jewish people, the prayer book in Hebrew became the symbol of a closer and more intimate bond of union, fostered and guarded no less loyally and tenaciously than the grand treasures of the race. At the same time the prayer book became a species of religious dialect which varied with locality and which communities could not forget or abandon even in exile. The secret of this seeming contradiction lies herein, that the unity of type must not be pressed to the extent of denying all variations. Judaism always recognized the fact that there are greater truths and lesser truths, catholic truths and individual opinions, forms which are essential and forms which are not essential. The policy of the United Synagogue is to apply this principle effectively. Our organization welcomes all those who stand on the solid ground of historical Judaism, who are loyal to Israel, his God and his Torah. To quote the last sentence of the preamble of our Constitution, "It shall be the aim of the United Synagogue of America while not endorsing the innovations introduced by any of its constituent bodies, to embrace all elements essentially loyal to traditional Judaism and in sympathy with the purposes outlined above." We wish all Jews to agree with us and are ready to walk with them step by step as far as they would go, and if they should stop, we will go on with some satisfaction that we have brought them so far. A great movement ought to be independent, yet it must not stand apart in isolation.

I spoke of the loyalty to Israel* as being a *conditio sine qua non* for membership in the United Synagogue. What we understand by loyalty to Israel is made quite clear in the preamble which describes as one of the aims of the United Synagogue "to preserve in the service the reference to Israel's past and the hopes of Israel's restoration." The resolution passed by you with reference to Palestine at the last year's convention, shows clearly that we are not only willing to pray for Zion's restoration, but also ready to work for it. The Declaration of the British Government in favor of a Jewish

---

*In the introductory portion of the address, which is here omitted.

Palestine can only fill every loyal Jew's heart with joy and gratitude. I believe that the time has come when the United Synagogue
should take an active part in the work for the restoration of Palestine. Most of the members of the United Synagogue, congregations as well as individuals, are enthusiastically engaged in this
kind of work, and it is high time that the voice of our organization
be heard in a matter so deeply affecting the spiritual life of the Jew.
Zionism was strong enough to defend itself single-handed agaisnt
its enemies, but it seems as if great danger is threatening it from its
friends, and the only organization representing historical Judaism
in America must come to its help.

Considered from an historical point of view, there is no such
thing as nationalism in general. History only knows particular
forms of nationalism. It is not the military or economic organization of a state which makes it a national body, but the spiritual idea
held by its people. When we speak of the Greek nation, we primarily think of the form in which the genius of this nation expressed
itself. And is not Jewish nationalism an empty phrase if we do not
connect with it Jewish religion which gave it its individuality? To be
conscious of a certain organ of our body is a sure sign of poor health;
as long as we enjoy good health, we are not aware of the different
parts constituting our organism. As long as the life of the Jew
functioned regularly he never differentiated nationalism and religion. The mind of many a Jew in modern times cannot find
Israel, but his heart cannot do without it, and hence the tragic
conflict between Jewish nationalism and Jewish religion. For us
who adhere to historical Judaism, Jewish nationalism without
religion would be a tree without fruit, Jewish religion without
Jewish nationalism would be a tree without roots. Let us work
with zeal and enthusiasm for the strengthening of the roots of the
tree of Israel, but without for a moment forgetting that we want
it to be a fruitful tree.

CONSERVATIVE JUDAISM AS A
UNIFYING FORCE *

By Rabbi Max Arzt

Dr. Max Arzt (b. 1897) served as a congregational rabbi for many years and has for a considerable period been Professor of Practical Theology and Vice-Chancellor of the Jewish Theological Seminary. His administrative functions, which included organizing the fund raising campaign at the Seminary, have involved him in exceptionally close contacts with congregations, rabbis and laymen throughout the country. He was President of the Rabbinical Assembly, has served in many areas of the Conservative movement and was one of the editors of the Rabbinical Assembly - United Synagogue Prayerbook. The article by him in this section is, thus, based upon rich knowledge of the various strands of thinking in the Conservative movement today. Its definition of Conservative Judaism as a unifying force is, in consequence, particularly worthy of consideration. The article appeared in the magazine Conservative Judaism *in June 1949.*

Conservative Judaism has been subjected to criticism by many of its affiliates because of the flexible and fluctuating nature of its body of doctrine and practice. The demand for concise definition has of late become more vocal than ever before. It is requested that before long the diversity of ritual conduct in Conservative congregations should give way to a uniformity and unanimity of religious policy and procedure. Then, at last, claim the precisionists, we will have a ready, unequivocal answer to the question: What is Conservative Judaism?

---

*For some of the historical data in this article, the author is indebted to Dr. Moshe Davis and Rabbi Herbert Parzen.

Our brethren in the Reform and Orthodox camps gleefully join this chorus of criticism and accentuate our failure to delineate sharply the boundaries of Conservative Judaism. They accuse us of endeavoring to be all things to all men, and describe Conservative Judaism as a tepid Orthodoxy and a timid Reform. While they admonish us to seek the road to exact definition, they are quietly invading the territory of vagueness and the domain of indeterminacy. Reform Judaism once contended that a plenitude of ritual was an obstruction to righteousness. It avowed that Zionism was a negation of Judaism's universalism and that the substance (if not the shadow) of Hebrew in instruction and worship was superfluous. One could then identify a reform congregation at sight, by means of the bareheaded congregation, the absence of the *Tallit*, the paucity of Hebrew prayers and the absence of such symbols as the *shofar*, the *sukkah*, and the *lulab* and *ethrog*. Reform rabbis were known for their conscientious objection to the *huppah*, to the Bar Mitzvah ceremony, to *kashrut* and to many other *mitzvot maasiyot*. Times have indeed changed, Reform Judaism has been seeking to retrace its steps. Indeed it now specializes in vagueness. It aims to enhance its fame by changing its name and prefers to be called "Liberal Judaism." It has made its peace with Zionism (though Zion and Jerusalem are still expunged from the Union Prayerbook), it no longer insists on bareheaded worship and the *tallit* has reappeared in many of its congregations. In the latest edition of the Union Prayerbook the full Aramaic text of the *Kol Nidre* has been included after having been banned from the Reform ritual for many decades.

In the expansion program of the Union of American Hebrew Congregations, "Liberal" congregations have been organized which conduct services on both days of *Rosh Hashanah* in which the covering of the head during worship is required and which announce *Yizkor* services for the last days of the festivals. In Brooklyn, there are Reform Temples which offer strictly Kosher catering facilities. Reform rabbis now readily accede to frequent demands for fully traditional wedding ceremonies, including the *huppah*, the *ketubah* and even the breaking of the glass. Indeed, the Columbus platform of 1937 virtually repealed the negation of tradition proclaimed in the Pittsburgh platform of 1885. Latter day Reform Judaism, alert to reality, will no longer submit to the constrictions of a definition.

Nor is the situation different in certain Orthodox circles. There one can discern a growing tendency toward indefiniteness. A steadily increasing number of *Yeshiva* graduates occupy pulpits in congregations where mixed pews are in vogue and they are recommended to these pulpits by the "Strictly Orthodox" authorities of their alma mater. Late Friday night services, confirmation of girls and prayers in English are tolerated and frequently introduced by "Modern Orthodox" rabbis. Bareheaded meetings and mixed dancing (the latter strictly prohibited by the *Shulḥan Arukh*) are held in the social halls of such Orthodox synagogues. Women are invited to speak from their pulpits at special services dedicated to Hadassah or to the Sisterhood. In a certain Southwestern community, an Orthodox rabbi was placed by his *Yeshiva* authorities in a synagogue where during the entire decade and a half of his incumbency a mixed choir accompanied the cantor on *Rosh Hashanah* and *Yom Kippur*. There is even a tendency to atone for the lack of orthodox constancy and consistency by resorting to the more evasive terms "Modern Traditional" or "Modern Orthodox" Judaism.

In the face of these developments how shall we interpret the growing demand of some Conservative Jews for exact formulation? Shall we become a distinct sect in American Judaism while others tend to move into the territory of all-inclusiveness over which we were alleged to covet imperial sway? Shall we abandon Catholic Israel at the time when others eagerly seek to adopt it?

We can clarify our position and yet avoid a retreat into sectarianism by a consideration of the origins of our movement and the motives that prompted its establishment. Conservative Judaism in America arose as a protest against the iconoclastic tendencies of radical Reform. The founders of Conservative Judaism constituted a "united front" against those who repudiated Jewish tradition and who would date the genesis of Judaism from the French Revolution. Accentuating the universalistic overtones of the prophets, the radical Reformers abrogated the authority of the Talmud and virtually obliterated the pattern of religious life that flowed from it. Their antinomian emphasis tended to make Judaism invisible in the home, and their misdirected patriotism led them to excise Zion from the Prayerbook and to de-Hebraize public worship and Jewish education. They began to tamper with the Jewish calendar, even venturing to imply that Sunday might be welcomed with the Sabbath psalm: *mizmor shir leyom ha-Shabbat.*

Alarmed because these teachings and tendencies were gathering momentum, men of orthodox conviction, such as Sabato Morais and H. Pereira Mendes made common cause with liberals, such as Marcus Jastrow, Alexander Kohut, and Benjamin Szold. They rose to the defense of "historical Judaism." Though aware of the differences in doctrine and practice which prevailed among them, they were supremely conscious of the need to avert the threatened dissolution of traditional Judaism. Somehow they all sensed that Judaism in America could not remain impervious to the currents of modern thought and the conclusions of scientific research. They knew that Judaism in America was destined to undergo changes necessitated by the American scene.[1] But they wanted Judaism in America to retain its organic identity with its historic tradition. At first, assured by Isaac M. Wise and his associates that they too fixed their gaze on this objective, the protagonists of the historical school strove to maintain the religious unity of American Jews. Isaac Leeser, in his personal life a rigid traditionalist, attended the abortive Rabbinical Conference held in Cleveland in 1849 at which Isaac M. Wise was elected chairman. Sabato Morais served on the Board of Examiners of the Hebrew Union College and Benjamin Szold delivered the address at the first graduation exercises of the College. In this address Szold pointed out that unanimity of religious thought and practice leads to atrophy and petrifaction and that diversity is a sign of vitality and creativity (*American Hebrew*, July 20, 1883). The "conservatives" seceded only after the Pittsurgh platform of 1885 repudiated Jewish tradition, officially discarded the hope for the restoration of Palestine and decreed the obsolescence of the main body of Jewish religious practice. They could no longer, in all

---

[1] In a series of articles published in the *Jewish Messenger* (vol. 38, nos. 18–22) Morais made a number of suggestions for the revision of the prayerbook and even contemplated the possibility of having the triennial cycle of the reading of the Torah introduced in American synagogues.

conscience, remain allied with those who, in their desire for change, were ready to amputate from Jewish life such vital elements as Hebrew, the traditional Jewish Sabbath day, and the dietary laws. When Morais and Mendes joined Jastrow, Kohut, Szold and other liberals in founding the Jewish Theological Seminary of America, they did not enter upon a mere pact of convenience. They believed that common endeavor in behalf of Jewish scholarship and a strong bias in favor of Jewish tradition would enable the conservative school to evince a unity that would permit and yet transcend the diversion of outlook and practice prevailing among them. They could not surrender the future of Judaism in America to extremists of the left who negated tradition and to extremists of the right whose monolithic attitude threatened to drive traditionalists of liberal tendencies into isolation or into the camp of Reform. Morais, in discussing preliminary plans for the establishment of a Seminary to foster traditional Judaism, first suggested that it be named "The Orthodox Seminary." He was readily convinced by Kohut to desist from his suggestion and the name The Jewish Theological Seminary of America was unanimously adopted. The historical school was not to be a new sect. It was to foster normative Judaism on the American continent.

The aversion to sectarianism was in even larger measure characteristic of Solomon Schechter. He said, "The Directors of the Institution, by terming it The Jewish Theological Seminary of America have distinctly shown their intention of avoiding sectarianism, for it is an especial American feature that no preference is given to any denomination or sect or theological *Richtung*. They are all alike welcome" (*Seminary Addresses*, p. 48). Thus Schechter envisioned the emergence of a form of traditional Judaism built on the broad basis of science and history, "which can hope to become a force and bring about that reconciliation among the parties to which every well-wisher of Israel is looking forward" (*ibid.*, p. 74).

Schechter's vision, also shared by his successor Cyrus Adler, inspired the further development of the Seminary in the past decade into a University of Judaism. This fruition of the Seminary's basic interest in the unity of American Jews was formulated and clarified by Dr. Mordecai M. Kaplan in an epochal address delivered at the 35th anniversary of the Teachers Institute in 1945.

Under Dr. Finkelstein's leadership, the Seminary's expanded program of academic activity and public education has transcended all factional loyalties in American Judaism. The Jewish Museum and the Eternal Light program have been an inspiration to all American Jews and indeed to countless Americans of other faiths. They are bringing within the orbit of Judaism, musicians, artists, men of letters and others who have hitherto stood on the *periphery* of Jewish life.

In the University of Judaism, recently established on the West Coast as a branch of the Seminary, Jews of all types of opinion and affiliation are members of the Board of Overseers of this new spiritual and cultural center. Firm in its loyalty to tradition, the Seminary has never overlooked its all embracing function as an exponent of, and spokesman for, the spiritual unity of American Jewry.

Likewise, in bringing into being the United Synagogue of America, Schechter aimed to establish a functioning organization "broad enough to admit the cooperation of all synagogues that are devoted to the conservation of traditional Judaism whether they call themselves Conservative or Orthodox." He furthermore stated "we regard it as a sacred duty that all such forces unite, irrespective of the differences which otherwise divide them . . . to conserve all the positive elements which they have in common" (*1913 Address*, p. 3). Thus he envisioned the possibility of the harmonious cooperation of congregations of varying degrees of conformance to tradition, provided that they were all fired by a strong desire to conserve and further the traditions to which they were all committed. Schechter delineated the wide area of common action which provided an ample consensus of agreement for the varying types of congregations that responded to his call in behalf of the United Synagogue of America. The preamble to the Constitution of the United Synagogue indicates the basis of such cooperative endeavor: "The advancement of the cause of Judaism in America and the maintenance of Jewish tradition in its historic continuity; to assert and establish loyalty to the Torah in its historic exposition; to further the observance of the Sabbath and the Dietary Laws; to preserve in the service the reference to Israel's past and the hopes for Israel's restoration; to maintain the traditional character of the liturgy, with Hebrew as the language of prayer; to foster Jewish religious life in the home as expressed in traditional observances; to encourage the establishment of Jewish religious schools, in the curricula of which the study of the Hebrew language and literature shall be given a prominent place, both as the key to the true understanding of Judaism, and as a bond holding scattered communities of Israel throughout the world. It shall be the aim of the United Synagogue, while not endorsing the innovations introduced by any of its constituents, to embrace all elements essentially loyal to traditional Judaism and in sympathy with the purposes outlined above."

This preamble, written in 1913, testifies to the vision and statesmanship of its author, Solomon Schechter. It implies that Judaism is not a closed system but a tradition with historic continuity and vitality developing and growing as it faces the challenge of a new era. In the emancipation era, Jews were catapulted from the ghetto into the life and culture of the modern scientific and industrial civilization. In the face of such a cyclonic transformation, the otherwise gradual process of development was greatly accelerated. In traveling at breakneck speed, one must hold fast as one turns a sharp corner. The preamble therefore sets forth the vital traditions to which American Jews must cling as Judaism makes the transition from the straits of the ghetto to the broad places of modern life. The Sabbath, the dietary laws and the traditional observances in the home are to be furthered. The Hebrew language must be fostered as the bond of unity among Jews in all lands and the key to sound Jewish learning. Hence, it must ever remain the predominant language of Jewish worship and the vehicle of an intensive Jewish education. The preamble affirms that the prayerbook must continue to express our historic association with the Holy Land and our hopes for its restoration.

Specific in underscoring these fundamentals, the preamble avoids further explicitness. It does not envision a rigid uniformity of belief and practice. Total conformance in matters of religion may have been possible in pre-democratic times and lands in which the social and intellectual climate induced unquestioned obedience. In the climate of democracy one cannot expect uniform obeisance to a regimen of religious expression, since life is too complex and personal temperaments and situations vary. In a democratic society, united endeavor among individuals and groups is possible only when a higher unity transcends their differences without suppressing them. In such a voluntary society, sectarianism and schismatic fragmentation are the inevitable results of imperial insistence on rigid particularizations of noble objectives. Unity can be attained only in the midst of diversity. The United Synagogue aims to include within its orbit all Jews who are essentially loyal to the fundamental traditions of Judaism. It invites the affiliation and cooperation of all whose sincere desire it is to strengthen loyalty to the Torah in its historic exposition.

In thus providing for unity in the midst of inevitable diversity, the preamble takes cognizance of the varied practices existing among its founding congregations. Some had introduced innovations such as family pews and the organ. These innovations were not outlawed, for by common consent such matters were left to the collective conscience of each congregation and to the guidance of its rabbi. Nor are the innovations endorsed, as such endorsement would have committed the more traditionally minded rabbis and congregations to the approval of that with which they were not in accord. Hence the preamble concludes with the following statement: "It shall be the aim of the United Synagogue, while not endorsing the innovations introduced by any of its constituent bodies, to embrace all elements essentially loyal to traditional Judaism and in sympathy with the purposes outlined above."

In the course of a few decades such innovations as family pews and ceremonies of confirmation or Bas Mitzvah for girls have become the norm in most Conservative congregations and in many "Orthodox" congregations. Life and tested experience have confirmed that which our generation has found to be beneficial to the strengthening of Judaism in our age and country. Other innovations such as the playing of the organ have not won such wide acceptance, perhaps because it still remains to be proved that the organ evokes a heightened devotional mood in Jewish worship. However, congregations using the organ are welcome in the ranks of Conservative Judaism if they endorse the major objectives of the United Synagogue.

In underscoring the maintenance of Jewish traditions, Conservative Judaism avoids the dehydrated liberalism and the religious colorlessness resulting from a nihilistic disavowal of tradition. At the same time, it has wisely resisted the temptation to draw sharp lines of distinction which always lead to fanaticism, intolerance and divisiveness. In its aftermath, World War II produced many tired liberals who yearn for dogmatic definitiveness. Averse to the old Orthodoxy, they seek to define a new orthodoxy based on their particular brand of diversity. It is less perplexing to be specific and definite. Then one enjoys the luxury of being able to state precisely where he stands and where others should stand on matters of religious belief and behavior. But as we have indicated above, such exactness leads to splinter divisions, and, therefore, militates against cooperative endeavor. Conservative Judaism has chosen the far more vulnerable alternative of accentuating the unity of American Israel under the banner of our historic tradition and of inviting the cooperation of all who are animated by love and reverence for that tradition.

In affirming the principle of unity in diversity, which in recent years has been so convincingly expounded by Dr. Mordecai M. Kaplan, Conservative Judaism places the accent on unity. Its hope is to inspire Jews to a voluntary ordering of their lives in accordance with the fundamental norms of our tradition. The growing movement for intensifying the Hebraic character and content of religious education will help to perpetuate the pattern of congregational worship and procedure. In their collective religious life, congregations evince a strong presumption in favor of traditional patterns. This is even true of latter day Reform congregations which have been profoundly influenced by Conservative Judaism.

More complicated and more chaotic is the status of personal piety within the ranks of Conservative and also Orthodox Judaism. Here there is an abysmal distance between the *Halakha* and the actual life of the people. Personal observance of the Sabbath, *kashrut*, and other essentials of Judaism is on the decline. In many communities personal conformance to the *Halakha* has almost reached the vanishing point. There is one heartening aspect to this distressing situation. The widespread disregard of the basic sanctities of Jewish life is no longer due to cynical defiance. It is due to indifference, ignorance, and neglect. A vigorous program of mass education and activation would arouse our people from their state of spiritual lethargy. The case for such

Sabbath "prohibitions" as refraining from mundane occupations, from shopping, from mowing the lawn, card playing, and the like, is unaswerable. Most religious-minded Jews will readily be convinced (though not so easily persuaded to change their lives accordingly) that Sabbath attendance at public worship, daily prayer, the kindling of Sabbath candles, and the chanting of *kiddush* and *zemirot* are, for Jews, indispensable ingredients of a zestful religious life. Their consideration of the major claims of the *Halakha* on their spiritual life will confirm the Psalmist's experience "I have considered my ways and turned my feet to Thy testimonies" (Ps. 119:59). Some observances, such as *kashrut* and the major home observances are, in the main, accessible to all. Others are not equally accessible to all people. The opportunities for personal religious observance and the degree of sacrifice entailed vary with the economic situation of the individual and with other compulsions of his personal situation. No code, not even a revised code, can conceivably take into account the many exigencies and complexities of modern life. Consistent *halakhic* conformance is not within equal reach of all persons even in so fundamental and so unchallenged an institution as the Sabbath. All religiously minded Jews agree that the ideal Sabbath is one of total abstention from mundane labors. But alas, only a small minority achieve this most desirable and most essential objective, so fundamental to Jewish life. More than in any previous age, Jewish tradition is abundantly observed only by those who heroically forfeit momentary material and secular satisfactions. We should each aspire valiantly toward the maximum of observance. It is, however, not given to us to sit in judgment over our fellow man in matters *bein adam lamakom*. We cannot ordain the sacrifices which each person must make in behalf of tradition since personal circumstances vary considerably. Sincere and persistent conformists can find their reward in a benign peace of mind and soul and in a heightened awareness of God's beneficent presence. But they should avoid the arrogant sanctimoniousness which categorically refuses to understand the circumstances that condition other people's religious life. On the other hand, those who feel that there are extenuating circumstances which preclude their conformance with some aspects of our tradition should not expect the ideal pattern of tradition to be adjusted to their measure. Thus the person who, residing a considerable distance from a synagogue rides to the synagogue, should not demand an official diminution of the Sabbath ideal by a blanket easement of the prohibition against riding. He should realize that it is still a highly desirable goal to avoid traveling on the Sabbath thus staying close to hearth and home, and to seek that refreshment of soul which comes with the leisurely gait and with freedom from the hustle and bustle of vehicular mobility. His present circumstances may preclude his attainment of this goal, but circumstances may change and full Sabbath observance may yet come within his grasp.

Because circumstances and personal situations differ so radically in our complex society, we shall have to learn and teach a twin type of tolerance: tolerance toward those who observe more than our optimum of personal piety, and tolerance toward those who do not attain our degree of religious observance. The former usually arouse in us a sense of guilt, hence we resent their extra measure of piety. The less observant induce in us a belligerent and fanatical self-righteousness. We shall have to blend our religiosity with understanding and humility.

Conservative Judaism should accentuate the living *Halakha.* Certain *halakhic* prohibitions, some with strong Biblical sanction, such as shaving and *shaatnez,* have become obsolescent even among otherwise meticulously loyal traditionalists. The temper of modern life has made aspects of the tradition inoperative. The collective conscience of the loyal elements in Catholic Israel no longer reacts to these "violations" as manifestations of wilful disregard of the Law or as indicative of religious unconcern. In dealing with such areas of obsolescence it is wise to practice the eloquence of silence prescribed by the rabbis "Even as it is a *mitzvah* to exhort the people concerning that which they will obey, so it is a *mitzvah* not to exhort them concerning that which they will not obey (Y. Terum., Ch. 5 end). The discreet silence of Orthodox rabbis on such matters registers their agreement with this principle.

There are however, situations where the Law must be adjusted by authoritative remedial action. I refer to the injustices resulting from the arrested development of the *Halakha* in matters of marriage and divorce. Here the fundamental social structure of our people is involved. Failure to take action constitutes an inexcusable delay in the amelioration of human tragedy. Our Law Committee should commission specialists in *halakhic* studies to formulate an *halakhically* reasoned re-interpretation of these laws and then submit the proposal to other rabbinic groups in traditional Judaism. Should these groups, after a period of time (six months or at most a year), fail to respond with the ratification of our proposal or with a more satisfactory solution of the problem, we need no longer hesitate to implement our decision. By utilizing proper channels of communication we can inform *Klal Yisrael* of the urgency of the problem and of the caution we exercised. Our action will then win overwhelming public approbation and respect.

The fluidity of Conservative Judaism's position on religious observance should be a stimulus rather than a deterrent to united action in behalf of more widespread personal observance. The main patterns of religious piety are abidingly valid. They are the vitamins of a zestful and meaningful religious life. The United Synagogue should plan and carry out a nationwide educational endeavor calling on our congregants to renew their covenant with the Torah by introducing into their lives and homes the highest optimum of religious observance available to them. Practices which have fallen into desuetude, even among observant American Jews, should not be stressed. But all that is vital and relevant should be dramatically expounded and given the widest possible dissemination. The opportunity for the revitalization of religious life is unprecedented. The establishment of the State of Israel has alerted the religious awareness of American Jews. They are now more receptive to Judaism because they no longer suffer from a sense of collective inferiority. The primacy of religion and the synagogue is being recognized even by those who formerly equated Jewish loyalty solely with philanthropy, defense activities and Zionist propaganda. The twentieth century Jew, like his fellow man of other faiths, has become disillusioned with the pseudo-religions of positivism, pragmatism, and communism — idolatries which have proven to be broken cisterns which hold no water. He suffers from spiritual homesickness and needs anchorage for his soul in a living tradition which can lead him to walk in the light of God's presence.

Though organized Conservative Judaism comprises only a fraction of American Jewry, it can have a powerful appeal to masses of our people. Its realistic and reverential attitude to tradition is animated by a profound concern for Jewish unity under the banner of tradition. The experience of chaplains in the armed forces revealed that the young American Jew prefers our *via media*. There are unmistakable signs that American Jewry is receptive to ideals which prompted the establishment of the Conservative movement. Ours is, then, the opportunity to reunite the House of Israel, to teach Judaism as a *Torat Ḥayyim*, and to restore the Torah to our people and our people to the Torah.

Part I

The Origins of Conservative Judaism

Section 2 — The History of a Movement

A NOTE ON THE HISTORY OF
A MOVEMENT

The Kabbalists spoke of *neshamot artilaot,* wandering souls which could not find a haven in a body. Many valuable ideas have had the same destiny, being fated to hover about in the intellectual atmosphere of an era without ever achieving embodiment in an institution or movement which could give them forceful expression and fulfilment. The ideas described in the preceding section suffered the same fate for some decades until they were at length embodied in effective institutions.

This section contains several selections on the institutions which were designed to implement the Conservative idea. The first of these was the Seminary and it has remained the dominant institution. However, the conception of the Seminary and its role in relation to Conservative Judaism has changed with the passage of time and several selections are included here to reflect the change. The second organization to come into being was the Rabbinical Assembly. There is, I believe, no statement which adequately describes its character and philosophy. However, some of the selections in the last section of this volume give a picture, in terms of specific issues, of the outlooks which it holds. The third major organization of the Conservative movement is the United Synagogue, of which variant conceptions are presented in two selections in this section.

All these bodies are rapidly changing in their own conception of their function and are expanding their operations by developing auxiliary agencies. It is probable that the statements printed here will need considerable reformulation within a few years.

A JEWISH THEOLOGICAL SEMINARY*

By Rabbi Sabato Morais

Brethren: This day, the ancient Psalmist Asaph offers the text to an address which will plead for the rehabilitation of a deserted religion. Listen, my fellow-believers, to the Levitish chorister of old, as he rehearses the wonders of the Lord. Asaph casts a retrospective glance on the past of Israel. He depicts the celestial interposition in behalf of a people enslaved and scourged; then recalling the purpose of a Divine selection, he says: "God established a testimony in Jacob, and appointed a Law in Israel which He commanded our fathers, that they might make the same known unto their children." "In order that a latter generation should also know, even the children that will be born, and these rise and tell their own children." "So that they may place their hope in God, and not forget the doings of the Divinity, but keep His precepts." A summary of Jewish principles is comprehended in those lines.

Mark it well. The heavenly imparting was not designed for a single age, not for one stage of civilization, but for ever. The God of Sinai committed it to our progenitors in trust, to be handed down to their progeny, for an ultimate object — that "they shall keep His precepts." Parental teaching is thus enforced, because it is the most direct and effective. In that light the greatest of prophets considered it; hence the emphasis which Moses repeatedly laid on the necessity of our inculcating our own selves ancestral doctrines on the supple minds of our offspring.

---

* Sermon delivered at Baltimore Chizzuk Emunah Congregation. It is an example of the thinking which led to the organization of the Seminary.

In these days of a restless attending to worldly pursuits; in this land of fast living; of a universal hurrying on to grow rich, we may almost despair of beholding a revival of sacred lore among all classes of Hebrews. But what parents deliberately or unwittingly cast aside, schools, seminaries, colleges, must lay strong hold on and plant firmly.

Who among my audience is on the side of the Lord? Thou, my brother, thou sister in faith of mine, who dost appreciate the teaching of Asaph, as to the aim of the Sinaic revelation — that the latest generation may cleave to the statutes — thou, who, loving the word of God and wishing its perpetuation, as transmitted by our fathers amidst appalling hindrances, art eager to shield it from peril, canst receive an eternity of name upon earth, and the approving smile of the celestial Legislator in immortality. A seminary of sacred learning will be set up. I acknowledge now with resolute boldness, lest I be charged at any period hereafter with having agreed to entangling compromises, I acknowledge that as far as it lies in *my* power, the proposed seminary shall be hallowed to one predominating purpose — to the upholding of the principles by which my ancestors lived and for which many have died. From that nursery of learning shall issue forth men whose utterances will kindle enthusiasm for the literature of Holy Writ, but whose every-day conduct will mirror forth a sincere devotion to the *tenets* of Holy Writ. The language in which the poetry of the soul chose to be clothed; the language which has in all truth annihilated distance and held a people, scattered throughout the habitable globe, in one fraternal embrace, the language unexcelled in terseness and vigor, must be revived. The future ministers in Israel shall become distinguished for their mastery of that grand language. Enamored with it they will not encourage or palliate a sin which aroused the righteous indignation of Nehemiah — I mean, our youths' reprehensible ignorance of Hebrew, the language of our national prayers. They will, on the contrary, shame our sons and daughters into a study which is now sedulously cultivated by Christians, to the end of gaining familiarity with the text, as written by the heaven-gifted beings who dipped their pens in inspiration.

As far as it lies in *my* power, those destined to ascend our pulpits shall draw knowledge at the fountain-head, not from stream-

lets running with corruption. The word of the Bible in its original
purity shall command profound attention; its purport, when
obscure, shall be sought at the hands of commentators, trustworthy
by reason of their thorough acquaintance with the construction,
the genius, the spirit of Holy Writ. Ewald shall not supersede our
Kimchi and Nachmanides, nor shall Luzzatto be set aside to make
room for Gesenius. Like the word of the Bible, so shall its history
also be studied in the original, not in Kuenen, Wellhausen, or
Robertson Smith; not in the works of Gentiles or Jews that deny
Moses the authorship of the Pentateuch, make our patriarchs
sheer myths, our priests tyrannical egotists, our Ezra a pretender,
our progenitors unmitigated dupes.

I lay great stress upon the need of a conscientious cultivation
of the Scriptures with the exegesis thereof, because I contend that
those revered volumes must chiefly serve as the armory sup-
plying Conservatism with weapons of defence. It is very far from
my thoughts to belittle Talmudism. I fully appreciate an ency-
clopedic literature created during more than six centuries by over
two thousand scholars, but seeing that persons who, like myself,
are in honor bound to enforce obedience to Mosaic precepts, the
performance of which has not an immediate connection with a
national residence in Palestine — (rabbinically termed, מצוות
התלויות בארץ); noticing, I say, that teachers in Israel are wont to
construe detached sentences, individual opinions, extravagant
utterances in the Talmud into a support of theories, subversive of
Judaism, I would insist upon a closer and deeper study of the
book, without which post-biblical literature lacks the foundation
stone; it is simply — a castle in the air.

As far as it lies in *my* power, the proposed seminary shall
vindicate the right of the Hebrew Bible to a precedence over all
theological studies. It shall be the boast of that institute hereafter
that the attendants are surpassing Scripturalists — if I may be
permitted the expression — though they may not rank foremost
among skilled Talmudists. The latter have, at times, degenerated
into hair splitting disputants — *pilpulists*, — but the Jew who has
imbibed a correct knowledge of the word of prophecy, the Jew
whose heart is thrilled by the lessons of wisdom, of goodness, of
godliness, unfolded in the oldest and most venerable of old books;
the Jew who has been made to realize the truth enunciated by the

illustrious Hillel, that in the Bible lies the germ of our national traditions, such a Jew will not work out his learning into a crown of self-aggrandizement, as Mishnaic sages would say; he will not go in quest of a popularity based upon a supposed originality which jars with the combined judgment of all the ancients. He will modestly cling to the tuition of the past, he will eagerly wish to create standard bearers to the Torah that it may be uplifted by unpolluted hands. To such a Jew may safely be committed the lead of a congregation in Israel. For "he is a messenger of the Lord of hosts," suasively withdrawing multitudes from sin, and bringing them nigh to the laver of purification. Ministers of a character so elevated, ministers who solely labor to the glorification of their Master, I hope and fervently pray, will issue from the seminary, which you can hasten to establish.

*   *   *   *

Brethren: In every stage of our history, when Judaism seemed to be grasping for breath, salvation providentially arose and the Torah lived. I am not disposed to denounce its deadly foes — unhappily abounding among men who should bare their breasts and receive the wound rather than pierce their fathers' creed with barbed arrows; but you all know by what perils our ancestral tenets are beset. You know that the covenant which Abraham — looking through a vista of unending ages, asked even ourselves his late descendants, inffaceably to seal, is exposed to the risk of being branded as infamous. The Sabbath of the Decalogue — the manifestation of God's creative will and Israel's testimony of that will, is declared beyond the reach of human obedience. The Passover, whose every ceremony evoked historical reminiscences of sublime import, is allowed to see leaven in the dwellings of persons in the public service of our religion. The Day of Atonement, formerly infusing a spiritual awe, is denied its conciliatory powers and wilful transgressors are reassured against the Scriptural punishment with which that day threatens them. The feast of Tabernacles — a faithful chronicler of forty years' eventful history, is relegated to obscurity, because its arrival finds the disciples of Moses inextricably engaged in "the fall trade." Superfluous it would be to allude to the laws which prohibit the eating of flesh with the blood thereof, of animals and fishes and amphibious creatures designated in the Pentateuch as an abomination to Israelites. You all know with what indifference the appointed guardians of that sacred book trespass against it, and with what untenable reasonings they preach the abrogation of its behests. None of you can be ignorant of the causes which embolden the reckless and the disaffected, but you can thrust back a fearful evil approaching with rapid strides, you can deliver posterity from recreancy, and keep it in our sacred fold to the glory of the One God. A bulwark of defence to our belief is being raised. In New York it shall tower high. You understand me, brethren. Efforts to promote a study conducive to godly actions have taken the initiative in that city. A circular has already informed you of the project and its scope. Another circular, defining the principles by which "The Jewish Theological Seminary" shall be guided, is in course of publication.

Trained by preceptors loyal to conservatism, real professors, making declaration of their fealty to Jewish doctrines — the scholars shall follow in the wake of their teachers, preaching the eternity of the revelation at Sinai, the venerableness of oral impartings, resuscitating the national language, commending the books which have preserved it, widened its scope and beautified it. But above all, those scholars shall luminously prove in their demeanour their belief in the immortal enunciations of Asaph. "God established a statute in Jacob, and appointed a Law in Israel, which He commanded our fathers that they might make the same known unto their children."

THE WORK OF HEAVEN*

By Rabbi Solomon Schechter

"Blessed be he that cometh in the name of the Lord." It is in the name of the Lord that we have invited you to join the United Synagogue of America, which is entering upon its existence this day. It is a real "work of Heaven," for which I invite your attention and participation — a work on which, in my humble opinion, depends the continuance and the survival of traditional Judaism in this country. The significance of these words will become clearer to you after a short explanation.

Let me premise that this United Synagogue has not been called into life with any purpose of creating a new division. While it will, as its name implies, unite us for certain purposes, which we deem sacred and indispensable to the welfare of Judaism, it is not our intention to enter into a feud with the existing parties. Life is too short for feuds, and the task before us is so great and so manifold, that we must spare all our faculties and save all our strength for the work of a positive nature, which I will outline presently. Moreover, feuds and controversies are only productive of bitterness and strife, which we are anxious to avoid. They would result in mere negative work, whilst the work before us, as already indicated, is of a distinctive, positive nature.

Indeed, what we intend to accomplish is not to create a new party but to consolidate an old one, which has always existed

---

* Address delivered at the Founding Convention of the United Synagogue in 1913.

in this country, but was never conscious of its own strength, nor perhaps realized the need of organization. I refer to the large number of Jews who, thoroughly American in habits of life and mode of thinking and, in many cases, imbued with the best culture of the day, have always maintained conservative principles and remained aloof from the Reform movement, which swept over the country. They are sometimes stigmatized as the Neo-Orthodox. This is not correct. Their Orthodoxy is not new. It is as old as the hills, and the taunt "new" can only be accounted for by the ignorance of those who took it into their heads that an observant Jew who has taken a degree in a college is a new phenomenon, representing a mere paradox. A better knowledge of Jewish history would have taught them that culture combined with religion was the rule with the Jew; culture without religion was the exception. There were cases, of course, of religion without culture, but these were to be found only in countries in which culture, such as it was, was confined to a small official class, consisting largely of clerics or priests, but in which the population at large had no share, whether Jewish or Christian. The "New" Orthodoxy, therefore, represents very little that is new. It was the normal state of the Jew in Spain; it was the normal state of the Jew in Italy; it was the normal state of the Jew in England and in Holland; it was the normal state of the Jew even in Germany, after the first calming down of the deluge, of the rationalism that came in the wake of the French Revolution, which swept over that country and the traces of which are more discernable on the shores of the North Atlantic than on the banks of the Rhine. The frame of mind which insists upon the unbridgeable chasm between the "Intelligenzia" and devotion and loyalty to the religion of the fathers is, at present, limited to the countries in the far East just emerging from a state of barbarism, as is the case with Russia. If we occasionally hear such sentiments expressed also in this country, we can only ascribe them to the pioneer state of mind from which we have not yet entirely emancipated ourselves. With very little time for reflection and serious study, the pioneer is too easily carried away by catch-words. And such war-cries as "Progressive Judaism," "American Judaism," and "Reform," have all the same charm for him in the spiritual world, as the advertisements of patent medicines and universal remedies usually exercise upon his mind in the material world. But as already indicated, there were always Jews who were not carried away by such big words. They knew well that a label means nothing. You may describe yourself a Progressive and find, after a careful analysis, that you are woefully backward, both in your philosophy and in your conception of history. You may call yourself a Liberal, and be as narrow as your sympathies and as limited in the sphere of your thought as your worst opponent. You may stigmatize Orthodox Judaism as un-American, and suddenly discover that real Americanism meant reverence for the Bible as the word of God, obedience to the authority of the Scriptures which lay at the foundation of this country, and love for institutions and memories of the past, that is a particular feature with the best American minds.

This Conservative, or if you prefer so to call it, this Orthodox tendency, represented by some of the noblest minds of American Jewry, to which several of the oldest synagogues bear witness, some of which have sent delegates to this Convention, received a fresh impetus by the immigration from the Eastern part of Europe, begun some thirty years ago. This immigration brought hundreds and thousands, mostly from countries which were never touched by the Reform movement, that had its birth, as indicated above, in Germany. Their presence brought to the consciousness of even some of the most thorough-going Reformers that the large majority of Israel still sought their spiritual salvation in the Torah and the Talmud and the Jewish Codes. The authority of various Synods in Germany was never recognized by these immigrants, if indeed they ever heard of them, and whatever the excesses of the individual may have been in the one case or the other, they have never been allowed any innovation in their synagogues or any alteration in their liturgy. If they were scolded as mediae- valists, they could point with pride to their prayer-book, which was the same in its main features as that from which Rashi and Rabenu Tam, on the one side, and Ibn Gabirol and Maimonides, on the other, said their prayers. They not only erected any number of synagogues, in which they worshipped entirely in conformity with the old Jewish ritual, but by the mere virtue of their numbers again brought the conservative tendency into prominence. Con- temporary with this immigration, a Conservative or Orthodox

Seminary was erected by the greatest leader of Orthodox Judaism in this country, Dr. Sabato Morais, the Rabbi of Congregation Mikve Israel of Philadelphia, who, with a chosen band of friends, which included the late Drs. Jastrow and Szold, labored in it for many years.

But grateful as every Conservative Jew must be for all that has been done till now and loyal as we all here are to the memory of such men as Isaac Leeser, Sabato Morais, Marcus Jastrow, Benjamin Szold, Alexander Kohut and many others, who did their best not to permit the standard of Conservative or Orthodox Judaism to disappear from us and to advance its cause, they still left much for us in which we might "distinguish ourselves," as the Talmud phrases it.

I have spoken of the immigrants and their wholesome influence in bringing about a wave of Conservatism which even impressed the Reform section of the Jewish community. But there was this drawback: Coming from a part of the world where, as pointed out above, any adherence to the "Intelligenzia" is almost tantamount to throwing off the yoke of the Torah and the Law, they still insist, or a large influential body among them insists, that secular education and modern methods in school and college are incompatible with Orthodox principles. In this, as you see, they agree with their most bitter opponents. They have, further, also this in common with at least the first Reformers in this country: that they dread the English sermon just as those Reformers did, the only difference being that the latter gave the preference to German and the former to Yiddish. Unfortunately, they differ from the Reformers in that they have never succeeded in creating proper order and decorum in their places of worship and have, besides, shown very little ability in the art of organization, which is the great strength of our Reform brethren. These our brethren are, undoubtedly, much stronger in numbers than the Reformers. But chaos reigns supreme among them, and just by this want of organization they are subject to a process of constant attrition which must become dangerous if the tide of immigration should, by more favorable conditions in the East, for which we all hope and pray, be stopped for a few years. This is the condition of affairs which cannot be permitted to go on without making an effort to step into the breach and create this Conservative Union.

I am very reluctant to denounce any party in existence. But close observation for ten years and more has convinced me that, unless we succeed in effecting an organization which, while loyal to the Torah, to the teachings of our Sages, to the traditions of our fathers, to the usages and customs of Israel, shall at the same time introduce the English sermon, and adopt scientific methods in our seminaries, in our training of rabbis and schoolmasters, for our synagogues and Talmud Torahs, and bring order and decorum in our synagogues, unless this is done, I declare unhesitatingly that traditional Judaism will not survive another generation in this country. Those of us advanced in years may be saved, but the younger generation will be swept away by a ruthless radicalism which even disquiets the better Reformed minds. And what will come after these few witnesses of Orthodox Judaism have passed away is too terrible to express.

I do not belong to those who despair of Judaism, even in my moments of greatest depression. I thoroughly believe with the old Rabbis that a general apostacy is impossible, the freedom of choosing another religion or no religion being granted only to the individual and not to the bulk of Israel. But I believe also, at the same time, in the homily of the Rabbis regarding man's efforts in the material life. "God promises Israel His blessing" (Deut. 15:18). But the condition is that He will withhold His blessing from them if they are mere lazy onlookers. We must labor and work. And it is for this purpose that this Union has been created.

Its scope is broad enough to admit of the co-operation of all synagogues that are devoted to the cause of the conservation of traditional Judaism, whether they style themselves Conservative or Orthodox. Yea, in view of the dangers threatening the historic faith dear to Conservative and Orthodox alike, we regard it as a sacred duty that all such forces unite, irrespective of the differences which otherwise divide them. Such co-operation should not be construed as the organization's approval of all those innovations which some of its constituent bodies may have introduced. The purpose of this Union is to conserve all those positive elements which they have in common.

The outlines of the work we have to do are given in the Preamble. But I may be permitted to offer a few general remarks. I wish, first, to remind you of the saying of Ben Zoma: "Who is wise? He who learns from all men." From the party describing itself as Reform, we should learn organization and method. Nothing in this country can exist without proper organization, backed by a large constituency, composed of members capable of denying, when necessary, their individual ambitions and advantages, in submitting to the mandates of the majority. We have to accept from the party usually describing itself as Orthodox the virtues of enthusiasm and intensiveness manifested by some of its members on various occasions. I hardly need tell you that my sympathies and convictions largely range on the side of this latter party. But I can never forget that there is such a thing as selfish salvation. I mean that salvation which is bought at the expense of sacrificing your children and the whole future of Judaism for the imaginary welfare of your own little soul. To banish the English sermon from the synagogue means to condemn our youth to ignorance of the teachings of Judaism, the sermon being in our days the only means of making the public acquainted with the word of God, the tenets of Judaism and the history of Israel's heroic sufferings. To object to strict order and decorum in our places of worship, means to expel our children from the synagogue, and to point out for them the way leading to the Ethical Culture hall and similar un-Jewish institutions. To oppose proper pedagogical methods in the instruction of our children, means to be instrumental in the bringing up of a rebellious gene-ration, which will not only be ignorant of Judaism, but hate and abhor it. I have seen such cases myself. To insist further that our rabbis and teachers should be trained in accordance with the methods prevailing in the old country, and even there considered obsolete, means to condemn Judaism to helplessness and to make it defenceless in the midst of a hostile world constantly at war with it, as well as to exclude it from the comity of the advanced nations, holding sway over our universities and other institutions of learning.

All these benefits, of an English sermon, of a decorous service and of methodic instruction in Hebrew and Hebrew literature of scientific research in our literature, and of rabbis and teachers trained in scientific research, must be accepted fully, without any reserve, by our constituents if traditional Judaism shall be able to hold its own, and in the end also to gain supremacy on this continent.

I am speaking of a continent, for nothing less than this is aimed at by the movement inaugurated to-day. It is not local. It is not even entirely national. It must extend over the whole of America, and be so far-reaching and far-extending, as to come in touch with the work of the whole of Israel. We do not ignore the local agencies that have sprung up within the last few years, such as the Kehillah, the Educational Alliance and several well-conducted Talmud Torahs and similar institutions. Our work must be of an independent nature, having, as just indicated, *Klal Israel* for its ultimate aim, but America as its immediate field of work.

Of such institutions which may be described as national, but, at the same time, Conservative or Orthodox, we have at present only one, the Jewish Theological Seminary of America. It was, as mentioned above, created by Dr. Morais and his friends, as a protest against radicalism, and this tendency prevailed after the re-organization, and is still prevailing. I do not care to speak "pro-domo," but its worst enemies — unless they belong to those who serve the Lord out of spite — will admit that it has proved a bulwark of Conservative Judaism within the last ten years, and even influenced more or less the other party. That some students, trained in the Seminary, have accepted Reform positions, while it is to be regretted, has happened both before and after the re-organization. But let no man who knows the conditions of most of our strictly Orthodox synagogues, the poverty prevailing there, the starvation wages which they grant to their rabbis, the constant strife within the congregation itself, the first victim of which is the rabbi, the ungenerous treatement of the young men on the part of those who consider themselves the pillars of the congregation — no man who knows these conditions will judge uncharitably those men who have not proved themselves strong enough to become martyrs of the cause. It is with the Orthodox they broke, not with Orthodoxy. I do not justify them. I only contend that if they sinned, they were also sinned against. The majority have remained loyal at a sacrifice impossible to be appreciated by those whose lines have fallen in more pleasant places, and are constantly proclaiming and admiring their own virtues. Of course, the Seminary is comparatively a young institution, but considering the want of material support on the part of the public, whose aid and sympathy it has a right to expect, it has accomplished, both as a religious conservative force and as a factor in Jewish scholarship, more than its best friends had any right to expect. Perhaps I may also indicate here that the authorities of the Seminary will, in the very near future, make the necessary provision enabling the faculty to give *Hatarath Horaah* to such students as may deserve such a distinction.

The Seminary has also created, as you all know, the Teachers' Institute, under the principalship of Dr. Kaplan, which is now preparing properly trained teachers for our religious schools. I need not dwell here on the importance of its activity. The New York community is already beginning to realize its beneficial influence in many respects, but I hope that the time may soon come when the country at large will share the benefit.

Having mentioned the Seminary and the Teachers' Institute, I must not omit to point to the Dropsie Institution as a centre of Jewish learning and to the Gratz College as an institution for the training of teachers; both institutions are represented here, the one by its president, and the other by one of its most important professors.

Now, to make this Union national in every respect, it will be our duty to establish a Bureau, which shall be in constant communication with our congregations; which shall also have the means of sending out Rabbis and preachers for the purpose of propaganda, not only to enlist new congregations, but to help such outlying communities in the various states as are in need of advice and counsel, as to the choice of Rabbis, the engaging and organizing of schools and schoolmasters, and providing them with literature and textbooks.

A part of the work of this propaganda shall be to make a strong personal appeal to all such congregations as have not accepted the Union prayer-book nor performed their religious devotions with uncovered heads. It is our duty to help them while they are wavering, and to bring them back to their loyalty and to strengthen the conservative sentiment that is not entirely extinct in them, and which, with encouragement and sympathy, would be soon brought back to consciousness.

It should again be the duty of this Union to make its influence felt with regard to the religious education of women, which is sometimes so woefully neglected in many old congregations. It is through them that we reach the children in a country like America, where the husbands are busy all the week. It is through them that we can save a great part of the Sabbath, and it is through them that the dietary laws will be observed in our homes. I would even suggest that the Union assign a certain portion of its work to women, and give them a regular share in its activities. They can become more than an auxiliary to us; indeed helpful in many respects where, as conditions are in this country, their influence is more far-reaching than that of their husbands.

As just indicated, our work must not remain confined to the synagogue. We want Synagogue Extension, but this in the sense our ancients understood it. The first place to which the influence of the synagogue should be extended is the home, becoming thereby a Jewish home. But the Jewishness must be something visible and tangible. A Jewish home without symbols, such as, for instance, the *mezuzzah*, is an anomaly, and is mere sentimental talk. A Jewish home, again, in which the dietary laws are not observed, is, more properly speaking, a non-Jewish home. The duty of the Union should be to help small communities in the process of organization to engage a *shochet*; but what is more important, it should be part of our activity to arrange for and to establish throughout the country places where kosher meals can be secured. This should be done with a special view to the needs of travelers. It is "on the road" where men, otherwise loyal to Judaism and eager to preserve its laws, after a hard fight with themselves, violate the dietary laws; and this which very soon results in abolishing them altogether, even in their homes.

This Synagogue Extension will further suggest the making of Jewish literature a factor in Jewish life. This question may be connected first with that of text-books. It is one of the crying needs of Jewry now. We are constantly establishing new schools, but we have nothing practical to put into the hands of the teacher or pupil. A committee should therefore be appointed with the purpose of preparing text-books under the supervision of experts, which should be of a doctrinal, of a historical, of an ethical and of a devotional nature. They should be written in such a way that teachers and pupils and educated laymen should all profit by them. The books of a devotional nature should be especially composed in such a way as to replace, in a certain manner, the old Yiddish-Deutsch devotional literature, which was the joy of our mothers, but is not any more intelligible to the new generation.

I cannot enter here upon details. This will be the task of the different committees, which you will appoint to-day. I rely upon their wisdom and insight, both to expand and to correct the views expressed above. But one thing at least, I must indicate: and this is, that the task before you, as indicated by this meager outline, is a great one. It is not local, but national, or rather continental. It embraces almost all departments of religious activity. It is planned with a view to establish Conservative Judaism on a firm foundation for posterity. It is especially calculated to anticipate and to make easier the work of the future generations, which shall be saved for traditional Judaism. Such a work, as I hardly need tell you, will require material sacrifice on the part of all those who inaugurate to-day this movement. We cannot do anything worth while without taxing ourselves to the utmost of our capacity. Comfort and salvation may also arise from other sources, but not until we have first done our full duty. I, therefore, recommend the appointment of a very strong and practical financial committee which will attend to this most important part of our activity.

In conclusion, let me thank all those gathered here for the confidence they have placed in us to appear here on this platform. As I have said, it is a "work of Heaven," to which you have been invited. And thus may the blessing of Heaven come upon all of you, so that the Divine Presence shall dwell in the work of your hands, which blessing alone can give it permanence and efficiency.

PREAMBLE TO THE CONSTITUTION
OF THE UNITED SYNAGOGUE*

The purpose of this organization is as follows:

The advancement of the cause of Judaism in America and the maintenance of Jewish tradition in its historical continuity,

To assert and establish loyalty to the Torah and its historical exposition,

To further the observance of the Sabbath and the dietary laws,

To preserve in the service the reference to Israel's past and the hopes for Israel's restoration,

To maintain the traditional character of the liturgy with Hebrew as the language of prayer,

To foster Jewish religious life in the home, as expressed in traditional observances,

To encourage the establishment of Jewish religious schools, in the curricula of which the study of the Hebrew language and literature shall be given a prominent place, both as the key to the true understanding of Judaism, and as a bond holding together the scattered communities of Israel throughout the world.

It shall be the aim of the United Synagogue of America, while not endorsing the innovations introduced by any of its constituent bodies, to embrace all elements essentially loyal to traditional Judaism and in sympathy with the purposes outlined above.

---

* Adopted in 1913.

THE STANDPOINT OF THE SEMINARY

By Dr. Cyrus Adler

The name of Dr. Cyrus Adler (1863–1940) is indelibly imprinted in the history of virtually every major Jewish organization between 1890 and 1940. He was the civil servant par excellence of American Jewish life. He was involved not only in the direction of the Seminary and the United Synagogue, but also in Dropsie College, the American Jewish Committee, the Jewish Publication Society, The Jewish Agency, Gratz College, and many other important organizations. Simultaneously, he pursued Oriental studies and edited the Jewish Quarterly Review *and the* American Jewish Year Book *and took a leading role in civic and national affairs. For many years, he was simultaneously President of the Seminary, the American Jewish Committee and Dropsie College and several other organizations. Indeed, he held so many presidencies that it is reported that a member of his family, when questioned about his occupation, replied that it was "being president."*

Unquestionably, Dr. Adler's pre-eminent role on the American Jewish scene afforded a platform for the Conservative view of Judaism which he represented in his official and personal capacity. But his main impact upon the Conservative movement resulted from his leading role in the re-organization of the Seminary in 1902, and in the direction of the Seminary during Dr. Schechter's presidency. Upon the death of Schechter in 1915, he became the acting President of the Seminary and subsequently the President. He remained President until his death and during his term of office the Seminary expanded its student body, built its current buildings and achieved a financial stability.

Dr. Adler's view of the Conservative position is made clear in the selection printed below. He was insistent that the Seminary was primarily an institution of higher learning rather than the proponent of a new viewpoint in Judaism. He assiduously avoided the idea that there was a Conservative movement or party and clung to the notion of a Conservative tendency. This position enabled him to receive support for the Seminary from people who did not personally share the Conservative viewpoint. However, it impeded the emergence of a well organized Conservative movement and limited the development of the Conservative ideology. Still, the forces which were to re-shape the Conservative tendency into a movement were already at work during Dr. Adler's lifetime. In the subsequent years the Conservative position has become more clearly that of a movement and the Seminary has expanded its conception of its role and has become more clearly identified as the advocate and head of the Conservative movement and ideology.

The statement printed below was delivered as an address to the Rabbinical Assembly in 1923.

Possibly it may be as well for me to tell you how the Seminary came to be, what were the motives that guided the founders, and then you will be in position yourselves to interpret the attitude of the Seminary, because the Seminary is a historical growth and was created to meet certain definite conditions which had arisen in America.

I was in early manhood when the Seminary was founded and remember most clearly the steps which were taken to establish it and the underlying thoughts which were in the minds of the founders, and I can say, without any hesitation, that the Seminary was not the creation of any particular party in Judaism. This statement may seem a little strange in these days of party strife, and yet it represents an actual fact.

It will not occupy very much of your time if I sketch for you the early history of the Jewish theological seminaries in America, because this brief history has to do with the founding of the Seminary and casts some light upon it.

The first Jewish college in America which actually opened its doors was the Maimonides College in Philadelphia, which operated under a charter of the Hebrew Education Society of that city and was founded by the Board of Delegates of American Israelites, a body which endeavored to combine all the congregations at that time in the United States into one effort both for the protection of the rights of Jews, the establishment of a college and the founding of a publication society. It did actually establish all these three agencies, and to that extent was not only the forerunner of several present national organizations, but more comprehensive than any one of them.

This College did not secure adequate support and closed its doors after an interval of about six years, but it had a double relationship to the Seminary. Two of the Faculty which composed it, namely, Dr. Sabato Morais and Doctor Marcus Jastrow, afterwards joined together in the establishment of our Seminary. You will also note that the Maimonides College was itself not a party effort, since Leeser, Morais and Jastrow were members of the Faculty and Leeser, its founder and head, proclaimed the breadth of its foundation in these unmistakable terms:

"Some may object to the movement, that it is not pledged to either Reform or Orthodoxy. These hateful words are always at hand when anything is to be done, from the election of a secretary to a society, to printing a book or establishing a college. The illiberal always ask: To what party does he or it belong? For our part, strange as it may sound, we belong to no party. We commenced life with certain convictions and have not swerved from them. We know only Judaism; and if you call it 'Orthodox,' you do so—not we."

In 1875, the Hebrew Union College was established, and this, too, was started on the same basis as the previous attempt in America, that is, Jewish science and Jewish knowledge were to be taught without any particular bias, and the students were expected to found an educated ministry or a body of Jewish scholars in America. While the impulse was given by Isaac M. Wise, who had already announced himself as a Reformer—Conservative Reformer he would have been called in these days—still others, who had in no wise departed from the tradition, took part in the foundation. If I am not mistaken, Louis N. Dembitz acted as Chairman of the Committee on Curriculum; Mayer Sulzberger attended the meetings which had to do with the founding of the College, and Doctor Morais himself acted as one of the examiners at the Hebrew Union College. I very well remember his having exhorted his own Congregation, Mikveh Israel of Philadelphia, to join the Union of American Hebrew Congregations and aid in the maintenance of the College, in order that we might have such an institution in America which would represent all Israel. This hope, however, was doomed to disappointment. Men like Doctor Jastrow never expected that one college could maintain itself for all the Jews under existing conditions. Leeser, in the meantime, had passed away, but Morais clung tenaciously to the belief that it was possible to create and maintain an institution which would satisfy the existing congregations in the United States. In 1878, Doctor Morais journeyed to Cincinnati and delivered the address at the closing exercises of the Hebrew Union College, in which he expressed the fondest hopes that the institution might provide an educated ministry for all the congregations in America. I cite this to you in order that it may be clearly understood that the founder of the Seminary, himself a Sephardi, of Italian birth, scrupulously adhering to the traditions in his Congregation and in his life, assenting to no changes whatever, was yet a man of sufficient breadth to be willing, in the interest of American Jewry and Jewish learning, to join hands with those of different views in the founding and maintenance of a college, and it was a man of that spirit who became our founder.

It was not until 1885 that there was any thought in his mind of another college, and the impulse for the creation of the Seminary came, not from any action of the Hebrew Union College, but from the action of the Central Conference of American Rabbis, which consisted of the Faculty and the then graduates of the College, who, at a meeting in this very city of Pittsburgh adopted resolutions which Doctor Morais declared "revealed unwarranted antagonism to the five Holy Books, a denunciation of the general character of the Pentateuch, a serious charge against Mosism as teaching imperfect ideas of the providence and justice of God." It was to combat these destructive views that the Seminary was founded, and the first steps toward it were taken within a week after the resolutions to which I have alluded were adopted.

The original call for the meeting which founded the Seminary read as follows:

"The undersigned, believing it imperative to make a strong effort for the perpetuation of historical Judaism in America, invite the coöperation of all Israelites who share their views.

"A meeting of ministers will shortly be held to take action in this direction. It is proposed to found an institution in which Bible and Talmud shall be studied to a religious purpose . . ." And later the purpose was stated: "To train ministers and teachers in a manner that their devotion to the law and traditions may inspire respect for Judaism's needs and promote the observance of its tenets."

Doctor Morais interpreted these formal statements in the following illuminating words:

"At the basis of our Seminary lies the belief that Moses was in all truth inspired by the Living God to promulgate the laws for the government of a people sanctified to an imperishable mission; that the same laws, embodied in the Pentateuch, have unavoidably a local and a general application. Those comprised in the first category lose their force outside of Palestine, the others are obligatory elsewhere; but both the former and the latter, being of necessity broadly formulated, needed in all ages an oral interpretation. The traditions of the fathers are therefore coeval with the written statutes of the five Holy Books."

While Doctor Morais formed the center of this group, and was immediately joined by Doctor Mendes, both of whom were ministers of Sephardic Congregations, three other men of great importance, Doctors Jastrow, Kohut and Szold, all of whom had adopted prayer books with modified services, recognized that a most dangerous tendency had developed which they, in spite of their minor differences, must unite in combating. Others who joined this company were H. P. Mendes, Henry S. Jacobs, F. de Sola Mendes, Aaron Wise, H. W. Schneeberger and Bernard Drachman. These men, therefore, banded themselves together primarily for the purpose of maintaining the thesis that the Biblical and Rabbinical Law as handed down and interpreted by the Rabbis and sages of Israel, was binding on the Jewish people, and that Judaism was an historical growth and not a mushroom sect whose character was to be changed from time to time by platforms or resolutions.

It must also be borne in mind that the Seminary was founded by men who, while having the traditional Jewish training, had also a western secular education and, strangely enough, they represented various western European countries. Morais came from Leghorn, Italy; Kohut from Hungary; Jastrow was born in Warsaw; Szold in Hungary; and Mendes had his training in England. Both Jastrow and Kohut were graduates of German universities, and Morais drew his inspiration from Samuel David Luzzatto. In other words, all of these men represented the training and the education of Western Europe and, excepting Kohut, had long residence in the United States.

It was natural that this group of men should look to the education of a Jewish Rabbinate which combined Jewish learning and adherence to tradition with secular knowledge. At no time in the history of the Jewish people, except in Eastern Europe, has there been any profound objection to the learning and the language of the nations among whom the Jews were settled. In the Babylonian exile, the Jews took up the Aramaic language and made it their current speech—witness the remains in the Holy Scriptures themselves. In the Hellenistic period they learned Greek and absorbed Greek learning and philosophy. When the Mohammedan Empire spread over a good part of Asia, North Africa and even Europe they studied Arabic philosophy, they adopted the forms of Arabic poetry, they re-learned Greek philosophy through Arabic, and many philosophical, ethical, and even legal books of the Jews were written in Arabic, and, of course, in Spain after Arabic they used Spanish, in Italy, Italian, and so on.

Thus in 1885, when the Seminary was founded, there was never any question but that secular knowledge and the English language were essentials to the Rabbinate in America and should be employed in the Seminary. At that time there may have been 500,000 Jews in the United States, of whom 400,000 represented the older settlers and 100,000 the van of the new immigration. When the Seminary was founded, therefore, it was the institution of the Orthodox, or Historical, or Conservative school, and there was . practically no question as to the propriety of the union of such forces for the maintenance of the Jewish tradition. As the immigration of the Jews from Russia, Poland and Galicia increased, a new question arose in America, and this new question was presented to the Seminary. For the first time Jews in America had to face an attitude brought over from Eastern Europe that secular learning, or indeed any learning which was not acquired from the Talmud and the Codes, or had anything to do with the Gentile world, could not be permitted as part of the training of a rabbi; in fact, unfitted him for the purpose, and that the English language itself was not to be employed.

This attitude, which had grown up in Eastern Europe, was different from the general trend of Jewish development, whether in Babylon, or the Persian Empire, or in Egypt, or in Spain, or in Italy, and was probably the outgrowth of conditions more bitter than had ever been experienced by Jews before and brought about the feeling that nothing which was employed by the non-Jews could be adopted. Such a state of mind caused the building up in this country of a *yeshiva*, where talmudic study alone was carried on—even the Bible was hardly formally studied.

The Seminary, on the other hand, following the methods existing in Western Europe and deriving something from the methods of the American colleges, had developed along lines similar to those of the Jews' College in London, the Seminaries at Berlin, Breslau, Paris, Budapest and even Constantinople, in which the real question was not so much that of a greater or lesser orthodoxy, as the combination of Jewish studies with secular knowledge. It was realized, of course, that since the secular education required time, and that all the attention of the student could not be given to Jewish studies, as it was in the *yeshivas*, improved scientific methods of imparting Jewish knowledge must be found.

I do not think that this is at all a new attitude. As I have indicated, it is the normal attitude which the Jews must have followed in the Babylonian academies, in the great schools of Northern Africa and Spain and in more recent times in the whole of Western Europe, where, in contact with the various civilizations, they maintained their own tradition and their own knowledge and yet partook fully in the knowledge of their day. It is needless for me to remind you that our ancient Rabbis knew astronomy and mathematics, that those in the Middle Ages studied physics and metaphysics and natural history, and that, therefore, the plan that we have applied is not a novelty but a steady development of several thousand years. It is true that in a section of Eastern Europe, in which the great bulk of the Jews lived, there had grown up a sort of abnormality—an abnormal attitude which, as it were, closed the Jewish mind in and limited it to its own literature, and even to a small section of that; always, of course, excepting a few of the greater minds, which can never be trammeled by any system, however narrowing.

It was these conditions which Doctor Schechter had to meet and, if possible, overcome. The Reform movement was showing a constantly increasing tendency to break away from Jewish history and tradition and base itself upon what it chose to call prophetic Judaism. The Orthodox party was growing more self-conscious and exhibiting the tendency to revert to the abnormal attitude of Eastern Europe. How did Doctor Schechter view the Seminary under these conditions? Listen to his own words:

"The religion in which the Jewish ministry should be trained must be specifically and purely Jewish, without any alloy or adulteration. Judaism must stand or fall by that which distinguishes it from other religions as well as by that which it has in common with them. . . . It permeates the whole of your life. It demands control over all your actions, and interferes with your menu. It sanctifies the season, and regulates your history, both in the past and in the future. . . . Judaism is absolutely incompatible with the abandonment of the Torah. Nay, every prophet or seer must bring his imprimatur from the Torah."

Ten years later he declared:

"Our work has been a hard one, considering . . . the great divisions among the people engendered by the extreme tendencies of the various parties, be they Reform or Orthodox, which could never understand a frame of mind that refused to be labeled by the names they wished to attach to it."

He gave as our ideal:

"The creation of a conservative tendency which was almost entirely absent or lay dormant in this country for a long time. Its aim was to preserve and to sustain traditional Judaism in all its integrity and by means of the spoken or written word, to bring back to the consciousness of Jewry its heroic past, which must serve as a model if we were to have a glorious future, or any future at all; but, at the same time, to remain in touch with our present surroundings and modern thought, and to adopt what was the best in them and, above all, to make use of modern method and system."

Judaism is, unquestionably, a way of life. This is not peculiar to Judaism, for it is the purpose of any religion to make good people, right living people, people who are trained to carry on the work of the world with a high spirit. Judaism has developed for this purpose a code of law, and under this code there are definite and positive acts to be done. A religious Jew believes that he must act in accordance with the Jewish law. The Reform movement held that this Jewish law was, in effect, abrogated. It was as a protest against this philosophy that the Seminary was founded.

The Seminary, therefore, insisted in the first instance, that the students must be persons who lived in accordance with the Jewish law. From this tradition the Seminary itself has never varied. It has not modified the prayer book, it has not changed the calendar, it has not altered the dietary laws, it has not abolished the second day of the holidays, and although some of its founders and some of its graduates have, without protest from the Seminary, attempted changes in the ritual, the Seminary itself has never adopted any of these changes.

Within the limits I have described, varying opinions on the part of the Faculty have always been permitted. The variation, it is true, is not very great; still, we do not persecute each other and we live reasonably well together. It may be that as a result of this broad-mindedness a Judaism will develop which is not partisan and may approach to a harmonization of these varying views. I do not mean by this an American Judaism. The Seminary, even before Doctor Schechter invented the phrase "Catholic Israel," still had such an idea in mind.

Doctor Morais, Sephardi that he was, proposed a union of the Sephardic and Ashkenazic and even of the Italian and Yemenite rituals, in the hope that the Jewish people might have a book of common prayer. The Seminary has always felt that the adoption of secular knowledge and American ideals did not require a change in the prayer book, always in the hope that just as the Hebrew language was the common bond of scattered Israel, so we might possess a uniform service, or at least a reasonably uniform service, which would make a Jew from New York, or Philadelphia, or Pittsburgh, at home in London, or Paris, or Constantinople, or Jerusalem.

The Seminary recognized that there are and always have been, and always will be, divisions in Jewry; that there are always people who call themselves conservatives; that there are legal minds and rationalistic minds, philosophers and mystics; that some Rabbis always favor the strict interpretation and others the mild interpretation. This is eternal and in the essence of human nature. If you take twins of the same family, give them the same attention, the same nurse, the same education, there is no guaranty that their minds will be alike. How much less can one hope to standardize the minds of a whole people.

But recognizing all these possibilities of divergence, the Seminary still aims to teach a form of Judaism to which all people could come, so far as fundamental values are concerned. A common language, the understanding of a common history and a common literature, are the strongest factors for keeping together the Synagogue—stronger in our opinion than any set of resolutions or platforms. Short of the very simple words of our charter, we have laid down no platform and adopted no creed, for we are of the opinion that religious platforms, like party platforms, are more often made to be disregarded than to be lived by, and that the surest guaranty for the steady maintenance of an enlightened Judaism based upon tradition was the teaching of the accumulated knowledge and information of the Jewish sages through all the ages.

I cannot wholly deplore the fact that there are differences among us. When have there not been? The differences which have arisen among the Jewish people in the past have not proved a wholly unmixed evil. It is to the Karaite heresy that Judaism owes a careful study of the Bible, Hebrew grammar and a reasonable exegesis. Probably the most distinguished works of the great Gaon Saadya were written under its inspiration. The philosophy of Maimonides was, as you all know, followed by the most bitter quarrel that mediaeval Jewry developed, and those that came after him actually destroyed his books, holding that such rationalism undermined the foundations of Judaism. This view the Seminary has never held. We welcome legalists, rationalists, mystics, always provided that they recognize the validity of the Jewish tradition and the Jewish law and are willing to live under it even though their explanation thereof may be different. Doctor Schechter, who at one time in his life was accounted a Liberal and as the years passed became more and more of a Conservative, held the view that the Seminary must always shelter men of different types of mind, that he always expected to have pupils who would berate him for his liberality or berate him for his conservatism, but that the greatest hope for Judaism would be a combination of the rationalist and the mystic, and that any generation which could produce such conditions would indeed produce great men and great rabbis.

Now this may be very far from what you have expected me to say as being the attitude of the Seminary, but had I said anything else, I do not think I should have correctly interpreted the Seminary, which, after all, is not a platform, is not a building, is not a library, is not even a fund, but consists of the masters and pupils who have labored for it and in it during these thirty-five years and more.

I see in it the ideals of Isaac Leeser, Sabato Morais and Solomon Schechter, each of whom, in turn, was the authorized leader of an American Jewish college devoted to the teaching of Judaism as historically handed down.

The Seminary is an institution of Jewish learning designed for the purpose of creating an educated Jewish Rabbinate in the United States. It aims to carry the student back to the sources of the Jewish law, history, liturgy, philosophy, theology and practice, believing that men so grounded in the knowledge and essentials of the great historic structure which we call Judaism will preach it and practice it.

Through these men the Seminary stands for the normal development in America of the main stream of Judaism, and it is willing to let any other body or group qualify or limit their Judaism by any prefix that seems best to themselves. The Seminary aims to open up the entire domain of Jewish knowledge to its students, by which it will best serve the purpose for which it was founded—to preserve in America the knowledge and practice of historical Judaism as contained in the laws of Moses and expounded by the prophets and sages in Israel in Biblical and Talmudical writings.

TRADITION IN THE MAKING

The Seminary's Interpretation of Judaism

By RABBI LOUIS FINKELSTEIN

Dr. Louis Finkelstein (b. 1895) is certainly the leading figure in the current shaping of Conservative Judaism. He occupies a commanding position by virtue both of his talents and his office as Chancellor of the Jewish Theological Seminary. Under his leadership the Seminary has grown in size, multiplied its functions and widened its area of concern. During this same period, and at least partially at his initiative, the organizational structure of the Conservative movement has been solidified.

The two selections in this book which were written by Dr. Finkelstein came from a period prior to his election to the Presidency of the Seminary. Both were delivered as speeches. "Tradition in the Making" was delivered at the 50th anniversary celebration of the Seminary in 1937. "The Things that Unite Us" was written some ten years earlier and presented at a Rabbinical Assembly Convention. They represent stages in Conservative thinking and enunciate principles which Dr. Finkelstein has implemented in the Seminary. However, there are other areas of his thinking and action, which are not reflected in these selections and which await, and will doubtless receive, written statement in the future.

Fifty years ago when this Seminary was founded, the conflict between religion and science, which formed one of the most important phases of nineteenth century thought, was at its height. Indeed, as late as the time when I was at college in 1911, we could still hear the last rumblings of the great battle. Scientific information had accumulated at such a rapid pace that it could not be completely digested or fully understood. As a result, even the foremost teachers of the age resembled, in a degree, the young sophomores, who having taken a course in Introduction to Philosophy, and learned to babble in terms of syllogisms, non-existence, and pseudo-reality, consider themselves the mightiest thinkers of all time, and feel nothing but contempt for even the most distinguished minds of earlier generations. The nebular theory of the development of the Universe, the Darwinian hypothesis of the origin of species and the descent of man, the higher critical speculations about the composition of the Pentateuch, and finally, the sociological and anthropological discoveries of parallels to Hebrew tradition among primitive peoples, seemed to imply the final doom of all religion.

The events of the past five decades have, however, demonstrated once more the truth of Bacon's famous aphorism, that "a little philosophy inclineth men to atheism, but depth in philosophy bringeth man's mind about to God." Today it would be difficult to find a scientist of high rank who fails to see in religion and the communion with God which it offers a valid and essential expression of the human spirit, basic to all possible human happiness.

What, indeed, are the facts which modern Science lays bare before us? They reveal to us a Universe of a size and magnificence which would have dazzled any thinker of earlier times, organic life of such a complexity and variety as to be all but incomprehensible to our minds.

When the writer of Job wanted to describe the greatness of God, he called upon the doubter to explain the manner in which "the wild goats of the rock bring forth," and the time when "the hinds do calve." "Canst thou number," he asked, "the months that they fulfill, or knowest thou the time when they bring forth?" "Gavest thou," he further inquired, "the goodly wings unto the peacock or wings and feathers unto the ostrich?" "Hast thou given the horse strength? Hast thou clothed his neck with thunder?"

How limited these wonders appear in the light of modern science, in spite of the lofty verse in which they are expressed. The miracle by which the unborn foetus knows precisely the time when it must separate itself from its mother and make its way into the outer world, which so amazed the ancient shepherd, is but one of the lesser marvels which come to our eyes.

The amazing precision of the ductless glands, which, like the most expert chemists, produce the drugs we need for our health, day by day, in just the amounts required for our health, growth and development; the wonder of the human heart, which beats so regularly seventy-six times each minute, from the moment of birth until death; the infinite complexity of the nervous system, which permits us to hear, to see, to feel, and to think; which like a never-failing guardian sends additional blood to the organs at the exact time when they need it, which stimulates the heart to more rapid action when the body is threatened by disease, which gives us the gift of refreshing sleep; had the inspired writer but known of them, what poetry might he not have poured forth in the praise of their Creator!

What would he have said had he known about the millions of living beings, too small to be seen by the naked eye, and who yet possess these functions of movement, growth and reproduction, which are characteristic of life? In what a magnificent and immortal flow of language might he not have described the singular truth, which modern science now insists upon, that all life—from the cleverest of men, the most mighty of beasts, the most gigantic of trees, to the tiniest of animalcules and germs—is descended from a primitive drop of protoplasm, which was invested by its Creator with the Protean gift of self-transformation; which became the fish and swam, which became the bird and flew, which grew into the mammal and suckled its young, and finally developing into man, speaks, thinks, remembers, and acts.

What could not a writer of Scripture have made with the discoveries of modern physical science!

More than two thousand years ago a Greek, trying to measure the size of the sun, set up two sticks in different parts of Greece, and came to the amazing conclusion that the sun is many times greater than the Peloponnesus. Astronomers now tell us that the sun is not only greater than the Peloponnesus and all Greece, but at least three hundred thousand times greater than the earth, and is itself one of the smaller stars, and, indeed, that our whole Milky Way, in which the sun occupies so modest a place, is only one of millions of similar galaxies, the light of some of which never reaches our telescopes.

With what reverence for the Mind which has revealed Itself to us through the Universe, must we be filled, when we think that "the marvellous order and beauty," to use Einstein's phrase, which controls these distant stars and galaxies in their wide courses, directs also those infinitesimal particles, so small as to be invisible even with the most powerful microscopes—the neutrons, the protons, and the electrons. There are millions of them in every fragment of matter which we touch, and yet there is not one which fails to act in accordance with the Divine Reason which expresses itself in the world.

What would Isaiah, who wondered at the blindness of the men of his generation, because they did not regard the work of the Lord, as it appeared in the simplicity of his day, have said of our generation, which has been granted so more complete a revelation, and yet continues in its unbelief! There is only one parallel in history to such willful blindness, and that is Israel worshipping the Golden Calf, within a few days after it had been permitted to witness the Revelation of the Divine Glory on Mount Sinai.

Incredible as is the world's resistance to the recognition of God, it is no more strange than the continued adherence of some of our younger men to the exploded theories of the Bible critics who denied the unique inspiration and greatness of the Hebrew Scriptures. Perhaps such an attitude was excusable fifty and even twenty-five years ago. Theologians and Bible students were blinded by the light which was coming to them from their new methods of research. The brilliance and daring of novel theories, like those of Graf and Wellhausen, were overwhelming and all but irresistible. But the spade of the archaeologist has done for the Scriptures what the test tube of the chemist, the microscope of the biologist, and the telescope of the astronomer have done for natural science. Archaeologists have shown, as Professor Albright indicated so brilliantly the other night at our Institute of Bible Studies, that the aspersions on the veracity of the Scriptures are themselves without foundation, and that, far from discrediting the narratives of the Scriptures, the monuments that have been discovered confirm them.

Together with these advances in Biblical study and natural science has come a deeper understanding of psychology and sociology, those infant sciences which give so much promise for the future of mankind.

The first students of primitive life, finding parallels to Israel's traditions in Africa and India, were prepared to deny the whole principle of Prophetic inspiration and to see in the great Prophets merely dervishes who happened to dance in Jerusalem. A deeper study of Prophetic religion and life has shown, however, that the Prophets are without parallel among any of the other traditions and that it may be said, with absolute truth and without the slightest exaggeration, that the Hebrew Scriptures are inspired in a sense in which no other literature of the world can be so described.

When we realize that the code of laws laid down in the Book of Moses and developed in the Talmud was not only superior to any code in antiquity, but in many respects to that of most modern countries; that the principles of universal peace, the equality of man, and the right of the individual to think for himself, which are fundamental in the religion of the Prophets are even now recognized by only a small section of the world; we suddenly become conscious of the truth that not only the Prophets, but the code of laws which the Prophets defended, is a Divine guide for conduct with which we cannot dispense.

Only a few blocks away from us, at Teachers College, experiments were performed in character training which definitely establish the fact that moral habits must be inculcated one by one, and cannot be given *en bloc* to the child or to an adult. Properly interpreted these experiments bear very nearly on the essential controversy between Paul, who rejected the Law, and the Rabbis who defended it. It is becoming increasingly obvious that it is not enough for the establishment and strengthening of moral character to hold up a symbolically perfect personality, but that it is necessary, by means of moral judgments, to train a person with regard to every question of right and wrong.

In asserting this truth, it is not our purpose to revive the ancient, unnecessary, and even unspiritual controversy regarding the rellative merits of Judaism and Christianity. The Judeo-Christian tradition, properly understood, is a single system of thought, of which Judaism is the core, and Christianity the periphery. It is a tradition which recognizes the discipline of Law as essential to human behavior, and which sees in proper conduct one of the most effective methods for a man to approach God. It is a fundamental principle of this system that a distinction must be made between the ceremonial and ethical elements in religion; and it is one of the great glories of our teachers that they were the first to discover the truth that while ethics is universal, ritual is not. The Jews have never asked the rest of the world to accept the discipline of Judaism with regard to ceremonial. We have asked the world to accept this discipline with regard to the ethical life, and Christianity in the main has accepted this task. Some groups of early Christians were hostile to these principles, but the greatest fathers of the Church and certainly the founders of it, realized that law is as much the basis of Christianity as it is of Judaism. Certainly it was a very legalistic Christianity which in the form of Puritanism laid the foundations of our own great republic. Yet from time to time, the revolt of man against discipline, whether intellectual or moral, expresses itself in a revival of the romanticism, which in earlier generations brought about the apparent conflict between Judaism and Christianity. Such a romantic movement was initiated early in the nineteenth century and has expressed itself in a rejection of the teachings of both the Pharisees and the Puritans, who in different ages, advocated almost precisely the same patterns of behavior. The saints who have made it possible for us to live free lives, both those of ancient Jerusalem, and those of modern New England, have been presented to us as bigoted fanatics and narrow-minded casuists by men who rebel against the necessary discipline of life. But the indictment is a slander both with regard to the ancient Pharisee, and with regard to the modern Puritan. The love and affection for humanity, the breadth of vision, and the depth of understanding which appear equally in the writings of the Pharisee and the Puritan, are among the noblest spiritual treasures of the human race. They represent movements which, finding their highest expression in the Hillels and Akibas of ancient Judea, and in the Miltons and Roger Williamses of sixteenth century England and New England, did more than any other to spread happiness among the peoples of the world, to make life more bearable and easy, and to carry mankind on further toward its goal of high intellectual development and deep affectionate feelings. As Huxley says, in a fine passage quoted by Doctor H. G. Enelow in his essay on the Pharisees, "Of all the strange ironies of history, perhaps the strangest is that the word 'Pharisee' is current as a term of reproach among the theological descendants of the sect of Nazarenes who, without the martyr spirit of those primitive Puritans, would never have come into existence. They, like their historical successors, our own Puritans, have shared the general fate of the poor wise men who save cities."

The truth is that we need Law and Discipline in life, but that this law and discipline must take continual cognizance of the goals which they are intended to serve. It is only in bureaucracies, in prisons, and in backward schools, that discipline is sometimes regarded as an end in itself. In civilized society it must be considered as a means to a further and more inclusive purpose. This has been described by Hasdai Crescas, who after Maimonides was perhaps the greatest mind produced by the Jews in the Middle Ages, as first, communion with God, and second, human happiness. In saying this, Crescas was but putting into philosophical terminology the Scriptural truth that the motives for righteous action are to please God, and to bring happiness to man. If Judaism is to perform these unctions, it must naturally take cognizance in every generation of the deeper understanding of God made available through research and the changing conditions of human life. Justice, truth, mercy, and love do not change—they are more real than the world in which we live. But their applications differ under varying conditions. What may be just in the jungles of Africa need not necessarily be just in the metropolis of seven million people. What is mercy to the well man may be cruelty to the sick man; and what is love under certain conditions may be the worst kind of hatred under others. It is one of the great achievements of Jewish law that it provides in itself the machinery for its interpretation, its expansion, and its application to changing conditions. The principles developed in our own American Constitution, whereby the Supreme Court is what has been termed an adjourned constitutional convention, occurs in Deuteronomy, where the Sanhedrin is elevated into a prolongation of the Revelation on Mount Sinai. This doctrine is expressed in that remarkable statement that: "Every truth which a careful student will discover in the future was already revealed to Moses on Mount Sinai."

For hundreds of years this adaptation of Judaism proceeded in its natural way and produced the glories of the Mishna and the Talmud and the early mediaeval rabbinic works. During the past few centuries, as Jewish life was narrowed by continually increasing oppression, this vitality of Jewish law has diminished and in our own time has all but disappeared. There are those who think that we have but two alternatives, to reject or to accept the law, but in either case to treat it as a dead letter. Both of these alternatives are repugnant to the whole tradition of Judaism, and it is to combat them that the Seminary was brought into being. Sabato Morais, who founded the Seminary, Solomon Schechter, who was its second president, and Dr. Cyrus Adler, who, happily with us, is its third president, have all accepted the fundamental principle that Jewish law must be preserved, but that it is subject to interpretation by those who have mastered it, and that the interpretation placed upon it by duly authorized masters in every generation must be accepted with as much reverence as those which were given in previous generations.

We, therefore, accept Judaism as a system of justice, but as a justice which, far from being blind, is very clear-sighted. To do this is to change Judaism from an ossified museum piece into a living and vital tradition. The Code of Hammurabi can rest unchanged in the Louvre. The Torah endures in human life and must partake of the vitality, the adaptability, and fluidity of all living organisms.

To effect this plan is not to break with traditional Judaism, but to return to it. There is no quarrel between us and Isaiah, Jeremiah, Hillel, and Akiba. If we are ready to do for our generation what they did for their generation, Judaism will not only be a light to us but will become for our time what it became for their time, a light for the world. Our quarrel is with those who, rejecting the doctrines of these great teachers, repudiate the discipline of Judaism on the one hand, or, on the other hand, refuse to give it the opportunity to live. Many of us look to the land of Israel as the place and to the Hebrew language as the natural vehicle for the full development and restoration of this vital Judaism, and indeed the presidents of this Seminary, the members of its Faculties, and its alumni have been among the foremost to contribute to the renaissance of Judaism which is associated with the rebirth of the Hebrew language and the restoration of the Holy Land. However, it is impossible for us who have the privilege and the responsibility of living in the greatest Jewish community ever assembled, to satisfy ourselves with contributing only vicariously to the restoration of Judaism. It is not enough to be a member of an organization that helps to rebuild

Palestine or promote the Hebrew language, to feel that one is doing one's part in bringing Judaism back to its normal life. Judaism demands of each of us: study and action, *ma'aseh* and *talmud*, regarding both of them as means for communion with God.

The promotion of Jewish learning at this Seminary is thus not at all to be dissociated from its religious work: one of the principles on which the institution is based is that Study is a fundamental part of Judaism. Whether Study or Deeds takes precedence in the tradition of our ancestors was, as you know, long a matter of dispute; but no one ever doubted that both were essential to it.

We regard this demand for Study and Practice not as one to be fulfilled only by a small professional group, who may be Jews for the rest of us. Each one of us must devote part of his day to Jewish thought and the Jewish mode of communion with God. To do this is not to offer a sacrifice for the preservation of a mystic entity called the Jewish people. On the contrary, it is essential for our individual welfare and happiness, as well as for the enhancement of our usefulness to the world. The preservation of the Jewish people which necessarily results from our devotion to our faith is but a further means to the fulfillment of these ends. The Jewish people must be maintained in order that their traditions may live; it is not the traditions that live in order that the Jewish people should be maintained.

There may be those who feel that they can live quite happily without either religious discipline or communion with God. But they are in grave error. The restlessness which characterizes us, the confusion which has come on our times, the increasing percentage of neuroses among us, and the general unhappiness of all of us in the midst of the greatest affluence the world has yet seen, have come upon us primarily because of the lack of that sense of communion with God which made our forefathers happy in spite of their poverty and their physical suffering. We resemble most closely those little children who, not having yet learned to interpret the symptoms of weariness and hunger, cry when bedtime or mealtime comes, and yet refuse either to go to bed or take their food. Living in a gilded palace, as it were, we are still miserable, for we are essentially orphans, having lost that most precious of all values in life, the sense of the Fatherhood of God.

The feeling of deprivation grows sharper and more poignant,

instead of less severe, as we grow older. The time comes to each of us when the burdens of life seem far too heavy to carry, when the brightness of youth begins to fade, and we notice the lengthening shadows which presage our end.

More than ever then do we become homesick; homesick, not for our houses or for our countries, but homesick for the universal Parent of all of us, for that deep affection which is the heart of the universe itself, for the mercy of God; yet a wall of iron has been placed between us and Him, and we cannot find Him. What greater good can a man achieve, either for himself or for the world, than to contribute his effort to piercing this wall, and bring the Father and the Children once more into loving communion with one another!

It is to this high task that we of this Seminary, members of the Faculty, members of the Board of Directors, members of the Seminary National Council, friends, alumni, and students have dedicated ourselves. Recalling that our forefathers who interpreted the science of their day in the terms of the religion, brought salvation to a whole world, it is natural to hope that we, their descendants, still bearing in our hearts a spark of the ancient fire, being if not prophets, the children and the grandchildren of prophets, will be able to bring about the synthesis between the modern intellectual life and the traditional faith that is needed for the happiness of our own time. Writers, philosophers, theologians may do their share today as they did two thousand years ago, but ultimately, the world will depend, not upon the literary contribution of a few, but the willingness of the whole people to devote themselves to the high ideal of Piety plus Learning, for it is in that combination that we, like our ancestors before us, see our most appropriate mode of communion with God.

That we of this institution should be able to make a lasting contribution of this type to the spiritual welfare of mankind may seem an enthusiastic fantasy to some. But they would also have regarded the faith of the ancient rabbis in their small Palestinian academies as unwarranted. I, for one, can never forget that of the whole ancient world, which included in itself the great schools of Athens, the magnificent libraries of Alexandria, and the great collections of Rome, none brought permanent satisfaction to the human spirit save the humble academy which met in the vineyard of Yabneh. Is it too much to expect that our academy, perhaps more imposing than that in Yabneh in size, but yet humble in spirit, may through its devotion, and through the peculiar circumstances which have brought it into being, and through the desire of those associated with it to follow the example set by our predecessors, still manage to serve the world? I think we can do it. And I believe that it is because so many of our neighbors of all denominations also feel that we have a special and important contribution to make to the spiritual life of the country and the world, that they joined so readily in the celebration of our semi-centennial.

When I was younger, I frequently wished that it might have been granted me to have lived in the first or second century and been one of those humble students, whose names have been for the most part forgotten, but whose life and labor contributed so much happiness and goodness for all the world. Now that I am growing older, I realize that we have no need to envy our ancestors. We can do better than that—we can emulate them. The call comes to us as it did to Isaiah: "Whom shall I send, and who shall go for us?" Certainly the answer which each one of us will make, will be that of the Prophet himself, "Here am I; send me!"

TOWARDS A NATIONAL SYNAGOGUE

By Rabbi Solomon Goldman

Rabbi Solomon Goldman (1893–1954) was one of the leading figures in the American rabbinate. He served as rabbi of congregations in Cleveland and Chicago which he directed with great skill into ever broader areas of activity. A fluent writer and a fine scholar, he produced several publicistic works on current Jewish life and several books on Bible and Jewish philosophy. His public activities were many and varied, including the presidency of the Zionist Organization of America and intensive involvement and leadership in many national and international Jewish organizations.

The selection printed below is excerpted from an address which Dr. Goldman delivered to a convention of the United Synagogue of America. It clearly reflects two elements which dominated his thinking during the last decade of his life. One was a feeling, which was carried into action, that a liberal and experimental approach should be employed in relation to the forms and practices of the synagogue. The other — most clearly mirrored below — was a conviction that the synagogue had to reassert its place as the central institution of Jewish life. Dr. Goldman was convinced that it could do so only if it achieved a broader conception of its role and if a conception of a national Synagogue overbore the notion of autonomous local synagogues. The selection printed here is thus both a critique of the United Synagogue and a picture, as Dr. Goldman saw it, of what its role should be.

This Convention has a grand and pregnant theme, 'An Era of Destiny.' What a magnificent phrase. And yet I confess that I am not in the mood for the theme . . . . . I would have for my mood found it more congenial to speak on a theme of a subject entitled 'An Era of Unfulfilled Destiny.' I confess that I miss the adjective. Or perhaps it is time that we courageously call together a convention and call it, in plain words, 'An Era of Failure.' With a subtitle: 'The Failure of the Synagogue.' I must warn you from the very start that I shall be parochial in my thinking and in my presentation. I know it is pleasanter to speak in grand phrases. It is true that the Jews love Judaism — and particularly the Judaism of 2000 years ago — three thousand years ago, still better. One can speak with sweeping gestures of that era because it was great. One is charged with parochialism by practically every Jewish leader in the country, when one gathers courage to speak about the synagogue . . . . But what shall I do? They have made me a watchman of my vineyard, and my vineyard is the synagogue. It is very pleasant to speak to Jews, of these vast movements that are before us, the hopes and problems of solving them. As long as you do that you are a man of vision and understanding. The moment you speak about the synagogue you are provincial. You are parochial. You are limited in your thinking. That in itself constitutes part of the failure of the synagogue and the rabbi. Some of the people argue, and not altogether without justice, that it is the failure of Judaism. I say there is a measure of truth in it, but the attempts should have been made, and I haven't yet seen the success . . . I thought the reason why the synagogue has thus far not succeeded was due to the fact that it did not have a good start in the United States. The foundation was not laid by competent hands.

Now, I ask, how has this come about in this land of freedom? What has become of our vaunted stubbornness? Why have we succumbed so precipitately? Why did we begin almost immediately after our arrival here to disfigure and disguise our identity — we, who for some four thousand years have been noted for the courage and dignity with which we maintained our distinctiveness and the zealous care and passionate devotion we bestowed on our heritage? The one answer of the many that might be considered is the fact that the first two Jewish communities to have settled in the United States were far too ill-equipped Jewishly and otherwise to have been able to lay a firm foundation for a Jewish life in democratic America.

The first settlers, the Sephardim, were small in numbers, unduly scattered and dispersed, to be in a position to achieve unity and cohesive strength. Though, prior to reaching these shores, they had been refugees for a century and a half, they had established but

little contact with world Jewry, and as a result came here in splendid isolation and dismal ignorance of Judaism. Having come to
regard themselves as constituting an aristocracy they talked, like
the Cabots and the Lodges, only to God, more frequently among
themselves, but rarely to an East-European or German Jew. Indeed, when, at the end of the eighteenth century, their fellow
Sephardees applied to the Revolutionary government of France
for emancipation, they made sure to emphasize that they were not
to be confounded with the miserable Tedescos, embracing in the
designation Tedescos all Jews whose forefathers had not enjoyed
the privilege of having been expelled from Spain. They assimilated
and dissolved, the surviving remnants holding aloof from the later
arrivals long after they had become preponderately Litvacks and
Galizianer. Distinguished as many of their numbers have been, and
conspicuous and significant as has been their role in the making of
America, they were not the ones to initiate an enduring American
Jewish life of any particularity of depth.

The second Jewish community to settle here, the German, was
larger in number, and, by comparison with the first, Jewishly better informed. Many of them were idealists and some of them were
inspired and consecrated Jews. Bernard Felsenthal, David Einhorn,
Samuel Adler, Isaac Meir Wise, Kaufmann Kohler, loved Israel
and the Torah and never ceased offering on the ancient altar their
gifts of mind and heart. However, German Jewry had suffered the
torments of intellectual and spiritual Anti-Semitism for so long a
time that it was left with a schism in its whole being, rendering it
unfit to achieve a harmony between its environment and its tradition. Large numbers of German Jews, the whole Mendelssohnian
entourage, abandoned Judaism. Those who remained in the fold
were seldom ever again happy. They preached more than they
practiced, debated more than they decided upon, and became
Jewishly uncreative. As a community their contribution to the folk
movements, which upheaved world Israel in the past century,
was almost nil, their impact having been for the most part negative
and against. They brought with them to this country this schism
of soul, this inner divisiveness and disquietude, this timidity and
unproud humility before the outer world, and not a little of the
Germanic contempt for the common man. They never could understand why the Jewish masses resented their overlordship and have

never realized why they have failed in this land of freedom to win a respectful hearing for the mission of Judaism, or why in the past decade or two the spiritual, intellectual, aesthetic, organizational, and here and there also the philanthropic leadership of American Jewry, has been slipping away from them.

The third immigrant community, the East-European, was markedly different from those that had preceded them. They arrived here by the hundreds of thousands and brought with them a larger accumulation of soul. They were the immediate heirs to a century of an awe-inspiring Jewish renascence, stirring events, overpowering movements, and extraordinary Jewish achievements. Their parents and their grandparents, their brothers and sisters, though living in the shadow of pogroms in Czarist Russia, and in fear of persecution in Roumania and the Austro-Hungarian empire, remained loyal to their heritage and retained their self-identity. They gave birth to Hasidism, established *yeshivot* without number, created in Hebrew and Yiddish two of the richest and most brilliant of literatures in the modern world, developed the Zionist movement, had the vision to reclaim and restore Palestine, thus preparing it, as if directly inspired by Him who watches over Israel, to receive the victims of Nazi and Fascist madness; revived the old Jewish arts and encouraged the cultivation of new ones; organized labor; fashioned model idealistic unions, and played a significant part in freeing Russia of the autocracy and tyranny of the Romanoffs and in stimulating its vast hordes to strive for a more abundant life. When they finally came to this country from the European hell, they brought with them a thirst for freedom and a desire to live as Jews. Unfortunately, they arrived very poor, many of them actually as the recipients of charity, and in woeful ignorance of Emily Post's rules of etiquette. Empty pockets, ghetto habits, and uncultivated manners made them self-conscious, shy, diffident. Plagued for the first time perhaps in their history by a sense of inferiority, they attempted quick transformations and metamorphoses, and assumed fantastic shapes indeed. Uppermost in their mind and heart was the desire to run away from themselves, to cease being what they were, to blot out the memory of Shnipishok and Ishishok, of Kasrilevka and Helm, to forget the father — the *melamed*, the *shames*, — his *tallis*, his piety, his *heder*. They copied and imitated and played the sedulous ape, even if

their painful exertions resulted in caricatures. Shrieked a sumptuously pearled, jewelled, and befurred madam to her neighbor,
similarly resplendent, across Manhattan's Central Parkway, "What
do you think of my *shiksa*, she spoiled my Christmas for me."
Shouted a dandy to the waiter in one of Miami Beach's thirty-five
dollar a day hotels, "You numbskull, I ordered *beigel*." Out of the
home went the pictures of Moses and Aaron, Maimonides, the
Gaon of Vilna, Moses Montefiore, making way for those of Spanish
matadors and German troubadours, clowns and courtesans. An
end was put to Jewish tradition, synagogue attendance, Jewish
education — to everything Jewish. For everything Jewish brought
back to the mind of this progeny of Molière's *bourgeois gentil-
homme* the ghetto and its poverty, and they were resolved on
pouring out the water to its last murky drop — even if it required
throwing out the baby. What an array of fantastic shapes and
forms have not America's first generation of East-European Jews
assumed! What an army of social climbers have not my eyes beheld!
How often have I not seen coat-tails and the prehensile tail swing
together.

Now, there are no slogans or stunts or improvised programs of
quick panaceas that we may rely upon to alter this situation. And
we must admit that no one in our midst has bodied forth the idea
to grip and transform American Israel. It is true that some of the
choice spirits in our midst have reinterpreted Judaism in a way to
have affected the American Jewish community. But it has not
happened. We shall apparently have to work slowly, gradually,
doing a piece-meal job over a long stretch of years. We must not,
however, delay too long in making a beginning in that direction.
For myself, I am convinced that if the synagogue and rabbi are
allowed to maintain their status quo for another generation they
will completely deteriorate and their influence be altogether expunged from the American Jewish community. They may even
cease to exist except in insignificant numbers. And I am no less
convinced that with the deterioration of the synagogue will come
the complete break-down of the American Jewish community. The
organizations, themselves, will not guarantee the creative continuity
of American Jewish life. I, therefore urge that we, as Conservative
Jews, members of Conservative synagogues and the Conservative
rabbinate, begin to grapple with organizational problems.

I don't want to point out that there is a narrowing out of the synagogue — in function and program and even in comprehending it. What we have witnessed in the United States is the disappearance of *The Synagogue*. In its place arose *synagogues*. And unless you will get this difference in your mind I am very much afraid that you will never create the United Synagogue and never come to grips with the problems we are facing. Synagogues there are, and many of them indeed far better as individual institutions than almost anything we had in Vilna. But remember, they are not The Synagogue. In Chicago I cannot find The Synagogue. As The Synagogue disappeared and the synagogues were being born, the organizations also came into existence. They, too, began to multiply. With The Synagogue they might never have competed. Something remarkable has happened: the institution which was at one time synonymous with the Jewish people, which was the national institution (when you said Israel you meant The Synagogue) — the one organization that became local was the synagogue. All the other organizations became national. All of these organizations, these lodges and branches and districts, have no meaning to the members. One who joins a chapter is joining a national body. Therefore, one who joins a chapter simultaneously becomes an enthusiast of all of the other Hadassah chapters in the city. Simultaneously, the synagogues are rivals. They are in conflict. Not only is the synagogue the one local institution and all the others national, and therefore in magnitude they outweigh the synagogue, but the synagogue is not first in your mind. You have other interests, good interests, in your mind, shaped by the organizations. But the organizations have limited objectives, insofar as their membership is concerned. They have made American Jewry today into a campaign for one thing or another. The synagogue must make other demands. It cannot say, Join and give money. It must say to you, You have *mitzvot*. Keep the *mitzvot*. Why don't we see your children in the Hebrew school? . . . . The organizations present the urgency of their objectives. The rabbi talks in long range.

. . . . The synagogue, we are told, cannot cope with immediate and urgent objectives. Yet, it suits the purpose of the organization to think of us in historic terms and it suits the synagogue to think of itself in terms of its position in history. The result is that the synagogue opens its doors to every organization. Appeals can be made for every movement and cause. . . . . These organizations feel that they have a historic right to call on the rabbi. This imposition saps the strength of the synagogue and the rabbi and they cannot attend to the duties to which they should attend. You take all of these factors together and you will see why we have reached the level in American Jewish life that we have and why the synagogue is today the weakest of all of the organizations. Why the synagogue could very well disappear and not be missed in any way. . . . . . They all talk of the centrality of the synagogue. Why isn't it happening? What is the delay? Why haven't we moved? Why haven't we made the progress we should have made? Because we have synagogues and not A Synagogue, and we have a rabbi who is a jack of all trades and therefore can hardly be a master of any one.

What is the remedy? First of all, I suggest creating A Synagogue to replace the synagogues. Professor Schechter didn't suggest as the name of our organization the United Synagogues, but the United Synagogue. And there is a difference. When the United States was founded, when the Constitution was written, the foremost men at the time wanted to name it the United State. Those who stood for state sovereignty wanted the United States. Professor Schechter wanted a United Synagogue, that is, an organic unity. The United Synagogues simply mean a number of congregations joining voluntarily for the consideration of certain tasks which can never be brought to the point of implementation. I propose the organization in the larger communities where there is one or more Conservative synagogues, of a Synagogue Association which those who are adherents of Conservative Judaism will join as members. This association will maintain the synagogues now in existence and build others whenever it will be necessary and feasible. Synagogues now existing in smaller communities shall become a part of a Regional Association. Communities where there are at present no synagogues shall become the responsibility of the Synagogue Association.

Under the proposed new Synagogue Association, the selection of rabbis for different congregations would be made by the Association, and not as in my own case, over a bridge game. Why shall not a Synagogue Association have ten or fifteen itinerant preachers? Divide these functions and let the Association see to it that these functions are thus divided. Then in due time, when a Jew will begin joining The Synagogue, and not a *chevra* with any special name, in his own neighborhood, you will discover that you will not have to preach at him that there is A Synagogue in the United States. Create The Synagogue! And then you will see that many of your problems will begin to be solved.

. . . . . Though I have understood the need of the ideological structure in our midst, that we must find the proper balance between the left and the right, I have come to the conviction on the basis of what I have seen throughout the country that our problem is psychological and organizational, and only next, ideological, great and vital as that problem is.

Although I can not look into the future I feel certain that within five years after the Conservative National Synagogue Association is formed, there will be a Reform Association and later an Orthodox Association in America. These will ultimately give American Judaism the American Jew.

Part II
The Philosophies of Conservative Judaism

A NOTE ON THE PHILOSOPHIES
OF CONSERVATIVE JUDAISM

The philosophy of Conservative Judaism has never been formulated in any official statement. Accordingly, its over-all outlook must be deduced from the general presentations made by recognized leaders or by active figures in the movement. A selection of such statements is presented here.

Philosophies, as a whole, tend to be very general, to involve issues of principle and to have little concern with practical utility. This is partially true of the outlooks contained in this section. They reflect views of Conservative Judaism as, in the opinion of the writers, it ought to be and not necessarily as it is. But the pragmatic quality of Conservative Jewish thought can also be discerned as a substratum of the thinking. The practical experience of the Conservative movement is mirrored in these philosophies and obviously modifies them. By and large these philosophies are not systematic statements. They reflect the fluidity, the ambivalences and the "life is stronger than logic" outlook which characterize the Conservative movement. It is obvious, too, that there are great differences of emphasis in these statements. But it may also be noted that they operate from substantially similar premises and come to closely related conclusions.

Some of the statements were designed for publication; others were speeches and bear the impress of the occasion upon them. It was deemed wise, in an anthology, to leave them substantially as they were presented, and thus to mirror the varied forms in which the Conservative outlook has been presented to the American Jewish community.

An attempt was also made, in choosing the material for

this section, to reflect the changes in points of view that the years have brought. In consequence, several different decades are reflected in the selections. To get a more rounded picture, the papers in the first section should be considered jointly with the ones here. Since there is some reason to believe that the outlooks of men who are primarily academicians and those who are primarily practicing rabbis differ, an attempt has been made to include statements of both types of figures.

UNITY IN DIVERSITY IN THE CONSERVATIVE MOVEMENT*

By Rabbi Mordecai M. Kaplan

The greatest leavening force in the Conservative movement for several decades has been Mordecai M. Kaplan (b. 1881). His influence manifested itself in a great variety of ways. He has been the most prolific writer on the Conservative ideology and the most exhaustive explorer of the religious problems raised by the American Jewish scene. Indeed, he is the one figure in the Conservative movement whose major works — and they are numerous — have centered about the problems of the Conservative ideology. He devised the term Reconstructionism to characterize his outlook and around it built an organization for the propagation of his ideas. The Reconstructionist Foundation is not quite a movement, but it has been a force which has profoundly affected thinking within the Conservative movement, has had a considerable influence upon the Reform movement, and has had a marked effect upon Jewish educators, social workers and a great many laymen. Dr. Kaplan has been in a particularly advantageous position to make his influence felt within the Conservative movement. He has been, for more than 40 years, Professor of Homiletics and Midrash at the Seminary. For an almost equally long period, he was Dean of the Teachers Institute. He has been the rabbi of an influential and experimenting New York congregation for many decades, has been the President of the Rabbinical Assembly and has continued to participate actively in almost every phase of the Conservative movement. Most significant of all, from the point of view of influence, is the fact that he has raised up a group of ardent disciples who have advanced his views far and wide in speech, in writing and in organizational activity.

Dr. Kaplan's influence has been particularly evident in what has been called the "left wing" of the Rabbinical Assembly. But a great many of his ideas and

---

* An Address delivered at the United Synagogue Meeting in June 22, 1947.

proposals have become the common stock of the Conservative movement and are not necessarily associated with his name. Thus, in the advancement of his ideas, he has achieved a greater acceptance than has been accorded to the specific philosophy of Reconstructionism.

Two selections from Dr. Kaplan's writing are included in this volume. Many more might well have been included, since he has written illuminatingly on every area of Conservative thought. However, these two embody a synthesis of much of his thinking and make plain his belief that unity in Jewish life does not mean uniformity and that the Conservative movement must have guiding principles, and not be merely an amorphous catch-all.

I

The trend in Judaism designated in this country as Conservative is associated with the Jewish Theological Seminary of America and with the two organizations that have emanated from it, the Rabbinical Assembly and the United Synagogue. Conservative Judaism properly traces its origin to Zacharias Frankel, the founder of the movement known as Historical Judaism, who lived a century ago. It has had no less a personality than Solomon Schechter to give it its initial impulse in this country. Nevertheless, both doctrinally and from the standpoint of practical directives, it is still inchoate and amorphous. The Conservative movement has had at its disposal the most creative men in the field of Jewish scholarship and those elements of the Jewish laity which are most active in the fields of congregational and educational endeavor. Despite, or perhaps because of, these advantages, it has been functioning to this day without an acceptable philosophy or program to guide its own adherents or to win new adherents.

Conservatism's lack of a philosophy and program has long been recognized. That did not faze some of the leaders of the Conservative movement. They, in fact, made a virtue of that lack. In the semantics of two or three decades ago, Conservative Judaism boasted of being adjectiveless Judaism. Later it came to be described as middle-of-the-road Judaism. As such, its main attributes, like those which the Medieval philosophers ascribed to God, were negative in character. It was identified as being neither Reform nor Orthodox. As we take stock of the assets of our movement, we cannot honestly say that its indefinable status has contributed to its effectiveness or progress. If we have made any organizational headway, it has been in spite, and not because, of our lack of a philosophy or program.

From the standpoint of bringing order out of the chaos in our inner life as a people, the Conservative movement has been merely marking time. Like so many other activities in Jewish life, it has been propelled less by any inner vitality than by the galvanic kind of energy which any skillful appeal to organizational loyalty can evoke. Organizational loyalty should not, however, serve as a substitute for clear, forthright thought and for the intrinsic enthusiasm which a cause should elicit. When it does so serve, it generates the surface appearance of activity, beneath which stagnation in ideas and creative values reigns undisturbed.

If we want to break the spell which keeps our movement from making any headway except in numbers, we should look for some psychological cause which could have produced that state of self-induced inhibition. We would then discover this situation: Those who belong to the Conservative movement do not happen to be of one mind theologically. They, therefore, labor under the mistaken notion that this diversity constitutes an inner contradiction in the movement, and that in the interests of the movement it should be replaced by unanimity in religious doctrine and regimen.

The truth, however, is that the very attempt to introduce uniformity by fiat must lead to highly undesirable consequences. It is bound to lead to a struggle for power among the various groups within the movement. Any one group which may be in a better position to assert itself than the others will seek to impose its ideas and its will on the others and treat their adherents as second class citizens who should be glad that they are at least tolerated. In the end, this method of dealing with diversity is certain to prove divisive. It may ultimately drive away the strong minority groups, and hold fast within the grip of a deadening uniformity those who remain.

It seems to me that a better and happier solution may be found for the problem created by the existence of diversity within the ranks of the Conservative movement. I venture to submit a plan that would neither ignore nor seek to suppress the existing diversity, but try to channel it in such a way as to render it productive of the most good. Following the advice of our Sages that we should emulate the good in our non-Jewish neighbors, we should take a page out of the experience of the Protestant sects. Though they are divided on what they regard as highly important doctrines and religious practices, they nevertheless, manage to cooperate within the frame of some of their most influential organizations and institutions. The Federal Council of the Churches of Christ in America consists of all the major Protestant denominations and many of the lesser ones. The five principal seminaries which train for the ministry, such as the Union Theological Seminary and the Divinity Schools of Chicago, Harvard and Yale Universities and the McCormick Theological Seminary, have from eight to ten denominations represented on their faculties and as many as twenty-two on their student bodies. There is no reason why we Jews who, despite our differences, have much more in common than those Protestant sects, should not be able to work together without trying to suppress our differences.

The only legitimate and fruitful conception of the Conservative movement is one which frankly recognizes the existence of more than one type of approach to the problem of Judaism. These groups should get to know themselves and one another and learn to cooperate in that which they hold in common, recognizing each other's right to foster their respective differences. For the sake of common action in behalf of the Conservative movement, it is neces- sary for them to become fully aware of what differentiates all of them from other groups, in terms of positive principles and of the many affirmative activities which those principles call for. Follow- ing the recognition of what the groups hold in common, each group should draw up a clear and comprehensive statement of its own guiding principles of belief and action. All that I shall attempt to do is to suggest what might constitute the common affirmative denominator, and to describe the actual differences in belief and practice that exist among us today, which it would be fatuous to deny and ruinous to try to suppress.

II

The areas of agreement amongst us are four in number. They are the following: 1) The indispensability of Eretz Yisrael for Jewish life in the Diaspora, 2) The primacy of religion as the expression of collective Jewish life, 3) The maximum possible plenitude of Jewish content, including the use of Hebrew, and 4) The encouragement of the scientific approach in Jewish higher learning.

These areas of agreement are so far-reaching and penetrating in their implications that the term "Conservative," far from being the negative designation which it is generally held to be, includes enough grounds and motives for common action to render the dividing differences of minor account, if not almost nugatory. This becomes evident when we consider what is involved in each of those areas.

1) The assumption that Eretz Yisrael and its rehabilitation as the center of world Jewry is indispensable to Diaspora Jewry is not held by the Conservative party merely as a Zionist or political proposition. It is held as a central element in its conception of Judaism as a way of life. That assumption had no place whatever in the school of thought which was the forerunner of the Conservative movement. Neither Zacharias Frankel, the first head of the Breslau Jewish Theological Seminary, nor Moritz Guedeman, Chief Rabbi of Vienna during the last quarter of the nineteenth century, would have subscribed to it. In fact, the latter was one of the notorious group of "Protest Rabbiner" who prevented the first Zionist Congress from being held in Munich. It is entirely owing to the initiative taken by Solomon Schechter that Eretz Yisrael has come to occupy the place of centrality in the philosophy of the Conservative movement.

Largely under the influence of Ahad Ha-Am, and due to his own deep insight into the sterility of Diaspora Judaism, on the one hand, and the fructifying power of participation in the upbuilding of Eretz Yisrael, on the other, Schechter took the position that such participation is more than a matter of politics; it is a matter of the spiritual well-being of the Jew. He thereby contributed to the Conservative movement its most important affirmation. That affirmation is chiefly responsible for the transfer of the spiritual center of gravity from abstractions about God and man to the concrete reality of the Jewish people. Therein the Conservative movement is worlds apart from either Orthodoxy or Reform, and in a way that does not merely negate their approach, but that evokes many a constructive principle of thought and action.

2) The primacy of religion as the expression of collective Jewish life as the second area of consensus among the adherents of the Conservative movement, is intended to negate the secularist revolution in Judaism. The emphasis on the concrete reality of the Jewish people is liable to bracket the Conservative movement with the secularist revolution. It is therefore important to stress that, for us Jews, mere existence as a people is meaningless. Our collective life as a people must be deliberately cultivated as a means of enabling the individual Jew to achieve his destiny as a human being. The Jewish way of life must help the individual Jew to be and do his best and to experience that sense of at-homeness in the world which only beneficent religion can give. There are wide divergencies of belief among the followers of Conservatism with regard to the origin and nature of the Jewish way of life. But whatever its origin or nature, they agree not only as to its religious function, but that without it the Jewish people would be like a body without a soul.

3) A third area of consensus among the adherents of the Conservative movement is the assumption that Jewish living must not merely be correct and conform to certain prescribed rules of belief and action. It must also be rich in content and ever creative of new content. This assumption is of particular relevance in the Diaspora under modern conditions. Jewish life has to be lived within the frame of an overpowering and all-embracing non-Jewish civilization which, by its sheer magnitude, tends to crowd out all Jewish interests from the consciousness of the average Jew. It is only with the greatest difficulty that he can manage to prevent those interests from being swamped completely. The temptation is, therefore, great to fall back upon some minimum regimen to satisfy the call of the past and the desire to be loyal to tradition. To yield to that temptation, however, is to allow oneself to be absorbed by the environment, without leaving a trace of Jewish identity.

The only way to meet the strong centrifugal pull of the surrounding life and culture is to intensify the centripetal tendencies of Jewish life. This can be achieved only by following the principle of introducing as much of the content of Jewish living as possible into every nook and cranny that has not as yet been flooded by the environing civilization. To that end we should discover a new use for ritual observances, new occasions for cultivating esthetic expression of Jewish values and emotions, new reasons for introducing the study of the Hebrew language into the high schools and colleges attended by Jewish students, to say nothing of its more intensive and extensive study in Jewish schools and its maximum use in worship.

4) The fourth differentia which is common to all groups within the Conservative movement is the encouragement of the scientific approach to Jewish higher learning. None who adheres to this movement is any longer satisfied with the type of study which prevailed in the past, and which is still upheld in the Orthodox *yeshibot*. All non-Jewish learning, by reason of its great prestige and utility is still regarded by the consistently Orthodox as a powerful rival to Jewish learning. Mathematics and the other exact sciences, are perhaps an exception, because of their assumed neutrality, from the standpoint of traditional religion. Such challenges as modern astronomy or geology seem to present to tradition are regarded as capable of being met by means of proper interpretation. But the biological sciences are considered as opening up dangerous vistas for doubt and disbelief. This is true to an even greater degree of the human sciences namely, psychology, sociology, anthropology and the comparative study of religion. Even if a way be found to study those human sciences so that they cannot do any harm to traditional religion, Orthodoxy strenuously opposes any tendency to apply their methods of research and reasoning to the content of Jewish tradition.

It is quite evident that this restrictive attitude toward the study of the past would have narrowed the scope of Jewish creative thought and effort. We should never have had any part of the Jewish past brought to life by great historians like Isaac Hirsch Weiss, Leopold Zunz, Zacharias Frankel, Heinrich Graetz and Simon Dubnow, if the Orthodox of the school of Samson Raphael Hirsch had had their way. The Historical School in Judaism, which laid the foundation of the scientific study of Judaism, produced very few who identified themselves with the Reform movement. That the overwhelming majority of those whose names belong to the roster of that school of thought were the forerunners of the Conservative movement is no mere coincidence. When the scientific approach to the study of Jewish tradition is motivated by the purpose of finding direction for the future, it has a twofold effect. It steeps one in the abundance of Jewish content and it gives one a sense of historical development. This twofold effect is most congenial to the Conservative movement. It fosters a feeling of continuity with the past without enslaving one to it.

The foregoing four principles are sufficiently important and inclusive for those who subscribe to them to constitute a distinct party or movement in Jewish life. We may even go further and say that the adherents of the Conservative movement not only subscribe to those four principles, but also recognize them as interdependent and mutually organic.

By an accident of history the Conservative movement has fallen heir to a name which many of its foremost adherents regard as unfortunate, and in a way, misrepresentative of its true character. For the adjective "conservative" generally denotes being fearful of change. The matter of name, however, is not too serious. It is what is put into the name that counts. Nevertheless, we should not permit the movement to be the victim of too many such accidents of history. We should just now be on our guard against that which is liable to prove a most dangerous accident, namely freezing of the status quo of the movement into a fixed and permanent form. That is all too liable to come about, if we permit any one school of thought which happens at a given time to be most vocal or most active, to speak in the name of our movement as a whole.

Indeed, the conspicuously wholesome feature about our movement has been the fact that it has been possible for a number of distinct schools of thought to arise within it. Now that we can afford to be sure of the common frame within which those schools of thought or distinctive groups may recognize their intrinsic unity, the danger of their going off on their own is virtually over. Hence, it is proper that we should identify such schools of thought and practice as exist among us. So far no formal or authoritative statement of principle has come from any one of the existing schools of thought. Perhaps this discussion will ultimately elicit the long overdue statements on their part. Those statements will have the authority necessary for the effective functioning of our movement.

Since the conditions and exigencies of life vary with each individual even within each group or school of thought, any description of the characteristic beliefs and practices of each group cannot be more than a stylized approximation to the actual facts. With this qualification in mind I herewith proceed to give in outline form the philosophies and programs of the three discernible groups or schools of thought in the Conservative movement, which, for purposes of discussion, may be designated respectively as Right, Center and Left.

III

A) The Rightists subscribe to the thirteen principles of the Maimonidean creed. In retaining the principles concerning the personal Messiah and bodily resurrection, they reserve to themselves the right to interpret those principles figuratively. They permit themselves such liberties of belief concerning the authorship of the Torah as an Ibn Ezra, for example, permitted himself. These liberties of course, are very limited, and intended only for the initiated. On the whole, they accept the traditional belief with regard to the supernatural origin and character of the Torah. They resort to Maimonides' *Moreh Nebukim* for the solution of textual difficulties and contradictions. Their theology coincides almost entirely with that formulated in Joseph Albo's *Ikkarim*.

In the matter of ritual practice, they are guided in the main by the *Shulhan Aruk* which they regard as authoritative and binding. While they recognize the need for change to meet new conditions of life, they put little faith in any existing rabbinical group as qualified to effect such change. Nothing less than the convening of a Synod recognized by the entire body of the Jewish people would satisfy them as competent to deal with the problem of changing any of the traditional laws.

In their ritual observances they follow strictly the letter of the *Shulhan Aruk*. They are at one with the strictly Orthodox group in the requirement of ritual baths for married women after their menstruation period. They consider the use of the razor for shaving forbidden. In the observance of the dietary laws, they adhere strictly to the prohibition of foods prepared by Gentiles. They would not eat even fish meals in non-kosher eating places. They abide by the prohibition of wine handled by a non-Jew. They would not turn on the electric light on the Sabbath. Some do not even answer the telephone on the Sabbath, ring the door-bells, or use the elevator, particularly one that is self-running.

The fact that many of their own people find it impossible to get along without infringing on the dietary laws and Sabbath observance does not elicit, from this school of thought, the least apology. They maintain that if Jews had really wished to abide by traditional law, they would not find it impossible.

In the prayer-book they would not permit any tampering with the traditional text of any part of the service. They do not accept the Sabbath and Festival Prayer-book published by the Joint Prayer Book Commission of the Rabbinical Assembly and the United Synagogue, because of the changes it has introduced in the petitions for the restoration of the sacrificial cult. The ritual of having the *kohanim* bless the congregation at festival services is strictly adhered to. The practice of praying thrice daily, putting on *tefillin* on week-days is strictly upheld. They do not, as a rule, permit the seating together of men and women during services. They do not have Confirmation exercises on *Shabuot*, because they consider such exercises as an innovation introduced from the Christian religion. They are, as a rule, averse to late Friday night services. In a few instances where they have Friday night gatherings, they take care not to dignify as services the exercises which are then held, including a sermon or lecture.

In marriage laws they refuse to make any compromise whatever in the matter of divorce, *halizah* or a *kohen's* marrying a divorcee, and follow strictly the letter and spirit of the *Shulhan Aruk*. They insist on the presence of ten men at the marriage ceremony and require that the witnesses who sign the *ketubah* be strictly observant of the traditional practices.

B) The Centrist group is, in large measure, the continuation of the school of thought, first articulated by Zacharias Frankel and later transferred to this country by Solomon Schechter. That school of thought has not made a fetish of consistency. "On the whole," says Solomon Schechter, "its attitude toward religion may be defined as an enlightened Scepticism combined with a staunch conservatism which is not devoid of a certain mystical touch." They might be said to hold that, in the basic principles of religion as well as of politics and economics, the human mind has so far proved unable to arrive at satisfactory solutions by means of strict adherence to logic. In fact, all such attempts have often led to tyranny and oppression, besides leaving the original confusions and uncertainties just where they were at first. Life and history have a logic of their own, which we cannot afford to disregard. From the standpoint of tolerance and freedom, better results seem, indeed, to have been achieved by the method of "muddling through" than by the desire to hew strictly to the line of reason.

One thing, however, is certain. The Center group no longer believes in the divine revelation as a historical event but as a theological concept. That difference is far more revolutionary than it sounds. As a historical event, "revelation" or the traditional term "*Torah min ha-Shamayim*" denotes a miracle that was visible and audible at a particular time and place. As a theological concept "revelation" denotes the natural experience of the human mind which reacts to anything as opening up new vistas of meaning and holiness. Despite the "Higher anti-Semitism" which Solomon Schechter rightly discerned in much of the Higher Criticism, he seems to speak with pride of the fact that "the first representatives of the Historical School were also the first Jewish scholars who proved themselves more or less ready to join the modern school of Bible Criticism and even to contribute their share to it." They could not possibly have been so ready to join the modern school of Biblical Criticism, if they had believed in the traditional sense of *Torah min ha-Shamayim*, or revelation as an historical event.

The closest that the Historical School has come to defining its theological position is the following statement by Schechter in his introduction to the First Series of Studies in Judaism: "It is not the mere revealed Bible that is of first importance to the Jew, but the Bible as it repeats itself in history, in other words, as it is interpreted by tradition . . . Since then the interpretation of Scripture or the Secondary Meaning is mainly a product of changing historical influences, it follows that the center of authority is actually removed from the Bible and placed in some *living body*, which by reason of its being in touch with the ideal aspirations and religious needs of the age, is best able to determine the nature of the Secondary Meaning. This living body, however, is not represented by any section of the nation, or any corporate priesthood, or Rabbihood, but by the collective conscience of Catholic Israel as embodied in the Universal Synagogue."

It follows from that statement that only such change as falls within the category of interpretation is possible in Judaism, as

Schechter conceived it. Since we Jews do not have any authoritative body, whether corporate priesthood or "rabbihood," analogous to that which the Catholic Church possesses, no amendment or new legislation could acquire the status of revelation.

Traditional Jewish law, however, is regarded by the Center group as itself sufficiently flexible and latitudinarian to permit, within its own frame, whatever indispensable changes the needs of the times call for. The fact that so far little has been achieved by the process of interpretation is charged up to the inertia of those who should have performed the task of interpretation rather than to any obstacle inherent in the tradition itself. Life, however, cannot wait. Thanks to the demands of the times certain changes have taken place in Jewish life, which those of the Center group feel will have to be sanctioned formally, as they are now accepted informally. Among those changes are the following:

There is a marked leniency in the observance of the Sabbath. Those who work on the Sabbath, or engage in business because of economic necessity, need not labor under a sense of sin. Even those who are not under such necessity are not expected to conform to the letter of the *Shulhan Aruk*. From this point on there is no established norm with regard to the details of Sabbath observance. Most turn on the lights, but some do not. Most do not ride, but some do. As many prepare breakfast and reheat their other foods as do not.

Similar leniency obtains in the dietary laws. Though in principle observed, in practice there is a marked departure from the letter of the *Shulhan Aruk*. As many draw the line between home and outside as do not. Most have two sets of dishes, few do not. No one has any scruples about eating fish and milk foods in hotels and restaurants. On Passover, however, there is a close approach to strict conformity to traditional laws concerning *hametz*.

In the matter of ritual purity, there are very few who still adhere to the law requiring the ritual bath. All scruples with regard to men's shaving with a razor are gone.

As far as worship is concerned the range of differences is rather large. The only departure from tradition common to nearly all congregations of the center group are the mixed pews and the frequent use of English in the prayers. Beyond that, there is no uniformity except with regard to covering the head in the synagogue. Most use no musical instruments, some do. Of those congregations which have mixed choirs very few engage non-Jewish singers. Nearly all have the first *Amidah*, and most have also the additional *Amidah* repeated by the cantor. The only changes in the prayer text affecting doctrine are the recent ones incorporated in the new Sabbath and Festival Prayer Book. Late Friday night services are regarded as entirely proper. In a few instances, even the Torah is read at that time, and on the Friday night before *Shabuot*, Confirmation exercises are held.

In most of the congregations the entire *Sidrah* of the week is read on Sabbath morning, in few, only a portion. Of the latter, most cover the entire contents of the Torah usually in a three years' cycle; very few, however, read each year the same part of the *Sidrah*, which they regard as of most interest. The traditional distinction of *kohen*, *levi* and Israelite is maintained in nearly all of these congregations.

The practice of having confirmation classes for girls and confirmation exercises on *Shabuot* has become quite general.

There is no uniform standard with regard to the recital of daily prayers, the use of *tefillin* by the men, or their wearing of a *tallit katan*. The same is true of washing before meals and reciting grace. The tendency to observe them is on the wane.

The most troublesome problem is that of the marriage and divorce laws. Most rabbis in this group treat the *ketubah* quite seriously, though they would not insist upon the witnesses being strictly observant of ritual practices. Some, however, treat it perfunctorily, or omit it altogether from the marriage ritual. Very few insist upon the presence of ten men at the marriage ceremony. Some would refuse to sanction the marriage of a divorcee to a *kohen*, but most would not. *Ḥalitzah* is virtually ignored, but with a sense of guilt. Most rabbis in this group refuse to officiate at the wedding of a divorced woman who has not received a Jewish bill of divorce, but they advise the couple to apply to a Reform rabbi; some merely avow their helplessness; a minority over-ride their scruples. For years the entire matter has been the subject of discussion and deliberation by the Rabbinical Assembly, without any practical results.

C) The third group, which might be designated as the Leftist, consists for the most part of those who have been influenced by the

Reconstructionist movement. That movement has been on the American-Jewish scene since the appearance of the Reconstructionist magazine in January 1935. Reconstructionism transcends the lines that divide the three synagogue denominations. Its primary aim is to find a basis of an affirmative character for unity among all who want to remain Jews and to raise their children as Jews and to have that unity translated into organic community life. However, it comes with a conception of Judaism and Jewish religion which, when accepted by members of the Conservative movement, necessitates their constituting a third group within that movement.

The two main principles of the Leftists are the following: a) To be a Jew means to be involved not only in a set of beliefs and practices usually identified as religion, but in the civilization or culture of a people, with all that such involvement implies. b) The Jewish religion in which the values of that civilization are utilized as a means of individual and collective salvation, though indebted for its unique character to the divine intuitions of its lawgivers, prophets and sages, has been subject to the laws and limitations of the human mind and spirit.

The principle that Judaism is to be reckoned with as a civilization instead of merely as a religion is not inconsistent with the views of either the Rightist or the Centrist group of the Conservative movement. It does not imply any idea or ideal that conflicts with traditional teaching. It is more than anything else a formula for the social strategy best suited to advance Jewish life. Instead of having Jewish life centered around the synagogue, Judaism viewed as a civilization calls for a distribution of authority and influence among the various organizations that carry on Jewish activities. Though the synagogue, by reason of its being the chief vehicle for the articulation of the meaning of Judaism, should normally be the chief mouthpiece of the Jewish people, both inwardly and in relation to the outer world, it should not aspire to be more than *primus inter pares*. This conception of the place of the synagogue in Jewish life should logically be acceptable, regardless of one's theological views concerning Judaism. But it is viewed by the Rightist and Centrist groups as a concession to secularism, for no other reason than that it regards the Jewish people as subject to the same laws of social groupings as are all other peoples.

The main differentia of the Leftist group, however, derives mainly from the principle that the Jewish religion has been subject to the laws and limitations of the human mind and spirit. That principle calls for a humanist conception of the origin, development and application of Jewish religion. It is not merely as a theoretic outlook, however, that this conception is stressed, but as suggesting the proper method of approach to all phases of Jewish teaching and preaching, from the most elementary to the most advanced stages of educational activity. It prescribes complete freedom of thought and inquiry, not merely as permissive but as imperative, no matter how deeply rooted the beliefs or traditions. It assumes that only through such freedom is it possible for the individual to arrive at a sense of personal involvement in and responsibility for the religion he professes, and to experience an inward drive to live in conformity with what he professes.

The question of distinctive Jewish practice, accordingly, is answered in the light of the two following principles: In the first place, since to be a Jew is to be a part of the civilization of a people, it must find expression in conformity to some system of law which regulates the social relations which obtain within that people. A people is not a voluntary society. It is a social organism into which one is born, and which can function as such only because those who belong to it abide by a system of law governing its social relationships. The two essential traits of that kind of system of law are, first, the fact that it represents the general will of the people, and secondly, that it is accompanied by some kind of sanction. The sanction need be no more than general disapproval, which may, or may not, culminate in ostracism.

In the second place, the principle, that the Jewish religion is to be viewed as having evolved naturally, gives rise to two corollaries touching Jewish practice. The first is that a distinction should be drawn between social and ritual practice. While social practice should be subject to some system of civil law, ritual practice cannot properly be included within the category of law. In tradition, where all kinds of ordinances, both social and ritual, are assumed to be part of supernaturally revealed Torah, there is warrant for a legalistic approach as well to social practice, for that approach implies implicit obedience and the exercise of sanctions in case of disobedience. Neither of these conditions can be expected to exist any longer in the modern world with regard to ritual practice, primarily as a result of the renunciation of the belief in the supernatural origin of the Jewish religion.

The foregoing does not negate the need of transferring some of the ritual practices to the social area of Jewish life where the concept of law does obtain. Thus, some minimum cessation from work on the Sabbath and festivals, observance of the rite of circumcision and the Jewish validation of marriage should constitute part of Jewish civil law. That would mean that they have to be lived up to as a requirement for being a loyal Jew. But it does not mean that the many detailed rules which are enumerated in the *Shulhan Aruk* as part of their observance would have to fall within the category of law

Another qualification to be reckoned with, in the case of ritual practices, is that their removal from the category of law does not negate the need of establishing some standards by which the individual might be guided in his desire to achieve through these ritual practices a spiritual kinship with his fellow-Jews. Uniformity of some kind is essential, if religious observances are to serve a purpose of that kind. In case, however, circumstances prevent a Jew from adhering fully to the established norm, he ought to know just how far he may diverge without destroying the sense of spiritual kinship with the rest of his people.

The function of Jewish civil law undergoes a radical transformation, once we reckon with Jewish religion as the product of an historical process. We are no longer limited by the principle that any law which is to be enacted must in no way run counter to the traditional law of our ancestors. As a living people, we have a right to amend and change any law that has come down from the past, now that we no longer accept the assumption that it emanated directly from God. Take, for example, the status of woman in traditional Jewish law. By no manner of interpretation is it possible to interpret the traditional law with regard to that status as one of equality with that of the man. The only feasible remedy is to legislate that the woman be given equal status with the man. That illustrates the only workable approach henceforth to the problem of Jewish civil law.

The Reconstructionist movement which is Leftist in form, has not been on the scene long enough to evolve a characteristic regimen of ritual observance. What it has to say about Jewish civil law presupposes a strong communal organization. Though an attempt has been made to evolve some theory with regard to ritual observance, as is done in "Toward a Guide for Ritual Observance," the practical aspect of ritual observance is still in the process of formulation.

It is thus evident that those who associate themselves with the Conservative movement, or are associated with it in the minds of others, are actually divided into three distinct groups or schools of thought. The foregoing is an attempt to describe them in terms of their respective ideologies and practice patterns.

It is by no means assumed that every rabbi or layman who is identified as Conservative at present can, or does, actually belong only to one of the three groups. The very lack of uniformity within each group and the lack, hitherto, of any recognized classification into groups of any kind has bred in most of us a natural resistance to being classified. But these facts should not deter us from proceeding with the process of formulating our points of agreement and of difference. That is the only way to free the Conservative movement from the blight of inactivity and the danger of petrification. Though I have been fair and objective, I may have failed to give a true picture of our present condition. I am more than eager to make good whatever error of omission or commission will be pointed out to me.

How would the approach here suggested work in practice? Whenever we solicit a congregation to join the United Synagogue, we should inform its members of the four basic principles to which they are expected to subscribe in common with all groups or schools of thought within the Conservative movement. As for the rest, they are to be given the choice with which group they prefer to identify themselves. This very method of joining the United Synagogue would provide both occasion and stimulus for the re-education of our men and women in the content of Judaism. It would get them to think about it as they have never done before. They would begin to realize what it means to be Jews.

In the Rabbinical Assembly, the constructive ideas and activities of each group would be granted a hearing. No one group would

be more authoritative than the others. The publications of the
Rabbinical Assembly would not be in the hands of the one
dominant group.

No doubt other specific problems are likely to arise with regard
to coordinating the functions of both the Rabbinical Assembly
and the United Synagogue in accordance with the plan here
proposed. But all these problems can be solved without creating
any rift within the movement as a whole, if both the United
Synagogue and the Rabbinical Assembly are willing to accept the
principle of unity in diversity as an essential characteristic of the
Conservative movement.

The basic question which we have to answer forthwith is: Are
we willing to accept these differences among us, to live with them
and, with the aid of the democratic process, try to resolve all
possible conflicts to which they may give rise. Or shall we go on
assuming that it is possible for the Conservative movement to
evolve some monolithic type of thought and practice? I submit that
such an assumption will do neither us nor Jewish life as a whole
any good. It will only hinder our efforts in behalf of our people and
our faith, and render us uncreative and spiritually sterile in the
future, as it did in the past. Driven underground, our differences
will only cancel out one another, leaving us completely neutralized.
Brought to the surface and granted the normal interchange in the
free market of ideas and ideals, our differences will enable each
group among us to further in its own way what we all agree on as
essential to the future of Judaism. We shall thus all be partners in
the great adventure which all of us who have anything to contribute
to the revitalization of Jewish life should be permitted to share.

A PROGRAM FOR AMERICAN
JUDAISM

By Rabbi Robert Gordis

*Dr. Robert Gordis (b. 1908) has written and lectured extensively on Conserva-
tive Judaism and the problems of the American Jewish community. He has served
as the rabbi of a Long Island, N. Y. congregation for more than 25 years, has been
President of the Rabbinical Assembly, editor of the Rabbinical Assembly-United
Synagogue Prayerbook, and has been involved in most of the activities of the Conservative movement in recent years. He has, in addition, taught Bible at the Seminary
for a good many years. His views, thus, are based upon wide and intensive experience
with every aspect of the Conservative movement. The selection included here is
reprinted from his book* The Jew Faces a New World *(1941), by permission of
the publishers, Behrman House, Inc., 1261 Broadway, New York 1, N. Y.*

The victory of life over logic is nowhere better illustrated than
in the emergence and progress in America of the movement known
as Conservative Judaism. At its inception, and for a long time after,
its spokesmen evinced no desire to create a new movement or
elaborate a philosophy. On the contrary, for many years the tendency was to deny that it constituted a new alignment in Judaism.
Under the slogan of unity in American Israel, its accredited leaders
often made a virtue of necessity and refused to set forth a systematic
program.

Its name, borrowed from English Orthodoxy, with which it had
a slight accidental connection, has proved increasingly inappropri-
ate as the movement has grown into an independent entity emphasizing progress and growth. None the less, inadequate as the name
may seem, no other is likely to displace it, a phenomenon that has
occurred more than once in history.

Because of its lack of a platform, it has often been decried, and not altogether unjustly, as a watered-down Orthodoxy or as a timid Reform. Thus it was possible for Dr. Philipson in the preface to the revised edition of his important work, *The Reform Movement in Judaism*, to describe it as the right-wing element in Reform, while Dr. Lee J. Levinger, in his *History of the Jews in the United States*, speaks of it as the left wing of Orthodoxy. In a sense, Conservatism has been particularly American, pragmatic rather than theoretical in approach.

The characteristics of the movement flow directly from the history of American Judaism during the past half century. Fifty years ago, American Jewry was divided into two hostile camps. On the one hand, were the Jews, mainly of German extraction, who had come to these shores thirty or forty years earlier and had already attained to respectable positions in the economic and civic life of their new country. With justifiable pride they regarded themselves as thoroughly American.

On the other hand, the last two decades of the nineteenth century brought vast masses of refugees from the pogrom-stricken areas of Russia and Roumania. These immigrants were definitely foreign in manner and outlook. They settled in the squalid and congested areas of the large cities, where they engaged in a desperate battle for existence. With their surplus energies, they struggled to retain their spiritual inheritance and transmit it to their children. As was only natural, the only Judaism they knew and recognized was that of their native lands, and so the Ghettos of the great cities were dotted with synagogues that kept the name and sought to recapture the spirit of Jewish life in Poland, Russia, Hungary or Roumania. The heroic efforts of these immigrants to preserve Judaism as they knew it were doomed to failure. It quickly became apparent that the small, dingy synagogues in the Ghettos were unable to win the loyalty or even command the respect of American-born children. The foreign teachers, or *melamdim*, who regarded their pupils as incurable savages fated to be their eternal enemies, succeeded mainly in impregnating their charges with a deep-seated repugnance for Judaism. The American-born generation tended to regard Jewish life in all its manifestations as a foreign burden which their parents had forgotten to leave behind them in Europe, but which they themselves would quickly lay aside.

The waves of Jewish immigration before and after the turn of the nineteenth century imposed heavy responsibilities upon the older Jewish communities in America, which were largely of German origin. These obligations they assumed with characteristic generosity. They provided centers of Americanization, settlement houses, hospitals, homes for the aged and other essential services for their immigrant brethren.

Nevertheless, a deep chasm yawned between the two groups. The sources of the antagonism were varied and deep-seated. Part of it was economic. The German Jews were frequently the employers, and the east European Jews the workers, in the sweatshops of the clothing industry. This factor was largely eliminated as time went on, as the recent arrivals soon became employers themselves and German-Jewish clothing concerns all but disappeared. Moreover, the rise of progressive textile unions, largely Jewish in leadership and membership, especially until the First World War, raised the living standards of the workers immeasurably and eliminated the worst abuses of the industry.

Another factor of misunderstanding lay in the varying lands of origin, with the concomitant prejudices, that set the German against the Polish Jew, the former being "American," the latter a "foreigner." This shortsighted snobbery had its counterpart in Germany, both before and after the advent of Hitler. But as the later east European arrivals integrated themselves in American life, the sharp edge of the antagonism was blunted. Nevertheless, it still remains a distressing symptom in Jewish life. The complete disappearance of this factor will come only with the welding of all the elements into an American Jewry, through decades of living in America and marriages among the various elements.

Finally, there was a deep chasm between the conception of Judaism held by the two groups. The recent European immigrants were Orthodox in sympathies, if not in practice. The older groups, barring a tiny number of Sephardic Jews, were devotees of Reform Judaism, which had established itself in America in a form far more radical than in Germany, and which proudly called itself American Judaism.

It was in 1885 that outstanding leaders of Reform met and adopted the Pittsburgh Platform, which served as their basic document for the next half-century. As has already been noted,

Reform Judaism denied the nationhood of Israel and declared that Jews were members of a religious sect, having no aspirations for the restoration of Palestine as the national homeland of the Jews. The Pittsburgh Platform also surrendered the entire structure of Jewish law as authoritative and binding upon modern Jews. Basic observances were dropped, and the groundwork laid for a new prayerbook, almost entirely in English. By this program the Pittsburgh Conference was only formulating in theory what was already widely practiced.

Deeply stirred by this official break with traditional Judaism, a small group of English-speaking Orthodox rabbis decided to create a theological seminary which, in contradistinction to the Hebrew Union College in Cincinnati, would stand four-square on the program of loyalty to traditional Judaism. Thus the Jewish Theological Seminary opened its doors in 1887. As a small struggling institution it lasted a decade and a half and finally closed its doors for lack of public support.

By this time, however, the mass Jewish immigration from eastern Europe made it more essential than ever to train American leadership for traditional congregations. In 1902, a group of Jewish leaders invited Solomon Schechter, Reader in Rabbinics at Cambridge University, to come from England to become the President of the Seminary. Under his dynamic guidance, it became a foremost institution for research and higher Jewish learning and within a few decades the spiritual fountain-head of a new alignment in American Jewry—Conservative Judaism.

While fifty years ago the ultimate triumph of Reform seemed inevitable, today another story can be told. Reform, incomparably the finest organized group in Jewish religious life in America, has not kept pace with the enormous growth of the Jewish community. The following figures, derived from the Annual Reports of the Union of American Hebrew Congregations, are illuminating. In 1903, when the Jewish population in the United States was 1,250,000, the number of Reform Congregations was 125, with a membership of 13,083. In 1940, the Jewish population numbers over 4,800,000, four times the earlier figure. The number of congregations affiliated with the Reformed Union of American Hebrew Congregations has increased threefold, from 125 to 301, with a membership of 58,461. To these figures should be added

55,000 Sisterhood members in 374 units and 125 Brotherhoods with an estimated 20,000 members. There are, therefore, all told, 125,000 official adherents of Reform Judaism, less than 3 percent of American Jewry. In addition, there are an indeterminate number sympathetic to the movement, though not officially enrolled. The work of the Union, of course, goes far beyond its affiliated units. Through its publications and activities, generously placed at the disposal of all groups, it has been instrumental in raising the level of Jewish cultural and religious life generally. Nevertheless, the Reform movement as such has experienced no phenomenal growth during the past four decades.

No reliable figures for Orthodox congregations are available, but it is generally conceded that Orthodoxy has consistently been losing ground as the process of Americanization has continued.

In contradistinction to Reform and Orthodoxy, Conservative Judaism is the most rapidly growing movement in Jewish religious life today. In 1913, when Dr. Solomon Schechter organized the United Synagogue of America, the national organization of Conservative congregations, it included 20 groups. Four years later, in 1917, there were 40. Today (1940) there are 275 congregations affiliated with the United Synagogue and 200 more associated with it less directly. There are 300 Sisterhoods in the Women's League, 100 Men's Clubs and 150 Young People's Leagues banded together under its aegis. It is estimated that approximately 250,000 men and women are enrolled in these congregations and in their affiliates, and the number is constantly on the increase. Today some of the greatest American congregations in point of numbers, prestige and general vitality are Conservative.

The spiritual leadership of these congregations is derived largely from the graduates of the Jewish Theological Seminary. Almost 300 of its graduates serve as rabbis in the field, many of whom have achieved positions of influence and importance in the fields of Jewish scholarship, Zionism and public life generally.

Moreover, the influence of Conservative Judaism on groups that have remained officially Reform or Orthodox has been considerable, even if frequently unacknowledged. The Central Conference of American Rabbis has revised the basic Pittsburgh Platform of 1885, principally because of the revolutionary transformations in Jewish life that are associated with Zionist achievement and the rise of anti-semitism. But it cannot be doubted that the success of the Conservative movement has also played its part in the trend back to tradition within Reform Judaism. As far back as 1928, the association of Reform laymen, the National Federation of Temple Brotherhoods, polled its members and announced that five-sixths of the men wanted Hebrew in the service, 96 percent favored more traditional Jewish music, 80 percent called for congregational singing, and almost 70 percent opposed the practice of Gentile singers in the choir. As outstanding a leader of Reform as Dr. Stephen S. Wise has publicly declared that had Conservative Judaism existed fifty years ago, Reform would not have struck roots in America.

Within the camp of Orthodoxy, too, there has been an approximation to Conservatism. The so-called modern Orthodox congregations are frequently indistinguishable in practice and spirit from avowedly Conservative synagogues and many of their rabbis frequently expound a similar philosophy of Judaism. That is not to deny the existence of uncompromising Orthodoxy in America, even of the Frankfort variety. Yet discerning Orthodox observers, in common with most others, recognize that the future of American Judaism lies with Conservatism.

During the past two decades, the program of Conservative Judaism has been slowly crystallizing. The time is now ripe for a formulation of its philosophy, which, however tentative, will reflect the growing consensus of thought among its leaders and laity.

In this process of clarification, two stages can be discerned: the first, the period of negative definition, the second, of positive formulation. During the first stage, the movement was largely concerned with emphasizing its distinctiveness from official Orthodoxy and Reform. While it did not know what it wanted, it knew very definitely what it did not want! Even now, most American Jews still approach Conservative Judaism in terms of what it is not, largely because its observances set it apart from the other camps.

Conservatism has learned much from both Orthodoxy and Reform, but it feels that they are inadequate to satisfy the spiritual needs of modern American Jews. Its critique of both these great movements may be graphically expressed in a well-known Midrashic parable: "Once there was an army marching between two roads, one of fire, and the other of snow. If it approaches too closely to the fire, it will be burnt; if it comes too near the snow, it will be frozen. What is the army to do but walk in the center and avoid both the snow and the fire."

Orthodoxy is well symbolized by the road of fire, for it possesses both its outstanding properties—heat and light. Orthodoxy has been the great repository of warmth and enthusiasm, marked by zeal for Judaism and the willingness to bring sacrifices for its cause. Through the years, it has fostered the sense of brotherhood, linking Jews together throughout the world, in spite of all divisive factors.

Besides, Orthodoxy has been the great protagonist of the light of Jewish learning in modern times. It created the *yeshibot* or Academies that dotted the map of eastern Europe. It insisted that learning was not the prerogative of a handful of rabbis, but the duty and privilege of every Jew. While other groups have acquiesced to the whittling down of the content of Jewish education in America, Orthodoxy has had the warmth and devotion necessary to keep the lamp of true learning aglow. The program of a maximum Jewish education in America has all too few devotees, but they are nearly all drawn from Orthodox ranks.

Yet fire is not only an instrument of good; it may become a scourge. Probably because of its intense loyalty to Judaism, Orthodoxy has all too often been intolerant of change or deviation from traditional patterns. Usually it has been unwilling or unable to adapt itself to new conditions and ideals. Even when it has adopted modern externals, it has remained inhospitable to modern thought and its implications. It goes without saying that troubled souls seeking the stability of an unquestioning faith will be drawn to it, especially in days of chaos and unrelieved suffering, because like Catholicism, it holds out the solace of certainty. But it cannot serve those who wish to live in the modern world, without the device of the compartmentalized mind.

On the other side of the road of fire stretches the road of snow, white, gleaming and silent. What better symbol than snow for Reform Judaism, which brought decorum and refinement into the synagogue and excluded everything extreme, noisy or grotesque. This insistence on the holiness of beauty by the side of the beauty of holiness worked a revolution in the modern synagogue. The importance of this contribution is difficult to appreciate fully, because it has become integral to all groups in Judaism today. Above all, Reform insisted that Judaism is hospitable to modern thought. It thus helped to bring the Jewish heritage once more into the main stream of human progress.

But Reform suffers from the defect of its virtues. Its negations were emphatic; its affirmations were pale and colorless. Snow is white and pure, but stoop and touch it—it is cold. While large numbers of men and women have found spiritual shelter in Reform, many others have felt it to be lacking in emotional warmth and intellectual zeal. In practice, if not in theory, it has surrendered to the appalling ignorance of Jewish cultural and religious values characteristic of so many American Jews in our generation. The new tendencies in Reform Judaism toward a return to more traditional practices and to a more intensive type of Jewish education would indicate that the objections have considerable validity.

Conservative Judaism chooses the center path, and eschews both the road of fire and the road of snow. It recognizes wholeheartedly the contributions that both movements have made to Jewish life. It honors Orthodoxy for its warmth and light, for the devotion and learning that have characterized it. But it refuses to accept its denial of change as the law of life, its opposition to modernism and its refusal to grow with time. It is grateful to Reform for its insistence on decorum and esthetic appeal in the service and its generally liberal attitude toward modern thought. Yet it seeks to avoid, at all costs, the perils of emptiness of content and spiritual anemia. Therein it parts company with both Orthodoxy and Reform.

But negations are not enough. A program of affirmation is needed if the movement is to avoid sterility and superficiality. Such a philosophy is now in process of articulation, drawing upon varied modern sources of Jewish thought.

The great German scholar and rabbi, Zacharias Frankel, is generally recognized as the founder of the movement as such. The circumstances surrounding the event are highly significant. When the Reform movement arose in Germany, it encountered the uncompromising resistance of the Orthodox rabbis of the time, who refused to admit the need of the slightest deviation from the accepted pattern. In order to clarify their own program, the rabbis who believed in the need for change called a series of synods which were held at Brunswick in 1844, at Frankfort in 1845, and at Breslau in 1846. Frankel attended these conferences. He listened in silence to the discussions on changing the Sabbath to Sunday, modifying the marriage laws, abolishing circumcision and similar themes. When, however, the apparently minor matter of the retention or abolition of Hebrew from the service came up for discussion and it was voted that Hebrew be retained only out of deference to the older generation, Frankel walked out of the conference.

He thus served notice that the national character of Judaism was basic to its vitality, and set himself apart from Reform, which declared that Jews were members of a religious community. Unlike the Orthodox, Frankel did not take easy refuge in the total acceptance of the past. Frankel was a first-rate creative scholar in the field of Jewish law and history. He was fully aware that Judaism has never been static, but has evolved continuously throughout its history. He felt that its survival in modern times demands the acceptance of the principle of historical development. Hence change is inevitable, but it will be gradual, and not extreme, and will flow from an inner necessity, rather than from the pressure of the environment to conform.

Frankel called his conception by the ponderous name of "positive-historical Judaism." He never worked out the implications of his position with sufficient clarity, particularly the central problem of the criteria for legitimate change. Nevertheless, he supplied two important elements for Conservatism, the recognition of *the indispensability of the national elements in Judaism* and the need for *untrammeled scientific research* as the basis for intelligent and constructive change.

The second great source of Conservatism is Solomon Schechter, who served as President of the Jewish Theological Seminary of America from 1902 to 1915, and made it a world center of Jewish learning. It was he who emphasized, in his own incomparable manner, the doctrine of Catholic Israel, the conception of a people and not of a religious denomination. In the preface to his *Studies in Judaism*, he pointed out that scientific research in the Jewish past, while not necessarily discarding Revelation, had in effect made the *historic practice* of the Jewish people the measure by which Jewish observances and ideals were to be judged. What was generally observed was basic and should not be tampered with. What had fallen into disuse had outlived its usefulness and could be eliminated. Law must follow life, the life of "Catholic Israel." What the bulk of Jews throughout the world observed was by that token normative and binding on all who wish to preserve their bond with their people. While Frankel had emphasized the need for unity with the Jewish past, Schechter stressed the need for unity with the Jewish present as well.

When Schechter came to America, the view was being enthusiastically promulgated that Reform was the only true American Judaism. With inimitable wit and brilliance, Schechter insisted that nothing can be called Judaism of any variety, American, French or German, if it breaks violently with the hallowed tradition of the past or with Jewish life in the present. Granted that American Judaism would not be a mere replica of Russian, German or Polish Judaism, nevertheless it would necessarily have most elements in common, since Jews everywhere were members of a single people.

While he thus defended the national elements of Judaism against Reform, Schechter pleaded against secular Zionism, declaring that a Torah-less nationalism was unworthy of the Jewish people. As a consequence, Schechter formulated the idea of *religious nationalism*, which is basic to Conservatism.

The third great source from which Conservative Judaism drew inspiration was, curiously enough, a man who was not identified with any school of religious thought. It was the great Hebrew thinker and essayist, Asher Ginzberg, who wrote under the modest pseudonym he made famous, Ahad Ha'am, "One of the people." His skeptical temperament and incisive intelligence made him the most devastating critic of the two major schools of Zionist thought in his day. During the last decades of the nineteenth century, the *Hibbat Zion* movement in eastern Europe had begun to plant colonies in Palestine. In 1889, Ahad Ha'am visited these colonies and published his broadside, *Lo Zeh Haderek*—"Not This Is the Way." Similarly, the political Zionism of Herzl, with its insistence on obtaining political recognition by the Powers of the Jewish right to Palestine, struck him as superficial and visionary. Ahad Ha'am felt that Palestine could serve principally as a spiritual center, where Jewish culture would be safe against disintegration.

Later events demonstrated that his criticisms were too sweeping. Practical Zionism, with its emphasis upon colonization, proved to be the concrete foundation of the Jewish homeland, and Herzl's far-fetched dream of a fully recognized, legally assured homeland for the Jewish people in Palestine was largely realized in the Balfour Declaration in 1917.

Nevertheless, Ahad Ha'am made a lasting contribution to Jewish life and thought. His criticisms impelled him to formulate his own philosophy, that of cultural Zionism, which has since been synthesized with practical and political Zionism. Though he underestimated the practical possibilities of Palestine, he comprehended what many enthusiastic Zionists at first refused to see, that it could not become the gathering place of all the Jews. Rather, its central value would reside in its being the spiritual center of the Jewish people, where Jewish culture would be the dominant and not the secondary civilization. Thus it would be free to develop and grow, without the perpetual dangers of stagnation and assimilation to which it is exposed everywhere else. From Palestine as their center, Jewish values in art, literature, science and philosophy would radiate to world Jewry, enriching and quickening Jewish life everywhere. This conception of *the interaction between Palestine and the Diaspora, which gave a significant role in Jewish destiny to both spheres,* remains his most fundamental contribution to Jewish thought. This position Conservative Judaism has adopted wholeheartedly. For Conservatism, Zionism is not an optional feature, but an integral element in Judaism. Palestine is not merely a refuge for oppressed Jews, or a historical memory, but the *sine qua non* for the spiritual health of the Jewish people and the preservation and development of its heritage.

Ahad Ha'am's conception of cultural Zionism does not exhaust his contributions to Jewish thought. He had a profound insight into Jewish group psychology and the havoc wrought by assimilation on the psyche of modern Jews. His analysis of these dangers has proved a rich arsenal from which Jewish leaders have drawn instruments of defense in the perpetual battle for Jewish survival.

Finally, Ahad Ha'am stressed *the centrality of the ethical content in Judaism* and, because of his wide familiarity with contemporary thought, was able to restate traditional ideas so as to make them relevant to modern needs. He thus helped in the revitalization of traditional religious values. Though, as has been stated, he was not religious himself and probably was unaware of the existence of the movement, the importance of his contributions to the theoretic structure of Conservative Judaism can scarcely be overestimated.

In utilizing Ahad Ha'am's thought for this new formulation of traditional Judaism, the late Professor Israel Friedlander rendered a signal service. In his too little known volume *Past and Present*, published in 1919, he prophesied a significant role for American Jewry as the next great center of world Israel. Particularly fruitful was his insistence that Judaism was a variegated *culture* rather than a mere religious tradition.

Dr. Louis Ginzberg, Professor of Talmud at the Seminary, and perhaps the greatest living Jewish scholar in the world, developed critical methods in the study of Rabbinic literature and law with incomparable brilliance and erudition. He focussed attention upon the social, economic and political foundations of that great spiritual edifice called the Talmud, and showed how Judaism had remained alive by reinterpreting its ideas and practices throughout its history, never losing touch with changing conditions.

The next great commanding influence in the creation of a philosophy for Conservative Judaism has been Professor Mordecai M. Kaplan. He elaborated *the method of the re-interpretation of Jewish tradition*. Basing himself upon the conclusions of Jewish scientific research, he emphasized that many institutions and practices that no longer seem relevant to modern life have undergone many changes in form and meaning during their history. Frequently, they can be restored to vitality by a process of reinterpretation, so that they receive new meanings, appropriate to the contemporary scene.

The same process may be invoked in the realm of ideas. Within the body of Jewish tradition, there exist concepts which today are not generally acceptable. Merely to discard them summarily would be a grave error. For in the past they served to meet basic human needs, which still must be satisfied if men are to find life worth while today. Hence these apparently outworn ideas should be studied from the point of view of the functions they performed in the past, and means must be sought to perform these functions, either by partially modifying the traditional ideas or by creating entirely new concepts. In almost every instance, however, one discovers that a good deal in traditional ideas and practices is still serviceable for modern Jewish religious life. All that is necessary is to discover the actual or potential values inherent in them. This is to be expected, since human nature changes slowly, if at all.

This process of reinterpretation is not new in Jewish life. The Bible itself contains countless examples of older primitive ideas and practices that were reinterpreted and made to serve more exalted ends. "The Day of the Lord," as conceived by the Jewish masses in Biblical times, was a chauvinistic doctrine that the day would come when Israel would enjoy a complete victory over its foes. The prophet Amos and his successors reinterpreted it to mean the triumph of righteousness over iniquity, so that even Jewish sins would meet their condign punishment on that day. Similarly, the Day of Atonement was raised from the purely ritualistic level, in which the scapegoat was the central feature, to the exalted standpoint of a day of moral re-creation, as reflected in the fifty-eighth chapter of Isaiah. The Talmud, as a whole, is essentially a massive reinterpretation of Biblical law, because of new conditions and advancing religious and ethical concepts.

The advantage of reinterpretation is that it permits growth and development without the loss of continuity, the sense of identity with Jewish tradition. In the past, these changes took place unconsciously, since the sense of historical development was virtually nonexistent. Henceforth, reinterpretation must be created consciously. In addition to this contribution to the philosophy of Conservatism, Professor Kaplan has followed Ahad Ha'am and Israel Friedlander, who spoke of Judaism as "a culture," and has popularized the conception of Judaism as a civilization.

Within the past few years, Professor Kaplan has launched a new movement under the name of Reconstructionism, which has adopted a more advanced theological attitude. While its proponents have insisted that the movement is above the time-honored alignments of Orthodoxy, Conservatism and Reform, both its friends and its foes regard it as the "left wing" of Conservatism. Nearly all the intellectual leadership in Reconstructionism comes from Conservative rabbis and educators, and its program is most nearly approximated in Conservative congregations. Most significantly of all, Professor Kaplan's years of teaching at the Seminary molded the thinking of nearly all Conservative rabbis in the field, long before the new movement was launched. It therefore seems clear that Dr. Kaplan's most fruitful contribution to

American-Jewish life lies in his influence upon Conservative Judaism.

These men, of whom Professors Ginzberg and Kaplan are fortunately among the living, were far from being in agreement among themselves, but for their students and disciples, and for American Jewry as a whole, they served to create the program of Conservative Judaism.

This program may now be formulated in a sentence: *Judaism is the evolving religious civilization of the Jewish people.* The implications of this attitude are highly important.

Its first great emphasis is upon the *evolving character* of Judaism. Judaism has never been static; it has always adapted itself to new thought and new conditions. Moses, the Prophets, Johanan ben Zakkai, Maimonides—each saved Judaism in an hour of crisis by adjusting it to the times. Not only the Talmud, but even post-Talmudic Judaism, continued this process of growth and development, though not as fruitfully as before. Only during the past three centuries has the free-flowing stream of Jewish tradition been congealed, because of the extraordinary deterioration of the Jewish status in the seventeenth and eighteenth centuries, and the disintegration and chaos occasioned by the "Emancipation" in the nineteenth.

That inner vitality and capacity for development must now be restored. Evolution, however, does not mean destruction. Reform saw the difficulties inherent in Jewish law under modern conditions and proceeded to abrogate its authority. Orthodoxy officially maintains the structure unchanged, and denies that Judaism has ever undergone development. Conservatism bases itself upon scientific research, which reveals the stages of development in Judaism, and is taking steps to restore the flexibility and power of adjustment which Judaism still abundantly possesses.

Moreover, Judaism is the *culture or civilization* of the *Jewish people.* It is not merely a religion, in the sense of a few articles of belief and a handful of practices, as Reform teaches, or a longer list of beliefs and practices, as maintained by Orthodoxy. It is a complete culture or civilization, possessing all the varied attributes of language and literature, art, music, customs and law, institutions and history. The Jew prays in Hebrew, not because God understands no other language, but because it is his language, and therefore is both the form and the content of his thought. His holiest sentiments must be expressed in the tongue that links him with his ancestors and his brothers everywhere. As Schechter said of Bible translations prepared by Gentiles, "We cannot afford to have our love-letters written for us by others." The practices and customs of Jewish life, its history and traditions are precious to the Jew because their *contents* reflect the noblest aspirations of which man has yet shown himself capable, and because their *forms*, growing out of his own group experiences, are closest to him.

The loyalty of the Jew to Jewish life is, therefore, entirely free from a scorn or dislike of other religions and cultures. On the contrary, adherence to Judaism makes possible his genuine appreciation of other civilizations, without condescension or a sense of inferiority. It places the Jewish heritage in its proper place within world culture.

What is more, since it is the civilization of the Jewish people, Judaism must have a locale, one corner of the world where it can grow and flourish. The Jews who live in America and throughout the world can perpetuate Judaism, but its untrammeled and natural development is possible only where Judaism is the dominant and not the minority culture, where it creates and in turn is molded by the atmosphere. Therefore, Palestine, as the center of the Jewish people, must be the living center of Judaism, and the more strongly and firmly Jewish life is established in the Homeland, the richer Jewish life everywhere will be. It is therefore clear that Zionist loyalty and action is far from being repugnant to Judaism, as extreme Reform and Orthodox leaders were wont to assert, or an optional feature, as is now contended in certain quarters. On the contrary, Zionism is integral and basic, a central article of faith in the creed of modern Judaism.

Last and most important is the stress upon the *religious* character of Jewish civilization. Judaism has many aspects, but religion is primary. The recognition of God in the world and the drive for ethical perfection are the two great Jewish contributions to the world—two that are really one. Perhaps other civilizations can survive without religion, but not Judaism. Our history, our customs, our law, our literature, even our music and art, are intimately connected with the religious and ethical ideas of Judaism.

Jewish nationalism and religion are the body and the soul of a living organism. Jewish nationalism without religion is in danger of becoming a Golem, destructive and brutal, as is all too self-evident today in fascist nationalism. Jewish religion without nationalism is a disembodied ghost, without vitality and staying power. Whenever Jewish religion without nationalism has been tried, as in Reform, it has failed. When nationalism without religion has been attempted, as in Jewish secularism, it has been unable to maintain itself, after the momentum created by the religious dynamic was exhausted. This has been demonstrated in all the varied forms of Diaspora nationalism. Even in Palestine, the saga of rebuilding has not been able to still the longing for an adequate world-view, which is being increasingly felt among the secular-minded elements of the *Yishub*. For man cannot live by bread alone, even if the bread be won through heroism and shared in justice.

Judaism as the evolving religious civilization of the Jewish people—therein lies the distinctive attitude of Conservative Judaism that makes it not alone the most rapidly growing movement in the present, but the most vital and promising tendency for the future, if it adheres to its program with intelligence and zeal.

It is obvious that in this outlook, whether carried through by officially Conservative groups or by others in essential agreement with it, American Jewry has a program that will broaden and deepen Jewish life immeasurably and ultimately affect the organizational character of the Jewish community. It includes a positive attitude toward Jewish tradition and an equally clear awareness of the necessity for change and development. It does not deny the patent fact of the nationhood of Israel, but places the emphasis properly upon the fundamentally religious character of its civilization. It is genuinely American, yet retains its bond of attachment to Catholic Israel and its zeal for the rebuilding of Palestine.

In his fascinating *Autobiography*, Lincoln Steffens tells of his days as a reporter on New York's lower East Side. On Yom Kippur he would see the young men smoking and laughing outside the synagogues, while within, the old men would read their prayers, with pain in their hearts. Steffens goes on to say, "The tears hurt, the weeping and the gnashing of teeth of the old men, who were doomed and knew it. Two, three thousand years of heroism, devotion and suffering for a cause lost in a single generation." The vitality and promise of Conservative Judaism hold out hope that the cause is not yet lost.

RECONSTRUCTIONISM—A CREATIVE PROGRAM

By Rabbi Milton Steinberg

Rabbi Milton Steinberg (1903–1950) whose statement on Reconstructionism is printed here, was an outstanding preacher and writer who combined felicity of phrase with creative thinking. He served as rabbi of the Park Avenue Synagogue in New York and exercised a wide influence through his many articles in periodicals and through his several books. He was closely related to the Reconstructionist Movement, having participated in the editing of its prayer books, serving as an editor of The Reconstructionist, *and advocating its thinking in speech and writing. The selection included here is taken from* A Partisan Guide to the Jewish Problem, *by Milton Steinberg, copyright 1945, used by special permission of the publishers, The Bobbs-Merrill Company, Inc., in which he advocated the Reconstructionist point of view. His later bent, however, was to be somewhat critical of the Reconstructionist philosophy, as is evidenced in his book* Basic Judaism *and in portions of his book* A Believing Jew.

Parturiunt montes. . . . . The mountains labor, and a definition is born; we toil mightily among ideologies, and father a conception. Judaism, we affirm, must be envisaged as the evolving religious civilization of the Jewish people. Well, what of it? How is the American Jew better off now that he has arrived at our particular formula (Reconstructionism)?

To this extent, certainly, he is farther along. He perceives much more clearly what he is dealing with. It is, he now knows, no simple and static entity. Rather is it a complex, many-faceted organism, rich in colors, diverse in members and ever changing. What is more, he also has some pretty clear intimations as to what he has to do. For, definition is not only description, it implies courses of action.

THE REALM OF RELIGIOUS BELIEF

Religious faith, in the sense of a theistic world outlook, is in many regards the neglected aspect of the Jewish heritage. Here is a tradition that can be said to have been born with the emergence of a particular conception of God; a people whose members by the thousands have endured martyrdom on behalf of their creed, whose greatest texts have been proclamations of faith, whose greatest heroes were saints. Yet, in its scheme of things today, the God-interpretation of reality is quite submerged. This not merely among Jewish secularists to whom irreligion is often a matter of conscience but even among professing Jews, indeed in the Synagogue itself. Thus Jewish preaching, as is notorious among those who know it well, tends to shy away from theology. Again, of all the voluminous contemporary Jewish literature, very little deals with issues of doctrine. Indeed, matters have come to such a pass that rabbis and Jewish theological seminaries must resort to books written by non-Jews for instruction in contemporary religious metaphysics and in the scientific interpretation of the Bible. In other words, the classic *Weltanschauung*, Judaism's major gift to the world, and the Book in which it finds purest expression lie fallow these days.

This neglect of religious interests among Jews is not only unprecedented in Jewish history, it is broader and cuts deeper than among Gentiles—a circumstance not hard to explain. For Jews, like Christians, have been exposed to all the influences which account for the general advance of secularism in modern times. In addition they have been affected by special factors touching them peculiarly. Their distractedness is one such. The Methodist as Methodist has a limited budget of denominational obligations. The Jew as Jew has all those plus all the items discussed in this book. Little wonder that he has little time or energy to devote to Jewish doctrine and practice.

A second, even more potent cause of inordinate secularism among Jews is their tardy entrance into Western society. Christianity took the intellectual revolutions—Copernican, Newtonian, Darwinian and Freudian—one at a time. Even so it suffered large dislocations under their impact. Judaism, isolated from the world for five hundred years, coming into the open only very recently, got their full weight all at once.

Nor in accounting for the retreat of the Jewish religion is it proper to overlook the psychic element. Many a Jew who is an *anima naturaliter religiosa*, who would normally arrive by himself at religious affirmations, cannot make peace with the Jewish religion, not because it is a religion but because it is Jewish.

Whatever the causes of the secularist drift in Judaism, Reconstructionism must resist it. Religion is, from its point of view, many things in one: an integral element in Judaism, indispensable to individual self-fulfillment, and a prerequisite for general social health. To this extent, at least, our definition helps us; it dictates a position on religion.

The formula goes further, characterizing Judaism as evolving— that is to say, as something that grows and unfolds, that sloughs off outworn elements and flowers into fresh expressions. God-faith and theology, therefore, must also evolve and be transformed in response to new insights and novel conditions. Another tangled issue is resolved: the question whether Jewish belief ought to remain fixed, as Orthodoxy argues, or to be regarded as modifiable.

Other positions on the Jewish religion are, of course, possible and proper. Judaism has a legitimate fundamentalist wing as has Christianity. With Jews, who are at ease in Orthodoxy, Reconstructionism not only has no quarrel; it has, so far as theology goes, no message.

It addresses itself rather to those who would like to make their peace with the Jewish religion but cannot; who, on matters of faith, stand at the temple doors "heart in, head out." To these it preaches adherence to the old, as it stands if possible, remade if necessary, and yet creation of the new. It insists, "On this lay hold, and from that withdraw not thy hand." In sum, it acknowledges the polarity, universal in human purposes, between tradition and progress.

This means, more concretely, three specific jobs. First, the Jew must establish a rapport with Jewish belief as it emerges from the past. Second, he must rethink, *reconstruct*, those elements which are unacceptable to the modern mind. Wherever the traditional and the contemporary are at loggerheads, every effort ought to be made to resolve the conflict with minimal damage to the former. But boldness is called for as well as conservatism, and one must be prepared to abandon as well as to preserve. Third, he must seek to make the Jewish faith creative once more, productive of novel insights, revelatory of hitherto unsuspected truths.

This balancing between the old and the new is less difficult than may be suspected. We have already noted that doctrine in Judaism has never been cast into crystalline, authoritative form. Hence it lends itself the more readily to being remolded closer to the needs of any given generation. Besides, there has always been latitude in Judaism. The individual has ever been relatively free to put his private configuration on the group outlook. Uniformity of religious opinion has not only never existed among Jews, it has rarely been sought after. There is, therefore, less radicalism than first appears in our proposal of a continuous, progressive reformulation of Jewish theology.

It can be carried off—this project of establishing a harmony between the Jewish tradition and modern thought. Thousands of American Jews, myself included, have done it. We see the universe through a God-faith which enables us to comprehend it the more thoroughly; which invests it with meaning and purposefulness; which lends intelligibility and sanction to our ethical values; which stimulates us toward moral self-realization and the broader service of our fellow men, and which, last of all, enables us to see our Jewishness as a part of a cosmic design unfolding on all sides of us.

This faith, to speak for myself, is a legitimate descendant of that cherished by my ancestors—so legitimate that I enter their world as preserved in writing and feel myself completely at home. This faith is, at the same time, a proper expression of contemporary thought—so proper that I am at ease in the science and philosophy of our day. Not that I do not run into metaphysical systems alien to my own. These I reject partly because they are incompatible with the Jewish tradition, but equally because, in my judgment, they are inconsistent with rigorous reasoning.

I would not be misunderstood. It is not my intention to suggest that in adapting Judaism to its world setting, one must make it a "religion of reason," an outlook composed only of demonstrable propositions, in which furthermore, all undertones of mystery and mood have been muted. Despite Hegel, reality is not all reason; despite the classical rationalists, the human personality is not pure intellect. A religion confined to the logically establishable, and indifferent to the emotional hungers of men would both mispresent the universe and feed its communicants stones for bread. Yet, to say that there may be more things in this world than are dreamed of in our philosophies is one thing. To maintain as an article of faith what is contrary to the intellectually probable is very much amother. This is not belief but its abuse. Reconstructionism seeks to obviate it for Jews.

From our definition, then, flows as the first imperative the retrieval of God in Judaism.

THE DOMAIN OF ETHICS

The Jewish tradition is immeasurably rich in ethical values. Of these, the world at large is familiar with only one segment, the Biblical. But Scripture does not begin to exhaust the wisdom concerning human behavior which Israel has massed through the centuries. Into Talmud and Midrash, into medieval pietistic works, a people that made a career of contemplating the good life and living it distilled its precious experiences. For much that they discovered analogues exist elsewhere. But some of the perceptions they achieved are unique; some of the fields they explored have never been surveyed by others. For example, Judaism contains a virtually unprecedented ethic of scholarship and the life of reason, an extraordinarily balanced approach to the body and its desires, an unparalleled awareness of the reciprocity between individual and social morality. Mankind would be much enriched were these treasures to be made public property. Unfortunately, and incredible as it may seem, many of the most important moralistic texts of Judaism still await translation.

Our concern at this moment is not with the world but with Jews. For them, Reconstructionism projects a second major line of endeavor: the recapture, reconstruction and refertilization of Jewish ethical vision.

The task to be undertaken in religion must be duplicated in morality, and with pretty much the same techniques.

First: the rediscovery of the past. The Jews of our time must come to know their significant writings and the principles they teach.

Second: a great sifting. Our generation, as each generation in its time, must scrutinize and appraise for itself the judgments and aspirations formulated by the past. What it finds alive, meaningful, permanent, it must take to itself. That which is valid in essence but not in form it must modify. That which has outlived its day, it must, despite all reverence for the past, put firmly aside.

Third: the repointing of Jewish morality. The key Jewish ethical insights possess the virtue of timelessness. But it is one of the deficiencies of things eternal that they have no special message for any given day. An aura of generality invests them. Always relevant, they never point particularly to any specific situation. The prophets of Israel were keenly aware of this. Whatever their moral abstractions, they straightway concretized them. So they no sooner asserted nature to be the handiwork of the God of all men than they denounced "them that join house to house, that lay field to field till there be no room." They went further, ordaining a jubilee year wherein the poverty-stricken peasant might again possess the field that had been sold from under him. Talmudic Judaism strove after the same objective, the conversion of ideals into habit, law and communal practice.

A similar task confronts modern Jews. Theirs is the assignment of exploring their ethical heritage to discover its meaning for modern times, of focusing its light on the obscurities of our day, the issues of individual morality, of war and peace, property and persons, freedom and authority, capital and labor.

Last of all: the evocation of new Jewish ethical expression. According to an ancient rabbinic epigram, the voice that sounded at Sinai was never silenced. What this signifies is that the proclamation of moral truth never ends. Now genius is a sensitive plant whose budding cannot be predicted or forced. There is no way whereby any group can guarantee that it will produce scientists, musicians, metaphysicians of the first magnitude. But every society ought to hope for such a consummation. The Jews, with their tradition of ethical questing and their present experience of pain and injustice, constitute a promising seedbed for prophets, saints, priests and scribes of the good life. It becomes, then, their duty and privilege to foster the cultivation of moral perceptions and values. In the past their husbandry in the field proved not unfruitful; it may turn out equally productive in times to come.

To anyone, Jew or Gentile, who views Judaism from without, ritual must appear unimportant, and preoccupation with it a misdirection of energy. After all, of what consequence can it be whether a Jew does or does not drive his automobile on the seventh day of the week, whether he partakes of, or refrains from certain foods. Such thoughts may suggest themselves to persons who stand outside Jewish life, never to those at home in it.

For, as any informed and practicing Jew knows, observance looms large in the Jewish scheme of things. So it has always been, the practices of Judaism having been cherished for two thousand years with the utmost fidelity and joyousness. So, though far less generally, it is still. The typical professing Jew of our day, like his forebears, knows well and values highly the Sabbath Eve with its candles, braided bread loaves and cup of Sanctification; the Passover Feast with its multifarious ritual symbols; the ram's horn sounding on the New Year; the austere solemnity of the White Fast of the Day of Atonement; the keening chant of the Black Fast of the Ninth of Ab; the prayer shawl; the first binding on of phylacteries after one's thirteenth birthday; the Kaddish prayer and memorial lamp for the dead; the Scroll of the Torah dressed in embroidered velvets and adorned with glistening breastplate and crown. These a Jew is likely to remember longest and most poignantly; in these and through these, faith and ethic embody and transmit themselves. This is for many Jews the countenance of Judaism, well known and passionately loved.

Little wonder that ritual has been a storm center, not only in the remote past but in recent years as well. When Reform emerged in Germany, it exhibited many radicalisms. But the one that most offended the Orthodox was its iconoclasm on observances. Indeed to this very day the line of demarcation between traditionalists and nontraditionalists consists, of all things, in that the former wear, the latter doff their hats at worship. This is, of course, not the whole story, but it is symptomatic. Again, when Dr. Kaplan published his volume *Judaism as a Civilization* with its many bold premises and unconventional conclusions, the most violent protest centered on his recommendation that certain details of Jewish usage be modified.

The ritual problem in Judaism is composed of two distinct yet inter-related issues: a social reality and a theoretical question. The social reality is the progressive disintegration of Jewish observance. There was a time, and that not so long ago, when virtually every Jew complied with the last and least requirement of the Law. That day is gone forever. While there are Jews who still adhere firmly to the traditional design, there are many more who have departed from it, either in part or all the way. The process has been gathering momentum through the years. The band of the observant dwindles, the number of the nonconforming grows apace.

The theoretical issue concerns itself with the role of ritual in Judaism. Is a system of practices essential or dispensable? If the former, must it be the historic system unchanged or can it be some variation of it? If the latter, on what basis ought modifications to be designed?

Reconstructionism insits that Jewish life requires a regimen of observances. By its theory, Judaism is a religious civilization. Every custom possesses, therefore, not one but two significances. Vis-à-vis the Jewish religion it is a rite; in relation to the culture, a folkway. So, when a Jew sets out to partake of a Passover Feast he effects dual purposes simultaneously. On the one hand he celebrates God the Liberator in prayer, song and symbolism. His behavior is cultic, almost sacramental. At the same time he is doing something analogous to reciting the Declaration of Independence on the Fourth of July. That is to say, he is reliving a significant moment in the past of his people, conforming to a social pattern of his group.

Whether as ritual or folkway, observance from the Reconstructionist viewpoint is indispensable to Judaism. For no religion can be complete or thrive without some pattern of rituals; and no society can exist, let alone be vigorous, without some fabric of mores.

But what shall be the shape of Jewish observances? The

unabatedly traditional? Some variant of it? Or the overtly non-traditional?

Here again Reconstructionism is explicit. And once more its conception of Judaism as evolving provides the warrant for its answer.

It is of the nature of a growing thing that it holds on to its past, and yet reaches toward a future. He who cultivates anything, whether a historic theology, an ethic or a system of practices, must guide himself accordingly. Jews, in other words, ought not to play fast and loose with their past, lest they lose contact with it, the root and strength of their present existence. On rituals as on so many other themes, the presumption is always in favor of the tradition.

A presumption, be it observed, not a rule. There are observances which, in the process of time, have been emptied of content; some, indeed, which, challenged by modern realities, can be maintained only by a heroic effort and then to no determinable advantage. Other practices could be made more effective spiritually were they to be changed in detail. Then there are *lacunae* in the Jewish regimen, junctures of large significance in the life of modern men toward which religion ought to have something ritualistic to contribute. To such situations historic Judaism, the creation of another age, often has nothing to offer. Reverence may have its place, but so also has boldness, the courage to renounce, to remake, to innovate.

But is not all this an invitation to anarchy? The Jewish group has no central authority to supervise changes in observance. Is not our policy a sanction to each individual to do with the tradition as seems right in his eyes? Is it not a counsel of irresponsibility? What else can be expected from it except the wildest disorder?

Undeniably, grave perils attend our proposal. Yet is there any other course except to risk them? Is not anarchy already upon us? Save for the limited and ever-dwindling ranks of the Orthodox, most Jews have long since arrogated to themselves the privilege of doing with Jewish observance as they please. Nor does Reconstructionism offer *carte blanche* to the individual. On the contrary, it has been careful to define precisely the criteria by which change must be directed. What is more, it is working for official sanction for new departures, preferably from established wings of Judaism such as the Conservative and Reform, but, failing action on their part, from the Reconstructionist movement itself.

It is freedom, not license, that Reconstructionism commends. Besides, what alternative is open to Jews who wish to live Jewishly but cannot be Orthodox? They must venture trial, error and experiment in the hope that eventually there may emerge a new norm of Jewish observance, a pattern at once traditional and yet entirely acclimated to modern America.

Admitted that the whole enterprise has in it something of a gamble. If so, it is a gamble which cannot be refused. Destiny forces it; there is no other prospect of success.

THE FIELD OF CULTURE

Creativity is the index of a community's vitality and its assurance againt times to come. It is the badge of vitality, because to live means to create. It is a guarantee against the future, because the more a society creates, the more meaningful its existence becomes for its members, the more they in turn will exert themselves on its behalf.

By this standard—the standard of new things in music, art and literature—how go matters with Judaism? A candid answer must bespeak both disappointment and satisfaction. In Palestine the Jewish spirit has turned incandescent. There a small but renascent community has poured itself forth in a flood of self-expression, intense, and diversely colored. In Poland—prewar Poland of course—a Jewry hobbled by intolerance and crippled by poverty still managed somehow to sustain a passionate spiritual existence, both contemplative and creative.

The picture grows darker as one turns elsewhere. Prewar Russia, by every expectation, should have been the site of a vigorous Jewish cultural life. Its Jewry had long been highly literate and devotedly traditional. Under the Soviets, Jews for the first time in history enjoyed political equality and social security. The Jewish community, moreover, recognized as a minority nationality, was protected in its own language and civilization; it was accorded even a distinct national home, in Biro-Bidjan.

Despite these favorable circumstances, Russian Jewry as a whole has not done too well culturally. Broad and uncontrollable factors account for this in part—the fierce absorption of Russians in the gigantic economic plans to which they had committed themselves, the tendency exhibited by almost all minority nationalities to drift toward Russification, the war. Among the causes, however, must be listed the Soviet policy on Judaism, its hostility to the Jewish religion, to Zionism and to Jewish culture, except the Yiddishists, its consistent segregation of Russian Jews from Jewries abroad.

All this may be water under the bridge. Because of the exigencies of the war, because of natural developments, the Soviet Union has very recently abandoned its isolationism; has modified its procedure, if not its theory, on religion; and, for the first time since 1917, has permitted contact between the Jewries of Russia and of the world. Furthermore, there now appears to be a fair chance of a revision of Communist policy on Zionism, Hebraism and Jewish Palestine. All in all, Jewish culture in Russia may from now on get a better "break."

There is reason for optimism as to the cultural future of Russia's Jews. But it is—and this applies to all Jews on the European continent—remote, not immediate. Everything else aside, the Jews of the Old World have been drained of blood and substance. Whatever strength remains they will need for survival and recuperation. Not for a long time are they likely to have energy to give to literature or art.

Of all Jewries only one, in addition to the Palestinian, can now be looked to for productivity. That one is, of course, the American, the largest and freest in the world, the only community of size that has not been ravaged by the Second World War. Here too the picture is somber in hue. American Jewry has been far less creative Jewishly than might have been expected in view of its advantages. And very sizable advantages they have been: freedom and security; economic resources sufficient to sustain cultural enterprises; a rich environment of American literature, music and art to buoy up specific Jewish interests; a Jewish community large enough to serve as a market to artists and a public to authors; an age-old Jewish tradition of devotion to intellectual pursuits. Like the vineyard of which the prophet sang, American Jewry is culturally "a choicest vine" planted in "a very fruitful hill." Like that, too, it has disappointed its cultivators.

In the nature of things, it cannot be proved that the Jews of America have been less creative than their background and circumstances warrant. The spirit, being neither ponderable nor measurable, does not lend itself to the striking of trial balances. And yet, even statistically, an impressive case can be made for the thesis.

The novel is perhaps the most characteristic of modern literary forms. How much a society does with it may be taken for a barometer of sorts. If so, American Jewry is far from well off.

I have before me a bibliography of novels of Jewish interest. The list does not pretend to be exhaustive; it does however contain every important piece of Jewish fiction done in English in recent years. Well over half the titles represent translations from the Yiddish, Hebrew or German. One-fifteenth were written by Christians, including, in one instance, an apostate from Judaism; another fifteenth by British Jews; one-twentieth by American Jews who, by background and education, are Europeans rather than Americans. Of the entire catalogue only twenty-one percent are indigenous to the American Jewish community. It is not irrelevant to add that none of these is of the first magnitude, comparable for instance with the "Joseph cycle" of Thomas Mann. On this record American Jews have been nearly sterile. They appear to even greater disadvantage when compared with the smaller and infinitely poorer Jewry of prewar Poland, or with the Palestinian community which, one-ninth of the size of the American, has been more creative not only relatively but absolutely.

Further evidence for our thesis is afforded by an extraordinary symposium entitled "Under Forty." Inquiries were addressed to a number of distinguished, younger American Jewish authors concerning their attitudes toward Jewishness and Judaism, and the influence of both on them. They were asked, among other things, whether they had "formed a conscious attitude toward their heritage"; and whether the Jewish tradition had played any role in their literary development.

These questions, soberly put, were answered with equal sobriety. All participants in the symposium revealed themselves to be acutely aware of their Jewish identity. Some of them seem always to have possessed this awareness, others to have had it forced on them by anti-Semitism. No matter how acquired, it has been an influence in their lives. Almost to the man they agreed that by virtue of it they were the more sensitive to the dangers of political and economic reaction and to the minority problem in all its manifestations. Conversely, they were the more passionately committed to democratic ideals.

Jewishness, as identity, quite clearly looms large in their thinking and feeling; Judaism, whether as religion or culture, comes off badly indeed. Of the eleven respondents, seven deny it any place in their scheme of things. One, indeed, goes so far as to deny that it can have any meaning for anyone. "There is," he writes, "much show and talk of affirmation, but only to the end that the negative, or neuter, elements may be made more acceptable." And as for the Jewish religion, "its function is to provide, chiefly for people of no strong religious impulse, a social and rational defense against the world's hostility." (Is it a coincidence that the author of these earnest but categorical assertions confesses that since childhood the word Jew has "struck straight to the unconscious where fear, shame, attraction and repulsion are indistinguishable"?) Only four of the eleven ascribe considerable influence on their inner lives to the Jewish heritage, and even these in varying degrees. To two at least, Judaism operates as a *fait accompli*, a childhood experience which, though never renewed, continues a potent memory. The reckoning ends then with only two of the writers regarding Judaism as actively meaningful to them.

On the basis of my own observations, I am inclined to believe that the distribution of attitudes among these eleven persons is not fortuitous, but mirrors with fair accuracy the standing of Jewish culture among the American Jewish intellectuals. That is to say, among them about two out of eleven are concerned with specifically Jewish values. Ernest Bloch, Maurice Samuel, Ludwig Lewisohn suggest themselves for illustration. Indeed, simultaneous with the publication of the symposium and in the teeth of the contention of one of its participants that there could be no worthwhile Jewish expression in this country, several of the great orchestras of this country presented Leonard Bernstein's *Jeremiah*, a work of distinctly Jewish inspiration. Unfortunately one swallow, even a flight of swallows, does not make a spring.

Now, I wish to be altogether clear. I do not conceive of the

American and Jewish cultures as being mutually competitive. Nor am I fired to jealousy by the spectacle of Jews giving themselves to pursuits unrelated to Judaism. The artist has a full right to go where his spirit listeth. Nor is he under any obligation to express himself through Jewish media. On the other hand, if he does elect to do so, he is equally within his rights, not only formally, but essentially. Jewish interests are as thoroughly legitimate on the American scene as any. The Jewish thread is a proper strand in the fabric of this land, to weave with it an entirely American act. As I see it, then, the Jewish artist has a choice between working on the larger loom or the smaller. Whichever he selects, he is equally worthy of his hire.

My point right now is a simple one. In the life of the American Jewish man of art and letters the Jewish identity and heritage are facts. As such he ought somehow, somewhere, whether as nuances to other themes or as major motifs, respond to them. And yet, as we have just seen, he will, if he is at all typical, fail to do so.

Why? The answers are many. Ignorance of Judaism, psychic blockings against it, lack of clear thinking about it, absorption in social issues so total as to leave room for nothing else, all these, as the symposium demonstrates, are episodes in the story. The nub, however, is that it must be so. Judaism is the secondary, ancillary civilization of American Jews. With the inevitableness of a body drawn by gravity toward a larger mass, they will drift naturally in the direction of the broader field. Of creative artists no more than a minority can be expected to seek self-expression in Jewish channels, and of these only a minority in turn to do so consistently.

Whence it follows that the American Jewish community for all its size and resources cannot be expected to sustain itself culturally. To put it bluntly, it is going to have to live on the largesse of other, more intensely Jewish Jewries.

But though Jewish art and letters in this land cannot but be largely derivative, the larger the volume of original output the better. In the first place, useful activity is not only a sign of group health; like exercise, it tends to superinduce it. Again, no matter what the worth of importations, the home-grown poem, song or painting, sprouting on the American scene, will both savor of it and be relevant to it. The odds may be heavy against indigenous Jewish creativity. Despite them, the game must be played. Every encouragement must be given by the American Jewish community to native authors, playwrights, composers, choreographers and sculptors. Fellowships, subventions and markets ought to be assured to persons of promise and works of merit. As matters stand now, he who puts his hand to a Jewish artistic enterprise will begin with difficulties in getting his piece mounted and end with a limited audience. The least American Jewry can do is to offset the crasser and more readily remediable disadvantages.

RECONSTRUCTIONISM AND ZIONISM

In the architecture of this book, Zionism is an unruly element. It cuts across all the lines we have drawn for the orderly division of our materials; it spills over into every field of Jewish interest. And all the time it is also an entity in itself. That is why it has been reserved for the fourth and last section of this volume.

And yet, in advance of the special presentation that still awaits us, I should like to pause briefly over the Reconstructionist view of Zionism. Not that the latter derives from the former. Zionism is too large, complex and tumultuous a movement to be bound to any single ideology of Jewish life. But we are now exploring the practical implications of Reconstructionism. Our argument will not be complete unless we inquire, no matter how briefly, after its position on this vast and crucial issue.

To put the matter bluntly, Reconstructionism leads directly to Zionism. Given the premises of the first, the second follows relentlessly.

1) No program for the perpetuation of Judaism can be indifferent to the welfare of the people who are its bearers. Palestine has saved the lives of myriad Jews in the past, it promises to redeem many more in the future. On this score, alone, Reconstructionism must indorse Zionism.

2) There is in Reconstructionism a heavy bias in favor of the historical in Judaism. The love of Zion, the hope of its rebuilding, the dream of the restoration there of at least a part of the Jewish people are etched deep and indelible in the consciousness of the Jewish traditionalist. In effect, it is next to impossible to accept the Jewish civilization without embracing Zionism at the same time.

3) The Jews constitute, as we have seen, not only a religious communion and a culture group but a people also. And every people ought to have some place in the world where its peoplehood can find total expression.

4) Reconstructionism implies Zionism because of the needs of Judaism, because of the persistent disadvantages we have just surveyed under which Jewish culture operates everywhere. The second civilization of Jews, Judaism is constantly under the necessity of refreshing itself from a free-flowing source. Somewhere in the world it must be the dominant concern of Jews. In other words, a Jewish Homeland must be established.

Reconstructionism on all these counts is Zionist. But it does not, therefore, sanction all vagaries of Zionism. Thus it stands against the secularism of Messrs. X and Y. Religious in its premises and objectives, it insists on the primacy of religion in every aspect of Jewish life. For, only when grounded in the historic Jewish faith and ethic can Zionism be vigorous and full-blooded, only when tempered by them can it be kept from nationalistic excesses, and only under their direction can it serve, as it should, the classic humanitarian purposes of the Jewish tradition.

By the same token, Reconstructionism offers no sympathy or asylum to the Zionism that sees only Palestinian Jewry and no other. There is a Zionist who is so thoroughly absorbed in his distant task that he forgets his Jewish obligations nearer to home. There is another Zionist who despairs of the possibility of Jewish life outside Palestine. Convinced that Diaspora Judaism is doomed, he concentrates his energies on the only Jewry that appears to him to have a chance. With such pessimism, Reconstructionism has no patience. It has confidence in the future of Judaism throughout the world. It objects to the notion that Palestine and the Diaspora are competitive and mutually exclusive. It holds such an alternative to be false and to obscure the job of modern Jews which is not a matter of "either . . . or" but of "both."

THE NEED FOR KNOWLEDGE

Even now we have not squeezed from our ideology the last juice of implication. Two enterprises remain to be extracted. The first, a decision as to the organization of the American Jewish community, is so much a theme by itself that we shall reserve it for special treatment. The other is, as it chances, no less than the chief cornerstone of the Reconstructionist program, that first and last thing from which all else proceeds, toward which everything reaches. I refer to its emphasis on Jewish knowledge, as broad and deep as can be achieved.

A concern over Jewish information and understanding is, needless to say, not the monopoly of any one school of thought. All survivalist ideologies are agreed that the Jew must be informed. It is only the assimilationist who can indulge in or tolerate illiteracy. The advocate of the continuance of Jewish life, be he secularist, religionist or Reconstructionist, can afford no such luxuries. By knowledge as much as by faith and works, Judaism in the past transcended the rigors of its lot. Only with these can it outlive its present crisis.

These days, unfortunately, ignorance of Jewish affairs is quite the rule among Jews. Modern Jews, educated on all matters of general import, are very commonly innocent of Jewish learning of any sort. They know no history, theology or sociology; not Bible, Talmud or prayer book; neither prophets, sages nor heroes. Literacy used to be law among them. Now, of all groups that possess distinguished traditions, they are perhaps the most untutored in their own.

Because knowledge is wanting, the people perish. I would not be guilty of oversimplification. Many of the ills that afflict Jews and Judaism are totally unrelated to what is present or absent inside Jewish heads. Thus, were every Jew a Maimonides, anti-Semitism would still be his heartache and dark peril. But other issues, if they cannot be resolved by information, certainly cannot be resolved without it. The diffusion of knowledge and understanding may be nowhere enough by itself. But in many situations it is half the battle, or else a precondition without which the battle cannot be joined.

For one must know himself, his foes and the lay of the land, or he will not fight intelligently. One must know who and what he is, that indeed he is a man and not a craven, or he will not fight courageously. And one must know what he is fighting for and why it is worth the effort, or he will not fight purposefully, resolutely.

Hence it comes to pass that the protagonists of the various

survivalist idelogies who agree on so little besides are so much in harmony here. Because of varying premises and goals, they may differ to a degree on the goals of instruction, its materials and its techniques. Beyond these they are of one heart: Jews must be won to an understanding of their history, their tradition— religious, ethical, ceremonial, cultural, institutional—of their literary monuments, of the Hebrew tongue, of their problem, of the proposals for its solution, of their group purposes and ideals.

Everything I am trying to say about the indispensability of knowledge to the Jewish tradition has been anticipated by the tradition itself. In myriad epigrams and metaphors, the teachers of Israel from Moses on insisted that only as Jewry was informed could it be assured of life. But nowhere has this thought been stated more colorfully than in a legend spun by ancient rabbis.

When Moses descended from Mount Sinai, they relate, he held in his arms, as Scripture informs us, the tablets of stone engraved by the finger of the Holy One, blessed be He. And such was the virtue of the inscription, that it was not Moses who carried the tablets, but the tablets which carried Moses. So it came to pass that his descent over jagged rocks, on the verge of crags and yawning chasms, was effortless and safe. But when the prophet neared the mountain's base and caught his first glimpse of the Golden Calf, when God's words and the idol were brought into confrontation with each other, a wonder ensued. The sacred letters detached themselves from the stone in which they had been inscribed and vanished into thin air. Moses was left holding a blank, inert thing, too heavy for him. It is not true, the sages assert, that Moses threw the tablets to the earth, so shattering them. The fact is that he had to let them go or be crushed. The lettered stone which had carried Moses was, once letterless, too much for him to bear.

It is not difficult to discern what the ancient rabbis are trying to say in their parable: given knowledge and insight, Judaism sustains the Jew; without them it is a crushing burden, too heavy for even the strongest to withstand.

STANDARDS FOR THE CONSERVATIVE
MOVEMENT IN JUDAISM

By Rabbi Simon Greenberg

Dr. Simon Greenberg (b. 1901) is now Vice-Chancellor of the Seminary. He was for many years the rabbi of one of the leading Conservative congregations in the country. He was at one time President of the Rabbinical Assembly and subsequently served as Executive Director of the United Synagogue.

Dr. Greenberg is represented by two selections in this volume. One is printed below and represents his view of Conservative Judaism. It was delivered as an address to the 1952 convention of the United Synagogue. The other is an article on Jewish education, a field in which he has shown especial interest and in which he has had wide experience both as an administrator and as a writer of text-books.

CONTROVERSIES FOR THE SAKE OF HEAVEN

It may well be that prudence would counsel the choice of another theme for this occasion. For the subject that I would re-examine with you is one that has in the past stirred considerable controversy. But two considerations have led me to disregard such counsels of prudence. The first is the fact that these *makhlokot*, these controversies have been *L'shem Shamayim*, for the sake of heaven, as proved by the fact that on the whole they have strengthened rather than weakened us. They protected us from intellectual stagnation. They helped to clarify our thinking and to keep our Movement vital, creative and relevant to our daily lives.

Moreover, I intend to turn our attention to the great, fundamental, articulated and unarticulated agreements that have shaped

263

the character of our Movement. For in addition to the verbal clashes in which we have from time to time engaged, we have at all times been occupied in joint constructive action. Out of that joint constructive action as well as out of the discussion there have emerged a number of clearly identifiable concepts which have all the characteristics of standards for conduct. Though these have never been formally voted upon and accepted by us at any national convention, they are, nevertheless, now widely recognized as the real forces that have been at work amongst us. They are *standards* in every significant sense of that word, for in their light we have formulated policy and passed judgment on our own acts and the acts of others.

The Conservative Movement in Judaism has been closest to the spirit of traditional, historical Judaism, above all in this: that *it did not define itself in dogmas or in publicly announced platforms*. But it did create, develop or adopt a number of concepts, and made them peculiarly its own. Within our Movement these concepts entered into a unique combination of interrelations, and proved to be the spiritually and intellectually fructifying leaven in our midst.

What are these concepts? How have they determined the character of our Movement in the past? How can they guide us in the future? I shall refer only to four such concepts and discuss them briefly.

1. *The Scientific Knowledge of the Whole of Judaism.*

The first of these concepts, in terms of chronology and perhaps also of significance, was created by the German Jewish precursors of our Movement, by men like Leopold Zunz, Zacharias Frankel, Heinrich Graetz. They spoke of "Jüdische Wissenschaft." We translated it rather clumsily into English as "The Science of Judaism." I prefer to think of it as "The Scientific Study of Judaism." Judaism, as we all know, has always stressed knowledge. But since the rise of the modern scientific method and the modern study of history, knowing our Tradition as our fathers knew it is not enough. The scientific study of Judaism calls for knowledge in terms of historical circumstance, of growth, development and adaptation. It calls for full and complete knowledge. Not knowledge limited to any one area or to any one era of Judaism—not only knowledge of the Bible, or the Talmud, or the medieval codes or the modern literary, legal or philosophical writings, but of all of them with equal thoroughness and equal reverence. It calls for first hand knowledge of original sources in their original languages and not for knowledge about our heritage through second hand media.

It is no accident, my friends, that it was the Conservative Movement that created the largest Jewish library, the largest collection of printed books and manuscripts dealing with our heritage that was ever in the possession of any Jewish community in all of our history. It is no accident that the Conservative Movement has always been unequivocally attached to the Hebrew language and that the faculties of our Seminary schools have maintained the very highest standards of thoroughness, comprehensiveness and exactitude in knowledge. It is no accident that at our Seminary we now have the Louis M. Rabinowitz Foundation devoted to the publication of the scientifically most exact texts of our basic religious literature. All of these are the inevitable outgrowth of the natural inclination of the leaders of our Movement, from its earliest beginnings to our own day, to measure all their actions by the standards of the concept of scientific knowledge.

One of the characteristics, therefore, of an understanding and devoted member of our Movement is this: Does he apply the standard of scientific knowledge in what he favors or disfavors in Jewish life? Are we constantly encouraging study of and contact with the original documents of our faith in their Hebrew originals or are we directly or indirectly encouraging a second-hand, a translated Judaism? Are we encouraging a one-era Judaism—be it a Prophetic Judaism, or a Rabbinic Judaism or a Hassidic Judaism? Are we advocating a one-area Judaism—be it an East European, an Israeli or an American Judaism? Or are we constantly striving for a scientific knowledge of Judaism, without any adjectives that would limit it geographically, chronologically or ideologically?

These questions refer not only to what is done at the Seminary. They have direct bearing upon the curriculum which we establish in our congregational schools, upon the place of Hebrew in our services and upon the kind of knowledge we expect from our spiritual leaders. It is the answers that each one personally gives to these fundamental questions as they refer to the local congregational activities that, in the last analysis, determine the character of our Movement as a whole.

2. Judaism—A Torah Centered Civilization

The second concept which became a fundamental standard for the Conservative Movement in Judaism is the modern articulation of the thought, repeatedly expressed by the Rabbis, that Judaism is not only one segment of life but embraces all of life. "Search the Torah again and again, for you will find everything in it," wisdom, history, law, ethics, truth, beauty and goodness. That description of Judaism formulated some nineteen hundred years ago was challenged for the first time during the nineteenth century. In the struggle for equal political rights for Jews in central and western Europe, a group arose which sought to limit the scope of Judaism to a few metaphysical dogmas and ethical principles. It was primarily against this narrow, sterile view of Judaism that our Movement fought and continues to fight, for the battle is far from won. Within our ranks in America the man whose voice was raised most vibrantly in the early days of the century in behalf of this broader, all-embracing view was that of the beloved, martyred Israel Friedlaender. It is high time for us to re-publish many of his brilliant essays in popular, reasonably-priced editions, and make them easily accessible to the rank and file of our people.

In a lecture on "The Problem of Judaism in America," delivered in 1907, Friedlaender said, "If Judaism is to be preserved amidst the new conditions, it must again break the narrow frame of a creed and resume its original function as a culture, as the expression of the Jewish spirit and the whole life of the Jews." * He decried the fact that "Judaism, which has curtailed its functions down to those of a creed, has no room for the talents of its children, so that its poets, artists, dancers, actors, writers, creative spirits of all kinds were enriching the culture of all peoples except their own." **

The broad comprehensive conception of Judaism as a culture

---

* *Past and Present*, p. 269.
** *Ibid.*, p. 271.

has been most fully developed by Professor Kaplan in his classic book *Judaism as a Civilization*. We all agree with his main thesis that Judaism is more than a creed, more than a ritual, but a rich, varicolored culture or civilization.

Hence, it is no mere accident that our Movement was at all times completely and unwaveringly devoted to Zionism, to the effort to re-establish an autonomous Jewish community upon the soil of Israel. We were loyal to Zionism in days of comparative ease and not only in days of distress because Zionism to us was always more than another typical, nationalistic movement of the nineteenth century, more than a philanthropic movement concerned merely with the rescue of the persecuted, more than merely an answer to anti-Semitism. We followed Ahad Ha'Am in his analysis of the situation facing us to the effect that not only Jews were threatened by anti-Semitism but that Judaism was endangered by the new social and political condition which faced us after the French Revolution. Hence, to us, Zionism represented, above all, the hope that in an autonomous Jewish State, Judaism would have the best possible environment within which it could again function as a culture or a civilization, affecting every aspect of life and stimulating every creative impulse within us to find expression within the framework of our Tradition. Our interests in the establishment of a Jewish State were, therefore, never exclusively or even primarily political or philanthropic. They were always, first and foremost, spiritual and cultural. The last decade has, unfortunately, compelled us, for the time being, to give primacy to the humanitarian and the philanthropic aspects of our relations to Israel. But the long-term, permanent foundations of our association with the miraculously re-established State of Israel are, and will remain, spiritual and cultural. We will look to a free and independent Israel because we believe that its political, social and economic framework can and should create the environment within which Judaism will flourish most gloriously as a full and many-sided culture or civilization. Its vitality on the soil on which it reached its noblest heights will, we believe, radiate strength and blessing not only to Jewish communities throughout the world but to all men striving for a better world.

But we shall not for a moment retreat from our faith that in this land, too, Judaism can maintain many of its historic aspects as a comprehensive culture.

In the light of that historic position of our Movement we can readily see that it was no mere accident that, at the suggestion of Dr. Kaplan, we called our school on the West Coast a University of Judaism; that, within our Movement, were created the Eternal Light and the Jewish Museum, the two media which, more than any other, have stimulated and utilized creative, artistic talents for the presentation and interpretation of the teachings of Judaism; and that from within our ranks there came the Institute of Religious and Social Studies, and the Conference of Science, Philosophy and Religion, as the expression of Judaism's intrinsic concern with all phases of human thought.

But we never for a moment lost sight of the truth that in Judaism, regardless how broadly conceived, the Torah was and should remain the heart and core, the indispensable root and the most prized fruit. In the words of Professor Louis Ginzberg, spoken when he was Acting President of the United Synagogue of America, we tried ever to remember that "the Torah stood forth throughout the history of Israel as the guiding star of its civilization." This concept of Judaism as a Torah-centered civilization has dominated the course of the Conservative Movement and remains, to this day, one of the indispensable standards whereby to judge the propriety of any proposed action whether it be on a national or on a local level. Under the impulse emanating from this concept we created and sponsored the Ramah summer camps. In this country they approximate as closely as possible the atmosphere in which Judaism as a Torah-centered civilization can be most intimately experienced.

That is why, within our ranks, the Synagogue Center was born and lives most vigorously. It is a new and more comprehensive embodiment of the traditional concept of the Synagogue as a *Bet Tefila*, *Bet Midrash*, and *Bet Knesset*. Preserving the central position, both architecturally and ideologically, for the Ark of the Torah and all that it represents, the Synagogue Center provides room within its ample circumference for study and recreation, music and art, dancing and the drama. All activities that make life happy, colorful, rich, pleasant and beautiful are there nurtured in the spirit and in the light of the Torah.

3. *Klal Yisrael—The Brotherhood of Israel.*

The third concept which has always been indigenous to our Movement and which was given new and unique expression in our midst is the Rabbinic concept of *Klal Yisrael*, which Dr. Schechter translated in his striking phrase, "Catholic Israel." There have been varying interpretations given to the terms "Catholic Israel" and *Klal Yisrael*. One thing is certain. Those who created these concepts sought to express thereby their inner desire to be identified not with any one sect or party in Israel, but with the whole of the Jewish people.

To be sure, there is never any lack of protestation on the part of individual Jews on the matter of their longing for a united Israel. But this desire for the unity of Israel is all too often little more than an impassioned zeal to remake all others into our own image. *All too rarely does it appear as a ceaseless effort to remake ourselves so that we may serve as the core through which differing and even conflicting elements may experience the sense of their common spiritual kinship.* Dr. Schechter expressed the hope that the Seminary might become a force for reconciliation in Israel. That force our Movement has ever sought to be by stressing our spiritual and historic kinship with all Israel. We refrained to the utmost, as a Movement, from emphasizing the differences between us and other groups. We never hesitated to admit, — on the contrary, we gloried in — the many things which we had in common with our brethren on the right or the left in religion, or with our brethren of no religion at all. It is not that we wanted to be all things to all men. Not at all. But we wanted to equal every man or any group in devotion to whatever we believed to be Jewishly positive and constructive in their lives. We wanted and want to match the most ardent Hebraist in knowledge of Hebrew, the most ardent Orthodox Jew in the practice of piety, the most ardent Reform Jew in determination to make Judaism aesthetically attractive and the most militant secularist in making Judaism contemporaneous and relevant. I think it is altogether to our credit that in the eyes of some we appear to be Orthodox, in the eyes of others Reformed and in the sight of still others, secular nationalists. That is the way historical Judaism always appeared to others. To the pagans Judaism was godless.

To the Roman patriot it was too universal. To the Christian it was too nationalistic.

To stress the difference between us and other groups in Judaism rather than the similarities between us may, for the moment, appear to be helpful in that it seems to clarify issues and draw clearly defined lines. It makes easier the creation of slogans and the rallying of followers to a party banner. But it is an advantage bought at the price of ultimate division and separation. The differences between the Karaites and the Rabbinites became clearer and clearer as generations passed. Unfortunately for Jewish history, there did not appear, during the eighth or ninth century, a third group with which the two implacably opposed groups could feel that they had much in common. Inevitably, therefore, the differences between them grew sharper and sharper. They drifted further and further apart until they could not recognize themselves as belonging to the same *Klal Yisrael*.

On the other hand, the lines of differences between *Hassidim* and *Mitnagdim*, which, in the eighteenth century, were very sharply etched, became more and more blurred with the growth and development of the *Habad* group, so that both the *Mitnagdim* and *Hassidim* had a common bond to one another through them. It is not that confusion in thought is a desideratum, but we must ever be on guard against the fallacy that imagines that life can ever be confined within a series of crystal-clear definitions or boundaries.

Humanity today is faced with the imminent danger of indescribable tragedy because one segment of it is so fearfully sure of its definitions, so terribly certain of its absolute truths, and has differentiated itself with such blinding clarity from the rest of mankind. There are those in America who would have America stress not the ideals and values it has in common with the rest of mankind, but only those which are peculiarly its own, so that we differentiate ourselves more and more from the rest of humanity and stand out over against it,—in our own minds benevolently, but in the minds of others, threateningly. This is the path of ruin for mankind and the path of disintegration for any group within human society.

The Conservative Movement has thus far remained true to the intuitive insight of historical Judaism which was, as Professor

Ginzberg has said, "National *and* Universal, individual *and* social, legal *and* mystic, dogmatic *and* practical at once." It has always seemed to me that the mere fact that in our sacred Scriptures the book of Leviticus is at the side of the books of Isaiah and Amos, that the Song of Songs is at the side of the book of Lamentations, that, above all, the books of Job and Ecclesiastes are bound in the same canon with the books of the Psalms, that this fact, in itself, teaches as much about the profound insight into life which guided the builders of Judaism, as much about the spirit of our historic faith, as anything found within the books themselves. Life can never be purged of its inescapable inner contradictions. And if, at times, we appear to harbor within our ranks contradictory drives and impulses, it is but further evidence of the vitality and the essential truth of our Movement, that it can keep the differences confined within the boundaries of a larger unity.

In psychology we know that the mind purged of a steady flow of contradictory thoughts is unbalanced, and the heart not pulled hither and thither by contradictory emotions is either all ablaze, or woefully apathetic.

We are a great unifying force in Israel, a great rallying center for *Klal Yisrael* precisely because we do not seek to differentiate ourselves from others. We gladly accept from others whatever appears to us to make Judaism more meaningful and attractive. We are not afraid of being called Reformed Jews because we accepted the practice, first characteristic of Reform, to confirm girls and boys, nor are we afraid of being called Orthodox because we observe the Sabbath traditionally, nor secularists because we believe in the existence of a politically independent Israel. We know that each one of these and many similar practices and ideas help to strengthen Judaism and to make it more meaningful to its followers. But that is not all. We also know that in accepting for ourselves these positive constructive ideas, we are not only strengthening Judaism but are also approaching just that much closer to some of our Jewish brethren, thus helping them to experience their kinship with us and, through us, with many with whom they would otherwise have no contact. Through us and with us, the secular Hebraist, the pious traditionalist and the cultured modernist discover their basic historic kinship, one with the other.

It is thus that many of us understand the concept of *Klal*

Yisrael. It obligates us ever to strive to emulate every constructive Jewish pattern, no matter what its source, so that all Jews may sense a spiritual kinship with us and through us with one another even as we consciously seek to maintain a spiritual kinship with them.

4. *Innovation Without Regimentation*

The fourth of the concepts that has consciously and subconsciously molded the Conservative Movement I would designate as "innovation without regimentation." It is contained in the pre-amble to the constitution of the United Synagogue of America. That preamble should be much more widely known. It would help to answer many questions about our Movement. It was written by very wise, learned and loyal men. It states that the United Synagogue "while not endorsing the innovations introduced by any of its constituent bodies, seeks to embrace all elements essentially loyal to traditional Judaism."

By that statement the founders of the United Synagogue expressed their recognition of the fact that, at no time in Jewish history, and least of all in periods of flux and transition such as ours, has there ever been a uniformity of practice and ritual. The exigencies of time, place and community require their own adjustments. The Mishna is replete with such statements as: "in communities where it was the custom to work on the eve of Passover, it was permissible to work. In communities where it was not customary to work on the eve of Passover, it was not permissible to work."

In such matters as the synagogue service, the Torah readings, the place of women in the community's activities, and in many other spheres, there was always considerable room for differences in practice. Now, the United Synagogue did not set itself up as a superior body whose business it is to introduce uniformity throughout its ranks. It has the responsibility to guide individual communities so that they might not, through ignorance, isolation or the blandishments of some false prophets, read themselves out of the main framework of the tradition of Israel. But the need and search for new forms of worship and observance are the sure signs of constructive and sincere interest. The worst enemy of any spiritual heritage is indifference.

In a country such as ours where there are Jews who no longer even have a recollection of the Sabbath but who still want to be Jews, men and women who can barely read the Hebrew alphabet but who want to pray as Jews, families isolated by vast distances from their houses of worship but who want to join their brethren in communal prayer on Sabbaths and Festivals, local adjustments, which in most instances are essentially pedagogic devices rather than legal innovations, have to be made. But let us not label one another with epithets of approval or disapproval as progressives or reactionaries, depending upon the number or the seeming boldness of our experiments. Above all, let us not ask that every *local* adjustment, regardless of how successfully it meets the *local* needs, be given formal national approval and be declared as standard national practice for the whole Movement. Let us not constantly create new "orthodoxies." We must avoid, on the one hand, the development within our ranks of such diversity of public services or ritual observances as to make us strangers to one another and to sever us from the main body of our historic Tradition. On the other hand, we must ever bear in mind that Judaism never achieved an absolute uniformity of practice within its ranks and that we, today, do not consider such uniformity either particularly virtuous or desirable. A certain amount of uniformity is indispensable if a movement is to have its distinctive character. It is necessary so that when we meet together we may pray as a congregation, and when a member of one congregation prays in another he should feel "at home" in the service. But we do not want to encourage the notion that there is some magic virtue in the order of the prayers, or in their number, or in their melodies. The synagogue service is in no way a mysterious magical formula. Its purpose is to inspire, to instruct, to purify and to exalt. Hence, we want always to make the service relevant to the worshipper even as we want to make the worshipper more receptive to the service. For only as the service remains essentially true to its own historical character can it serve as a bond between the worshipper and his ancestors as well as between him and his contemporaries. We must bear in mind always that we are a people whose unity, in the last analysis, always depended upon a general consensus. Within the framework of American democracy there is no other basis for our unity. Hence we consider it among the primary responsibilities of the United

Synagogue to keep the lines of communications open at all times among our congregations so that all may be informed what each is doing. But, nationally, we accept and practice only that which is historically tested and authenticated, and that to which an overwhelming consensus has given approval in theory and practice.

That is how the concept of diversity within unity has been applied in our Movement. That is how the notion of change within continuity has been functioning within our ranks. And if, as the result of this freedom to experiment within bounds, we should be accused of harboring inconsistencies, we shall not either deny or be affrighted by the charge. The restless, searching spirits amongst us who, from time to time, venture off the beaten path, very often return with fresh experiences, new insights and novel discoveries which become valuable and permanent additions to the sum total of our religious heritage. They always stimulate our thinking. As long as the main body of our Movement proceeds along the broad highway of historical Judaism we can afford, and we should even welcome, the departure of occasional "scouting parties" into side paths and unchartered fields. We must never tire in our effort, by word and by deed, to help them maintain intact their lines of communications with the main body.

Let me repeat these four tested standards:

1. Scientific knowledge of the whole of Judaism.
2. Judaism as a Torah-centered culture or civilization.
3. *Klal Yisrael* as a challenge to fashion ourselves into a center around whom and through whom Jews of all shades of belief and opinion may experience their common kinship.
4. Innovation without regimentation.

OUR HISTORIC TASK AND OPPORTUNITY

These, to me, are the four concepts that have dominated the thought and action of our Movement. There are other concepts that have played their part. These four, however, were and are the most significant and pervasive. They are the standards which as a Movement we have followed with an extraordinary degree of consistency in the past. They will, I hope, remain the guiding standards of our Movement in the future.

In the great historic tasks of rebuilding Jewish life, both in Israel and throughout the world after the unprecedented tragedy of this past decade, the Conservative Movement has a great role to play. Jewish knowledge is to be nurtured, Jewish brotherhood is to be fostered and Jewish intellectual horizons are to be kept wide. The extent to which our Movement will succeed in fulfilling nobly its historic task will, in the final analysis, depend not only upon the national organizations, but primarily upon the quality of the leadership of the local units that make up our Movement, namely the congregations. Will the lay as well as the rabbinic leadership of our congregations ponder profoundly and prayerfully upon these standards of our Movement and tirelessly seek to apply them to the day-to-day activities of their own congregations and communities? Will our congregations be able to rise above their historically ingrained isolationism? Will officers and members of congregations come to see that they are part of a large national Movement and that their local effectiveness is inextricably intertwined with the effectiveness of the Movement as a whole? Much more depends upon this awakening of a sense of identification between the local congregations, the Seminary, the Rabbinical Assembly and the United Synagogue, than appears on the surface.

Deeply conscious of the wounds of mankind and of Israel that are to be healed, and of our obligation to be messengers of healing, let us pursue our tasks with faith, with courage, with devotion and with prayer.

> "Heal us O Lord
> And we shall be healed
> Save us and we shall be saved
> For whatever of glory there is in us
> Is but of Thee."   (Jeremiah, XVII, 14)

NEW GOALS FOR CONSERVATIVE JUDAISM

By Rabbi Morris Adler

Rabbi Morris Adler (b. 1906) is a leading figure in the American rabbinate and the rabbi of one of the major Conservative congregations. He has taken an active role in the Law Committee of the Rabbinical Assembly and has been Visiting Professor of Homiletics at the Seminary. The selection which bears his name was delivered as an address to a United Synagogue Convention in 1948. While it represents his own point of view, it is included here, partly, as an expression of the outlook of a man who has been pre-eminently a rabbi serving in a congregation. It may, as a result, be closer to the thinking of the congregational rabbis than some of the other selections included in this section.

I believe it to be a happy and significant augury for that which will follow, that the subject of this session has been defined as "New Goals for Conservative Judaism." It is essential recurringly to become disenthralled from principles long and reverently maintained and examine them anew. Liberty is not the only human good that is secured at the cost of eternal vigilance. For a faith and tradition to remain vitally relevant to life, eternal vigilance is no less necessary. Life refuses to be embalmed. Truth cannot be permitted to remain in a state of suspended animation. Every generation must perforce live in a social context of forces, pressures and relationships unique to it alone, and the truth of the ages must be explored for the particular emphasis and interpretation which meets both its specific and universal needs.

To freeze our views at one front means to move farther and farther from the dynamic center of contemporary living. Every movement must guard against the slow descent of accepted thought towards the inactive commonplace. John Milton had the same danger in mind when he wrote that "truth is compared in Scriptures to a streaming fountain. If the waters flow not in perpetual progression they sicken into a muddy pool of conformity and tradition."

Life requires constant review and examination of our conceptions, for an unreflective existence must inevitably become fatally detrimental to the portencies that may still inhere in our uncritically held doctrines, as well as blind us to the just and necessary claims of the life about us. Many of us feel that a survey and examination of our goals is a not-to-be postponed need, for our movement must make the transition to a new stage in its development.

The primary motivation out of which Conservative Judaism arose and became organized was the necessity to negate prevailing conceptions held by the camps to the right and the left of us. We reached against existing movements. Orthodoxy was unacceptable and Reform undesirable. It is a useful function at specific points in the historic process to question, to challenge and to refute philosophies that have become embodied in movements and organizations. Partisans of either extreme may scoff at a viewpoint that seems to subsist on denials. But consciously or not, the Conservative movement made a notable contribution when it refused to be impaled on the horns of the dilemma of either wholesale acceptance in its entirety of an unchanged and unchanging body of Jewish tradition, on the one hand, or such a diluted and distorted interpretation on the other, as worked violence upon the historic pattern and integrity of that tradition.

Denials and negations play a fruitful part in the history of ideas. Every idea involves both affirmation and denial; acceptance and rejection; inclusion and exclusion. The rabbis, with rare insight at such a point in the development of religious ideas, boldly stated, "To reject idolatry is accounted as all but affirmation of the Torah." And elsewhere the Talmud remarks, "He who rejects idolatry is called a Jew."

In the Decalogue the majestic affirmation contained in the first word is immediately followed by the emphatic negative expressed by the second. Jeremiah, when called to prophesy, was told that his mission would be, "To root out and pull down, and to destroy and to overthrow; to build and to plant."

No apology or defense is necessary, therefore, for the negations which were implicit in our position from the outset, although our positive formulations were by comparison pale and feeble. We spoke of the process of development which courses through all of the recorded history of our tradition, and meant thereby to negate the viewpoint of a static and immutable law, on the one extreme, and to reject the doctrine that the authority of Jewish law had completely lapsed on the other. We stressed the integrity of the Jewish motive in refutation of those who favored an easy and convenient capitulation to the environment. In the same breath we spoke of the flexibility and fluidity of our social heritage as Jews, in opposition to those who desired to congeal it and keep it insulated against all interaction with modern life. We spoke of modern Judaism and by it expressed our objection to a Judaism that was not modern, and a modernity that was not Jewish. Our affirmations were more apparent than real. They could be fully comprehended only in terms of a frame of reference constructed largely of our negations.

Ladies and gentlemen, we must face the truth that we have been halting between fear and danger; fear of the Orthodox, and danger of Reform. We have set our watches by their time pieces. The time has come for our emergence from the valley of indecision. We must move forward to a stage in which Conservative Judaism revolves about an axis of positive and unambiguous affirmations. This will require a measure of boldness and vision on our part which as a movement, I am sorry to say, we have not thus far manifested.

For one thing, there is a growing grass-root demand for such an exposition and clarification of our position as cannot be achieved by reliance on the eloquence of our denials and disavowals. There is a growing impatience on the part of our people, the members of these 400 sisterhoods and 350 congregations—a growing impatience on their part, with the timidity or reluctance which inhibits our forward movement.

For another thing, the struggle with both Orthodoxy and Reform has lost much of its intensity and much of its meaning. Indeed, the whole battle has shifted to a new ground. The formulae of three or four decades ago no longer address themselves to the immediate or central problems of American Jewry.

Leaving for the moment the aspect of those who escape from Jewry and concentrating upon Jews who live within the framework of our organized community, we shall have to conclude, I feel, that our chief work must be to combat the inertness which, like a spreading paralysis, has settled in vital areas of American Jewish life. Inertness in our midst is of two varieties. First, we have the inert multitudes. You in Chicago know of them. We in Detroit are not unfamiliar with them. If they constitute the periphery, then perhaps for the first time in Jewish history, the periphery outweighs the center.

Multitudes of our people are untouched, uninformed, uncovenanted. They have not enough Judaism to live it, nor enough interest to reject it. They go on in routine indifference. Only now and then does some climactic circumstance briefly touch them to evoke a fitful response. Their personal lives are uninfluenced by the fact of their Jewishness. They take their values from the circle in which they move, from the business they operate, from the fashions in thought and action that are current about them. These and these alone serve them as Decalogue and Torah, the inheritor of and substitute for their tradition. Uncommitted, they represent a pre-historic and pre-Sinaitic tribe in our midst. Some of these we shall probably never reach. They have been too long in the deep freeze. Others may yet be stirred if somehow we could devise the challenge and establish the organization that is electrically endowed with resurrecting powers.

There are others just equally inert, but on the side of Judaism. You find them crowding the membership rolls of our numerous organizations, synagogues and Zionist districts. I suggest we spend a month dropping members who have not lived up to our traditions. It is not non-Jewishness that is routine but Jewishness. Judaism has become for them a glacial heirloom which they have strangely fallen into the habit of guarding. On the surface they are affiliated, but theirs is a frigid and uninspired affiliation. There is about it no glow, no incandescence of the spirit. It does not have the compelling warmth, the transforming power of a great experience. Unimpassioned themselves, they communicate but little to their children. Theirs is a creed without color, a faith without fire.

Nor can we face our new obligations without an abiding and vivid awareness of the overwhelming cataclysm which, in our day, has deprived us of the most potent and creative source of Jewish vitality and content in the Diaspora. The hope of *Galuth* Judaism lies with us, and the challenge to our understanding is written largely on the surface of contemporary Jewish life. It is a challenge which cannot be met by stepping up our techniques of fund raising or consolidating defense agencies. The statistics of our loss do not suggest the enormity of the cultural and spiritual depletion we have suffered. The millions who were done to death had maintained a society rooted in rich Jewish feeling and in the manifold variety of Jewish experience and expression. Their death marks a crisis in the conscience of mankind. It also marks the death of an epoch in Jewish history, midst horror and agony.

Lewis Mumford did not exaggerate when he said that a thousand years of history swept by between 1930 and 1940. Into that self-same decade were telescoped crucial changes in the complexion, destruction and inner strength of world Jewry. Modern Jewish history is generally believed to have begun with the French Revolution. It is the history of modern Judaism in distinction to modern Jewish history, or the history of Jews. The history of modern Judaism did not begin until more recently. As a matter of fact, in a real sense we are in the midst of its period of origin. Reform Judaism was not so much the organic result of a changed life as the convulsively improvised response to it. The large, rooted Jewish communal life in Eastern Europe, preserving in unpartitioned fullness the dynamics of our past tradition and history, endowed us in America with spiritual power and provided us with a stream of types and personalities fashioned in its social foundry.

When we spoke of reinterpreting or reconstructing the tradition, we were placing a superstructure of interpretation upon a base sufficiently solid and strong to support our revisions. Whether we were aware of it or not, our amendments to Judaism had as their background that full-blooded Jewish center with its Volozhins, Vilnas, Odessas and Warsaws—the home of Gaon, Baal Shem, student, scholar and saint. Today our adaptations have as their background inertness, flatness and a process of pervasive corrosion and disintegration. Ours is the God-like task of creating a world to supplant the world that has gone down in destruction and ashes. Ours is not simply the task of reforming alone, but also of forming; not solely of reconstructing but likewise of constructing; not merely of re-interpreting but more importantly of interpreting Judaism to Jews. The Jews for whom we are called to devise a Jewish philosophy and rationale are not Jews whose conceptions of Judaism have become outdated and are in need of revision, but are individuals with no conception of Judaism at all. Our approach to the problem must therefore be seen in this new perspective.

Nor must we fall into the error of placing unreasonable reliance for our salvation as a Jewish community upon Eretz Yisrael. At the convention of the United Synagogue we do not have to protest our Zionism. If there is anything upon which we are indivisible and united, it is on the role which Palestine plays in our thinking. In every community where there is a conservative congregation, its membership and rabbi form the backbone of the local Zionist movement. So I speak without any fear of being misunderstood or that my Zionist loyalty will be suspected.

The role of Eretz is secure and central in the economy of Jewish life but its influence is not exclusively the coefficient of its own spiritual power. The students of Chassidism tell us that Chassidism conceives of God as "One who is good and does good." From Him there emanates in a perpetual stream divine grace to fill the atmosphere of the universe. But, alas, that divine grace does not always enter the world of mortals, for often it does not meet with the capacity on the part of men to receive the celestial influences from above. It is thus with Eretz Israel. Eretz may practice affluence without exerting influence.

The ability to export currents of cultural power must be matched by the ability to receive them. Ours must be a spiritual absorptive capacity. This quality depends upon the kind of Jewish attitudes that dominate our own community, the character of Jewish personalities that we develop, the caliber and effectiveness of our leadership and institutions in creating a climate hospitable and congenial to an influx of incoming, enriching, positive influences streaming from Eretz Israel.

The goals we recognize as being proper to our movement rest on our Jewish aspirations and upon a number of premises we believe to be irrefutable. No transplantation of a rooted Jewish life from one community to another is possible. Even as life is traffic between personality and environment, history results from the meeting of culture and experience. Our environment and experience differ radically from the past. It is inevitable that our Jewish culture and Jewish personalities will differ to the same degree. An organic Jewish life must be related to the particular setting in time and space in which it finds itself. The great Jewish centers that arose in Babylon, Spain, Franco-German settlement, Eastern Europe, developed their own physiognomy in terms of their historic era and social background. A Judah Halevi is inconceivable in Germany, a Judah Hasid unimaginable in Spain. Such a process of interaction with the environment did not, in the past, and need not, in the present, spell a breach in the continuity of the total Jewish experience.

American Judaism, likewise, if it is to enrich the lives of Jews, must be inextricably related to the conditions and circumstances of our society. Our life is marked by a greater involvement on the part of masses of Jews with the cultural, political and social forces and forms in the larger group in the midst of which we live. Our relationship to that larger group and its milieu is characterized by a community of interest and an identification of purpose which were never shared by as large a portion of a Jewish settlement in any previous period. Many needs hitherto filled exclusively by Jewish instrumentalities and outlets are now filled by American life. Less time, energy and need for specific Jewish experience is the inevitable result. There can be no iron curtain dividing our Jewish from our American lives. A convention such as this must see itself vis-à-vis the problem of our people and tradition in our time, and likewise vis-à-vis the American scene in which we have a deep stake and of which we are a part. We cannot abdicate our American obligations and interests any more than we should renounce our Jewish beliefs and concerns.

This revolutionary impact upon the daily course of our lives is likewise felt in our attitudes, ideas and conceptions. It is not only the behavior of Jews that has changed, it is their mentality. To meet that impact it will be necessary to achieve a pace of adjustment to it, which corresponds to the rapidity with which change has come into our lives. No gradual and slow process of interpretation or geologic rate of adaptation will suffice either to evolve a Judaism compatible with our needs and our new mode of existence or with effecting a narrowing of the growing gap between Jews and Judaism in this country.

Lloyd George once said that the most dangerous thing in the world is the attempt to leap a chasm in two jumps. That is what we have been trying. There have been other periods when the historic dislocation was so great that the customary process of interpretation geared to a slow moving, normally developing society had to be abandoned, although legally the procedure of change followed, or seemed to follow, the traditional legal pattern. The change from sacrifice to prayer, from temple to synagogue service, constituted basic changes which were more than orderly re-interpretations within the framework of the tradition. Life made imperious demands which Judaism could not deny.

It is not within the province of this presentation to deal with method or extent of change. Laymen have a great stake in it. We are talking about the pattern of Jewish living, of your children and mine. However, if the above analysis has any validity, it implies that you must exert pressure through your congregation and through your rabbi. That in such spheres of Jewish law as Sabbath, dietary laws, divorce laws, laws relating to the problem of the *agunah*, laws touching the priesthood, we cannot any longer be content with revisions by the strict, slow process of law. Nor can we transfer that responsibility to any other community, not even to Eretz Israel.

We must clearly and unambiguously articulate our conception of ritual observance as it is implicit in our philosophy and our behavior. The standards, insights and values which are permanently naturalized in our outlook as modern men cannot be segregated when we deliberate upon our problem as Jews. Observance is not for us a supernaturally ordained regimen, but the vehicle of Jewish discipline and unity and the stimulus to refinement of our spiritual life. We must deal with the system of practice in the light of such a view of it and stop hiding behind double meaning phrases. Nor do I have any patience with the frequently reiterated fear that any change is dangerous, since it will lead to a flood of changes. Such a fear simply means that we leave change to the haphazard environmental influences or to the anarchic will of any individual. It means a perpetration of a chaotic status-quo and the elimination of human control and will from governing men's affairs.

If our faith is so feeble that it may catch its death of cold when we open the slightest aperture in its closed self containment, then we must surrender all hope of preserving it under the present conditions of our life. The trouble with our movement is that we have good brakes but we lack an accelerator. Our own paralysis in effecting a bold and reasoned adaptation, both to the inner world of our own ideas and needs and feelings, and to the outer world in which we live, is not equalled by a comparable paralysis on the part of the forces of life. Even as we sit here this evening they continue to nullify, destroy, revoke, erase with frightening thoroughness, the laws we cherish. We owe it to our people to guide them in energizing Jewish practice so that it serves contemporary purposes, and free ourselves from those superstitions from which we came to liberate American Jews.

And we must seek a clarification of our basic philosophy of Judaism which once again in unambiguous and unmistakable language will express those views which among ourselves and at our conference we do not hesitate to affirm. The fact that there are differences of view in our midst does not mean that there is not a body of concepts upon which there is widespread agreement. We can, I feel sure, unite on a statement which need not be final or dogmatic on such basic elements in our tradition as "Nature of Torah and its origin;" Messiah; Chosen People; Resurrection of the Dead; Reward and Punishment; Providence. Such a statement would not alone organize our common views, but also begin to prepare those cohesions which can unite our individual synagogues into a single movement. Thus far we are united only by an organization and by a school. We must develop that inner cement of a common conception — else our movement, for all of its techniques, will disintegrate or become impotent.

We must seek to make of our movement a factor and force in another transition, the transition of American Jewry from aggregation to center, from settlement to community. Obviously, the very existence of a large aggregation of Jews acts as reinforcement to the powers of survival and as a dam upon the corrosive and disintegrating impacts upon our group integrity. The rabbis even proposed a blessing to be recited when one sees large gatherings of our people.

Aggregation, however, is a physical fact, a statistical phenomenon, whereas a community is the product of historic, cultural and spiritual forces. An aggregation is in a sense a pre-historical, sub-conscious society which rises to the threshold of historic power when proximity and numbers are translated into an inner co-hesiveness. The common descent of individuals becomes, in the case of a community, fortified by common activities, interests, loyalties and an inner sense of social and spiritual togetherness. The very recency of the settlement of large numbers of Jews in our land is, of course, a factor in our failure to reach the level of community status. The responsibilities which world conditions thrust upon us to engage in welfare activities on a large scale since World War I for the relief and rehabilitation of Jews in other lands have given a one-sided direction to our collective Jewish life.

But the confusions and timidities of our official leadership, and the inadequacy of our formulated conceptions, play a not unimportant part in the retardation of our communal develop-ment. A conscious goal of our activities must be the achievement of a community life, marked by self-acceptance and self-identifica-tion as Jews and the placing of ourselves in the line of historic continuity and progress. American Jewry in its present immaturity still suffers from a type of isolationism in time, not viewing itself under the aspect of Jewish history.

We can and should contribute to the attainment of the larger perspective. A settlement, functioning on the sub-community level, sees its primary functions in terms of elemental motivations, such as fear and pity. Neither of these is a healthy base for community organization. They breed a paternalistic leadership regarding it-self as the guardian of a constituency composed of waifs and dependents. The Jewish community must become democratically organized and admit to representation the masses of Jews who are presently disenfranchised. We must give evidences of greater thought on this problem and seek to play our part in the establish-ment of such a community.

The tempo and temper of modern life have brought about emotional disturbance, spiritual confusion, personal instability. While a community is more than the sum of its individuals, it has of course no meaning apart from the life of those individuals. The malaise of numbers of such men, victims of the stresses and tensions of contemporary society, cannot but react on the soundness of the whole community. In a more organized and planned manner must we equip ourselves to deal with the personal problems of our people. The rabbi must be trained in handling insecurities, fears, loneliness, guilt complexes and other symptoms of basic maladjustment of men and women. Our synagogues cannot overlook this field, and should accept as not the least of their functions, the obligation consciously to aid in bringing about better emotional balance and more wholesome attitudes towards self, towards others, towards the whole of life on the part of those in the community who need guidance and psychological reinforcement. I believe that if we are aware of the problem and accept our responsibility with regard to it we shall muster the wisdom necessary for meeting it.

The age in which we live confronts us with a spiritual challenge and opportunity which we cannot overestimate. Our locale is the American scene, though as Jews the range of our responsibility and zealous interest extends far beyond it. We are, however, part of American life in more than any accidental or even physical sense alone. We are woven deeply into the fabric of America and live a considerable part of our lives in the wide area of mutuality common to all Americans. The spiritual problems of America are our problems, and the perplexities and conflicts of our time touch us deeply.

Every age is in a sense a crucial age, and every epoch a time of transition. Life is dynamic and flows restlessly from level to level. The present unites the past with the future. We are the children of our ancestry and the forebears of our posterity— biologically, socially and culturally. That is the transitional aspect of any period in history. The decisions any one age makes are "crucial" since they have consequences far beyond its own duration. The crucial and transitional character of an era has, however, rarely expressed itself in such global and explosive manifestations as in our own. The newspaper daily brings us corroboration of this estimate. We do not touch the root of the problem of our time, until, having probed beneath its economic and political expressions, we come to the real and basic malady which is spiritual and moral in essence. We have not the ethical sensitivity adequate to the news conditions of life — the interrelatedness into which we are, perforce, thrown with all the people of earth, the immense skill for destructiveness which we wield. And here I might mention that it was my doubtful privilege to walk amidst the ruins of

Hiroshima. It wasn't the ruins that depressed us then, because by that time when we came to that fateful city, we had seen much of the Orient in shambles. We had seen Tokyo, one of the greatest cities of the world, reduced to ashes, but as you walked through the streets of Hiroshima you were aware that something had entered human life, a new dimension of destruction; a new havoc, global in its scope, had now come into human history for the first time. And you wondered whether that power would be used to destroy us so that even historians would not survive to write a decent epitaph on the collective grave of mankind.

These new facts in our life require a larger vision and larger loyalty than we have attained. There is needed a moral revitalization, a spiritual reinforcement of our political policy, an ethical wisdom with which to make economic decisions that are wise and just. These problems must re-echo in our life and we must seek through our religious tradition to add to the strength of the moral forces of our land. Our faith in the possibility of ordering our lives through human intelligence and goodness, and the passion for justice with which our tradition is vibrant must flow through our movement into the mainstream of American life. Until we are well on the road to world understanding, world justice and world peace, we are "dead men on a furlough," "playing golf across the burned hills of hell."

To attempt a program of the magnitude that has been here suggested, we shall have to draw closer one to another. We shall have to join synagogue to synagogue in a disciplined purposeful movement that becomes a spiritual force. We shall have to overcome parochialism, timidity and confusion within our own ranks.

Aristotle points out that the distinction between a craftsman and scientist is that the former develops skill in the "sphere of being," the latter in the "sphere of coming to be." We have a great opportunity to work in the "sphere of coming to be" of an American Jewish life, informed with dignity, spiritual power and Jewish understanding. May it never be said of us that faced by a great opportunity we lacked the will and vision to meet it. May American Jewry, through us, fulfill the ancient prophecy, "And they that be of thee shall build the old waste places. Thou shalt raise up the foundations of many generations. And thou shalt be called the repairer of the breach, the restorer of paths to dwell in."

TOWARD THE FORMULATION OF GUIDING PRINCIPLES FOR THE CONSERVATIVE MOVEMENT*

By Rabbi Mordecai M. Kaplan

INTRODUCTION

The establishment of the State of Israel is the second challenge of the modern world to the survival of Judaism. The first challenge came about 150 years ago, when Jews began to be emancipated from political and economic thraldom and to be admitted into the body politic of western mankind. We have not yet recovered from the impact of that first challenge. Coming on top of that, the challenge implicit in the creation of the new State has hardly penetrated our consciousness. Those of us who are active in Jewish life are too pre-occupied with the desperately urgent overseas needs of our people to have a mind for what is happening to Jewish life here. We assume that the large scale campaigns for U. J. A., Federations and the defense organizations are evidence of an inherent vitality in American Judaism. We point with pride to the many synagogues and community centers which have been built recently. We forget, however, that, except on the High Holidays, the average synagogue attendance of our congregations seldom amounts to more than ten percent of their memberships, and that the memberships themselves in the large cities, where 85 per cent

---

* An address delivered at a Conference of the Rabbinical Assembly, December 1949.

of our people live, amount to less than ten percent of the Jewish population. We forget that the Jewish birthrate in this country is perilously small. We forget that more and more of our children are getting less and less of a Jewish education. We forget that more and more of our Jewish social workers in the ramified activities of Jewish life care less and less about what is going to happen to our Jewish heritage, so long as they can keep anti-Semitism at bay.

To none but incurable or professional optimists can our present situation appear as anything less than bewilderingly complex, and the prospects of a future for Diaspora Judaism as anything but dim. In his latest book *Promise and Fulfillment*, Koestler reiterates his assumption that for Jews to retain their group identity in the Diaspora is to perpetuate an anachronism. Those who do he considers sentimentalists who have no right "to place the ominous knapsack now void of contents on their children who have not asked for it." As for the State of Israel, he is certain that "within a generation or two it will have become an entirely 'un-Jewish' country." Granted that Koestler has never known Judaism, that he is far too alienated from it to comprehend its inexhaustible vitality and its pathos, and that he is too dejudaized to appreciate the hopes for the renaissance of Jewish life that have been focused on Eretz Yisrael. But the fact is that he is too much the student of human nature and society for us to brush him aside. Moreover, in his opinion concerning Diaspora Jewry, he is voicing what is actually in the mind of most Jewish opinion-makers in all walks of life, even among those who are active participants in the upbuilding of Israel. Even if those opinions were no more than the expression of wishful thinking, the very circumstance that so many Jews of light and leading should wish to see Judaism liquidated is enough of a danger signal for those of us who are concerned with its conservation and enhancement. We should, therefore, take thought and reappraise our efforts with a view to concentrating them where they are most desperately needed.

We synagogue Jews must begin to realize that *our response to the first challenge, the challenge of the emancipation and incorporation in the general body politic, has virtually incapacitated us for an effective response to the second challenge, that of the establishment of the State of Israel.* The first response has divided us into four distinct groups, each with its own ideology. The ideologies have become largely outdated.

Their dividing lines are considerably faded, so that they merge into one another like the colors of the rainbow. But the four groups have established their own organizations and institutions and have developed their own loyalties. The question is what shall these groups do? To ask them to realign themselves is to expect water to run uphill. On the other hand, as will be shown presently, there is nothing so urgent nowadays as for all Jews throughout the world to present a common spiritual front against the menace of Jewish self-liquidation. The only feasible strategy is for each existing group to do two things: 1) propose some formula as a common meeting ground for all groups on the highest possible level of common purpose, and 2) redefine or reformulate those of its principles and practices that had led it to take issue with the other groups. In line with this strategy, I submit the following analysis and program for the Conservative group.

It is necessary, in the first place, to recall how affirmative Jews—by which term I mean those who wish to remain Jews—responded to the challenge of the Jewish emancipation. That challenge, it must be remembered, was accompanied by the challenge of what is known as the "Enlightenment," or modernism, with its displacement of traditional ideas about God, man and the world. Jews became divided into four sections: Reform, Orthodox, Conservative and Secularist. According to Reform, the justification for Jewish survival was henceforth to be based upon the need for maintaining Jewish religion as a historically evolved ethical monotheism. Orthodoxy has stressed the need for keeping alive the only religion that can claim to have been supernaturally revealed. Jewish secularism has taken the position that Jews possess a national culture which, when secularized in keeping with modernism, is for those who share it its own justification. Conservatism, formerly designed as "positive-historical Judaism," at first took an intermediate position between Reform and Orthodoxy, and since the rise of Zionism, between Reform and Secularism. That explains why Conservatism has found it difficult to formulate as clear an ideology as the three other groups. That, however, has not prevented Conservatism from being a constructive force in Jewish life. It has offered a haven to affirmative Jews who could not conscientiously hew to the line of any of the other three ideologies.

Secondly, it is necessary to realize wherein that fourfold grouping, as it exists at present, incapacitates Jews to respond constructively to the challenge which inheres in the establishment of Israel. The question which Jews everywhere will have to answer is: What is henceforth to be their status as an identifiable society? Or, what is to be the basis of their unity? That sounds very much like the very question that Napoleon put to the Jews when he convened a body of Jewish notables whom he labelled "Sanhedrin," and who were expected to sign on the dotted line. Or like the question which non-Jewish statesmen have been trying to answer, whenever they sought to vindicate civic rights for Jews. But the truth is that the question of status with which the rise of Israel confronts us is an entirely different one. The old question was that of status vis-à-vis the non-Jewish environment, or the state of which we were citizens. The adoption of religious pluralism in Western Europe, or of separation of State and Church in the United States, has settled that question once and for all, except in the minds of pettifogging Jews and non-Jews. However, the new question is: What is henceforth to be the status of Jews in relation *to one another and to the Jewish group as a whole?*

The lack of a definite answer to that question, an answer that should satisfy the average affirmative Jew, stands in the way of a normal relationship of the individual Jew to the rest of his people. That abnormality is becoming particularly acute as a result of the prevailing attitude of Jews in Israel. They naturally assume that the only understandable status of Jews in relation to fellow-Jews is that of nationhood. They interpret the establishment of Israel as *kibbutz galuyot,* as a call to all Jews who wish to remain Jews to migrate to Israel. That assumption cannot but place in a predicament all who wish to continue living as Jews elsewhere. It is a more serious predicament, both psychologically and from the standpoint of Judaism, than even the one in which Jews found themselves when they had to define their position as Jews in relation to the states that conferred upon them the rights of citizenship.

The need of extricating ourselves from this predicament is dictated not merely by our interest, as a Conservative group, in strenghtening our own institutions, but by the fact that the matter of inner status—in contrast with outer status vis-à-vis non-Jews—is decisive of the fate of Judaism as a whole. Whatever any individual or group can do to clarify that inner status is a service in the benefit of which all Jews can share.

Why is the matter of inner status of such decisive and, at this time, of such urgent importance? The answer is: Because being a Jew is, first and foremost, a matter of belonging, even before it is a matter of believing. *We belong as Jews before we come to believe as Jews.* By the time the Jewish child becomes self-aware, he finds himself a Jew. He realizes that, whether he likes it or not, he belongs to an historic group. Outside Eretz Yisrael, he cannot take the fact of his belonging for granted. First his parents and then he, himself, must do something about it; they must either accept it or abjure it. In either case, they have to make use of some kind of rationale. On the other hand, if they shy away from the question altogether, they can only end up with inner conflict and spiritual malaise.

Insofar as being a Jew is a matter of belonging, it presupposes some congregate entity with a definite status, just as being a soldier presupposes the existence of an army. One cannot be a Jew individually, as one cannot become a soldier merely by putting on a soldier's uniform. Axiomatic as all this is, it is generally overlooked. No wonder it comes like news when a Hillel director writes in the following vein: "Entrusted with a student community representing different religious, social and economic backgrounds, he must provide his students with a sense of Jewish identification and a sense of Jewish community." What that rabbi, like most of his colleagues, does not realize is that most well attended courses on Judaism and the most successful socials are not enough to provide "a sense of Jewish identification and a sense of Jewish community." Belonging to a congregation at best gives a sense of Jewish identification, but hardly a sense of Jewish community, if by community we mean an active bond of creative unity with fellow-Jews. The reason it is impossible to inculcate that kind of community sense is that *there is at present no consensus among Jews as to what is to unite them, or what their status is as a society in relation to one another.*

If Jews were merely an ethnic or kinship community, they would have no reason, other than a sentimental one, for fostering their unity. Even the assumption that the religion which united the Jews in the past was evolved by them in accordance with the operation of historical forces, aided by a line of prophets and sages, is not sufficient as a basis for continued unity or specific group status. Most of the spiritual values in Jewish religion which have a universal significance have become the common property of mankind, and are not a sufficient reason for Jewish survival. To maintain that the Jews throughout the world constitute a nation, and that their status is one of nationhood, would, in the face of present reality, be nothing less than absurd. That reality is the creation of the State of Israel. That means that those who wish to belong to a nation that is predominantly Jewish have to live in Eretz Yisrael.

What alternative status remains for Jews outside Eretz Yisrael to that of ethnic community, religious community, and nation? So long as we leave that question unanswered, we lack the essential motivation for living as Jews, a motivation that can come only from belonging to a group or society that knows what it is and is passionately eager to retain its character. The finest engine in the world, set on the best steel tracks on the soundest roadbed, cannot be made to run without fuel, or electric power. It would have been impossible for the automobile to come into use and to give rise to a new great industry, if the enormous resources of gas and oil had not been discovered at the same time. So long as we Jews in the Diaspora have no definite group status, all our efforts to increase synagogue attendance, or the religious school population, or center activites, cannot produce lasting results, because the motive power necessary to sustain them is lacking.

We cannot subscribe to the proposal of various Orthodox groups outside Israel that the Rabbinate in Eretz Yisrael be recognized as the authoritative body to legislate and speak for world Jewry. That kind of political ecclesiasticism might conceivably have an appeal to ten per cent of the Jewish population in this country. Our most urgent task, therefore, is to find what status shall unite Jews in Israel with those outside Israel, as well as all affirmative Jews, to whichever of the four previously described sections they belong. No section of Jewry is exempt from that task. In what follows I shall attempt to set forth, first the main principles which might constitute a meeting ground for all the four groups in American Jewish life, and secondly the principles on which the different trends in the Conservative movement itself might unite.

I

1. The need for adopting the status of peoplehood.

The Conservative section should propose for the over-all uniting bond of Jews throughout the world the status of people (*Am*). "People" is an old traditional term into which new content will have to be put, if it is to serve the purpose here proposed. Most of the old content will have to be retrieved. For those who are no longer at home in the traditional universe of discourse, that old content will have to be restated and reinterpreted, in terms that are in keeping with their modern outlook. But what is of much more importance is that its theoretic implications and practical applications be fully set forth.

Our entire tradition throbs with the emotion which the sense of oneness with the people of Israel evoked from the Jew. The most passionate outcry of the Jewish soul is not "The Lord, He is God," but "Hear O Israel, the Lord our God, the Lord is One," as if to imply that before you can grasp the true meaning of God's unity, you have to identify yourself with the people of Israel. The concept Israel is, in tradition, given a significance coordinate with that of God and of Torah, as may be gathered from the popular oral dictum that God, Israel and Torah are one. In the Rabbinic writings, Israel is designated as not only a nation but as a *kenesset*, or *ecclesia*. That new term was invented in order to focus attention on the distinctive kind of inner status by which Jews wished to identify themselves. To fortify their awareness of this unique status they added a most unlikely book to their sacred canon, the Song of Songs, in order to symbolize what that status implies for Israel's relationship to God. We miss what is great in the medieval sacred poetry of a Halevi, an Ibn Gabirol or a Samuel Hannagid, if we fail to note the passionate love that it breathes for the people of Israel. Hasidism escapes our understanding if we do not discern at the heart of it the mystic apotheosis of the Jewish people.

It is only in the modern movements in Judaism which are a reaction to the challenge of modern civilization that the Jewish people ceased to figure in the consciousness of the Jew as more than a vague concept emptied of any soul stirring content. The only exception is Solomon Schechter's attempt to put back such content into it. It is that which he tried to express by means of the rather unfortunate term "Catholic Israel," unfortunate because of its English High Church undertones. But what it meant to him still applies. "Since the interpretation of Scripture," said Schechter, "or the Secondary Meaning is mainly a product of changing historical influences, it follows that the center of authority is actually removed from the Bible and placed in some *living body*, which by reason of its being in touch with the ideal aspirations and religious need of the age, is best able to determine the nature of the Secondary Meaning. This living body is not represented, however, by any section of the nation, or any corporate priesthood, or Rabbihood, but by the collective conscience of Catholic Israel as embodied in the Universal Synagogue." Schechter was eager to find some concrete way of placing the awareness of that "living body" in the center of Jewish consciousness. It was that which made him an ardent Zionist, and reconciled him to so outstanding a secularist as Ahad Ha'Am.

The time has come for all affirmative Jews to recapture that long lost experience of oneness with the people of Israel past, present and future. That should be easy for those who subscribe to the historicity of the miracles recorded in the Pentateuch. It is also attainable, however, by those who regard those stories as legends. The miracle of the Jewish people itself, in its struggle not only to survive but to find meaning in its survival, is enough to evoke the emotional response of *ahavat Yisrael*. In recent years that response has come to be recognized as qualified to fill the void left in the hearts and minds of Jews, which have been emptied of the traditional religious dogmas. Out of that growing sentiment we need to distil a vivid awareness of the "living body" of the Jewish people, together with a warm sense of the interdependence of all Jews, which constitutes their peoplehood. The basis for that sense of interdependence is the fact that *every Jew depends upon his fellow-Jews for the energy, resources and courage wherewith to be a Jew*. That interdependence is now in need of being given formal recognition by means of a formal covenant to be entered into by all sections of Jewry and to be morally binding upon all affirmative Jews. Peoplehood so understood should be accorded that same devout respect as is accorded to such bodies as churches. That involves deepening the meaning of religion, so that *peoplehood, in satisfying some of the deepest yearnings of the human spirit, could come well within the category of religious concepts.* On the other hand, it also involves such broadening of the meaning of religion as to render it compatible with theological pluralism. Religion, in that sense, has room for diverse interpretations of its function and place in human life, and for a variety of ritual practices to accompany those interpretations.

The fostering of the sense of peoplehood and the translation of it into an effective program of Jewish life and growth call for the acceptance of the following principles for world Jewry as a whole.

2. The indispensability of the Jewish community in Israel as the hub of the Jewish people.

With the diverse civilizations and cultures among which the Jewish people seemed destined to remain dispersed, a few abstract religious dogmas and rites, even if they were generally subscribed to, would have failed to give all Jews an active sense of unity and interdependence. The truth is that, despite the religious uniformity that obtained among the Jewish communities in pre-modern times, they had little connection with one another. Each was an island unto himself. What the Jews lost through disparateness of communities they made up by their common devotion to the Torah and the Rabbinic interpretation of it. Now, however, the disparateness itself has to give way to unity. Never since Jews have been scattered have Jewish communities been so drawn together, on the one hand, by the dire need for help, and on the other, by the generous desire to be of help. But for want of any common objective to produce a sense of common destiny, the drawing together of the different Jewish communities has been sterile. Where the uniting factor has been the need of combatting the common enemy, anti-Semitism, it has inevitably given rise to a sense of common destiny, only to awaken rebellion against such a destiny. The Zionist movement received its main impulse from that rebellion. The desire to avoid, wherever possible, controversial issues and the need of confining itself to practical projects have prevented Zionism from concerning itself with the task of providing a common objective that might give all Jews, wherever they chose to live, a sense of common destiny.

Now, however, that the State of Israel is a reality, the Jewish community which is there will have to function as a hub in holding together the different segments of our people throughout the world. Interest in its growth, not only economically but socially and spiritually, must never flag. What has been often referred to as a two-way passage must be established between Israel and every segment of world Jewry. Not only should young people of leadership calibre acquire some part of their education of a general or technical character in the educational institutions of Israel or in one of the collective colonies, but Israel's youth of the same calibre should be given an opportunity to get part of their training in countries where Jews live in large numbers. One way of assuring a profound interest in the development in Israel on the part of the Diaspora Jewry is, no doubt, that self-involvement which comes with investment in industrial or agricultural undertakings. Such investment should be neither philanthropic nor speculative. The rate of interest should be in keeping with the public welfare of the Israeli State. Such investment should be treated as the modern form of the highly important *mitzvah* of *yishuv Eretz Yisrael*.

3. *The recognition of theological diversity as legitimate and normal.*

Even on the assumption that tradition was infallible, it never was possible to accept the requirement of uniformity of belief and practice as a prerequisite to Jewish unity. That very assumption, however, is today challenged as never before. With most Jews in our day acquiring basic literacy in non-Jewish schools, and absorbing there the general spirit of questioning and criticism, it is altogether improbable that we shall ever again develop a consensus on the infallibility of tradition. Freedom of thought and the right to differ are today no longer merely intellectual but moral issues. To deny freedom of thought in Jewish life at the same time that, as citizens of the democratic states where alone they are likely to enjoy human rights, Jews have to be among the foremost defenders of freedom of thought is to render them subject to debilitating schizophrenia. We surely cannot afford to jeopardize the mental health and moral integrity of our people. If these require, as they unquestionably do now more than ever in the past, that Jews feel unrestricted in their thinking, provided it is done in the sincere pursuit of truth, *it is essential to explore all available means to Jewish unity, so that it shall be unnecessary to depend upon uniformity.* We cannot hope to build Jewish life on a negation of democracy. Democracy implies that there are enough interests in common among human beings to unite them, without demanding of them to think alike and act alike. If our conception of religion is to measure up to the highest ethical aspirations of mankind, it surely cannot disregard that ethical standard of democracy. It is, therefore, in the interest of religion itself that freedom of thought and its natural outcome, diversity of theological views and interpretations, be henceforth accepted as normal and legitimate.

4. The broadening of the concept of religion to enable the Jewish people to designate itself as a religious community.

Though this principle superficially resembles that which the Reform movement enunciated in response to the challenge of the Emancipation, it has a radically different denotation and connotation. In the first place, this principle asks for something that does not yet exist, and that certainly did not exist in the early days of the Emancipation. It asks that we Jews who have contributed to the religious life of mankind continue to be creative in the sphere of religion. The creativity it asks for is to take the form not of imparting abstract doctrine but of being a living illustration of what we mean by religion. That has always been the method of Jewish religious creativity. That method we should now use to illustrate what we mean by religion in the modern world. *To us as a people, religion must henceforth mean the self-expression of a historical community in terms of the highest spiritual aspirations for the individuals who compose it, as well as for all other communities in the world.*

We Jews are impelled to foster that broader conception of religion, which permits theological differences, not only in order to reconstitue our unity, but also in order to make ourselves understood by our neighbors. To our neighbors the only understandable reason for wishing to maintain our corporate unity and identity can be some particular version of religon. A version like the one suggested, which allows for theological pluralism, is one that mankind is as much in need of today, as it was in need of monotheism when paganism was dominant. By accepting that version of religion we would not be repeating the step taken by the Reform movement, when it renounced all hopes of nationhood and claims on Eretz Yisrael, and declared that religion is the only bond of Jewish unity and that Jews constituted only a religious community. On the contrary, we would be giving to the concept religion a much broader and deeper sense, one far more in keeping with the part that religion has actually played in human life, than could have been contemplated by the founders of the Reform movement. Moreover, we would at the same time be vindicating a far more intensive and dynamic unity among Jews themselves than could have been possible with the conventional notions of religion current in the days of those founders.

5. The need for Jewish education.

If we do not agree on theology, we agree on the centrality of Torah, in its broadest sense, as the search after the way of life that leads to salvation both individual and social. Torah was never intended to function as a "liberal" education, but as a mass education. It was not meant to be a leisure class privilege but a universal obligation. Though it could not serve as a means of earning a livelihood, it has always been conceived as indispensable to the art of living. We need not have uniformity of either thought or practice, but we must have universal Jewish education. The one heresy that Judaism can never tolerate is that of ignorance. Note what it is that leads Koestler to believe that Jewish parents in the Diaspora have no right to place "the ominous knapsack" of Jewish life on their children. It is because he finds that knapsack to be "void of contents." That is what Jewish life feels like to the traditionless Jew, or to the one to whom the tradition was transmitted in such mechanical fashion that he cannot see its relevance to the problems that agitate us today.

The general ignorance, pertaining to Judaism, that prevails among American Jews is staggering. Never did so many of our people know so little about so much of our spiritual heritage. Were the consequences of such Jewish illiteracy limited to intellectual deficiency, it would be deplorable enough. Unfortunately, they include the loss of inner peace and self-respect. If we fail to develop in our children an awareness of their spiritual ancestry, there necessarily remains a vacuum in their minds as to their Jewish identity. That vacuum is bound to be filled with the derisive imagery and derogatory opinions concerning Jews and Judaism that they encounter everywhere in the cultural and religious works of western civilization. Even if they receive an elementary Jewish training, but fail to continue their Jewish education during their college years, when to the derogation of Jews is added the challenge to the basic teachings of Judaism, they are likely to go through life spiritually crippled.

Furthermore, the most arduous efforts in behalf of Jewish education are certain to be neutralized by the ignorance of Judaism on the part of those who play a leading role in Jewish institutions and in Jewish activities of overseas influence. No one will suspect that those institutions and activities probably fall short of what they might have accomplished had our leaders been better informed concerning Judaism. Most people will undoubtedly conclude that Jewish knowledge must, indeed, be superfluous, since it is possible to enjoy the prestige and power of Jewish leadership without it. Some years ago, I pleaded for the establishment of a University of Judaism which would offer a basic understanding of Judaism not only to rabbis and teachers but to all who wished to serve Jewish life either in a professional or lay capacity. I still regard such a University as a *sine qua non* of Jewish vitality and unity.

It is quite evident that we can want no greater common denominator amid all the diversities among affirmative Jews than the one inherent in a renewed emphasis on the need of making provision for elementary and adult education of all Jews in the significance of their tradition, in the history of their people, in the situation confronting them at present, and in the truths bearing on the philosophy and theology of Judaism.

6. In the United States and Canada Jewish peoplehood should be mediated through local organic communities.

The most perplexing element in the problem of Jewish survival is, no doubt, the fact that to live as a Jew outside Israel is not only to move against the stream, but that, although all American Jews are, in a sense, in the same boat, there is no such thing any longer as compelling everyone of them to pull his own weight at least. Most Jews prefer to rest on their oars. To cooperate with their fellow-Jews in the upkeep of Jewish life is now optional. That makes it increasingly harder for the few who are loyal. There is only one remedy, and that is to render Jewish life a source of personal good and satisfaction. This means that *the awareness of belonging to the Jewish people must be rendered concrete and incarnate in some visible association, being part of which would bring some advantage to each individual Jew*. Merely to inculcate in the Jew a sense of awareness of his belonging to the Jewish people, and to stop at that, would be to engender in him a vague haunting sense of responsibility the exact nature of which he could not grasp — a kind of feeling which is vividly portrayed in Kafka's *Trial*.

The only way in which the peoplehood of the Jews can be made an object of flesh and blood experience is to create the human instrument without which peoplehood would remain a mere potential energy without the dynamo to actualize it. The dynamo which is needed to convert the spiritual force of our people into active energy for living as Jews is the organic community. Jews who wish to remain Jews have to be made to realize that the only way in which they can hope to attain their purpose is to form themselves into workable organic communities, these communities in turn to form a network of co-operating bodies in all matters of common interest.

The reason for stressing the organic character of the communities is that they are to be entirely different in structure and spirit from the so called communities of our day. What we have at present are not communities but miscellanies of Jews. There are organizations, societies, institutions aplenty. But they are a kind of organized chaos which gives one more a sense of frustration than of fulfillment. When we analyze them, we find them to be of two kinds, those which are purposive, in that they aim at some definite objective like social service, Zionism, defense, or in that they are meant to satisfy the need of belonging, like congregations, clubs, and fraternal orders. The purposive organizations do not concern themselves with the Jewish future of those who belong to them. Of those that seek to satisfy the need of belonging, the congregations are the only ones which attempt to spell out belonging into affiliation with the Jewish people. If they were at least united among themselves in making that purpose of theirs so prominent as to transcend their theological and class differences, the chances of Jewish survival would, undoubtedly, be considerably augmented.

But there would still be no ground for complete assurance, because to entrust the Jewish future of any aggregate of Jews to a small fraction of its members is undemocratic and unsafe.

Since the will to live as a Jew depends so much upon personal preference, every Jew must be enrolled in the endeavor to make the need for belonging a motive for wanting to belong to the Jewish people as a whole and not merely to a clique, or club, or congregation, or even a fraternal order. Translated into action, that means the formation of workable organic communities. What would render them organic would be the fact that they would function mainly as a means of helping every Jew that belongs to them to fulfill himself as a Jew, as an American and as a citizen of the world. It is not necessary at this point to go into the details of organization and affiliation, except to state that *the principle of organic community calls for the enrollment of all Jews, rich and poor, learned and ignorant, religious and non-religious, who are willing to live as Jews and to bring up their children as Jews. The acceptance and promulgation of this principle and all that it involves is the foremost duty of all Jewish spiritual leaders.*

Organic community would thus be the deliberate outcome of the attempt on the part of Jews to do what their neighbors have had to do as Christians. When the modern nationalist state began to emerge, and the hegemony of the Roman Catholic Church began to be challenged, the various Protestant churches found themselves in need of rethinking the problem not only of church dogma and church practice, but also of church polity. The very structure of the society to which the faithful belonged was a question not of practical politics but of religion. In Protestant Christianity, to this very day, the question as to what kind of social structure is best calculated to mediate the function of the church to each individual Christian is of high *religious* import.

The bearing which all this has for us Jews is a twofold one. In the first place, the experience of our Christian neighbors with the problem of polity indicates that when social changes in the world around us necessitate the reconsideration and reorganization of our own social structure or polity, we are involved in as much of a fundamentally religious problem as when the general world outlook necessitates our reconsidering and reorganizing our beliefs and practices. Moreover, whatever social structure or polity we

Jews finally agree upon as most conducive to the survival of Jewish life, no matter how many institutions or organizations conventionally designated as secular it will include, the structure as a whole will, for us Jews, have the same religious significance as the church has for our Christian neighbors. If organic community will prove to be the kind of polity best suited to perpetuate Jewish life, it will be entitled to all the rights, privileges, and immunities of all other religious bodies.

9. *The need for a formal covenant to be openly entered into by all segments of Jewry including the segment in Israel.*

In ancient times the beginning of a new epoch in the career of our people was generally marked by a formal covenant. We read of a covenant as having been entered into by the Israelites at Sinai, at the end of their journeying in the Wilderness, and at Shechem not long after their entry into the Promised Land. Of special significance are the two covenants by which our ancestors declared their allegiance to the Torah, one under Josiah and one under Ezra and Nehemiah. The act of signalizing the beginning of a new epoch by a formal covenant focuses attention upon the new elements that have come to play a role in the life of a people. It calls forth the awareness that is needed in order to reckon adequately with the new conditions under which the people must henceforth live.

In ancient times, men were not in the habit of taking note of the existence of new conditions that called for collective readjustment in attitude or way of life. If, nevertheless, in those times our ancestors deemed it necessary to take cognizance of new conditions by the formality of covenants, it is hard to understand why we should be loath to take cognizance of the revolution which is being wrought in the life of our entire people by the establishment of Israel. Of course it is not the revolution that should be the occasion of a covenant, but the new *modus vivendi* which is to emerge of it. Assuming that a *modus vivendi* will be arrived at by collective world Jewry — for without it there can be nothing but a lingering vegetative existence at best — the prospect of sealing it with a covenant in the very near future should be kept in mind. Even the very thought of such a goal would be an incentive toward furthering the means to its attainment.

The need on the part of dispersed Jewry for a formal declaration of its unity arose, indeed, the moment that unity was challenged. And challenged it was in twofold fashion as soon as Jews began to be incorporated into the general body politic, first, by those rulers of the Central and West European states who demanded of the Jewish citizens, as the price for such incorporation, the severance of all active association with the rest of world Jewry, and secondly, by the natural tendency of each local Jewry, which took on the image of its new national allegiance, to become estranged from every other local Jewry. We would probably by this time have become not merely tribalized but disintegrated beyond hope of ever being reintegrated, had not anti-Semitism made it necessary for those who managed to escape its claws to salvage those who remained in its grasp.

Now that the persecuted of our people have a haven of refuge, and that there is a possibility that the fury of anti-Semitism will subside, the danger of fragmentation is upon us once again. Indeed, the very intensification and normalization of Jewish life in Israel are apt to breed in the Jews there a "holier than thou" attitude toward their fellow-Jews in the Diaspora. That can only lead to the widening of the gap between the Jewry in Israel and the rest of world Jewry. The consequences of any such sense of distance are bound to be fatal to both. Israel would shrink into an insignificant satellite nation, moving in the orbit of one of the great world powers, and world Jewry would be condemned to complete absorption and disappearance. If either eventuality is to be averted, *we must at once begin to agitate for a great demonstrative reaffirmation of Jewish unity throughout the world, in order to keep alive the prophetic vision of the role to be played by our people in the salvation of mankind.* Such a reaffirmation should take the form of a solemn covenant to be enacted in Jerusalem. Every segment of Jewry should be represented there, and the day on which it would take place should be celebrated each year as Jewish unity day, the day when we shall have become an *Am berit*, a Covenant People.

The eventuation of that covenant calls for long range preparatory planning. In the meantime, as an integral part of that preparation, it is necessary to institute an appropriate ritual of initiation, which will habituate as large a number of men and women as possible in the significance of Jewish covenantship. The initation should be participated in by them on their attaining the age of full maturity, or at any time thereafter. The ritual should set forth the meaning of Jewish unity and its implications for the life of the individual as well as for the relation of Jews to one another and to the non-Jewish world.

II

The foregoing seven objectives which are the practical corollaries of the status of peoplehood constitute a program which the Conservative group should advocate as a common meeting ground for all Jews who want Judaism, in whichever way they conceive it, to survive and flourish. *What is of concern to Jewry as a whole should always take precedence over what can be of concern only to a fraction of Jewry.* The chances that any fraction of Jewry will succeed in attaining what it is after are naturally greater the more the stability and permanence of Jewry as a whole are assured. For that reason, while there are many matters of special concern to the Conservative group, they should always be dealt with, not necessarily after the over-all program has been provided for — that would be an entirely unreasonable postponement to expect — but at least simultaneously with the over-all program. Let it not be said that the Conservative group seems to live in a kind of spiritual shangri-la where the realities of contemporary Jewish life never reach it, and that it is too absorbed in its own interests to realize fully the moral and spiritual crisis in which we are all involved. But once we undertake to cope with the general problems and begin to take steps to implement all inclusive objectives like those suggested above, it is entirely in order for us to deal with the specific problems that grow out of the distinctive backgrounds and assumptions of the Conservative movement.

1. The need of coping with the problem of Jewish law.

There is first the problem of law. After almost half a century of existence of the Rabbinical Assembly, its various atempts to deal with that problem have gotten no further than answering questions of law in terms which might emanate from a village *dayyan* in Lithuania. Excellent use has been made of the *Shulhan Aruk* and some of the other classic authorities. With three notable exceptions—the responsa on the subject of *Kohanim* published in the Proceedings for 1928, the *takkanah* for *agunot* sponsored by the Committee on Jewish Law during the war, under the inspiration of the late Louis Epstein, and the Rabbinical Assembly Prayer Book, there has been nothing produced by us, which in any way differs from what could have been obtained from a similar group, with much less experience in the world, much less concern for the future of the Jewish people, and much less of either vital religion or high statesmanship.

While the views on Jewish law among us are probably as numerous as our members themselves, we can generally be grouped under three headings. There are the Rightists, for whom the present situation seems quite satisfactory. There are the Centrists, who regard the present situation as anomalous, but who believe that any advances in the field of Jewish law ought to be predicated on our ability to discover authority for it within the traditional literature. There are the Leftists—among whom, as everyone here and elsewhere knows, I count myself—who have been hoping that the Law Committee would resort to traditional law for the rendering of decisions whenever the conditions under which the law arose were anywhere near like those which still obtain today. Otherwise the committee would venture beyond the traditional law, and render decisions on the basis of certain desirable consequences of a moral and spiritual character to Jewish life. The theoretic basis of the Rightist group is clear; it is that of Jewish law as it has been lived throughout the centuries. The basis of the division between the Centrists and Leftists has never been clearly formulated. The fact is that underlying the approach of the Centrist group is the same *theocratic* conception of the law as that which underlies the Orthodox approach. What for us Jews might be the alternative to a *theocratic* conception of the law has never been thought through. At the convention in Chicago in 1948, a Law Committee was appointed, in which all the three foregoing trends were represented. That Committee has met several times in the course of the year. It reported at the regular annual convention last June, and will report again at the forthcoming convention. That report should be thoroughly discussed, and the Committee should be instructed by the Convention whether to proceed along the lines of last year's activities or adopt a new approach, or whether the Committee itself should undergo reorganization. The Rabbinical Assembly should feel perfectly free to proceed with the problem of Jewish Law as its own wisdom dictates.

A priori it might seem impossible for the three groups into which the members of the Rabbinical Assembly divide themselves in their attitude toward Jewish law to find a common basis for consensus in matters concerning which there is a legal pronouncement in our tradition. The fact, however, is that the present Law Committee which consists of representatives of the three groups, Right, Center and Left, has managed to avoid getting itself into a state of deadlock, and has succeeded in achieveing consensus on some very important questions. That is due to two provisions: 1) that both majority and minority rulings be reported, leaving it to the members of the Assembly to follow whichever ruling they choose, and 2) that the Law Committee formulate standards in Jewish ritual and non-ritual practices which lie outside the scope of traditional law. How far this empirical procedure will get us only time will tell.

In the meantime, to make sure that the present effort shall bear fruit, *it is necessary that the Rabbinical Assembly give recognition which is not grudging, but welcome, not merely de facto, but de jure, to the three points of view with regard to Jewish law represented in it.* To some that may sound as heresy and as surrender to expediency. Personally, I should not take such a tragic view of the situation. On the contrary, in the light of what has been said above with regard to the recognition of diversity as not only normal but also legitimate, there is no reason why we of the Conservative movement may not exemplify the workability of such recognition in our own midst. If the matter of Jewish law were the only one in which we would have to depend for common approach and action, such diveristy might be serious. But there are so many other issues, on which we can unite and which at the same time differentiate us, from other groups, that we need have no worry about a *raison d'être* for our continuing as a distinct movement. The positive results, which would not have been achieved without what unites us among ourselves and differentiates us from every other group, are a sufficient vindication. The very freedom and latitude which have made it possible for us to work together in spite of our differences are by no means the least valuable traits of our movement. To these traits our movement, no doubt, owes much in the way of Jewish creativity.

2. The need of rendering Jewish life abundant.

The chief manifestation of the creative potential of the Conservative movement is the tendency of all who play a role in it to stress the need of rendering Jewish life as abundant and as full of soul-enriching content as the conditions under which we live permit. *We are all agreed that we should, on principle, always aim at the maximum possible in every form of Jewish self-expression, whether it be education, prayer, or the observance of the Sabbath and festivals.* In that regard we are no different from the Orthodox. But we tend to go far beyond them, and it is that tendency which we should stress and deliberately cultivate.

Permeated as we have been with the idea that welfare and salvation of the Jewish people are the nuclear realities to be considered in all our activity in behalf of Judaism, we have naturally come upon the realization that the entire gamut of esthetic values has to be placed in the service of Jewish life. Music, drama, the dance, literature, architecture, painting and sculpture can and should be utilized to express and enhance the values expressed in living as Jews. These are not to be merely ornamental. In fact, their very character as a distinct dimension of the human spirit would thereby be destroyed. They must be functional, in that they should articulate to the emotional response to life, which is intrinsic to the ethical and spiritual values in Judaism. We cannot be satisfied with merely having our Jewish heritage intellectually compatible with the most advanced thought of the day. There is not enough in the intellectual appeal to engage the entire being of the Jew. *To secure his whole-hearted devotion, Judaism must be so presented to the Jew so as to make him fall in love with life, with the world, with mankind.* He will then be impelled to find some appropriate esthetic medium for the expression of his feelings. That is the goal toward which we should move in all our efforts. Esthetic expression of Jewish life pursued in that spirit is spiritual experience of the highest order, and properly belongs to religion at its best.

It is quite evident that this approach to Judaism would enlist in its service a large share of the extraordinary amount of esthetic talent that is to be found among Jews. At present such talent contributes to the alienation from Jewish life of those who possess it, because Jewish life offers them no opportunity to express that with which their entire being is identified. Their alienation has in turn served as an excuse to the average Jew for not displaying any eagerness to cultivate his Jewish heritage, which, lacking esthetic appeal, strikes him as something remote and abstract.

The corollary which follows from this significance of esthetic values for the enhancement of Judaism is that we must aim to create a milieu that is Jewish. In natural dread of segregation and the ghetto, many of our people have come to assume that whatever is audibly, visibly or tangibly Jewish is likely to ghettoize us Jews, to set us apart from the general population. So prevalent is this assumption that many who would resent being regarded as assimilationist or as irreligious consciously or unconsciously deprecate and discourage any form of Jewish self-expression outside the synagogue. They are fearful of being or appearing too Jewish. While we can understand those apprehensions, we must realize where they are liable to lead us, if not counteracted. Counteracting them calls for the reeducation of our people in the part played by milieu, or cultural and social atmosphere, in shaping our higher life, and in having them understand that a verbalized Judaism, a Judaism which is merely a way of speaking, must inevitably become a source of ennui and boredom for the non-professional Jew. We must Judaize our homes and every institution, center or locale where we carry on Jewish activity, by creating in them a colorful distinctive Jewish atmosphere through every available esthetic means.

Another very important tendency of the Conservative movement, which it is essential to place in the general pattern of its thinking and to fortify by means of specific measures, is that of stressing the knowledge of Hebrew as indispensable to a first hand appreciation of our spiritual heritage. That tendency must now be given a rationale in terms of the new realities that constitute the Jewish scene and of new needs which confront us. The first such need is that of experiencing the very reality of the Jewish people. We hope that each organic community will mediate that reality to the individual Jew by means of what it will do to satisfy his sense of belonging. But even that is not enough. In comparison with the impact which the reality of the surrounding civilization has upon the Jew in the Diaspora, the impact even of an organic Jewish community is apt to be weak, and the reality of the Jewish people is bound to escape the individual Jew.

When you understand a sentence of any language, you experience at first hand something of the inner life and mind of the people whose language it is. If the language is that of a living people, you establish active contact with that people when you read anything in that language. If we want to bring up our children not only to call themselves Jews but to feel as Jews, we have to inculcate in them a feeling of the aliveness of the Jewish people. That cannot be done in any other way than through the medium of Hebrew. Hence Hebrew must figure prominently in our educational activities. We must see to it that wherever possible Hebrew should be taught as a language in the high-schools and colleges with large Jewish student bodies. To achieve that we have to break down the resistance not so much of non-Jews as of Jews, both parents and educators, who are mainly responsible for the slow progress which the movement to establish Hebrew in the general educational curricula has been making.

*   *   *   *   *

The foregoing presentation is not intended to preclude any alternative formulations of what should be the position taken by our movement. However, even if the specific suggestions herein made be wide of the mark, I nevertheless believe with all my heart that the future of our movement depends upon the acceptance of the following principles:

1. That it is to the highest interest of the Conservative movement to formulate a plan that would offer a common meeting ground for all affirmative Jews whether Orthodox, Reform, Conservative or Secularist.
2. That the Conservative movement should legitimatize the three groups in its own midst.
3. That the problems of Law and Standards and of Jewish life abundant are the main areas in which the distinctive character of the Conservative movement should find expression.

These principles will prove their worth only when they are embodied into a program of action and education. We should not expect all our congregations forthwith to fall into line with that kind of program. Our colleagues who head congregations which have joined our movement only in recent years will find the going hard. Let them not be soured or disheartened. Let them remember that a program based upon these principles calls for spiritual adventure no less heroic than that which culminated in the establishment of the State of Israel. Like all adventure, it entails struggle, sacrifice and infinite patience. We must, however, be prepared to take a leap of faith similar to that by which, according to Rabbinic legend, Nahshon ben Aminadab caused the waters of the Red Sea to divide for our ancestors who had been liberated from Egyptian bondage. We of the Conservative movement are so circumstanced as to be able to see Judaism in steady and integral perspective. For that very reason we are impelled to take a leading part in renewing the covenant which God has made with our people that His spirit and His teaching are never to depart from our children and our children's children.

THE THINGS THAT UNITE US*

By Rabbi Louis Finkelstein

We are all, members of the Rabbinical Assembly, vaguely aware of our fundamental unity of aim and point of view. We have our differences but, even without analyzing them, we know that they are slight in comparison with our basic agreement in essentials. Taking this agreement for granted, we prefer to discuss, when we meet, those aspects of our work and faith which divide us. This is stimulating to the mind and it emphasizes our individuality, but may tend to obscure in our own minds our basic unity. We are apt to develop the psychology of brothers in a large family, who to all outsiders look and act alike, and yet are continually bickering with one another about their minute differences of taste and manner. Who know better than we rabbis how frequently families are disrupted because a husband or wife suddenly discovers an affinity with some stranger with whom only a few casual commonplaces have been exhanged? It is only later when the harm has been done and cannot be remedied, that the realization comes that "then was it better with me than now."

As I have been listening to the papers read at our Convention and following the activities of our members I have been profoundly impressed with the need of analyzing and reducing to a rational basis our indefinite consciousness of unity. In this paper I could attempt nothing more than to take the first steps toward such an analysis. Only the more obvious truisms about our relations

---

* Address to the Rabbinical Assembly Convention, 1927.

are pointed out; the more difficult task of studying them and clarifying them must be left to further discussion. Hence you must not expect to hear what you do not already know; the purpose of this paper is not to reveal the hidden but to summarize the known

The subject inevitably divides itself into a number of headings regarding each of which there is among us fundamental agreement as well as difference in shade of opinion. I shall point out under each title as clearly as I can the extent of likeness as well as of disagreement.

I. THE CONCEPTION OF GOD

So far as I can see we all agree that the visible world of which man is a part is but an island in a sea of truth which transcends it, and which is most clearly reflected in the human mind and conscience. The evils and cruelty which form an integral part of the material world are for us not the final reality; behind them and giving them meaning is the Ultimate Good, whose validity is testified to by the human mind though not dependent on it. The spiritual truths which have always been associated with the name of God are valid independently of man's knowledge or practice of them. The prophets and lawgivers of Israel were men who more clearly than any others felt the presence of God and came most directly in contact with His spiritual being. They knew less than we about the actions and movements of physical being, but incomparably more about the laws that govern spiritual life. They felt constantly in their daily lives the presence of God that we sense only in moments of ecstasy and under particularly favorable conditions. They knew what was right by intuition, by meta-logic if you will. Their works are therefore great in the sense in which no other literature, no matter how great or how beautiful, is inspired. To see the beauty of the world as Homer or Dante or Shakespeare saw it, is an approach to an understanding of its deeper meaning; but it is not the whole of it. The prophet was not merely a poet, he was also a man of God.

God thus revealed himself to Israel through the Torah and the prophets. We say He chose Israel in the sense that Israel was more keenly aware of his Being than other people. In Israel's recognition of God we become aware of the Divine selection of

Israel. It is therefore literally true that the inspiration of the Torah and the Prophets is the expression of God's choice of Israel as His people.

For the God who revealed Himself to us through the Torah and the prophets we have the same love that the prophets and the sages felt for Him. Our heart yearns for Him like that of the psalmist whose soul "thirsted for God." We are not talking empty metaphors when we say that we feel the presence of God in the synagogue, especially on the High Holidays like Yom Kippur when our people are assembled there in greatest numbers; that at times when our minds are properly attuned we feel the exaltation of His inspiration when we read the Bible or study the Talmud or recite the prayers. But on the other hand, with all the great Jewish thinkers of the past from the writer of the Book of Chronicles, the authors of the Septuagint, and the Targumim, and with the authorities of the Talmud to Maimonides and Jehuda Ha-Levi, we feel that if God is to be made intelligible to men of intelligence as well as to others, the conception of Him must be stripped of its anthropomorphisms which satisfy only the needs of the uninitiate. We fear that the last three or four centuries have produced in Israel a deterioration of the conception of God just as they resulted in a deadening of the feeling for the Torah. And we must teach our children and our following to feel the presence of God and, at the same time, not to think of Him merely in human terms. We can as little reconcile ourselves to reducing Judaism to a cold and dispassionate doctrinism as we can hope to maintain in an age of widespread education a conception of God that marks a definite retrogression from that attained by Judah Ha-Levi and Joseph Albo. We are thus a unit even in our understanding of the ultimate basis of all religious life, and insist that only in our faith, which is frankly based on our emotions and intuition, but which we seek to formulate with proper recognition of the scientific facts that have been established, is there room for the conception of God that can remain living and effective in our children's minds.

II. OUR ATTITUDE TOWARD THE TORAH

Our attitude toward the Torah differs from that of other schools in our application to the practical life of religion of the principles and feelings which find their theoretical expression in the historical school of Jewish studies. The fundamental premises of this school may be summed up in two statements: (1) that Judaism is a developing religion which has undergone an historical and definable change through the periods of the prophets and the rabbis; (2) that this change was not one of deterioration and ossification but of growth, self-expression and foliation.

No student of history can fail to see that the Judaism of the Second Commonwealth developed, particularly toward the end, a new and widespread affection for the ceremonial observance of the Torah as well as for its study and exposition. It is in vain that we search the prophets, especially those who lived before the exile, for anything like Hillel's or R. Akiba's devotion to study for its own sake, or their readiness to sacrifice everything in order to observe the commandments. The leaders of Jewish thought in the Second Commonwealth were legalists and legislators; those who had prepared the way for them were primarily poets, prophets, visionaries and critics of the existing order.

Even in the First Commonwealth the legislator and prophet were closely associated. The codes of law in Exodus, Leviticus and Deuteronomy, though expressed in prosaic form, are so far above all contemporary codes that they can only be recognized as prophetic and divine in the same sense that the fiery words of Isaiah and Jeremiah are prophetic and divine. But there was a change of emphasis from the First Commonwealth to the Second, and perhaps it can be best summarized by saying that in prophecy Judaism was in its twenties, and in Rabbinism it had reached it-forties. This change does not warrant the use of a different terminology for the two periods. We regard it as preposterous and unscientific to distinguish the Judaism of the Second Commonwealth from that of the First by calling the faith of the prophets the religion of Israel rather than Judaism. It would be just as fair and correct to call America before 1860 by some other name, say Columbia or Indiana, because during the Civil War American opinion underwent a profound change. Pharisaism and Rabbinism are for us the legitimate and natural outgrowth of prophetic Judaism; they are more—they are its fullest expression.

Because on the one hand we regard the laws of the Torah as prophetically inspired, and because on the other we regard the legalism of the rabbis as the finest and highest expression of human ethics, we accept both the written and oral Law as binding and authoritative on ourselves and on our children after us. The Torah is for us the way of life, and Rabbinism merely the fruit into which the blossoms of prophecy ripened.

But, and here our modern outlook asserts itself, we do not regard the observance of either the written or oral Torah as an alternative to eternal perdition. The punishments with which our fathers threatened us for deviating from the ways of the Torah seem to us too naive and unsophisticated. The conception of God that lies at their basis is too immature for us and for our children. We are rather prepared to accept the dictum of the rabbis that "the punishment for a transgression is the transgression itself." If by salvation is meant spiritual peace, the satisfaction of living a worthy and good life, certainly salvation can be attained only through the observance of the commandments. But we are entirely unwilling to cajole or intimidate our following or our children into being loyal to the Torah through threats and the fear of punishment.

We are drawn to the Torah with the bonds of love for it and for its norms. We love its ceremonies, its commandments, its rules, and its spirit. We delight in its study, and find in it comfort and consolation, discipline and guidance. And it is this response to it that we want to hand down to our children. We owe our affection for it to our ancestors who have guarded it through 2000 years of suffering, and we feel that it would be a betrayal of them to yield in our adhesion to it now when we have at last attained freedom and emancipation.

These were doubtless the forces that kept our ancestors loyal to the Torah. Their fear of punishment was merely a rationalization of what was essentially emotional. We are conscious of the real urge that animates us and we are unwilling to deceive ourselves as to its essential quality. We certainly dare not, even for the sake of the Torah, establish its observance on the basis of what has come to seem to us a false rationale.

Our love for the Torah is only in part rationalistic; in the main, we need not be ashamed to confess it, it is emotional, intuitive and mystic. We find much in the Torah of which the validity can be established by science and logic. But we do not base our observance of it on mere intellectualism. We can give no mathematical reason for the joy which the Sabbath brings us. If our neighbor does not feel it he lacks the *neshamah yeterah* which he can better obtain by living our life than by listening to our arguments. Doubtless had we been born Hottentots, we could not have discovered the Torah of our own will and accord. But we are not Hottentots, and have behind us our Jewish individual and racial memories. It is these memories that are part and parcel of us and that bind us to the Torah with ties which we have no desire to sever.

III. OUR ATTITUDE TOWARD CHANGE IN CEREMONIAL

The Torah is for us not merely a joy; it is Israel's most effective protection from disintegration and assimilation. With this fact in mind, we cannot overlook the multitudes of our people who regard what are for us garlands of roses and chains of love as shackles of steel and iron. With an effort they break themselves free of these fetters, and, like Spintho in Shaw's play, run straight into the mouth of the lion.

In order to hold these men within the comity of Judaism it has been proposed to lighten their burden. Obviously, if a breach is to be made in the levee it is better to make it deliberately, thoughtfully, intentionally and intelligently so that we may control the waters. Far better that than to permit the flood to carry away home and farm, hamlet and village. Such voluntary breaches in the wall of Judaism have been made heretofore, but always their utility was first demonstrated to the satisfaction of the scholars and leaders. Today there is such a lack of authority in Judaism and the rabbis are so hopelessly divided, that it appears impossible to convince even an appreciable fraction of them of the necessity of concerted action. Some of our number have felt that these conditions demand urgent and immediate steps. They simply could not wait for the "blind mouths" to become seers and feeders and they have taken matters into their own hands.

To change the established law, even by interpretation, without concerted action of wisely recognized authorities is admittedly a revolutionary process. Yet the purpose that fills the minds of all of us is to maintain the Torah. None proposes to yield the marriage law or the Sabbath; the most rash among us have suggested only the abrogation of some customs, ceremonies and prohibitions that have arisen in the course of time, and of which the value is no longer evident to all. After all, Resh Lakish did say, "Sometimes the transgression of part of the law is the saving of the whole of it." There is all the difference in the world between proposing a change in a single law for the sake of saving the Torah and disregarding the whole of the Torah.

Still, it cannot be denied that the attitude of permitting changes in the usage of Israel by individual congregations and rabbis is untraditional and revolutionary. Revolutions can be justified in only one way—by being successful. It was revolutionary for the Babylonian Amoraim to set themselves up as judges and rabbis without the traditional Palestinian *semicha*; it was revolutionary for R. Gershom to gather a synod for the purpose of making new enactments; it was revolutionary to write down the prayers and codify the law. All of these changes, of which the least is far more radical than any proposed among us, were justified by the fact that they helped to save Judaism in crucial periods. The necessity was recognized by *Klal Yisrael*, and what had been a break with tradition became itself tradition. The American Declaration of Independence was adopted in violation of the established political order, but that did not prevent it from becoming the basis of a new order in whose tradition it is the most precious document. The will of the American people made regular what was essentially irregular, and so the living will of the Jewish people has often made proper what was at first and in essence improperly done.

If the shifting of values and the introduction of new devices will actually bring Jews back to God, to the Torah, and to the synagogue, they will doubtless be accepted. They will then take their place besides the Maccabean innovation which permitted war in self-defense on the Sabbath day; beside the Tosafistic leniencies in regard to the wine of Gentiles; besides R. Isaac Elhanan's new interpretation permitting the remarriage of a woman whose husband was drowned at sea.

But pending such proof of the value of these changes, and

pending their acceptance by all Israel, some of us prefer to stand aside and watch like Eliezer at the well "steadfastly, holding our peace, to know whether the Lord hath made their way successful or not."

As to the proposed innovations and new interpretations, there is none of us so bigoted as to refuse to cooperate with those who are attempting them, provided always that the ultimate purpose of the change is to strengthen the attachment of Israel to the whole of the Torah, and that it does not defeat its own end by striking at the fundamentals of Judaism. We could not countenance, for instance, the substitution of Sunday for the Sabbath as the main day of worship, although most of us have acquiesced in the alteration of our school curricula so as to place primary emphasis on conversational Hebrew rather than on prayers and mechanical reading, and have in one form or another accepted the late Friday evening synagogue assembly, which frankly aims to meet the religious needs of those who do not attend on Sabbath morning. To permit Sunday to supersede the Sabbath would be such a clear break with all of our past that no gain could justify it, but Judaism is definitely strengthened in this land whenever Jews who do not attend the traditional service, do come to some Sabbath gathering.

We are a unit in opposition to any attempt to put Judaism in a strait-jacket. Many, through ignorance or lack of vision, do not hesitate to insist that a practice once established shall always be retained. One is reminded of the retort made to a group of such bigoted stereotypists by the famous saint and scholar, R. Israel Lipkin-Salanter, half a century ago. The synagogue in Kovno which had been built a century earlier had, like all Lithuanian synagogues, never had a stove. When someone proposed to install some heating apparatus, opposition was raised on the ground that it would be untraditional, "It has never been done," the instransigents argued. "Why depart from the ways of our fathers?" R. Israel overwhelmed them in a moment. "Do you mean to say," he asked those who preferred to shiver traditionally rather than be comfortable in a new way, "do you think, that because our ancestors have done a foolish thing for a hundred years, we must continue their folly forever?" And the stove was installed.

IV. OUR ATTITUDE TOWARD ISRAEL

Much of the difficulty about change in the law is due to a lack of faith on the part of the Jews whose lives were narrowed by persecution. The study of Jewish history has been much neglected, and thus it has occurred that even students have grown up unaware of the accomplishments of Israel in the past. To us the development of prophecy, of the Talmud with its system of law, its codes and commentaries, of mediaeval philosophy and of Jewish poetry, are all evidences of the creative spirit of Israel. We believe with Hillel, that if the children of Israel are "not themselves prophets, they are descendants of prophets," and have in themselves potentialities of return to their ancient exalted state.

What future creations lie latent in the still growing mind of Israel we do not know. But we would encourage every attempt to create the new, provided it is not positively self-destructive. Jewish art, Jewish music, the renaissance of the Hebrew language as a medium of daily intercourse, and above all the rebuilding of the Jewish homeland, have all our enthusiastic support. We cannot accept the formula that Israel lives only for the sake of its mission of monotheism; we believe that great as monotheism is, and greater still as are the ethics of Israel, there may be yet other creations in the spirit of this people. In this we disagree also with those, who, while exalting God and the Torah, deny the power of Israel's creativity. Does not the Talmud say that Elijah was rejected as a prophet because he sought the honor of God but had neither faith nor patience with Israel?

On the other hand, we cannot agree with the various secularist groups even in the conception of Israel which they hold in common with us. We cannot, with our knowledge of anthropology and sociology, and our awareness of the infinite harm that such claims have done to other people, insist or even admit that the Jewish people has a superior germplasm. We refuse to be jingoistic, chauvinistic or bigoted in weighing our own personality. Israel is a great and ancient people; it has done great things and there is no reason for doubting its ability to create further. We love it as our people. We recognize that it has weaknesses of which we are aware, and may have more of which we are unconscious. In any event, our loyalty to it does not depend on our belief in its singular excellence. We decry any attempt to establish loyalty to it on such a basis, firstly, because it is building on quicksand, and secondly, because it is like the exaggerated and preposterous claims of Teutonic and Nordic superiority.

V. OUR ATTITUDE TOWARD PALESTINE

From what has been said, it is evident how closely we are related to each other, in opposition to other groups, in our attitude toward Palestine. We want to see Palestine rebuilt; we have for it, too, an intuitional, unreasoning and mystic love. We want to see Palestine rebuilt as the spiritual center of Israel, for in that way it can serve our people best and help solve some of our pressing problems. But aside from its help in maintaining the spiritual integrity of our dispersed communities, we look on Palestine as we do on the Torah—as an ultimate, a thing that is good in itself, whose welfare we seek for its own sake. Our formula, therefore, may be expressed thus: We want Eretz Israel established as a Jewish community; if possible as an autonomous one. We should like to persuade its present generation of colonists and workers that the interests of their people demand their observance of the Torah, and the interests of Truth their recognition of God. And yet if our arguments should prove of no avail, we, unlike all other religious groups who accept Zionism, are willing to trust the future to God and to His people.

VI. OUR ATTITUDE TOWARD THE HEBREW LANGUAGE

Every Jewish renaissance, from that of the Maccabees until our own time, has been accompanied by a revival of interest in Hebrew as a language. The Book of Jubilees, written in the first half century of Maccabean independence, stresses again and again the fact that Hebrew was the language of creation and of the patriarchs. One of the effects of the Revolution of 70, and also of the Bar Kokba rebellion, was to stimulate the use of Hebrew so that in the household it was the vernacular. R. Meir insisted that just as one must teach one's child the *Shema*, so must one teach it to speak Hebrew. We are therefore entirely sympathetic to the establishment of Hebrew as the language of conversation, Jewish literature and learning. We wish to encourage it in every way, again as a means of maintaining the integrity of the Jewish people and the Jewish spirit, and also because, like the Torah, Israel, and Palestine, it is an end in itself. We find ourselves in opposition to those who have permitted the excision of Hebrew from their prayer book, and have dropped it as a subject for instruction in their schools. A Hebrew-less Judaism we conceive to be an impossibility, or, rather, as Dr. Hertz states in his recent work, "A Hebrew-less Judaism has no future because it cannot be justly said to have a present."

On the other hand, we feel that Hebrew will always remain a holy language—that is to say, its use ought to be a religious duty rather than a chauvinistic whim. Nor can we agree with those Hebrew writers who neglect the literature of the last 1800 years from the Mishnah to our own times, and prefer phrases constructed on the basis of modern Arabic to those of traditional Hebrew. We regard some of the modern Hebraisms as sterile mongrels and oppose them because they desecrate the language which is to us as sacred as the books which were written in it. We desire in every part of our spirituality to keep alive the traditions of our people.

VII. THE SEMINARY

We thus find ourselves united in a number of important conceptions in which we all believe. Within our ranks there are wide differences of opinion as to the exact meaning of some of them, and the realtive emphasis to be placed on each of them. And yet one cannot believe that these slight differences among us would justify any separation in our ranks, in view of our substantial unity of outlook and the difficulty of serving our cause even when we are together. After all, to put the whole matter in a word, we are the only group in Israel who have a modern mind and a Jewish heart, prophetic passion and western science. It is because we have all these that we see Judaism so broadly, that we can agree with almost all elements in the constructive suggestions proposed by them, but break away from them in their arrogance and lack of foresight. And it is because we are alone in combining the two elements that can make a rational religion that we may rest convinced that, given due sacrifice and willingness on our part, the Judaism of the next generation will be saved by us. Certainly it can be saved by no other group. We have, then, before us both the highest of challenges and the greatest of opportunities. It is the knowledge of this, above all, that unites us and makes us one.

Our unity is symbolized for us by the Seminary, that institution of which we are all either the natural or adopted children. In its diversified faculty we find our own differences ably reflected. As our Alma Mater we all owe it loyalty and gratitude, and these we give the more willingly because it serves as a source of encouragement for us when sometimes we falter, and as a center around which we can always gather.

Through it we become not only comrades in arms, but also brothers. After we have said everything about our similarities and likenesses, there remains but one thing to be said, and that is we are all of us "Seminary men."

Part III
The Attitudes of Conservative Judaism

Prayer and the Prayerbook
Jewish Law
Education
The Community
Zionism

A NOTE ON THE ATTITUDES
OF CONSERVATIVE JUDAISM

The ultimate test of any system of ideas is how it functions in specific situations. In this section attention is directed to the application of the ideology of Conservative Judaism in certain areas of Jewish life. Thus, selections on prayer, education, law, Zionism and the community are included. Many other areas of Jewish activity and thought, however, are not represented by a selection. This is primarily due to the fact that there has been little writing about these subjects of a character which can be said to represent the thinking of Conservative Judaism.

The epitaph on the tombstone of Christopher Wren, who lies buried in Westminster Abbey which he designed, notes that his monument lies round about him. Much the same can be said of Conservative Jewish thought about many areas of Jewish life. The thinking has not been formalized in written statements, but it is represented in the practices of Conservative congregations throughout the country. The patterns, the attitudes and the practices in these congregations are applications of the Conservative approach and in consequence they show a substantial degree of homogeneity. The writings about them which might be included in such an anthology as this, are still to come.

The selections which are included reflect the general bent of thinking in Conservative Judaism. Where two selections on the same theme are presented, as is the case with prayer, or where a majority and minority view are included, as is the case with law, they reflect different strains of thinking which wield power in the movement.

PRAYER AND THE PRAYERBOOK

A NOTE ON PRAYER

Prayer has become a problem in modern Jewish life. On the one hand, there is a long tradition of a people dedicated to prayer and a prayer-book which has been compiled over the course of the ages. On the other hand, there are the undeniable facts that ours is not a prayerful generation, that a great many people cannot read the Hebrew prayers and that a great many more cannot understand them, that some of the phrases and concepts in the prayer-book are out of consonance with modern thinking and finally that the public services are very long. These circumstances have led to varied experiments with the prayer-book in an attempt to find a formulation which would be acceptable to the average Jewish worshipper. They have led, in most Western countries, at the very least to the printing of a translation in the language of the country side by side with the Hebrew prayers. In the extreme situation, represented by the Reform movement in the United States, most of the Hebrew has been removed from the prayer-book, a great many prayers have been eliminated and the remainder has been recast in form, expression and often in content. In less extreme circumstances, the prayers have been printed both in the Hebrew and in translation, so as to facilitate public services for groups who are not at home in the traditional prayerbook or in the Hebrew language. Some of these editions have taken liberties with the text; some with the translation; some have eliminated portions of the service. In this country alone, a sizeable number of different editions of the prayerbook have been published over the course of the last century by organizations and by individuals.

Since prayer and public services lie at the heart of any religious system, no Jewish religious body has been able to ignore the problem of making prayer more palatable to the modern Jew. Both the Conservative and Reform bodies in American Judaism have long been dedicated to the proposition that religious involvement and attendance at services could be increased by improvement of the prayer-book and better organization of the public services. The so-called "modern" Orthodox congregations have more recently accepted the same thesis. These sanguine hopes have not been justified by experience, as men like Abraham Heschel have pointed out. Nonetheless, forms and standards of public worship have been established for which specific types of prayer-books are necessary and the pattern of experimentation seems destined to continue.

The two selections printed below represent two approaches to the problem of prayer which have been entertained in the Conservative movement. Both of them start from the premises mentioned above, that there is a need to make prayer more palatable to the American Jew and that this can be achieved through manipulation of the prayer-book and the services. The Rabbinical Assembly - United Synagogue prayerbook is very restrained in the conclusions it draws from these premises; the Reconstructionist prayerbook is much more radical. However, it should be noted that both prayerbooks are alike in making the Hebrew language and the conventional organization of the services central to their presentation. The former prayerbook is the normative one in the Conservative movement and is widely used. The Reconstructionist prayerbook is used by only a few congregations, but the type of thinking represented in it enjoys a somewhat wider support among rabbis even if most of them are not prepared to go as far as the Reconstructionists or to accept the Reconstructionist prayerbook as the best possible product of such thinking.

INTRODUCTION TO THE SABBATH
AND FESTIVAL PRAYERBOOK*

By Rabbi Robert Gordis

This Sabbath and Festival Prayer Book is presented with the hope that it will serve the needs of all who are striving to perpetuate traditional Judaism in the modern spirit.

The past century and a half has witnessed a number of attempts to achieve a living synthesis of the old and the new, of Jewish tradition and the contemporary scene. To attain this goal in the realm of public and private worship, a number of teachers of Conservative Judaism during the past few decades published prayer books for the various occasions of the year under individual auspices. The only collective enterprise in the field was the United Synagogue Festival Prayer Book, undoubtedly the most attractive traditional Mahzor hitherto issued. As time went on, it was increasingly recognized that the principles and techniques of a traditional Prayer Book for the modern age needed to be reconsidered. Everywhere the conviction grew that the time was ripe for the issuance of a Prayer Book that would express the viewpoint of Conservative Judaism and bear the official imprint of the Rabbinical Assembly of America, representing the spiritual leadership of the movement and of the United Synagogue, the lay congregational organization.

Three fundamental principles guided the Commission in the preparation of this prayerbook:**

---

* From the Foreword to the *Sabbath and Festival Prayerbook* of the Rabbinical Assembly and the United Synagogue.

** For a more detailed treatment of the principles and techniques of procedure required in preparing a modern traditional ritual, see Robert Gordis, "A Jewish Prayer Book for the Modern Age," in *Conservative Judaism*, Oct. 1945.

First is the principle of continuity with tradition. Continuity is important for every faith and culture, but infinitely more so for Judaism. This is true not only because, as Ranke declared, Jews are the most historical of peoples, but also because loyalty to tradition is the strongest bulwark against the centrifugal forces that threaten Jewish survival everywhere. This emphasis upon maintaining tradition is no blind ancestor worship. Whatever other virtues our generation may possess, it cannot pretend to a genius for religious expression, a gift which is so beautifully exemplified in the traditional Prayer Book. This consideration does not free us from the obligation to strive perpetually after fresh and creative devotional forms. But it should prevent us from rashly laying hands on the product of the piety of earlier generations.

Relevance to the needs and ideals of our generation is the second basic principle. A Prayer Book is not a museum piece. It must express our own aspirations, and not merely those of our ancestors, however much we may revere them. This problem of relevance has two aspects. There are modern ideals that are expressed inadequately or too briefly in the traditional liturgy. This lack can be met with relative ease by supplementing the accepted service and thus incidentally stimulating religious and literary activity. The second and more difficult aspect lies in the fact that there are passages in the traditional Prayer Book that no longer seem to express the convictions and hopes of our day. Such passages require sympathetic study and skillful treatment in order to be made relevant to our age.

Intellectual integrity, the third criterion for a modern Jewish Prayer Book, demands that we do not seek to deny or evade the difficult problem of bringing tradition into focus with contemporary life. Thus, we cannot take refuge in the procedure of printing a traditional Hebrew text and a parallel English version that has little or nothing in common with the original.

These basic principles, continuity with tradition, relevance to the modern age, and intellectual integrity, are obviously not easy to harmonize. The extent to which one or another principle ought to prevail in a given case will naturally be the subject of differences of opinion. Our procedure has varied with the circumstances involved in each instance.

In many cases, apparent divergences of outlook between tradition and the modern age disappear when the true intent of the Prayer Book is grasped and its mode of expression is understood. The concept of Israel as a people chosen by God which is so prominent in Jewish tradition, is a striking case in point. To eliminate it from the Prayer Book because it has been vulgarized and misunderstood in some circles would mean surrendering to error and incidentally perpetuating an injustice upon the prophets and sages of Israel who understood the concept aright.

Moreover, in affirming God's election of Israel, we stand on solid historical ground. The great religions of Christianity and Islam, the modern humanitarian ideals and the basic principles of democracy are all rooted in the Hebrew Bible. They testify to the central role that Israel has played in the religious and ethical development of Western man.

Recalling this historical truth is no mere concession to group vanity. If our generation is to accept loyalty to Judaism willingly and joyously, notwithstanding the disabilities of Jewish life and the many temptations to desert the fellowship of Israel, it requires a sense of consecration, a conviction that the Jewish people has played and yet will play a noble and significant role in the world. They must feel that Jewish loyalty is nothing petty and insular, but that on the contrary, it ministers to the progress of humanity. This concept is therefore a psychological necessity as well as a historical truth, and therefore, an indispensable factor for Jewish survival today.

Besides, the idea of the election of Israel is invariably linked in Judaism with the great instruments of Jewish living, the Torah and the Mitzvot. In every instance, the Prayer Book associates the election of Israel, not with any inherent personal or group superiority, but with the higher responsibilities which come to the Jew as the custodian of Torah and the devotee of the Jewish way of life. This is no modern reinterpretation, but an instance of the correct understanding of both the letter and the spirit of tradition.

There are, to be sure, instances where the modern attitude varies from the traditional understanding of a concept. Often, it is possible to reinterpret traditional phrases in order to express our own convictions. Thus, the word *abodah* which in Hebrew means "religious worship" was referred by our ancestors to public worship in the Temple which centered about the sacrificial system. The word may quite properly mean for us the entire system of public religious worship. Nor need the prayer for the re-establishment of a great religious center in Jerusalem include for us, as it did for our fathers, the hope for the restoration of the sacrifices. The same connotation exists in the Festival Musaf prayer *Vehashev Kohanim L'avodatam U'Leviim Leshiram U'lezimram*, etc. There our rendering voices our aspiration for the restoration of Temple worship on Mount Zion with the Kohanim pronouncing the Priestly benediction and the Levites offering song and psalmody as elements in the historical continuity of Israel's religion. The rendering of the phrase *mehayyai hametim* "who calls the dead to everlasting life" is linguistically sound and rich in meaning for those who cherish the faith in human immortality, as much as for those who maintain the belief in resurrection. It may be added that the older rendering of this phrase is itself a reinterpretation of a still older Biblical idiom.

In all our striving for intellectual integrity and historical truth, it must not be forgotten that the Prayer Book is couched in poetry and not in prose. It must be approached with warm emotion and not in a mood of cold intellectuality. Thus, the emphasis in the Prayer Book upon the Messiah need not mean for us the belief in a personal redeemer, but it serves superbly as the poetic and infinitely moving symbol of the Messianic age. To have eliminated reference to the Messiah from the Prayer Book would have meant the impoverishment of the Jewish spirit, the loss of one of the most picturesque elements of Jewish belief, culture, music and art. The Prayer Book, like all poetry and truth, has things in it too exalted for literalness.

There will naturally be instances, however, where re-interpretation is impossible and the traditional formulation cannot be made to serve our modern outlook. Such preeminently are the passages dealing concretely with animal sacrifices. Passages like *ezehu mekoman* and *pittum haketoret* or the phrase *v'ishei Yisrael* "the fire offerings of Israel in "*Retzeh*," can be dropped without injuring the rubric of the service. The deletion of the Musaf service as a whole, however, would mean destroying the entire structure of the traditional liturgy, besides eliminating several valuable ideas and aspirations from the Prayer Book. Primarily, the Musaf service voices our hope for the restoration of Palestine as the homeland of the Jewish people. But that is not all. Also implied in the prayer is the recognition that sacrifice is essential for the fulfillment of all human ideals. Then too, we cherish the hope that Palestine will again become significant not only for Israel but for the spiritual life of mankind as a whole. Finally, it is characteristic of Judaism to recall the sacrificial system which represents a legitimate stage in the evolution of Judaism and religion generally. As Israel Abrahams wrote, "This is the virtue of a historical religion, that the traces of history are never obliterated. . . . The lower did not perish in the birth of the higher, but persisted." For all these reasons, neither the deletion of the Musaf nor its retention unchanged would satisfy the basic principles of a Jewish Prayer Book for the modern age.

The Prayer Book Commission* accordingly decided upon the following procedure. Both *Tikkanta Shabbat* and *Umipne Hata'enu* are retained as a reminiscence of Israel's glorious past by changing the tense of two verbs and a few other minor modifications. The other ideas we wished to express are embodied in a *Bakashah* preceding *Tikkanta Shabbat* and *Umipne Hata'enu*. Both for the sake of variety and in order to interpret the distinctive spirit of the Sabbath and the different Festivals, two distinct *Bakashot* have been included.

Another section of the Prayer Book where re-interpretation did not suffice is to be found in the Preliminary Blessings *shelo asani goy, ebhed, ishah*. As their position near the benedictions dealing with the Torah indicates, these blessings express the sense of privilege that the Jew felt in being able to fulfill the Torah and the Mitzvot, which were not obligatory in equal measure for non-Jews, slaves and women. However, the negative form in which these blessings are couched caused Jewish leadership much concern through the ages. Supported by the trend of tradition, the Commission decided to rephrase the blessings in the positive form.

In a few instances, the traditional text was made more relevant to our aspirations by adding brief supplementary phrases. Thus, the Babylonian prayer, *Yekum Purkan* with its prayer for the welfare of the scholars preserves a noble Jewish tradition appropriate to

---

* The members of the Commission were Rabbis Robert Gordis, Morris Silverman, Max Arzt, Simon Greenberg, Jacob Kohn, Israel H. Levinthal, Louis M. Levitsky, Abraham A. Neuman and Elias L. Solomon.

our age, in spite of its archaic flavor. All that was required was the addition of the phrase *bekhol arat galvatana* "and in all the lands of our dispersion." In the following blessing, *Mishebarah 'avotenu*, we have added the phrase *ubhebhinyan eretz yisrael* "for the upbuilding of Palestine" to express our conviction that therein lies one of the great mitzvot of Judaism today.

In *Sim Shalom*, the concluding blessing of the *Amidah*, it was felt that the univeral note should be made more explicit. Basing itself upon a reading in the Siddur of Rabbenu Saadya Gaon *sim shalom ba'olam*, the Commission therefore has amplified the passage to read: *sim shalom tovah ubrakhah ba'olam ḥen vaḥesed v'raḥamim alenu v'al kol yisrael amekha*.

The creative approach to tradition means not only the surrender of out-worn material and the reinterpretation of what can still be made viable, but also the enrichment of the Prayer Book by new material. Consequently, a large number of supplementary readings, both for unison and congregational reading, have been included. This material, both in prose and verse, is drawn from all ages of Jewish experience and is concerned with all the fundamental elements of Israel's life and thought. These readings may be integrated with the weekly Sidrah or the sermon themes. In addition, many of them are appropriate for the special occasions of the year. To this end, a list of suggestions for such use will be found in the back of the volume. The sources for all the supplementary readings are indicated in a special Index.

While the content of the Prayer Book is naturally our first concern, the form is scarcely less important. Here, too, certain principles and techniques emerged in the course of the work.

Hebrew and English differ radically in spirit and structure and a literal translation is often a distortion of the meaning. Thus much of the objection raised to the concept of the Chosen People is due to a failure to recognize the intent of the Hebrew text, which uses a coordinate clause where English uses a subordinate construction. Nor is this all. Hebrew is an Oriental language abounding in imagery. The use of many synonyms, which was stimulated by Biblical parallelism, is a characteristic feature. To eliminate these synonyms in the Hebrew means to commit the literary sin of judging Hebrew style by Western standards. On the other hand, to translate them all violates the spirit of the English language. Obviously, a briefer formulation is required in the English, while the Hebrew text requires no change. In general, the reader deserves an idiomatic English version exactly as the worshipper requires an authentic Hebrew text. Hence long phrases may be shortened, the word-order may be varied and the syntax modified when necessary. The changes of person and number that are characteristic of Biblical literature and hence are frequent in the Prayer Book should be brought into harmony with one another in the English. For the requirements of an English version are that it be clear, succinct and true to the meaning and spirit of the original.

Conscious of our limitations, the members of the Prayer Book Commission venture to hope that this Prayer Book may help advance the great cause of spiritual revival in American Israel. We have sought to keep before us the ideal proclaimed by Chief Rabbi Kook of blessed memory, *hayashan yithadesh, hahadash yitkadesh,* "The old must be renewed and the new become sacred." For the privilege of sharing in this enterprise, we are humbly thankful to Almighty God.

INTRODUCTION
TO THE RECONSTRUCTIONIST
PRAYER BOOK

By THE EDITORS*

INTRODUCTION

On presenting this revised prayer book, we wish to indicate what impelled us to undertake its preparation. We are well aware that great numbers of our people are attached to the traditional prayer book by sentiments of deep and sincere piety and deplore any deviation from its time-honored text. In their opinion, such deviation impairs the spiritual unity of the Jewish people and the continuity of its sacred tradition. We too are eager to preserve the Jewish worshiper's sense of oneness with Israel and to maintain the common memories and the feeling of a common destiny, which the services of the traditional synagogue have always fostered. But due regard must be paid to certain other considerations besides the unity of Israel and the continuity of its spiritual tradition. Otherwise, Jewish worship is in danger of disintegrating, and Israel's spiritual heritage of being dissipated.

Many modern Jews have lost, or all but lost, their sense of need for worship and prayer. They rarely attend religious services, and

---

* The Editors were Rabbis Mordecai Kaplan and Eugene Kohn. They were assisted by Rabbis Ira Eisenstein and Milton Steinberg. Research work and some Hebrew translations of English material were done by Rabbi Joseph Marcus.

even when they do, their participation is perfunctory. The motions survive; the emotions have fled. The lips move, but the heart is unmoved. Unless this apathy to synagogue services is overcome, it will spell the end of worship among Jews; and the end of worship means the decay of all spiritual values and the vulgarization of human life. Since the traditional service has not sufficed to preserve the spirit of worship among Jews, we have found it necessary to suggest new forms of Jewish liturgical expression. To be sure, this need has been recognized for over a century, and various attempts have been made to satify it. All such attempts have been worthy efforts to revitalize Jewish worship. But we have felt that, by reason of their theology and their conception of the Jewish people, they have failed to rekindle in the Jew the spirit of worship.

That spirit depends upon experiencing the reality of God and having a sense of oneness with Israel. The profound changes, however, in life and thought during the last century-and-a-half have made it necessary to restate what these experiences mean in terms of the thinking of our day. Only such a restatement can awaken in the heart of the modern-minded Jew the desire to worship.

EXPERIENCING THE REALITY OF GOD

If prayer is to be genuine and not merely a recital of words, the worshiper must, of course, believe in God. He must be able to sense the reality of God vividly, as an intense personal experience. Our ancestors possessed such a sense of the reality of God, and could, without hesitation, say with the Psalmist, "I set the Lord before me continually." The modern Jew, however, is disturbed by the current conception of nature. Nature is generally viewed as blind, mechanical and unresponsive to man's prayers. This view of nature leaves in his mind no room for God or for worship. Therefore it is necessary for the modern Jew to strive to formulate his idea of God in terms which can serve to inspire him with faith and courage, and which at the same time conform to his knowledge of the world. Just how each Jew will conceive God will vary according to temperament and outlook. For purposes of common worship, however, it is essential to arrive at an idea of God, broad enough to bridge the differences in individual outlook and capable of resolving the inner conflicts which paralyze the impulse to pray. The following idea of God may serve as the basis of a common faith for the Jews of our day:

Reality — the sum of all that is — should not be regarded as entirely subject to forces operating mechanically. Such forces exist. Science has identified them for us and justified our confidence that they apply universally and without exception. We believe in natural law. But natural law does not account for everything. We know, for example, that, as persons, we are more than bodies acting like mechanical robots. To be sure, everything that we think, feel or do takes place through the instrumentality of our bodies and in conformity with natural law. Nevertheless, our bodies and the laws governing them do not account for all that we are. They tell us nothing of what life means for us, of our yearnings, our desires, our hopes and fears, our loves and hates. So, too, the world about us cannot be wholly explained in terms of nature. There is a universal Spirit that transcends and uses nature in some such way as the human spirit transcends and uses the bodily organs of men. Science, which concerns itself with nature's laws, answers only the question: How? It does not answer the question: Why? It cannot tell us to what end or purpose we should direct our lives. The answer to that question, or rather the very question itself, implies a Power both in and beyond nature which moves men to seek value and meaning in life. That Power is God.

We cannot afford to live merely for the passing moment, not even for more inclusive ends confined to the brief human life-span; we must live for ends, only partially envisaged, that link us with the life of all mankind, and, beyond that, with the life of the universe, with God. Human life has worth only when its interests extend beyond the service of self. Only then do we feel that we are fulfilling our destiny as human beings and find joy in that fulfillment. Only by serving God can we achieve salvation.

Each of us should learn to think of himself as though he were a cell in some living organism — which, in a sense, he actually is — in his relation to the universe or cosmos. What we think of as a coherent universe or cosmos is more than nature; it is nature with a soul. That soul is God. As each cell in the body depends for its health and proper functioning upon the whole body, so each of us depends upon God. Were each cell in us capable of being aware of its dependence upon the whole of us, and were it to express that awareness, such expression would, for it, constitute worship. Each time we hail and glorify the "Thou" in "Blessed be Thou, O Lord, our God, King of the Universe," we enter, in however infinitesimal a degree, into communion with the Spirit that maintains the unity of life and directs that unity toward our salvation. Such communion should normally elevate our will to God's will. Our will is to make the most of life; God's will is that we utilize all of life's possibilities for our salvation. This is the nearest we can get to translating the belief in God into living experience.

To God, the source of our will-to-salvation, we must turn from time to time in appreciation and gratitude for all the gifts of life, for the heritage of habits, traditions, standards and ideals, and for the accumulated wealth of tools and skills to which we are heir and by means of which we can carry further the process of universal growth and happiness. To this same source of our will-to-salvation we must turn to ward off disheartenment at the seemingly insuperable difficulties which stand in the way of universal growth and happiness. If we are to have faith in man and man's future, if we are to have the indomitable courage to meet the onset of evil doers, if we are to be confident that the sacrifices made in behalf of a better world order are not in vain, then we must be in active communion with God of whom our best self is a minute but real emanation. To achieve that communion is the object of worship and prayer.

HAVING A SENSE OF ONENESS WITH ISRAEL

The prayers of the Synagogue imply the will of the worshiper to become one with the collective being of the Jewish people and its spiritual aims. The worshiper must, therefore, have a definite idea of what such oneness involves. It must mean that we are conscious of being members of the Jewish people, that we sense our kinship with it, that we accept a personal share in its history and destiny. It must mean that we recognize the unity of Israel, past, present and future, in all parts of the world. It must mean that we strive to understand Israel's hopes and aspirations and to make them our very own. Communal worship should be the occasion for thus immersing ourselves in the living reality of *kelal yisrael*, the totality of Israel.

But with the advent of the Jewish emancipation, that purpose has become difficult of achievement. The Jewish people is now an integral part of the body politic of many nations. This has altered not only the political but also the spiritual status of Jewry. Our sense of oneness with Israel must, therefore, be expressed in terms which conform to modern thought and are relevant to the present situation. We must recognize that Judaism and the Jewish people have evolved and are evolving, that tradition never achieves finality, that to deprecate all change is to stunt growth. It is with a living Israel that we seek to identify ourselves, an Israel with a land, a language and a culture, an Israel that ever remakes itself in the light of changing conditions and needs.

In order that the religious services should help the worshiper achieve oneness with the Jewish people, they should, as far as possible, be carried on in Hebrew. It must, however, be a Hebrew that is understood and appreciated, and not one that is repeated by rote. Throughout this book, in addition to the traditional prayers and the readings written originally in Hebrew, the new material written originally in English appears, wherever feasible, also in a Hebrew translation.

Another means of achieving oneness with Israel is awareness of our relation to Palestine. The immemorial hope of the Jewish people to rebuild its ancient homeland is reflected throughout the text. But, in addition, much attention is given to the great contemporary enterprise of rebuilding Eretz Yisrael, as the most significant common effort of the Jewish people to realize its ideals in the modern world. The faith, the courage, the vision and the strength of the resurgent Jewish spirit are articulated in those prayers and readings which touch upon the Zionist striving. Perhaps no other cause is as potent as Zionism to kindle the feeling of oneness with the Jewish people.

Still another means towards the same end is the intimate contact with the rich cultural heritage of Israel, which spans the centuries and the vast distances that separate the modern Jew from the generations that preceded him. With that end in view, there have been brought together in this text the words of Jewish prophet and sage, philosopher and ethical teacher, poet and mystic, from many periods and many lands. Though their thoughts are couched in an idiom different from that of our day, their words express the abiding need to experience the worthwhileness of life and to achieve salvation. Since they speak the common language of the heart, they strike a responsive chord in us.

MODIFICATION OF TRADITIONAL DOCTRINE

In order to retain the continuity of Judaism and, at the same time, to satisfy the spiritual demands of our day, it is necessary to make changes in the content of the prayer book. To preserve the authority of Jewish tradition, it is necessary to retain the classical framework of the service and to adhere to the fundamental teachings of that tradition concerning God, man and the world. However, ideas or beliefs in conflict with what have come to be regarded as true or right should be eliminated.

Some have attempted to obviate the need for change in the traditional prayers by reading into them meanings completely at variance with what they meant to those who framed them. This practice is fraught with danger. To read those new meanings into the traditional text by way of translation is to violate the principle of forthrightness. To assume that the average worshiper will arrive at them of his own accord is to expect the unattainable. Our prayers must meet the needs of simple and literal-minded people, even of the young and immature. We dare not take the chance of conveying meanings which do not conform with the best in our religious thinking and feeling. Not that prayers need be prosaic in their literalness, but their figures of speech must have clear and true meanings. People expect a Jewish prayer book to express what a Jew should believe about God, Israel and the Torah, and about the meaning of human life and the destiny of mankind. We must not disappoint them in that expectation. But, unless we eliminate from the traditional text statements of beliefs that are untenable and of desires which we do not or should not cherish, we mislead the simple and alienate the sophisticated. The simple will accept the false with the true, to the detriment of their spiritual growth. The sophisticated will feel that a Jewish service has little value for people of modern mentality. Rather than leaving such questionable passages to reinterpretation, we should omit or revise them.

In keeping with the foregoing, the text of the traditional prayers has been modified to bring it in line with the following changes in doctrine:

The Doctrine of the Chosen People:

Modern-minded Jews can no longer believe, as did their fathers, that the Jews constitute a divinely chosen nation. That belief carried for them the implication that the history of mankind revolved about Israel. It is not difficult to understand how they came to hold such an Israel-centered view of history. Belief in God's choice of Israel arose at a time when all the surrounding nations were idolaters and polytheists. It expressed for our fathers their intense experience of the reality of God and their intense awareness that their people was the only nation which recognized its responsibility to the God of all mankind. This belief was later fortified by the fact that the Christian and Moslem peoples, among whom the Jews then lived, also accepted it. They insisted however, that God had subsequently rejected the Jewish people. It became all the more necessary, therefore, for the Jews to reiterate the doctrine of Israel as the Chosen People.

In the modern world, all this has been changed by a number of political and cultural developments — the rise of democratic nationalism, the separation of church and state, the admission of Jews to citizenship and the waning belief in supernatural revelation. Thus the basis of the belief that the history of all mankind revolves about our people has been destroyed. However, even without that belief, we can and should continue as a people dedicated to the purpose of testifying to the reality of God and of serving Him. But we must acknowledge that other peoples can and should be dedicated to the same purpose.

We should, therefore, not retain the traditional text of those prayers which make invidious comparisons between Israel and the other nations. Our prayers should express a more modest conception of our role in history. The present text affirms the aspiration of Israel to make its own distinctive contribution to the enhancement of human life, but assumes the equal right and obligation of other peoples and communities to make theirs. It exhorts Israel to live up to the best of which it is capable, but avoids comparison of Israel's achievements and capacities with those of other groups.

The Doctrine of Revelation:

Tradition affirms that God supernaturally revealed the Torah, in its present text, to Moses on Mount Sinai. But the critical analysis of the text by modern scholars and the scientific outlook on history render this belief no longer tenable. We now know that the Torah is a human document, recording the experience of our people in its quest for God during the formative period of its history. The sacredness of the Torah does not depend upon its having been supernaturally revealed. The truth is not that God revealed the Torah to Israel, but that the Torah has, in every successive generation, revealed God to Israel. It can still reveal God to us. Though we no longer assume that every word in the text is literally or even figuratively true, the reading of the Torah enables us to relive, in imagination, the experiences of our fathers in seeking to make life conform to the will of God, as they understood it. We thus make this purpose of theirs our own and are inspired to seek God also in our own experiences. And those who seek God find Him. Our discovery of religious truth is God's revelation to us.

The study of Torah in this spirit is properly the central act of worship. It is, moreover, indispensable to our survival and growth as a people. The Torah so conceived is indeed a "tree of life" everlasting, planted within us. But it cannot serve this purpose as long as the Synagogue bases the authority of the Torah on the dogma of supernatural revelation, which the modern mind rejects. We have, accordingly, deemed it necessary to stress the sacredness of the Torah in other ways than by affirming that it was supernaturally revealed to Moses on Mount Sinai.

The Doctrine of the Personal Messiah:

Modern-minded Jews no longer look forward to the advent of a personal Messiah, who, by supernatural intervention, will redeem Israel from exile, and usher in an era of universal justice and peace. Certainly, there is still every reason to believe, as our ancestors did, that the Golden Age of mankind lies in the future, that history is morally determined, that the Kingdom of God can and will be attained in time. But we must now think in terms of universal redemption through the struggles, hopes, vision and will of all good men. Our prayer must henceforth be that Israel may contribute its share to the universal effort in behalf of a world of freedom, justice and peace.

While the prayers for the restoration of Israel's national home are retained and even elaborated, they are not to be construed as implying the return of all Jews to Palestine. Our prayerful concern should include those who will continue to live in the lands of their nativity, and should voice the hope that they be permitted to do so in peace and freedom.

The Doctrine of the Restoration of the Sacrificial Cult:

The institution of animal sacrifice was in ancient times the accepted mode of worship, and for centuries Jews prayed for the opportunity to reinstate that mode of worship in a rebuilt Temple in Jerusalem. Instead of the prayers which express that hope, the present text contains the prayer that we may learn to make sacrifices of our resources and energies in behalf of worthy causes, and that a restored Eretz Yisrael may once again inspire us to serve God.

Since the distinctions between *Kohen, Levi* and *Israelite* have always been associated with their respective functions in the Temple cult, these distinctions are no longer cogent. All references to them as still playing a part in Jewish life are omitted.

The Doctrine of Retribution:

Our ancestors believed that obedience to the moral and ritual laws of the Torah resulted in favorable rainfalls; and that disobedience caused the rain to be withheld. This was undoubtedly an aspect of their intuition that the moral law was as integral to the structure of the universe as natural law, and that both kinds of law were interwoven in the destinies of men. To the extent that obedience to the moral law spells happiness and peace for mankind, and disobedience spells disaster and war, that intuition was correct. But that the very rainfall is influenced by human conduct, we know, is not true. The present text, therefore, is so modified as to emphasize the ever timely truth that the material prosperity and well-being of society depend on its conforming to the Divine law of justice and righteousness.

The Doctrine of Resurrection:

Men and women brought up in the atmosphere of modern science no longer accept the doctrine that the dead will one day come to life. To equate that doctrine with the belief in the immortality of the soul is to read into the text a meaning which the words do not express. That the soul is immortal in the sense that death cannot defeat it, that the human spirit, in cleaving to God, transcends the brief span of the individual life and shares in the eternity of the Divine Life can and should be expressed in our prayers. But we do not need for this purpose to use a traditional text which requires a forced interpretation. This prayer book, therefore, omits the references to the resurrection of the body, but affirms the immortality of the soul, in terms that are in keeping with what modern-minded men can accept as true.

The revision of the traditional prayers to conform to the foregoing changes of doctrine should advance the major purposes of this prayer book. That revision should help the worshiper to experience the presence of God in his personal and communal life. And it should so unite the worshiper with Israel as to put him in possession of the living truth which Israel has learned concerning man's task on earth.

JEWISH LAW

A NOTE ON LAW

Every movement has its own panacea for the problems which it confronts. Reform Judaism has clung to "modernization" as the answer to the problems of Judaism; neo-orthodoxy is committed to "Torah-true Judaism." The Conservative movement has for many years placed great emphasis upon restoring flexibility to Jewish law.

The lengthy section on Jewish law included in this volume is intended to reflect the fact that Jewish law and its interpretation has been a primary concern of the Conservative movement. Indeed, there seems to have been a tendency to believe that changes, interpretations and modifications of Jewish law were the testing stone of the Conservative movement. In consequence, there has been, over the course of the years, a very considerable concern with the problem of establishing a harmony between Jewish law and Jewish life. Some groups in the Conservative movement have advocated radical action; others have hesitated to engage in any action at all.

The Conservative movement has met the problem in two ways. Certain forms of synagogue procedure, such as the seating of men and women together at a service, were widely adopted by congregations and never subjected to examination and legal debate. Other matters of Jewish law were dealt with by the Law Committee of the Rabbinical Assembly and by special Law Conferences involving both the Assembly and the faculty of the Seminary.

In 1948, after years of inconclusive debate, the Rabbinical Assembly adopted a formula which is still employed. The Law Committee of the Assembly which had been hesitant to raise any major questions of Jewish law and had been very traditional in its attitudes, was considerably expanded in size. An attempt was made to give representation on the enlarged committee to all wings of thinking in the movement. A procedure was evolved whereby answers to legal problems which received the unanimous endorsement of the Committee are voted upon by the Rabbinical Assembly and generally approved. Issues on which the Committee itself is divided are presented in the form of majority and minority reports but are not voted upon by the Assembly. The Responsa on the Sabbath which are printed below belong in this second cate-

gory. *And a great many Responsa have been issued and await publication which belong in the first class.*

Thus far a considerable number of minor matters have been approved by the Law Committee and the Assembly, but few fundamental problems have been taken up.

The major legal action taken by the Conservative movement was in the area of Marriage and Divorce Law. For this specific area of Jewish law, a different method of treatment was developed. A Joint Law Conference was called which involved both the Rabbinical Assembly and the Seminary faculty. This group was regarded as a body with the power to adopt takkanot (enactments). It created a steering committee which recommended a new form of marriage contract (ketubah) so that the problem of divorce might be more readily handled in the future and also proposed that a Rabbinic Court (Bet Din) be set up to deal with cases arising under the new ketubah. These recommendations were subsequently adopted and implemented. Presumably, any further proposals for changes in marriage and divorce laws would be handled in the same manner.

After several years of experimentation with a more active policy on Jewish law, it is possible to draw certain conclusions. The Conservative movement is now in a better position to implement its philosophy of flexibility in Jewish law. But at the same time a process of disenchantment has set in for many with the philosophy. While it is recognized that flexibility in Jewish law is necessary and desirable, it no longer seems that this is the touchstone of the Conservative movement. The conviction which many of the rabbis had held that an active policy on Jewish law would at once validate and guide the Conservative movement seems to be waning. There is instead a growing feeling that it is not enough to have an active policy on Jewish law; the active policy, to be meaningful, must be directed to more fundamental issues. There is, secondly, a growing recognition that flexibility in Jewish law is only one part of the broad issue of a clarification of Conservative ideology and practice. And there is the further feeling that changing the attitudes of the Jewish community and heightening its religious awareness involves far more than flexibility in Jewish law.

TWO VIEWS OF SABBATH OBSERVANCE

A RESPONSUM ON THE SABBATH

(Rabbis Morris Adler, Jacob Agus and
Theodore Friedman)

This is the first of two sets of responsa on the questions of riding and the use of electricity on the Sabbath. The responsum printed below is the collective effort of three men who prepared it for the approval of the Law Committee of the Rabbinical Assembly. It secured the support of a majority of the Law Committee and it was subsequently presented at a convention of the Rabbinical Assembly (1950). However, in conformity with the policy of the Assembly not to give approval to legal provisions which have not been unanimously approved by the Law Committee, it was not voted upon. It thus remains as the opinion of a group of men, but has no official status. At the same convention a series of papers, which are also printed in this volume, were presented as minority reports. This paper, however, is particularly valuable as the reflection of the approach to Jewish law entertained by many members of the Rabbinical Assembly, and as an example of the manner in which they analyze and interpret and seek to apply Jewish Law.

The authors of the paper are Rabbi Morris Adler, who is mentioned elsewhere in this volume, Rabbi Jacob Agus, one of the most vigorous and creative exponents of Conservative Jewish thought whose writings are currently available in volume form and are therefore not included in this volume, and Rabbi Theodore Friedman who has contributed considerably to the clarification of problems of Law and ideology within the Conservative movement.

Sheelah:

As a rabbi in Israel, I turn to you, my Colleagues, for assistance in a question both theoretic and practical which has caused me concern and anxiety. One cannot serve a congregation for any time without being depressed and disheartened by the widespread disintegration of Sabbath observance among our people. This breakdown of one of the major institutions in Jewish life is too deep and too prevalent to be countered by preachment and exhortations. Sermons declaring the pre-eminence of the Sabbath in Jewish life, or extolling its spiritual beauty and social significance are politely received by our congregants but exert no influence on their practices or habits.

Yet the American Jew is not innately resistant to religious forms and values. I find among many in my congregation, a fine receptivity to Jewish teaching and a marked interest in Jewish affairs. Some recognize the lack of spiritual satisfactions in their present mode of living and evince eagerness not alone for instruction in Jewish ideas but likewise for guidance in their practical conduct as Jews.

They are Jews who not only have been born into the modern, industrial world, but have also been educated in its institutions and have been mentally and psychologically shaped and moulded by its approaches, attitudes and activities. To ignore this fact and to speak to them as if they were the identical counterparts of their East European forbears is to engage in futile rhetoric. On the other hand to overlook the spiritual alertness and interest as well as the healthy Jewish pride and desire for Jewish identification which motivate them, is to doom to atrophy those characteristics which hold forth greatest promise for the future of American Jewish life. To do nothing, or to mouth easy formulas that have a respectable past behind them, is to abandon to the haphazard forces of the pervasive secular environment, much of the richest potential for Jewish living in this land.

I know, dear Colleagues, that the question of the Sabbath, as indeed of Jewish religious life, has agitated you as it has disturbed every earnest and thinking Jew. It cannot be met on a level of individual action since the problem is far too aggravated for such a necessarily fragmentary approach to it. In addition, were every rabbi to work in terms of his individual judgment, the confusion and disharmony in our midst would be greatly intensified.

Our Conservative movement must marshal its forces to meet the problem I have described. I therefore turn to you to ask for guidance in instructing my people as to our view as a movement on the Sabbath disciplines, our best thought as to its proper observance and a practical program by which its meaning may be better understood, its spirit more widely shared, its sanctities more greatly respected by the congregations that look to us, as Conservative rabbis, for guidance and instruction.

PLACE OF SABBATH — PAST AND PRESENT

Teshubah:

The question raised by our colleagues penetrates to the basic core of Judaism and touches likewise the most difficult and aggravating problem in contemporary Jewish life. A question of such scope cannot be simply or readily answered. We have deliberated through many months and have focussed upon this problem our most earnest thought. We seek a solution, humbly and prayerfully aware of the fact that we are dealing with one of the central sanctities of our tradition. The feeling that a Sabbath-less Judaism is no Judaism governs our consideration and motivates our reverent approach to the complex issues which are associated with so fundamental a problem. The colleague who has directed his quest to us has rightly suggested that as spiritual leaders in Jewry we would be remiss in our calling, were we content to leave the Sabbath to its fate, to be further buffeted about by the compelling pressures of the changed outer world in which we live and by the dictates generated by a greatly altered inner world of ideas and attitudes which we have come, as modern men, to inhabit. To overlook the former is to sacrifice relevance; to ignore the second is to violate integrity. Our duty as rabbis is not exhausted when we cite the law as it has been understood and practiced, and ignore the conditions of life in the midst of which, or the thoughts of men by whom that law is to be followed. One of the great responsibilities of this age in our history is to release the life-giving and life-enriching powers that inhere in our tradition, by relating that tradition to modern life. Changing conditions threaten an inert system of law. The Halachah lived and functioned in our history because it has traditionally been characterized by resiliency and responsiveness to life. The very designation of Jewish law as Halachah suggests its capacity for movement, and reveals the intent of its architects and builders to charge it with a genius for vital adaptability to the moving and changing scene.

It is out of a faith in the significant meaning which our historic tradition can and should have for us today and out of our conviction that modern Jews have a capacity for spiritual living and Jewish loyalty that we seek an answer to the question addressed to us by our colleague.

The preservation of the Sabbath spirit and of Sabbath practices is an indispensable element in any program for the Jewish future. The Sabbath has always served Israel as a "sanctuary in time," when, released from the deadening drudgery of daily duty, the Jew could soar to the highest realm of his human possibilities. The Sabbath was the most eloquent manifestation of the covenant with God into which Israel had entered and to the fulfillment of which its history is dedicated. The Sabbath helped to naturalize the Jew in a world of spiritual values and sensitivities, and made the Shekinah, the presence of God in human life, felt and experienced by even the humblest. It is impossible to overstate the role the Sabbath played in the spiritual and social economy of Judaism, or to exaggerate the widening circles of influence which it sent forth to the farthermost bounds of Jewish life.

We feel convinced, however, that never before was the Sabbath called upon as urgently to play its creative part in Jewish living as in our time. We could understand most vividly the full meaning of the saying of our sages שקולה שבת כנגד כל מצוותיה של תורה (ירושלמי ברכות פ״א).[1] Into a world whose landscape is dominated by visible and massive monuments to human ingenuity and power, the Sabbath quietly but firmly brings the humbling and saving message of man's dependence upon God. Our modern environment, built as it has been by the drives for possession and dominion which it stimulated, needs the spiritual overtones of a day overflowing with moral and religious content. The competitive character of the society we live in not only fosters man's acquisitive appetites, but also encourages the view that man stands in the relationship of competitor and antagonist to his fellow-men in the incessant struggle for worldly reward and gain. Sabbath peace and holiness represent not simply a temporary interruption of the daily struggle,

---

[1] "The Sabbath is equal in value to all the precepts in the Torah."

but renew within men the deeper and greater truth that men are brothers under the Common Fatherhood of a Universal God.

One of the pathetic characteristics of our day in history is that multitudes of men are so caught in the vise of the instrumentalities and machinery of living that they never glimpse the goals of life. The Sabbath can bring the modern Jew close to the basic and eternal issues of life, its highest purposes and its noblest meanings. Much has been written of the merciless strains and tensions in which modern living involves us. Millions are in quest of peace of mind. The fast pace of metropolitan life, the relentless pressures of economic striving and activity, the multiplicity of the interests and distractions that crowd in upon us, leave modern man either in a state of perpetual confusion or chronic weariness or futile purposelessness. The Sabbath helps unite the disparate phases of our life into an organized whole by relating means of livelihood to significant purposes and goals. Mental uneasiness and ennui which are so often characteristic of modern man result not only from a gnawing sense of futility but also from the atrophy of spiritual, creative and imaginative faculties with which he has been endowed. It has been said that "melancholy is the ache of an unused faculty." The Sabbath brings release from such a state of inner depression, by giving expression to the latent spiritual powers of man. In the midst of a society whose massive corporateness and whose vast mechanical operations lead to a devaluation of the individual, the Sabbath exalts the cosmic dignity of man and emphasizes the indispensable and unique worth of each being. By its spirit, the Sabbath proclaims the holiness of life and the holiness of each individual life.

The Sabbath forges vital and enriching linkages which the modern Jew needs as a man and as a member of an historic group. The Sabbath unites the Jew with his people not on the level of a joint philanthropic enterprise organized to meet an emergency, nor again on the level of a defense against the defamation of the Jewish name or the denial of Jewish rights — but rather in terms of deeply-felt and experienced identification with the life and history of a people dedicated to a purposeful and benign destiny. Through the opportunities for study and prayer which in the pressure of life, the Sabbath alone offers, the Jew enters the rich world of Jewish ideas and feelings and becomes kin to those eternal contemporaries in Jewish life — prophet, sage and poet. The Sabbath quickens the spirit and fortifies the meaningful cohesiveness of the Jewish family by rededicating the family altar and by providing a fund of shared spiritual experiences and delights, this in an age in which the family is being subjected to centripetal forces and multiple corrosions. Thus from the Sabbath there can flow into the life of modern Jews numerous streams of spiritual balm and enrichment.

WHY HAS SABBATH OBSERVANCE BROKEN DOWN?

While it is difficult to measure exactly the extent of Sabbath violation among the members of our congregations, no one will dispute the assertion that the Sabbath observers among our people constitute but a tiny minority and a dwindling minority at that. Thus, the breakdown in Sabbath observance is certainly the most flagrant and widespread instance of the disintegration of Jewish religious life of our times. It is, moreover, highly symptomatic for it is the direct outcome of a complex of new forces that now play upon and will continue to mould the lives of our people. An analysis and understanding of these forces in their economic, social and ideological aspects, are indispensable if we are to honestly stand up to the challenge they present and seek the means whereby to confront it.

The shift of the center of Jewish life from Eastern Europe to America brought with it, almost overnight, the end of that social self-containment or semi-isolation in which the great masses of our people had lived for generations. The social life of the East European Jew was lived out almost exclusively within the confines of the Jewish community itself. In a sense, the same was true of the Jew's economic life. In the larger cities, the density of Jewish population and its concentration in certain industries made it fairly manageable for Jews to set their own pattern for the work week. Jewish artisans in these cities catered largely to Jews and as independent craftsmen could, without excessive difficulty, avoid working on the Sabbath. Where the Jew was not an independent entrepreneur and thus free to fix his own day of rest, he was, as likely as not, relatively free from the competition of the non-Jew and was thus under a minimum economic disadvantage in keeping his shop closed on the Sabbath.

With the Jew's arrival in America, the situation changed radically. Here, Jewish economic activity had to gear itself, for the most part, to the general pattern of American life, a pattern which fixed Sunday as the universal day of rest. Thus, multitudes of Jews who did not, for one reason or another, enter the employ of factories operated by Jews in almost exclusively Jewish occupations, such as the needle trades, were immediately confronted with the problem of going jobless or working on the Sabbath. Where the choice was not so acute, then, at the very least, the refusal to work on the Sabbath meant the deliberate acceptance of a lower standard of living. We shall presently see why so few, though reared in the tradition of Sabbath observance and previously practicing it, chose not to work on the Sabbath. Many Jews who were unaccustomed to factory work and who had no particular craft at hand entered the retail business. Such small enterprises faced a situation where Saturday was the main shopping day. To keep their places of business closed on the Sabbath was tantamount either to running the risk of bankruptcy or permanently remaining small entrepreneurs. What was true of the small businessman was equally true of the Jew who entered the free professions. The professional man had to adjust his work week to the habits of his clients, a growing number of whom were non-Jews.

Several factors help explain why so few Jews upon their arrival in America chose to maintain Sabbath observance even if it did not involve a permanently lower standard of income. The whole spirit of early 20th century America was one of economic expansionism. An essential element in the American dream, a dream soon entertained by the new Jewish arrival, was that of a continual rise in one's economic status. Indeed, it was the hope for just such advancement, as it was the driving force behind other immigrant groups, that impelled many Jews to pull up stakes and come to America. Earlier Jewish immigrants, predominantly of the Reform wing, had already set the pattern of working on the Sabbath. The phenomenon of large numbers of Jews, some of whom were the leading figures in American Jewry as it was then constituted, working on the Sabbath, was a novel sight to the East European Jewish immigrant. It was obvious to the new arrival that

Sabbath violation in no wise rendered one Jewishly declassé as it might in Eastern Europe. This sight, that of Jews keeping their places of business open on the Sabbath and yet enjoying the regard of fellow Jews, was a powerful factor in the choice described above. Added to these factors was one which, while moving on a level quite other than that of economic and social forces, yet moved in the same direction — the ideological factor.

Its roots run back into the soil of the late 19th century when the winds of doctrine of the Haskalah began to play on the mood of the East European Jew. In total effect, the Haskalah and its spiritual derivatives, such as Jewish socialism, led to a weakening and slow dissolution of the ties that bound the Jew to his spiritual tradition. One of the most striking of these effects was the placing of the ideal of economic advancement in the forefront of the consciousness of the Jew, a position it had long since occupied in the catalogue of modern man's values. The old ideal of humble acceptance of one's lot was almost completely displaced by this new ideal; new, that is, for the Jew. It accorded perfectly, as we have seen, with the regnant spirit of an expanding capitalism. Thus, "aufarbeiten sich," became one of the central drives in the life of the American Jew. When, in the scheme of things, this new value, for the fulfillment of which so many opportunities were at hand, came in conflict with the observance of the Sabbath, it was the latter that gave way. It was only the exceptional soul that had the spiritual hardihood to withstand the all but irresistible pressure of both economic circumstance and ideological drive.

Thus, Sabbath violations became the rule rather than the exception in American Jewish life. For many, indeed for a growing proportion of the members of our congregations, their violation of the Sabbath represents merely a practice they have inherited from the previous generations without ever having themselves seriously considered the alternative of Sabbath observance. They are in this regard like תינוק שנשבה לבין העכו״ם ושכח עיקר שבת. [2] Where some sense of the sanctity of the Sabbath still remains among our people, the feeling is rife that since they do follow their usual employment on the Sabbath, it would perhaps be self-delusion, or, what is worse,

---

[2] "A child who was brought up in captivity among Gentiles and forgot the very principle of the Sabbath."

hypocrisy, if they made any effort at all in the direction of Sabbath observance other than that of refraining from work. This conviction leads, of course, to the gradual elimination and disappearance of all forms of Sabbath observance. It is a trend best described as a descending spiral. Unless halted and reversed, it will soon reach an absolute nadir and the single greatest Jewish religious institution will have passed out of the lives of the great mass of the members of our congregations. It is in our time, then, that the opportunity presents itself for doing something constructive towards the revitalization of Sabbath observance. One man, says the Midrash, can right an object that is falling; once it has fallen to the ground, five men cannot pick it up.

HOW CAN WE REVITALIZE SABBATH OBSERVANCE?

A program for the revitalization of Sabbath observance must seriously reckon with the realities of modern life. These realities as they relate to Sabbath observance possess a twofold character, economic and spiritual. It is the merest truism to state that the overwhelming majority of our people are not presently spiritually prepared to forego the opportunity for economic advancement in favor of Sabbath observance. It is equally true that in many instances the abandonment of work on the Sabbath would entail a complete disruption of a family's economic basis. Any program for Sabbath observance in our time that does not honestly reckon with these facts is doomed to futility. However, we should continue to hold out as our ultimate objective observance of the Sabbath by cessation from all gainful employment; an objective that a shift in circumstance, such as the universal adoption of the five-day working week, may permit an increasing number of our people to realize. In our efforts in behalf of the program that we propose, this ultimate goal must be made both vivid and explicit. But that goal will lose its contact with reality unless, in the meantime, we keep alive in the lives of our people, through a positive program, the sense of the sanctity and high spiritual value of the Sabbath. So, then, one must begin with our people in the situation, economic, social and spiritual, in which they presently find themselves. A journey around the world begins with a single step.

The program that we propose, then, is not to be regarded as the full and complete regimen of Sabbath observance, valid for all Jews for all times and for all places. On the contrary, it is aimed to meet the particular situation that confronts us, a situation without parallel in the long annals of Judaism. Our program seeks to reintroduce into the lives of our people as much Sabbath observance and spirit as we may reasonably hope our people will, with proper education, accept.

This program is devised, moreover, with an acute awareness of certain special conditions which obtain at present and which, as far as we can see, will become ever wideningly operative. We refer to the fact that the introduction of the automobile and other means of rapid transportation have made for the geographical growth of the average American city. More and more, our city populations are being decentralized and the number of people who find themselves living in widely scattered suburbs is increasing. Large segments of the population regard riding to the locale of their activities — economic, social recreational and religious — as a normal feature of modern life. This program reckons with these facts in a positive way, insofar as they relate to the question of Sabbath observance. To continue unmodified the traditional interdiction of riding on the Sabbath is tantamount to rendering attendance at the synagogue on the Sabbath physically impossible for an increasing number of our people. In the program here presented we indicate why and under what circumstances and for what purpose this ban may, in the discretion of the local rabbi, be modified.

PROGRAM FOR THE REVITALIZATION OF THE SABBATH

We call upon you and upon all our colleagues of the Rabbinical Assembly of America, in concert with the United Synagogue of America, to launch a campaign for Sabbath observance among our people. The campaign should have as its immediate goal the acceptance on the part of the people of the following basic indispensable elements of Sabbath observance. Emphasis on this immediate program should in no wise militate against the ultimate objective — the cessation of all gainful employment on the Sabbath.

It is in the conviction that only the immediate can lead to the ultimate that the following program is proposed.

(A) The ushering in of the Sabbath at home through the kindling of the Sabbath candles, the recitation of the Kiddush, the blessing of the children, the singing of Sholom Aleichem and other zemiroth.

(B) All preparations for the Sabbath, such as the Sabbath meals, the tidying of the home, as well as personal preparation, should be completed before the onset of the Sabbath. It is also suggested that there be introduced the custom now prevailing in Israel of adorning the house with flowers for the Sabbath.

(C) Attendance at public worship at least once on the Sabbath.

(D) A portion of one's leisure time on the Sabbath should be devoted to the reading of Jewish sacred literature, particularly the weekly Torah portion.

(E) One should refrain from all such activities that are not made absolutely necessary by the unavoidable pressures of life and that are not in keeping with the Sabbath spirit, such as shopping, household work, sewing, strenuous physical exercise, etc.

(F) The type of recreation engaged in on the Sabbath should be such as is calculated to enhance one's spiritual personality in its intellectual, social, and esthetic aspects.

(G) Refraining from the use of a motor vehicle is an important aid in the maintenance of the Sabbath spirit of repose. Such restraint aids, moreover, in keeping the members of the family together on the Sabbath. However, where a family resides beyond reasonable walking distance from the synagogue, the use of a motor vehicle for the purpose of synagogue attendance shall in no wise be construed as a violation of the Sabbath but, on the contrary, such attendance shall be deemed an expression of loyalty to our faith.

We are well aware in, the above connection, that in accordance with Jewish law one may worship at home as well as in the synagogue. We are equally aware, however, that the practice of private prayer has unfortunately fallen into such disuse that only the very minimal number of people engage in prayer unless it be at a synagogue service. Indeed, it is a well-grounded supposition that were it not for synagogue attendance on the Sabbath, there would be no prayer for most of our people from the end of one week to the other. Moreover, when almost every Jew had some measure of competence in understanding the Torah and our sacred literature, many Jews could and did spend some time in studying Torah. Today, however, this condition no longer obtains. The average Jew's knowledge of Torah and his Jewish information are gained through the synagogue and in great measure through the sermon which both instructs and inspires our people to live in accordance with our faith. Hence, in our time regular attendance at the synagogue has become a *sine qua non* for the maintenance of Judaism. We are, we sincerely believe, acting in accordance with the spirit of our rabbis when they declare אין שבות במקדש. — "The Sabbath prohibition of *shebuth*[3]" does not apply to the carrying out of the temple ritual. We similarly state in our program for the revitalization of the Sabbath that the traditional interdiction of riding on the Sabbath for the purpose of attending the synagogue service may, in the discretion of the local rabbi, be modified under the conditions we have described above.

PRINCIPLES IMPLIED IN THIS PROGRAM

(1)

Every effort to restore standards of observance among our people is likely to be met with cynical skepticism, as if the process of continuous deterioration were a foregone conclusion. Actually, there were many occasions in Jewish history when the seemingly hopeless process of decay was arrested and even reversed by a determined and courageous act of reconsecration. The Jewish religion does not favor the emotional excesses of the Christian "revivalist" movements, but it fosters the principle of voluntary acceptance of a pattern of life. Thus, we find that in the biblical period the children of Israel concluded covenant after covenant with the Lord, in which they pledged themselves to abide by a set of disciplines and ways of living. The covenant drawn up by Ezra and signed by eighty-six "heads of family groups" is a case in point. Consisting in a pledge to observe a few fundamental precepts, it became the cornerstone of a renaissance of Judaism. The same

---

[3] A quasi-labor activity prohibited by the Rabbis in connection with the Sabbath. The purpose of the prohibition was to erect "a fence about the law."

covenant principle was later employed in the Pharisaic movement, which laid the groundwork for the magnificent spiritual labors that are contained in the Mishnah and the Talmud. By a similar process of voluntary acceptance, Jewish communities pledged themselves to abide by the regulations of the Talmud, then of the Gaonim, and later the German-Polish-Lithuanian communities accepted the Shulḥan Aruch with the emendations of Rabbi Moses Isserless in the same spirit.

It is sufficient to take note of a question addressed to the Gaon Y'hudai, in which a community inquires whether laymen "should put on *t'fillin* when they say their morning-prayers and recite the *Sh'ma*, or is this requirement meant only for a great man. Is it not better for an ordinary layman not to put on *t'fillin*, because it looks like an act of arrogance since all the congregants do not put on *t'fillin?*" Here is a precept on which the Talmud lays great stress. Its neglect in the great ages of German-Polish piety was virtually inconceivable. Yet, less than two centuries after the completion of the Talmud, entire communities failed to observe the mitzvah of *t'fillin*. This situation was corrected by means of determined efforts of education, culminating in the re-acceptance of standards of piety. It is to a nation-wide effort, conceived in the spirit of the love of God and reverence for our tradition, that we must now dedicate ourselves.

At the same time, we must learn to adjust our strategy to the realities of our time and place, in keeping with the realistic genius of the great builders of our faith. Thus, our Sages cautioned us, *tafasta m'rubah lo tafasta* — "to overreach is to court failure," when you attempt to grasp a great deal, you will grasp nothing. They also advised all builders of fences in Judaism, "it is better to build a fence of ten handbreadths that is likely to stand than one of a hundred handbreadths that is liable to fall," *tov assarah t'faḥim v'omed mimeah t'faḥim v'nofel* (Aboth D'Rabbi Nathan). It is also well to remember the sage advice, *mutav shelo lomar davar sheaino nishma* — "it is better not to say a thing which will not be heeded."

(2)

In this spirit it is our consensus that riding to the synagogue on the Sabbath and the use of electric lights in the course of this journey or for other purposes are comprised in the general category of *oneg shabbath*, the delight of the Sabbath. Before discussing in detail the precepts and laws relating to these two specific enactments, we wish to point first to the general principle of community enactments.

The power of a community to enact ordinances in the field of religious life is virtually unlimited, provided its ordinances are made with the consent of the resident scholars and provided further that they be inspired by the purpose of "strengthening the faith," and intended only for their own time and place. The general impression that Jewish Law is rigidly inflexible and incapable of adjustment or adaptation is completely erroneous. (To be sure, in the Orthodox interpretation of Halachah, there is a core of laws called *d'oraita*, Torahitic, which can never be changed, but which can be temporarily suspended for good and valid reasons. There is also a category of rabbinic ordinances, *d'rabanan*, which can be revoked permanently only by a re-constituted Sanhedrin or by a court, "greater in wisdom and in numbers" than the ancient courts in Palestine). In crucial periods, our Sages did not hesitate to make special enactments for their own time or for a limited period of time, in order to meet the challenge of new circumstances.

(3)

This power of the communities to make special enactments in behalf of the faith, through their spiritual leaders and lay representatives, is in turn a corollary of the principle of development in Jewish Law. The labors of outstanding scholars in the past century have uncovered for us the view of Judaism as a mighty living stream, adjusting the flow of its healing waters to the contours of the country that it traverses. The great masters of Jewish learning in the modern period, such as Zunz, Frankel, Schechter, Tchernowitz and, may they be separated for life, Ginzberg and Finkelstein, have blasted for all time the notion that Halachah is ideally or ever was, in its creative periods, a frigid and frozen mold, into which life may flow, but which it may never bend. Nor is this principle of development discountenanced in our ancient tradition. Thus, an ancient Tannaitic Midrash inquires, how could Moses learn the whole Torah in forty days on the mountain? Is not the Law, in all its details wider than the earth and deeper than the sea? In reply, the Midrash asserts that "rules," *K'lalim*, were given to Moses at Sinai, rules of interpretation and application which were later crystallized into laws. The human share in the making of the Law is beautifully illustrated in the Talmudic account of the dispute between Rabbi Eliezar and Rabbi Joshua ben Chananya, when the latter ruled against "the echo of a Divine voice," *bath-kol*, declaring *lo bashama ·'n hi*, it is not in heaven. Similarly, the fanciful story of Moses ma₁ , eiling at the innovations of Rabbi Akiba reflects this historic insight of our Sages.

The share of the people in the creation and repudiation of laws is taken for granted in Jewish tradition. The Torah became binding upon Israel only when the twelve tribes accepted it voluntarily at the foot of Mt. Sinai. The power of the *minhag* to make laws and break them is well-known. It was the duty of the highest rabbinic court to declare an ordinance invalid if the majority of the people did not accept it in their daily practice, אי איכא הגוי כולו, אין; אי לא, לא. When otherwise observant people were living in habitual violation of a Torahitic ordinance and it was considered likely that they would not obey the law if told about it, the rabbis advised that the people be not told that they transgressed the law so as not to induce either feelings of guilt or a mood of rebellion. *Mutav sheyihyu shoggim v'al yihyu mezidin.*

Numerous illustrations may be cited of laws and practices, which have become so obsolescent that few, if any, Jewish leaders would now campaign for their reintroduction. Thus, the prohibition against milk and bread made by Gentiles, the requirement to dip newly purchased dishes in the *mikvah*, or to abstain from newly harvested grains, *chodosh*, are examples of laws that have quietly lapsed. We may recall also the lapse of the laws governing the lending of money, of *sh'mitath k'safim*,[4] the inauguration of *heter iska*[5] and its subsequent obsolescence. To sum up, the human share in the making of Jewish Law is both undeniable and inevitable.

The greatest authorities of the Medieval and early modern

---

[4] The injuction calling for the remittance of debts in the Sabbatical year was circumvented by the *prozbul* which permitted the turning of the debt over to the court so that it remained collectable.

[5] A documentary device which was designed to make possible the lending of money on interest by making the lender a silent partner in the proposed business transaction.

period were cognizant of this need. Thus, Maimonides who formulated the principle of the irreplaceability of the Torah, (*zoth hatorah lo t'hai muhalefeth*) stressed the duty of rabbis to formulate and enact special regulations for their time and place. The court may revoke these ordinances, for a time, even if it be smaller than the first courts, for the rabbinic ordinances are surely not greater than the words of the Torah itself, which the courts are entitled to revoke on a temporary basis . . . Even as the physician cuts off a hand or a foot in order that the patient might survive, a rabbinic court may teach the violation of some *mitzvoth* for a time, in order that the totality of Judaism might be preserved. Thus, our ancient Sages declared, "Desecrate for him one Sabbath in order that he might keep many Sabbaths" (משנה תורה, הלכות ממרים, פ"ב, הל' י"ד).

The great scholar of the eighteenth century, Rabbi Jacob Emden, declared, "that many *mitzvoth* come into being at different periods in Jewish history, both in respect of permitting the prohibited and in prohibiting the permitted . . . Thus, it is clear as the sun that the commandments are dependent upon the time, the circumstances and the people of every age. They were not at one time set up in a pattern that is complete and final, but they are subject to additions and modifications, as changing times require."

In the same spirit, the famed glossator of the Shulchan Aruch, Rabbi Moses Isserless declared in a responsum, "that when new circumstances develop, which were unknown to the ancient authorities, it is permitted to institute new enactments" (שו"ת, רמ"א, כ"א).

THE PROBLEM OF ELECTRICITY

The question whether electric lights be regarded as a form of fire in the Sabbath Halachah, first came up for discussion about sixty years ago. A great number of responsa on this subject was written. Some of the authorities declared kindling of electric lights to be an *issur d'oraita*, — a Torahitic prohibition — basing their view chiefly on the principle that the kindling of the smallest conceivable fire is prohibited, *havarah l'ma shehu*. Other students maintained that electric lights belong to the category of *issur d'rabanan* (a Rabbinic prohibition). Several reasons are presented in support of this view, notably the opinion that it is not *m'lachah shezricha l'gufa*,[6] since no such work was performed in the building of the *mishkan* (B. Shabbat 94a definition of Ri); the power that causes the filament to radiate light comes from the city's central dynamo and the action of turning the switch is therefore merely *grama*[7] which according to the severest view is *shebuth*;[8] and, thirdly, the argument that is sometimes given that though kindling of the filament is not fire, filament is heated and therefore such action would fall into the category of *bishul* (cooking), which is an *issur d'oraita*, is refuted by the Talmudic observation in another connection that an activity is *bishul* only when it is performed in the customary manner, *ein derech bishul b'kach*.

We propose the acceptance of the view that electric lights are not Torahitically prohibited. This form of activity belongs to the sphere of rabbinic legislation, or the realm of *shebuth*.

There is a difference of opinion among the Codifiers as to whether a prohibition of *shebuth* can be set aside for the sake of a mitzvah. The performance of the rite of circumcision on the Sabbath includes this permission. From this core, Maimonides generalizes that all forms of *shebuth dishebuth*[9] may be allowed, for the sake of a mitzvah. The Itur declares that, for the sake of a mitzvah, the prohibition of ordering a Gentile to do even a Torahitic *m'lachah* — i. e. *shebuth*, is set aside. Following this opinion, the practice was permitted, in many places, to tell a Gentile to stoke the furnace on the Sabbath, on the ground that "everybody is sick in relation to the exposure to cold" (Rabbi Jacob of Orleans quoted by Beth Yosef in Tur Oraḥ Ḥayyim 276). A late authority declares that this permission is now generally taken advantage of, even when the weather is mild, in reliance on the authorities, who permit *shebuth*, if no pain or suffering are involved (Mogen Avraham, *ibid.* בשביל הגדולים דסוברים דמותר שבות במצטער).[10] Most authorities

---

[6] See note 12.

[7] An indirect cause.

[8] See note 3.

[9] Telling a Gentile to perform work on the Sabbath is regarded as *shebuth*. When the work itself is only Rabbinically (rather than Torahitically) prohibited, the situation is *shebuth dishebuth*. Maimonides permits this sort of action for the sake of performing a *mitzvah*.

[10] "Adopting the view of some great authorities who say that one may overlook a prohibition of *shebuth* if one is faced with discomfort or distress."

could not consent to this lenient interpretation. Signing a bill of sale in non-Hebraic script in order to conclude the purchase of a home in the land of Israel is permitted. Thus, work that is distinctly prohibited by the rabbis, with some authorities attaching to it the penalty of stoning, is permitted on the Sabbath for the sake of a mitzvah (Tur Oraḥ Ḥayyim — Hagaha 306). Later authorities dispute this interpretation, claiming that it is permitted only to tell a Gentile to execute a bill of sale (Aruch Ha-Shulḥan-Oraḥ Ḥayyim 306, 22). Elijah Gaon of Vilna, permits all forms of *shebuth* when discomfort is caused (*matir kol shebuth*, Oraḥ Ḥayyim 276, 15).

It is obvious from the above that there exists no unanimity of opinion concerning the reasons that justify the lifting of a *shebuth* prohibition. The purposes of alleviating discomfort and assisting in the performance of a mitzvah are certainly present in the questions we are discussing. In addition, our decision depends on the utilization of the liberty to choose between authorities and to apply general principles — liberty which is properly within the province and authority of *Takkanoth Ha-zibur*.[11] We think of Halachah as an instrument of the people, for the enrichment of the spiritual life of our people and not as an end in itself. Furthermore, in modern life the use of electricity is essential to the normal comforts of living. Great stress was laid in our tradition on the duty of having one's home brightly illuminated in honor of the Sabbath. Therefore, in the spirit of a living and developing Halachah responsive to the changing needs of our people, we declared it to be permitted to use electric lights on the Sabbath for the purpose of enhancing the enjoyment of the Sabbath, or reducing personal discomfort or of helping in the performance of a mitzvah.

THE PROBLEM OF RIDING

The use of an automobile involves the following activities: the kindling of lights, the indirect combustion of gasoline to produce power, and locomotion from one domain to another. We have already dealt with the kindling of lights in the previous section. The combustion of gasoline to produce power is a type of

---

[11] Enactments undertaken for the benefit of the people.

work that obviously could not have been prohibited before its invention. All acts of burning are prohibited only when performed for specifically described purposes, such as: cooking, heating, lighting or the need of its ashes. Burning for the sake of power was not included in this list. Of course, some heat is produced in the act of combustion, but this result is neither intended nor desired by the motorist. Hence, it falls in the category of פסיק רישא דלא ניחא ליה, which is permitted by the latest authorities. The combustion of gas in the carburetor is therefore the type of work, classed as *m'lachah sheainah ẓ'richah l'gufah*, according to the definition contained in Tosafot, Shabbat 94a — נראה לר״י, דמלאכה שאינה צריכה לגופה קרי כשעושים מלאכה ואין צריך לאותו צורך כעין שהיו צריכין לה במשכן, אלא לענין אחר, כי הצורך שהיתה מלאכה נעשית בשבילו במשכן הוא גוף איסור המלאכה ושורשו.[12]

While Rashi defined *m'lachah sheainah ẓ'richah l'gufah* differently, we favor the definition of the Tosafists in this matter. Finally, locomotion from one domain to another (e. g. מרשות היחיד לכרמלית) is a rabbinic prohibition; since today there is no רשות הרבים, there can be no Torahitic interdiction involved. As a matter of fact, on the basis of the strictest interpretation of the law, riding would not be prohibited on Sabbath in a public vehicle driven by a non-Jew. Hence we deal here with a prohibition instituted by the rabbis. Their main reason for the prohibition of riding a horse or in a wagon was the fear that it may lead indirectly to the violation of the Sabbath. Thus they said that one may not ride on an animal because the rider may be tempted to break off a branch to use as a whip גזירה שמא יחתוך זמורה (ביצה ל״ו:). The additional reason was given that riding causes a Jewishly-owned animal to labor on the Sabbath שאתה מצווה על שביתת בהמתך (ירושלמי ביצה פ״ה) —.

Obviously, neither reason applies to the automobile. The apprehension that the driver might be moved to fix the car in the event of a breakdown is remote, since its complicated mecha-

---

[12] A labor which, while it necessarily results in a transgression, is neither intended nor desired. Thus *m'lachah sheainah ẓ'richah l'gufa* is a labor which is not performed for its own sake. The Tossafot definition is that it is a labor which is performed, but not for the need for which it was performed in the tabernacle (which is the basis of the rabbinic description of types of work) but rather as the means of achieving another type of benefit — e. g. combustion not for the purpose of burning but of achieving movement.

nism generally requires the services of an expert. 'א 'ל ביצה תוספות
ד"ה תנן: פירש רש"י שמא יתקן כלי שיר, ומיהו לדידן שרי, דדוקא בימיהם
שהיו בקיאים לעשות כלי שירים שייך למיגזר, אבל לדידן אין אנו בקיאים
לעשות כלי שירים ולא שייך למיגזר.[13]

The above analysis leads us to the conclusion that riding
in an automobile on the Sabbath is at most a rabbinically inter-
dicted activity. When this act prevents the fulfillment of the mitzvah
of attending public worship it shall not be considered a prohibited
act. We base this conclusion upon the numerous precedents in the
Halachah for the setting aside of a rabbinic prohibition when a
great mitzvah is involved, such as the mitzvah of Yishuv Eretz-
Yisrael (Baba Kama 80b, Maimonides Hilchoth Shabbat 6:11, 6:9)
and in the case of witnesses who came to testify on the appearance
of the new moon the law of *thumin*[14] was relaxed by a *takkanah*
(ordinance) of R. Gamaliel the elder (Mishnah Rosh Hashanah
4:5). We may also cite the frequently quoted general principle
regarding the easing of *shebuth* prohibitions when a great mitzvah
or public welfare is involved.

חפצך אסור, חפצי שמים מותר. (Shabbat 150a).[15] As we have already
indicated participation in public service on the Sabbath is in
the light of modern conditions to be regarded as a great mitzvah,
since it is indispensable to the preservation of the religious life
of American Jewry. Therefore it is our considered opinion that the
positive values involved in the participation in public worship on
the Sabbath outweigh the negative values of refraining from riding
in an automobile. When attendance at services is made unreason-
ably difficult, without the use of automobile, such use shall not be
regarded as being a violation of the Sabbath.

We cannot too strongly emphasize that our views in regard
to the use of electric lights and the automobile on the Sabbath
are not separable from the total program for the revitalization
of the Sabbath as herein suggested. To take these elements out of

---

[13] Tosafot, Betzah, 30a. — The Talmud enjoins that one should neither clap his
hands on the Sabbath while singing nor dance, lest he injure, and thus be led to
repair, a musical instrument. Rashi remarks that we may "in our time" both clap
hands and dance for "in our time" people are not versed in repairing musical instruments. It has become the work of professionals, so there need be no fear that the
ordinary person will undertake it and thus violate the Sabbath.

[14] The limitation on the distance one is allowed to walk on the Sabbath.

[15] Work which you desire to perform for your own benefit is prohibited, but
if it is designed to achieve some religious objective, it may be permitted.

the context of the entire national and local effort required for the strengthening of the basic institution of the Sabbath, would be to subvert the spirit and the purpose which animate our decision. On the other hand, it shall be understood that in their wisdom and in the light of the conditions prevailing in their respective communities, individual rabbis may find the easements here proposed unnecessary for the achievement of the larger goal herein envisaged. We take into consideration the fact that different situations in particular communities may dictate the application of varying methods.

The crucial question in the issue before us is whether we of the Conservative movement are well advised to labor on behalf of the Sabbath in our own way. Rooted in the consciousness of our people is the conviction that Judaism is the business of the entire Jewish people and that Jewish Law should be changed, if at all, only by the duly constituted authorities of a reunited Israel. Indeed, in ancient times, the present divisions in Jewish life could scarcely have been envisaged. However, we are neither able nor willing to turn back the clock of history. Diversity of opinion is a direct function of democratic freedom, so that whenever outside pressure was relaxed, the variety of thought and feeling which always existed within the Jewish community came to the surface.

Today, the choice before us is not unity or diversity; the first quality is illusory in any positive program of religious dedication. The second quality is inescapable. The only alternatives we face are a policy of continued inaction by all groups, permitting Sabbath observance to sink out of Jewish life, or a resolute attempt, on as broad a front as possible, to set a floor below which respect for the Sabbath-institution shall not fall among our congregants. In setting forth this program of Sabbath-observance for our congregations we hope to contribute toward a reversal of the trend of deterioration in all three groups. We earnestly trust that both the Orthodox and Reform movements will be moved to set up and implement similar programs of reconsecration for their respective memberships, with a consequent gain for American Judaism as a whole. Far from widening the present cleavage in American Jewry, such efforts are bound to make allegiance to Judaism more meaningful and to lead to the emergence of a common core of reference for Judaism and respect for its institutions.

The division of Jewry into communities, maintaining their own forms of ritual observance, is not an unprecedented development. Even before the rise of the Reform movement, there were Ashkenazic and Sephardic communities living side by side and employing a parallel set of rabbis, shochtim and cantors. Similarly, the rift between *Mithnagdim* and *Ḥassidim* demonstrated the capacity of Judaism to make room for a variety of emphases in religious expression, within the general pattern of loyalty to the tradition.

CALL TO ACTION

We call upon our colleagues in the Conservative movement to give to the program of Sabbath-revitalization pre-eminence in the many duties they are called upon to discharge. אחינו וחברינו, as rabbis in one of the most difficult and confusing ages for Judaism, we must consecrate our greatest efforts to the preservation of the most sacred institution in Jewish life. In our congregations and in the life of our communities we must, by every means at our disposal and through all the influence and energy we command, bring a heightening consciousness of the sanctity of the Sabbath. We must rally about us the most loyal and understanding members of our congregations and prepare a concerted attack upon Jewish indifference, neglect and ignorance. Our movement nationally must mobilize its best talents and its most dedicated spirits and make of the renewal of Sabbath observance the main object of our efforts. This breach in our wall must be repaired and none among us must rest or divert his energies to other work until American Jewish life is made safe for the Sabbath. We regard this responsum as but the humblest of beginnings in that direction.

By tireless activity, by earnest planning and unwearying persistence it may yet be given to us to bring back the Sabbath to its former glory as a reservoir of Jewish spiritual strength, renewal and inspiration. We earnestly pray

ויהי נעם ה' אלהינו עלינו ומעשה ידינו כוננה עלינו ומעשה ידינו כוננהו.

> And Let the pleasantness of the Lord God be upon us
> And establish Thou the work of our hands upon us
> Yea, the work of our hands establish Thou it.

REFERENCES AND SOURCES

Electricity:

1. The use of *electricity* for the purpose of *boiling* or *cooking* on the Sabbath. All authorities prohibit it:

1) שו״ת בית יצחק, יו״ד, סימן ק״כ.

2) שו״ת, אחיעזר, ח״ג, סימן ס׳.

3) הרב כעגקין בהקונטרס לוח היובל: דיני עלעקטרי בשבת.

2. Electricity for the purpose of *light*. The authorities disagree:

1) שו״ת, בית יצחק, יו״ד, סימן ק״כ – חייב משום מכבה.

2) שו״ת, בית יצחק, יו״ד, סימן ל״א – מסופק קצת בכיבוי אם הוא חייב.

3) שו״ת אבן יקרה, מהד״ג, סימן קס״ח – מבעיר או מכבה אור עלעקטרי בשבת, או מכבה ביו״ט, חייבים עליה מדאורייתא.

4) בשו״ת מהרש״ם, ח״ב, סימן רמ״ז – חוקך בזה אם בהבערה וכיבוי של העלעקטריציטעט יש בו מלאכה דאורייתא, כיון שלא היתה כמוהו במשכן, – וכנש״כ החתם סופר, או״ח, סימן ע״ג, לעניין מכסה הגשמים כיון שלא היה אוהל כזה במשכן אין בו מלאכה של תורה.

5) בשו״ת מחזה אברהם, סוף סימן נ״א, השיב שם על דברי המהרש״ם, דכיון דמקרי אש א״כ כל האשות בכלל.

6) בשו״ת מחזה אברהם שם, סימן מ״ב, מצדד לומר דהוא דרבנן, דסיבוב הכפתור אין כח ראשון להבערת החשמל, דממילא נתחברו החוטין, והוא רק גרמא שהוא שבות לעניין זה דמותר לעשות ע״י נכרי.

7) בשו״ת מהר״ש (ח״ה, סימן צ״ה) להרב מראדיישל, כתב ג״כ דהוא גרמא, וסמך עצמו על דברי המחזה אברהם הנ״ל, והעלה לפי זה שמותר להעמיד שעון אוטומטי בשבת על ידי גוי, משום דהוי רק שבות דשבות ובמקום הפסד.

8) בלבוש מרדכי להרב ממאד (ח״א, או״ח, סימן ט״ז-מ״ח), כתב ג״כ דהוא רק דרבנן.

9) בשו״ת מהרש״ג, ח״ב, סימן קל״ו – אצלו הוא כספיקא דאורייתא.

10) בשו״ת אחיעזר, ח״ג, סימן ס׳, כתב בהבערת וכיבוי העלעקטרי הוי איסור תורה, ואין זה גרמא, אלא כח ראשון, וגם לא כל הגרמות שוות, וכבר נתפשט הוראה זו בכל ישראל לאיסור.

11) מלכי בקדש להרב הירשענזאן, עמ' 19–38, מצדד לומר שאור החשמל איננו
אסור מדאורייתא, ואפשר שאין בו איסור כלל.

Travelling:

1. ועוד רצה רשב"ם להתיר ליכנס בקרון בשבת, ונכרי מוליכו חוץ לתחום,
וחזר בו משום שמא יפגעו בו ליסטים או שמא ישכח וירד ואין לו אלא ארבע
אמות (תוספות, עירובין מ"ג א' ד"ה הלכה).

2. כתב רבינו שמואל זצ"ל . . . וכאשר התרנו להפליג בספינה, כך מותר להפליג
ולהעלות ישראל בקרון והעכו"ם מושך בקרון, ובלבד שלא תמשך בהמה
בקרון. דאיכא משום אין רוכבין ע"ג בהמה, ובלבד שלא יצא חוץ לקרון, אבל
איכא למיחש שמא יפגעו בו ליסטים, א"נ אשתמיט ונחית מן הקרון, משו"ה אסור
(אור זרוע, הל' עירובין, סימן קמ"ו).

3. פסק מעין זה הוציאו רבני וינוצה להתיר רכיבת קרן בשבת להרופא אליהו
מונטלטו שהיה רופא הדוכס של דוכסית טוסקנה באטליה, ואח"כ רופא מלך
צרפת, יען היה היה חרד מאד בשמירת שבת (הצופה לחכמת ישראל, תרצ"א,
עמ' 196–7).

4. חוט המשולש או דברי נרגן, ע"י איש ר"ך הנקרא פלא בן זאב, אדעססא 1874,
עמ' 59–68.

–תשובה שבה מתיר לנסוע על מסלת הברזל בשבת, ורק
בדבר מצוה.

5. שו"ת משפטי עוזיאל, או"ח, סימן ט': בדין נסיעה בקרונות קיטוריות
או חשמליות בשבת, ושמתנהגות ע"י לא יהודים "אין כל
טעם לאסור רכיבתן משום שמשתמש בבהמה, ולא משום שמא יחתוך זמורה,
ולא משום אמירה לגוי, הלכך נראה שמותר לרכוב בהם בשבת
ויו"ט כדי ללכת הילוך של מצוה לבית הכנסת ובית
המדרש וכדומה. אולם מטעם אחר יש לצדד לאסור הנסיעה בקרונות
אלה . . . וכן כתב הרמב"ם נאמר בתורה תשבות אפילו מדברים שאין מלאכה
חייב לשבות מהן . . . . .
מסקנא דדינא: אסור לנסוע בקרונות חשמליות או מכונות קיטוריות שהן
של יהודים אפילו אם הנהגים הם לא יהודים . . . במקום שכל התושבים הם
לא יהודים מותר ליהודי לנסוע בקרונות של לא יהודים ושמתנהגות על ידם
בתוך העיר בתנאי שלא יצטרכו לשלם דמי כרטיס נסיעה בשבת ויו"ט, ואף
זאת אינו אלא לשם הילוך של מצוה כגון ללכת לבית הכנסת וכדומה, אבל
לא לשם טיול, ומכל שכן לשם צורך מסחרי".

6. מלכי בקדש להרב הירשענזאן: (עמ' 19–38)
מותר לנסוע ב„סאבווי" בשבת, ורק אם אינו נושא שום חפצים עמו.

A GROUP OF PAPERS ON SABBATH OBSERVANCE

Section A

A MODERN APPROACH TO A LIVING HALACHAH

By RABBI ROBERT GORDIS

The responsa printed below were offered as separate papers but collectively represent the point of view on riding and the use of electricity on the Sabbath, of what was at the time the minority group in the Law Committee of the Rabbinical Assembly. In the course of this discussion, theological questions are dealt with as well as legal questions, and psychological attitudes are propounded as well as scientific data. Thus, in the complete set of responsa a great many of the attitudes of members of the Rabbinical Assembly are brought to the fore.

An examination of the two sets of responsa makes it clear that there is disagreement, save on the question of the use of electricity. However, the papers share a concern for Jewish law and for the process of interpreting it.

The authors of these responsa are all distinguished in their field. Rabbi Bokser has written ably on several fields of Jewish law; Rabbi Gordis is described elsewhere in this volume; Rabbi Neulander has served as chairman of the Law Committee of the Rabbinical Assembly.

I

The indecision and the lack of clarity in the attitude of our movement toward the problems of the observance of Jewish law are not accidental. They flow from our failure thus far to articulate adequately our conception of the Halachah. To be sure, important aspects of the approach of Conservative Judaism to the Halachah have been illumined by the papers and discussions of many of our most distinguished scholars and thinkers during the years gone by, but much more needs to be done.

In setting forth this brief statement of our viewpoint on the Halachah as a preface to the discussion of the Sabbath law, we are aware of the fact that it may not prove acceptable, in whole or in part, to all the members of the Rabbinical Assembly. Yet it is our belief that the majority of the Rabbinical Assembly will find in it a presentation, however inadequate, of their own basic philosophy. We are convinced that it represents the fundamental approach implicit in Conservative Judaism as it has unfolded during the past half century, and that only along some such lines as these is there any hope for a vital Jewish religious life in our time.

We are conscious, too, that this standpoint is shared in most essentials by scholars and thinkers who are not associated with our movement. The responsa of such varied figures as the late Rabbi Hirschensohn, author of *Malki Bakodesh*, and the late Professor Jacob Z. Lauterbach of the Hebrew Union College, whose papers are to be found in various publications, the writings of Dr. Simon Federbusch, the interpretations and ordinances of the Chief Rabbinate of Israel, the pattern of life evolving in the Poel Hamizrachi colonies, and the quest for a vitalized ritual and ethical standards expressed in such Israeli publications as *Yavneh*, *Sinai*, and *Ba'yot* are far from uniform in character. Programmatic differences and organizational cleavages divide these and similarly minded individuals and groups from one another and from Conservative Judaism. Nonetheless, they share with us a conviction as to the viability and inherent worth of the Halachah on the one hand, and on the other, a faith that it possesses the resources to meet the needs of modern life as effectively as it did in the past.

Basically, our concept of Jewish law, which may be defined *as a modern affirmation of the central role of the Halachah in Jewish life*, rests upon two pillars. First is a return to the spirit and the techniques of the most creative periods of Jewish law, the age of the Bible, the Mishnah and Gemara. This creative spark continued to glow, though more faintly, in post-Talmudic times, down to our own day. Second is the utilization of the insights and conclusions of modern Jewish scholarship as an aid in the reinterpretation of traditional attitudes toward the Halachah, and in the formulation of the process necessary for its revitalization.

Within the brief compass of this paper it is impossible to present fully the grounds underlying our position, or analyze objections and contrary opinions at length. This has the disadvantage of giving this introductory paper a categorical and dogmatic cast, which is furthest from our desires. May the following paragraphs be understood in the spirit in which they are intended כשואל ולא כמשיב, as a contribution toward a philosophy of Jewish law for Conservative Judaism.

II

Basically, the sanction of the Halachah lies for us in its Divine character. We regard the Law, both Written and Oral, as the revelation of God. What Moses, the prophets, sages and rabbis taught, from Sinai to our day, is divinely inspired. That it has functioned so effectively, not merely for the preservation of Israel, but what is much more significant, for the enhancement of human welfare and the elevation of human character, buttresses, but does not supplant, our faith that its source is God. Hence we accept as fundamental to vital Jewish religion, the principle of *Torah min hashamayim*, "the Torah as a revelation of God."

Like our predecessors in rabbinic, medieval and modern times, each of us is free to give the term a greater or lesser degree of definiteness and literalness of meaning. The common core in all such views, however, and the irreducible minimum, is the belief that the Torah, which encompasses the ethical and ritual tradition of Israel, inaugurated at Sinai and carried forward through Biblical, Talmudic and post-Talmudic times to our own day, is an emanation of God, a revelation of Divine truth. This conception does not mean, for us, that the process of revelation consisted of the dictation of the Torah by God, and its passive acceptance by men. To be sure, this is implied in some, but by no means in all, rabbinic references to the subject, such as the explanation offered for the presence of the last twelve verses in Deuteronomy, which describe Moses' death: עד כאן הקב״ה אומר ומשה אומר וכותב מכאן ואילך הקב״ה אומר ומשה כותב בדמע "Until this closing section, God spoke, Moses repeated and wrote it down. When this passage was reached, God spoke and Moses wrote in tears" (Baba Batra 15a).

Revelation depends not merely upon its infinite and Divine source, but upon its finite and limited human instrument. Just as traditional Judaism found no derogation of the creative power of God in describing man as שותפו של הקב"ה במעשה בראשית "the partner of the Holy One in the work of creation," so Revelation is not impugned by viewing it as another aspect of this eternal partnership or cosmic symbiosis, where God כביכול depends on man, as truly as man depends on God.

That traditional Judaism recognized this variable human factor in Revelation is abundantly clear from our sources. The Bible itself distinguishes between the immediacy of relationship possessed by Moses and that of the other Prophets (Num. 12:6 ff.): אם יהיה נביאכם ה' במראה אליו אתודע בחלום אדבר בו לא כן משה עבדי בכל ביתי נאמן הוא פה אל פה אדבר בו ומראה ולא בחידת ותמונת ה' יביט "If there be a prophet among you, I the Lord do make Myself known unto him in a vision, I do speak with him in a dream. My servant Moses is not so; he is trusted in all My house; with him do I speak mouth to mouth, even manifestly, and not in dark speeches; and the similitude of the Lord doth he behold."

This distinction the rabbis amplify in their parable of Moses as a star-gazer with a clear telescope (אספקלריה מאירה) unlike the other prophets who had blurred instruments of vision (אספקלריה שאינה מאירה) (Yeb. 49b). The Talmudic comparison of Isaiah to a city-dweller looking upon the king (בן כרך שראה את המלך) and of Ezekiel to a בן כפר or rustic gazing in unfeigned astonishment at an unfamiliar spectacle (Hag. 13b), represents a distinction as well as an evaluation.

III

Not only does Revelation differ in content and depth, varying with the individual, but it is not limited in time. In other words, it is not an event, but a process. After the period of the Patriarchs, Sinai marked the commencement, not the conclusion of Revelation. The theophany on Sinai may be conceived of literally, mystically or philosophically, but it represents a basic historical fact without which all the subsequent history of Judaism and indeed of the

Jewish people is inexplicable. In increasing measure, contemporary Biblical scholarship is recognizing this truth and accepting the historicity of Moses and the Mosaic character of at least part of the Pentateuch. But scholarly analyses aside, for the Jewish religious consciousness, Revelation's first and greatest single hour, was at Sinai. However, as Rabbinic literature abundantly recognized, there were revelations after Sinai. (Cf. Bernard Bamberger, "Revelations of Torah After Sinai," *HUCA*, 1941). The relationship between these stages and Sinai is expressed in an utterance of R. Joḥanan: שהראהו הקב״ה למשה דקדוקי תורה ודקדוקי סופרים ומה שהסופרים עתידין לחדש "God showed Moses the derivations in the Torah and the words of the scholars, and whatever the scholars were to originate in the future" (Meg. 19b). The verb *ḥadesh* "create anew," makes it clear that the rabbis recognized that their function was active not passive, creative, not repetitive. The same view reaches classic expression in a passage which has been misinterpreted by some of its professed advocates, no less than by some of its strongest opponents: אפילו מה שתלמיד ותיק עתיד להורות לפני רבו כבר נאמר למשה בסיני "Even that which an able pupil was destined to teach before his master was already said to Moses on Sinai" (Y. Hag. I, 76d). What this statement sets forth is the belief, which we share, that the entire development of Jewish law after Moses is implied in the giving of the Torah on Sinai, and that the organic unity binding it all together gives to it all the same Divine sanction.

This concept may be succinctly summarized in the words *Torah missinai*. Incidentally, this phrase, as far as we have been able to discover, unlike *Torah min hashamayim*, does not occur anywhere in Talmudic literature, except in the Mishnah Abot 1:1 משה קבל תורה מסיני, where, however, it is not set forth as an article of faith. As a technical term, it is essentially late, being often used in modern Orthodox apologetics interchangeably though incorrectly, as a synonym for *Torah min hashamayim* and it is then taken to mean that the entire Torah, Written and Oral, was given to Moses on Sinai. Such a dogma means to pass judgment on a question which only historical and literary scholarship can legitimately decide, and which, contrary to widespread impression, is of little consequence for religious faith. At all events, for us both phrases summarize the belief that Jewish law, in its entire history and unfoldment, bears the same relationship to the Revelation at

Sinai as a spreading oak to its original acorn, in which all its own attributes are contained.

That this concept does not commit us to a static concept of Halachah is clear from the Talmud itself. By the side of the passage just quoted, which emphasizes the *unity* of the Halachah throughout time, must be set the profound legend in Menaḥot 29b which describes its *growing and changing character*:

בשעה שעלה משה למרום מצאו לקב״ה שיושב וקושר כתרים לאותיות. אמר
לפניו רבש״ע מי מעכב על ידך אמר לו אדם אחד יש שעתיד להיות בסוף כמה
דורות ועקיבא בן יוסף שמו שעתיד לדרוש על כל קוץ וקוץ תילין תילין של הלכות
אמר לפניו רבש״ע הראהו לי אמר לו חזור לאחורך הלך וישב בסוף שמונה שורות
ולא היה יודע מה הן אומרים תשש כחו כיון שהגיע לדבר אחד אמרו לו תלמידיו
רבי מנין לך אמר להן הלכה למשה מסיני נתיישבה דעתו "Moses found
God adding decorative crowns to the letters of the Torah. Upon asking the reason, the Lawgiver was told, 'In a future generation, a man named Akiba ben Joseph is destined to arise, who will derive multitudes of laws from each of these marks.' Deeply interested, Moses asked to see him and was admitted to the rear of the school-house, where Akiba was lecturing. To Moses' deep distress, however, he found that he could not understand what the scholars were saying, and his spirit grew faint within him. Then he heard Akiba say, 'This ordinance that we are discussing is a law derived from Moses on Sinai' and upon hearing this, his spirit revived." Hence the Sages could say: דברים שלא נגלו למשה נגלו לרבי עקיבא וחביריו "Things not revealed to Moses were revealed to Rabbi Akiba and his colleagues" (Bamidbar Rabbah 19:6, Vilna edition). It is significant that the same verb is here used of Moses as of the interpreters of the law a millennium and a half later.

Revelation is therefore a never-ending process, suffering all the vicissitudes of human life, because, human beings, weak and imperfect and varying widely in their profundity and insight, are creative partners in the process. Moreover, the process does not end with the Mishnah or the Gemara, Saadia, Maimonides, Jacob ben Asher or Joseph Karo, Rabbi Isaac Elḥanan Spector or Rabbi Abraham Isaac Kook. It also follows that not every stage is equally creative and fruitful. We venture to hope that the Rabbinical Assembly, dedicated to the cause of a meaningful and vital Judaism, may prove one of the instruments of divine revelation, and that its contributions will ultimately enter the mainstream of living Jewish tradition.

A corollary of this recognition of the divine character of the Torah, is our faith in its capacity to meet all the problems of life, however radically conditions may become altered. This conviction, to be sure, cannot be demonstrated mathematically. Yet it may be supported by the history of Jewish tradition, which has proved capable of growth and development through all the shifting fortunes of the Jewish people, both in Palestine during the periods of independence, autonomy or subjugation, and in the Diaspora, whether in the Greco-Roman world, or the various Christian and Moslem societies.

IV

It is highly significant in this connection that frequently institutions develop new rationales under changed conditions. To cite a paradoxical example, it would not be difficult to argue that in the simple, largely sedentary life of Jewish householders in Polish and Austrian villages of the nineteenth century the traditional Sabbath with its complete cessation of mobility, was scarcely necessary! In those communities, moreover, Jewish worship and study, which we associate with the Sabbath, found ample expression in the life of the people during the week. On the other hand, it is precisely in our harried and hurried age, which has all but lost the *locus standi* for the individual and the sense of unity in the family, that the *menuḥah shelemah*, "the complete and perfect rest" of the traditional Sabbath is most necessary for the physical and psychic health of the people.

Thus the difficulties that modern Judaism encounters in inculcating the observance of these time-honored prohibitions on work-a-day activities, far from justifying their surrender, actually testify to the burning need for the traditional Sabbath, and to the vital function which it, and it alone, can play in modern life. For in rapidly growing degree the hazards of modern life lie not so much in the area of physical fatigue and exhaustion, as in the field of mental and nervous disorders, as well as other diseases of hypertension like high-blood-pressure, heart ailments and stomach disorders, and perhaps even cancer. Considerations such as these do not categorically rule out the modification of the Sabbath laws, but they should guard us against a superficial approach to the problem.

This is not to deny that in many fields the Halachah today is far from being in consonance with the conditions and ideals of contemporary life. The fault, however, lies with the bearers of tradition, who have failed to maintain the momentum of intepretation and growth established by earlier and more creative spirits. Conditions in Israel have already forced action in several fields, notably that of the marriage law, where the Halachah is demonstrating its protean capacity to meet the issues of a new age. That process must be restored to all aspects of Jewish law and life.

V

The character of the Halachah creatively viewed is parallelled by its universality of scope. Beginning with the Decalogue, the Book of the Covenant and the Holiness Code, Jewish law has always concerned itself with man's entire life, individual and social, and has expressed itself both in ethical and ritual enactments. While tradition considers both the ritual and ethical elements of Jewish law as binding, it is a distortion to maintain that it regards them as of equal significance. The authoritative statement of Rab: לא ניתנו המצוות אלא לצרף בהן את הבריות "The Commandments were given in order to purify human nature" (Gen. Rabbah 44:1) clearly recognizes ritual as the means, and the ethical life as the goal, of religion. Nor is this attitude limited to the Haggadah. No other "commandment between man and God" can rival the Sabbath in importance. Yet the Halachah, which establishes the norm מפקחין פקוח נפש בשבת "Saving a human life takes precedence over the Sabbath" (Ket. 5a; cf. Yoma 85a, etc.), insists that even life itself must be sacrificed rather than violate the basic religious and ethical commandments of idolatry, immorality and murder: אין לך דבר העומד בפני פקוח נפש אלא עבודת כוכבים וגלוי עריות ושפיכות דמים בלבד (Ket. 19a; cf. Sanh. 74a). It is noteworthy that even of these three, Rabbi Ishmael permits the practice of idolatry under duress, except if it be publicly committed, where its impact upon the people as a whole would be disastrous: א״ר ישמעאל מנין שאם אמרו לו לאדם עבוד עבודת כוכבים ואל תהרג מנין שיעבוד ואל יהרג ת״ל וחי בהם ולא שימות בהם יכול אפילו בפרהסיה ת״ל ולא תחללו את שם קדשי ונקדשתי. Thus for him only two commandments, and these both ethical, remain supreme under all circumstances (Sanh. 74a). The same hierarchy of values is implied in the familiar Mishnah: עבירות שבין אדם למקום יו״כ מכפר עבירות שבין אדם לחבירו אין יו״כ מכפר עד שירצה את חבירו. "For transgressions between man and man, Yom Kippur cannot atone until he appease his fellow man." (Mishnah Yoma 8:9). In sum, while both the ritual and ethical elements of the Halachah are binding, the latter are more important than the former — that is the classical position of Jewish tradition, which modern Judaism can wholeheartedly accept.

The researches of Jewish scholars from the days of Frankel and Weiss to those of Chernowitz and Ginzberg reveal that the Halachah has a history. Hence to decide what the law requires on any given issue means not the discovery of a point, but the plotting of a line on a graph, where tradition is one coordinate, and contemporary life the other. To disregard either spells death to Judaism. In other words, it is important to know not merely where the Halachah stands, but in what direction it is tending. This is possible only by exploring in each case the *ideals* which constitute its spirit and motivation and the *circumstances* under which it arose.

VI

Having ascertained the position of the Halachah on any given issue and decided which *conditions* and *ideals* of contemporary life are to be reckoned with, it remains to determine the *method* of its *development*. In exceptional cases Rabbinic Judaism had recourse to legislation through *takkanot* and *gezerot*, positive and negative enactments, and this procedure is by no means to be summarily dismissed from consideration. However, many factors suggest that this device be used sparingly, if at all, today, and that only after the dominant method of interpretation has been proved inadequate. The *takkanot* and *gezerot* of earlier ages presupposed a far greater degree of homogeneity of outlook and practice in the Jewish community than exists today, and a correspondingly greater recognition of the authority of the rabbinate than any rabbinic group, particularly the Rabbinical Assembly, now enjoys. Moreover, during the past few centuries, the influence of historical conditions in Eastern Europe where the bulk of world Jewry was concentrated, impelled the *Aharonim*, who were their legal authorities, to adopt an ever more passive attitude toward the Halachah, avoiding any bold creative activity, and relying on the principle ספק איסורא לחומרא "When in doubt the severer opinion is to prevail." As a result, the flexibility and the power of growth of Jewish law have been severely curtailed in modern times. Common sense would dictate that we walk before we run, and that interpretation be utilized to the utmost before recourse be had to legislation.

Historically, the growth of Jewish law through interpretation proceeded through two methods. The first, which many scholars regarded as the older, was the method of *Midrash* "the searching of Scripture." It consisted of the analysis by scholars of the text of the Torah, both literally and through special canons of inter-pretation in order to deduce the laws from it. The *Tannaitic Midrashim* of the schools of Rabbi Ishmael and Rabbi Akiba, of which the *Mekilta, Sifra and Sifre* have reached us virtually intact, while others have survived only in part, are the literary monuments of this technique. The limits of this method, however, were reached early and its results were relatively circumscribed, with the result that it was not generally utilized after the second century c. e.

Instead, the method of *Halachah* or *Mishnah* proved far more fruitful. This approach derived its impetus not from the text of Scripture, but from the context of life. By and large the process would begin with a felt need among the people, of which the scholars became conscious. The spiritual leaders would then deter-mine for themselves whether the particular need or aspiration was socially desirable and spiritually valuable. If not, they would oppose it, or seek to suppress and minimize it. Thus, Professor Ginzberg has suggested that the absence of angelology in the Mishnah was due to the desire of the redactors to eliminate, or at least reduce, this element in Jewish folk-belief. That angels bulked large in the religious consciousness of the people is clear from the Apocrypha and the Pseudepigrapha, the Gemara and the late Midrashim.

If the scholars concluded that the expressed need or ideal was worthwhile, they would seek to bring it into the mainstream of Jewish tradition by finding a basis for it in the text of Scripture as amplified by the seven norms of interpretation of Hillel, the thirteen principles of Rabbi Ishmael and the elaborate thirty-two rules of Rabbi Eliezer, son of Rabbi Jose the Galilean. That two scholars representing contrary points of view could each validate his position by finding a Biblical support, indicates that while at times the Biblical text itself was the ground for the divergence, by and large the impetus was the differing evaluation of what was desirable and necessary, and therefore in the spirit of the Torah.

In the vast majority of instances recorded in the Talmud, this motivation is implicit, but often enough it is explicit. To cite one or two examples: In arguing with Rabbi Akiba regarding the punishment of the priest's daughter, who had yielded to immorality, Rabbi Ishmael calls out to his colleagues: וכי מפני שאתה דורש בת ובת תצא זו לשרפה "Because you press the meaning of the Vav in the word *ubhath* shall this girl be punished by burning?" (Sanh. 51b). The complicated laws of ritual impurity were consciously set aside by the Sages, as far as the soil of the land of Israel was concerned, out of regard for the sanctity of the land and the national interest.

Thus the Talmud declares: עילה מצאו וטיהרו ארץ ישראל (Ket. 20b; Nazir 65b) which Rashi explains: עלילה בעלמא מצאו חכמים והחזיקו בה לתלות בה ולטהר את ארץ ישראל "The Sages discovered an excuse and grasped it, in order to lean upon it and declare the land of Israel free from ritual impurity" (*ad loc.*). The city of Jerusalem was also exempted from these disabilities on similar grounds.

Even when this motivation was not specifically set forth, the process proceeded along these lines. It has its parallel in the American system of judicial review, in which laws enacted by the States or the Congress may, upon appeal, be brought before the Supreme Court, which then seeks to relate them to the Constitution.

It may be added that while no analogy is ever complete, it applies in all essentials even to the doctrine of the immutability of the Law, the impossibility of formally abolishing any enactment of the Torah. Technically, the Constitution of the United States, which lays no claim to Divine origin, may be amended. Yet after more than a century and a half of the most eventful history in the life of a great nation, scarcely more than a dozen amendments have been added to the original Bill of Rights. On the other hand, hundreds of thousands of laws have been passed by municipal, state and national legislatures, all of which are potentially or actually brought into relationship with the existent Constitution through the process of judicial review.

Undoubtedly there are instances to be found where the Supreme Court justices reach their decisions on purely formal grounds, with the letter of the Constitution determining the results. But more often than not, as is indicated by the bifurcation of the bench into "liberals" and "conservatives" and by the Court's change of viewpoint with the passing of time, the judges begin by deciding in their own minds whether the law is calculated to advance the goals laid down in the Preamble of the Constitution "to form a more perfect union, insure domestic tranquility, provide for the common defense, promote the general welfare, and secure the blessings of liberty." If they are persuaded that such is the case, the law is "constitutional" — that is to say, it is in the spirit of the Constitution. Like the lawyers who have defended the given statute, the Court then proceeds to validate it by relating it to the letter of the basic law of the land.

That this technique of discovering the law is indistinguishable from creating the law, students of legal philosophy like Morris R. Cohen have long pointed out. Viewed from the standpoint of the letter of the law, that is true, but from the standpoint of its spirit, interpretation is not only a lifegiving but a genuine process. It must be revived in our own day. Jewish religious leadership must become actively aware of the problems of our time, evaluate the various solutions proposed and relate the preferred conclusion to the body of Jewish law, through the interpretation of the existent Halachah. It would be as unjust as it is unpractical to dismiss this method as having failed; actually, it has not been tried.

VII

As we proceed to utilize traditional Jewish law for modern life, we shall discover that it possesses several other valuable resources within it. Such is the *existence of categories* within the structure of Jewish law. Like every living legal system, it recognizes that there are gradations in acts, both positive and negative. The warning of Rabbi Judah Hanasi: הוי זהיר במצוה קלה כבחמורה שאין אתה יודע מתן שכרן של מצוות "Be as careful with a light commandment as with a weightier one, for you do not know the relative reward of the commandments" (Abot 2:1) is designed to stimulate the observance of the lesser commandments, the existence of which it obviously conceded.

Similarly, all violations are not of the same severity, as is self-evident from the various degrees of punishment imposed in rabbinic law, such as the four modes of execution, which themselves vary in severity, *kareth*,[16] flagellation and the various fines (*kenas*). To be sure, we are not likely today to reintroduce these penalties; Rabbinic law, with its insistence upon *hatra'ah* and other safeguards against unmerited punishment, has seen to that. But the gradation of acts that exists in Rabbinic law, both with regard to forbidden and meritorious deeds, is an extremely fruitful concept which should be utilized by the modern Halachist in deciding contemporary issues.

The highest level of permissibility and favor consists of acts which are beyond the line of religious and moral duty. These deeds Jewish tradition calls *Kiddush ha-Shem* "the hallowing of God's name," when they involve fundamental religious values and the collective honor of Israel, and *lifnim mishurat hadin* "within the line of the law" when they relate chiefly to the individual in his civil relations to his fellow-men. On the other hand, adherence to a higher standard of piety than the law requires with regard to ritual commandments (*mitzvoth bein adam la-Makom*) is described in rabbinic literature by the phrase: קדש עצמך במותר לך.[17] From the medieval age onward, Jewish life knew also of those who chose to be *mahmirin le'atzman* "more stringent with regard to themselves than the law requires." Though these acts of this type might differ in temper and motivation, they were all performed in obedience to a categorical imperative — the desire to maintain the loftiest standard possible of adherence to God's will, free from the fear of punishment or the desire of reward.

The next level of permissibility consists of the prescribed *mitzvoth*, the performance of which is regarded as praiseworthy. As has already been noted, these, too, are not all of equal importance or significance in Jewish law.

It is worth noting that acts that we might be disposed to

---

[16] Literally — "cut off" — a term variously interpreted to mean an untimely death decreed by God for the transgressor or that he die childless.

[17] Sanctify yourself and abstain even from that which is legally permitted.

regard as religiously or ethically "neutral" do not develop a special term in traditional Judaism. This is no accident, but flows directly out of the life-affirming character of the Jewish religion. For Jewish tradition regards such acts as the satisfaction of one's bodily needs, the enjoyment of life's pleasures, the cultivation of one's skills and the preparation for a useful career not as neutral, but as positive *mitzvoth*, which are obligatory for man because they are calculated to testify to the glory of God and enhance it. Hence, Judaism ordains that every licit human experience is to be sanctified by a special benediction.

Within the *abheroth* or religious offenses, a similar hierarchy is to be found. The severest transgressions are those within the competence of human courts to punish, either by capital or physical punishment or by financial penalty.

Another widespread category in Jewish law consists of acts which the Codes describe as *'asur lekhathilah ubedi'avad patur* "acts which in advance are forbidden, but which once committed, are not punishable." Even in so sacred an area as that of the family, the Talmud recognizes that certain marriages which violate negative commandments, while forbidden in advance, are nonetheless valid (*kiddushin tophesin behayyabhei lavin*).

Rabbinic courts recognized that certain transgressions were beyond the competence of human justice. Offenses such as these they describe variously as *'anush karet* "worthy of extermination by God," or *patur bedinei adam vehayyabh bedinei shamayim* "unpunishable by human agency but punishable by the laws of Heaven." This is explained in greater detail in the Tosefta (Shevuot, Ch. 3) אינו חייב לשלם מן הדין ואין השמים מוחלין לו עד שישלם.[18]

VIII

It is a commonplace that the most difficult decisions facing us in life do not involve a clear-cut choice between right and wrong, but rather a conflict between two ideals, which special circumstances place in opposition to one another. Here the decision must necessarily be painful, for one value will need to be sacrificed

---

[18] "He is not obligated to pay the sum, by law, but God will not forgive him until he does pay."

in order to preserve the other. What is more, different individuals will decide in varying fashion, depending upon their scale of values, their temperament and other subjective factors. It is in areas such as this that freedom of the religious conscience operates, a fact to which Dr. Louis M. Epstein called our attention in a valuable paper several years ago. That a conflict of ideals or practices may arise in special cases would not justify a legal system in denying the validity of either ideal. Now the rabbis were keenly aware of instances where the individual might be faced by such a conflict and thus be compelled to violate the law. Rabbinic law showed its keen insight into human nature, as well as its solicitude for the maintenance of the entire structure by several categories. Such is the category of *patur 'abhal 'asur* "unpunishable but forbidden," which is applied by the Mishnah for example, in the familiar Sabbath law: המכבה את הנר מפני שהוא מתיירא מפני גויים מפני לסטים מפני רוח רעה או מפני החולה שיישן פטור כחס על הנר כחס על השמן כחס על הפתילה חייב "He who extinguishes a lamp on the Sabbath because he is afraid of robbers, an evil spirit, or to enable a sick person to sleep is unpunished; if his object is to save the lamp, the oil or the wick, he is punishable" (Shab. 2:15).

In a not inconsiderable number of instances, the rabbis were confronted with practices they could not favor, but where they felt nothing would be achieved by embarking on a campaign against them. Either they were deeply rooted in the life of the people or the motives underlying the action were praiseworthy, or at least understandable, or there was little likelihood of any change at that juncture because of prevailing conditions. In such cases, the Talmud tells us לא מיחו חכמים בידם "the Sages did not protest publicly against the practice." These affected such varied elements as the liturgy, agricultural law, the marriage law, relationships with the Gentile community and the prerogatives of royalty (Cf. Mishnah Pes. 4:8; Ket. 1:5; Git. 5:8; Sanh. 2:4; Men. 10:8; Tos. Shek. 1:12; Y. Suk. II, 52d; B. Ket. 3b).

Categories such as these suggest to the modern Halachist that he may at times wish to utilize a similar approach with regard to acts which arise out of genuine practical necessity, but which he is unable either to approve enthusiastically or forbid categorically. In particular, the rabbinic category of *patur 'abhal 'asur* may be reinterpreted by us as constituting the concept of "not recommended," with the decision in each case one which only the individual involved can make for himself.

IX

Two more observations are in order with regard to the creative functioning of the Halachah. Common sense dictates a realisitic approach to the contemporary problems of Jewish law, both with regard to the people for whom it is intended, and the areas of life where this process of interpretation is likely to prove most fruitful.

Attention has been called elsewhere to the need of recognizing the obvious fact that many modern Jews have all but completely surrendered the concept of Jewish law in practice, and to only a slighter degree in theory. To modify Jewish law in order to bring it into conformity with their way of life is tantamount to amending the Constitution of the United States so as to harmonize it with the viewpoint of an anarchist, however high-minded he may be. Such well-intentioned efforts can only succeed in undermining Jewish law for those sections of the Jewish people who still reverence it and seek to live by it, without winning over those who have strayed from the Jewish way of life. On the contrary, all experience teaches that the task of winning back the erring and the estranged, heartrendingly difficult as it is, is more often successfully achieved by traditional religion than by its non-traditional forms. This consideration aside, it is self-evident that only Jews who accept the concept of Jewish law and seek to observe it, can legitimately expect to mould the character of Jewish law and help determine its needs, direction and aspiration. *Klal Yisrael*, or Catholic Israel, as a body competent to create in Jewish law, includes only such Jews as recognize the existence and authority of Jewish law. When the Talmud said פוק חזי מה עמא דבר "Go see how the people conduct themselves" (Ber. 45a; Erub. 14a) it referred to a period when virtually all Jews qualified by this test. Had there been a large number of *Elisha ben Abuyas* or general Sabbath violators in their day, the Rabbis would not have consulted *them* as to how Sabbath observance should be conceived of.

Finally, after several centuries during which the entire field of Jewish law has lain fallow, it is obvious that all the broken fences cannot be mended at once. Hence, we should first take up the strand of development in those areas where our efforts are likely to have the most effect, and where the need is most acute. In the Diaspora, at least, the influence of the rabbinate is restricted largely to two areas — family law and synagogue life. Without ruling out action elsewhere, it is both our duty and opportunity to deal courageously and reverently with such problems, fundamental problems, as the disability of women in Jewish law, which still exists in the synagogue service, marriage law and religious life generally. Mixed pews which have become the norm without recourse to the Halachah, and the *agunah* proposal, which had recourse to the Halachah without becoming the norm, represent fields of productive thought and action which are open to us today. Other aspects of the same problem are the calling of women to the Torah, the *Bat Mitzvah* rite and the counting of women in the Minyan.

The Sabbath Halachah, especially the problems of traveling and the use of electricity, are so fundamental to Jewish life and the future of Judaism in America, that we are justified in approaching them from the standpoint here presented — the affirmation of the viability of the Halachah in meeting the problems of our age and its inherent value in ennobling human life and making man worthy to be God's partner in the universe.

Section B

THE HALACHAH ON TRAVEL ON THE SABBATH

By Rabbi Ben Zion Bokser

The Sabbath has been the most sanctifying influence in Judaism. Its place in Jewish life is richly extolled in literature and folklore, ancient as well as modern. It attained its hold on our people, however, not because it was glorified in the Aggadah, but because it was zealously served by the Halachah. Maimonides alluded to this when, in discussing the elaborate disciplines of the Sabbath Halachah, he states: "No opinions retain their vitality except those which are confirmed, publicized and by certain actions constantly revived among the people" (*Moreh*, II 31). Judaism shows here its most characteristic genius. It does not attempt to teach by dogmatic affirmation, but by a discipline injected into the pattern of life itself.

The Sabbath rose to its highest significance by the positive purposes to which it was set. The festive character of the Sabbath meal, with the entire family participating, the stirring songs which cast their spell on all who shared in the experience were the dramatic events that made deep impressions on the people. The sessions of study, the group reading of Psalms, the weekly review of the Biblical portion, gave the positive content of this great day.

From a social as well as a psychological point of view, however, the prohibitions played an equally vital role. It was the prohibitions which freed man from immersion in the world, and thus helped create the distinctive Sabbath atmosphere which pervaded the Jewish home, and became part and parcel of the Jewish personality. The negative elements in the Sabbath Halachah prepared the day for its highest possibilities as a source of relaxation as well as of sanctification. The rabbis were clearly aware of it when, commenting on the verse in Exodus 31:14 which characterizes the Sabbath as "holy unto you," they point to its negative rather than its positive attributes, to the closing of places of business and the cessation from labor. כי קדש היא לכם מגיד שהשבת מוספת קדושה על ישראל. מה לפלוני חנותו נעולה שהוא משמר את השבת מה לפלוני בטל ממלאכתו שהוא משמר את השבת (Mekilta, *ad loc.*).[19]

The prohibition of travel on the Sabbath was a vital contribution to preparing the day for its mission to sanctify life. The basis of this prohibition is the verse in Ex. 16:29 "Abide ye every man in his place; let no man go out of his place in the seventh day" (שבו איש תחתיו אל יצא איש ממקומו). Originally directed at the gatherers of manna in the wilderness, this verse was seen in a more general light, as an interdiction of all movement on the Sabbath beyond one's domicile.

Rabbinic sources offer us two general reasons for the objection to travel, both related to the goal of liberating man on the Sabbath day from labor as well as anxiety and distraction. The first consideration is expressed in the principle of *teḥumin*, the need of fixing one's domicile in a particular place, and then limiting one's motions within a prescribed radius of that place. The original interpretation of the Biblical verse was literal, and the place of permissible movement was confined to the home plus an additional 2000 cubits (שבו איש תחתיו אלו ד׳ אמות אל יצא איש ממקומו אלו אלפים אמות Yalkut, *ad loc.*).[20] The tendency to socialize the Sabbath finally wrought a change in interpretation and the home was then taken in the widest possible sense, to include one's city, supplemented by the usual radius of 2000 cubits of additional movement. The terminus of allowed movement could moreover be pushed farther away when necessary through an *erub*, a conscious designation of the desired place outside the city as part of one's home by depositing there some food as a token of home. A traveller who chanced to be away from a city at the advent of the Sabbath could, by an act of conscious designation known as *kinyan shebitah*, fix his home anywhere and then he was free to move within the 2000 cubit radius of that place.

---

[19] "It is said 'for the Sabbath is holy unto you'. This is intended to teach us that the Sabbath adds sanctity to the people of Israel. People ask why is this man's store closed, why is this man not working today? The answer is — he observes the Sabbath."

[20] The Biblical phrase 'abide ye every man in his place' refers to a place of 4 cubits — i. e. the home. The phrase "Let no one go out of his place" refers to the extreme limit of permissible walking on the Sabbath, i. e., 2.000 cubits.

Travel on the Sabbath by riding an animal was also forbidden for the additional reason of seeking to avoid involvement in incidental labor, such as possibly cutting down a twig in order to prod the animal on its way. There is also the suggestion that one who rides an animal might easily move beyond the confines of the *tehum* and cross the area around the home which is the zone of allowed movement on the Sabbath לא רוכבין על גבי בהמה שמא יצא חוץ לתחום ש״מ תחומין דאורייתא אלא גזירה שמא יחתך זמרה (Bezah 36b).[21]

There are other elements in the Sabbath Halachah which regulate movement, but they all testify to the same underlying goal. The rabbis did not seek arbitrarily to stifle the free movement of life. They sought to reject tension, undue exertion. They sought to mold the Sabbath into a day of serene, relaxed living. Thus they banned the *pesia gasa*, the hurried walk of the busy days of the week. The Tosefta generalized: "One may not run on the Sabbath to the point of exhaustion, but one may stroll leisurely throughout the day without hesitation." (אין רצין בשבת כדי להתעמל אבל מטיילין כדרכו כל היום כלו ואינו חושש). The Sabbath was to be a day of peace and the Halachah was engaged in fashioning the usual rabbinic fence that was to keep man from crossing over into the domain where the world and its cares stood ready to devour his serenity and his rest.

The Sabbath law was as flexible as every other branch of the Halachah. Under some cicumstances the prohibition against riding was waived, simply because other values at stake were deemed more pressing. Thus it eventually ceased to operate altogether in the case of ocean travel. The difficulty of facing travel in such a way as to avoid being on the boat on the Sabbath was clearly the most significant factor. It would have paralyzed movements from Palestine to other parts of the world, which in many cases depended on schedules beyond the control of the individual passengers. In some instances the journey as a whole was of more than a week's duration, and it was clearly impossible to halt the ship for the Sabbath observing passenger.

That the rabbis originally looked upon ocean travel as included

---

[21] "It is not permitted to ride on an animal on the Sabbath, lest it lead to going beyond the permissible travel limits on the Sabbath. Can we deduce from this that the limit for such travel is Biblically fixed? No! The prohibition of riding stems from the fear that the rider may break off a branch to use as a whip."

in the category of prohibited movement is manifestly clear from our sources. The Talmud in Shabbat 19a provides: "One must not undertake a boat voyage less than three days prior to the Sabbath . . . On the other hand, the short distance from Tyre to Sidon one may undertake even the day preceding the Sabbath." (ת״ר אין מפליגין בספינה פחות מג׳ ימים קודם לשבת . . . ומצור לצידון אפילו בע״ש). In time the law reckoned with life and the formula was eventually worked out, allowing even the boarding of the ship on the Sabbath itself, provided one has deposited there some of his belongings, thereby designating it as his home for the Sabbath through an act of *kinyan shebitah*.

It is significant from our point of view that even travel on land was in some exceptional cases suspended in consonance with other considerations, deemed even more pressing than Sabbath rest. Thus a witness testifying as to the appearance of the new moon was permitted to travel on the Sabbath. He was to come riding on an animal on the Sabbath day (Mishnah Rosh Hashana 1, end): מי שראה את החדש ואינו יכול להלוך מוליכין אותו על החמור . . . מחללין את השבת [22] (ויוצאין לעדות החדש שנא׳ אלה מועדי ה׳ אשר תקראו אותם במועדם). In the face of danger to life the prohibition of travel was of course to be waived as was every other provision concerning Sabbath observance.

Do the conditions of modern life call for revision of the Sabbath Halachah concerning travel? There has been much agitation in recent years demanding a change. It is also pertinent to note that this element of the Sabbath Halachah is being widely ignored even by Jews who otherwise believe in and practice the disciplines of Judaism. There are certain facts about life in the modern world, it has been argued, which make the restriction on travel especially irksome. Our cities are large and people do not live in compact neighborhoods. Members of the same family, even when living in the same city, are often so far from each other that they can be reached only by travel. Many people find it difficult even to reach a synagogue on the Sabbath, unless they travel. The mechanization of travel through modern means of transportation has minimized

---

[22] "If a man saw the new moon but could not walk, he may be taken on an ass (on the Sabbath) . . . they may profane the Sabbath and go forth (even with a burden) to bear witness about the new moon, for it is written 'These are the set Feasts of the Lord, even holy convocations which ye shall proclaim in their appointed season' (Lev. 23:4)."

the element of work involved, and, therefore, it has been suggested, that the old objection to it ought not apply.

The consideration of modern conditions suggest, however, other factors as well, which would argue against lifting the ban on Sabbath travel. We must judge our question in the light of the two principles enunciated by the rabbis in their prohibition of Sabbath travel. The first is the principle of *teḥumin*, of safeguarding the home that it may be the proper medium within which the sanctifying power of the Sabbath was to be experienced. An analysis of the facts involved suggest that this principle is far from being obsolete, and that, on the contrary, it has taken on in our day additional cogency as an argument for banning Sabbath travel. The complexities of large city life which have diversified the interests and occupations of individual members of the family and have subjected them to different time schedules has proven a serious menace to the stability of the family. The Sabbath as a sanctifying influence on the lives of people depends on its being set within a fixed home and on uniting the entire family for the Sabbath experience. If on the Sabbath, too, members of the family will each go his way and pursue a private schedule of social or recreational life, the Sabbath experience will drop out of our lives altogether. The principle of *teḥumin*, while in itself not entirely pertinent to our problem, since travel under present conditions is not intended to cross beyond the confines of the city boundary, yet points to a principle which has lost none of its validity. If we want to preserve the Sabbath, then we must create fixed home experiences and limit movement away from home, in order that the family be kept together. There can be no Sabbath atmosphere, none of its sanctifying or relaxing elements, without the rejection of the things that undermine the home's fixity and threaten the stability of the family as an integrated unit of human life.

An analysis of the nature of travel under modern conditions, moreover, fails to bear out the contention that it is free of the element of work. The precaution against possible need of cutting a twig to prod an animal (שמא יחתוך זמורה) has its parallel in the need of guarding against mechanical failures in the car. Anyone driving an automobile is painfully aware of the possibility of a flat tire or other failures in the vehicle, and of the distractions and the anxieties which are incidental to them. One cannot set out to

travel, whether in a private or public vehicle without money, papers
of all kinds, writing materials and various other appurtenances,
which contradict the atmosphere of the Sabbath. The rabbis were
brilliant interpreters of human nature when they developed the
principle of *mukzah*, banning the very handling of the objects that
are used in our week day tasks, putting them out of our minds.
Thus were we to escape the associations which they suggest
and which will destroy the mood of the Sabbath. Travel involves
the utilization of objects all of which carry associations disturbing
to Sabbath peace. No one can attain the *neshamah yeterah*, the
"over-soul" of the Sabbath, unless one withdraws physically as
well as mentally from the mundane affairs, their associations, and
the very objects which represent them for us.

There is, in addition, the element of exertion and work in
the effort of driving a car or even to travel on a public vehicle.
There is, of course, combustion caused in the motor which is
an indispensable in the vehicle's movement. But there is work
in a more direct sense. The tension of driving in traffic, of pressing
against crowds, of being subject to noise, of waiting in line — all
these are extremely exerting to the nerves of people. They make
any trip a tiring experience. The Sabbath is meant to free us not
only from the work that tires the body but from the experiences
which tire and weary our nervous system. The tensions of modern
life have taken a frightful toll, above all, on the nerves of people.
They have attacked not so much the body, as the spirit. Modern
man is especially in need of periodic emancipation from the
machines and the complexities they create for him. Modern man
needs the Sabbath urgently, desperately, as a vital healing of the
ills which beset him. And we shall never have the genuine Sabbath
unless we eliminate travel on that day.

Weighing all the circumstances, we are prompted to reaffirm
the ban against Sabbath travel. The fact that the ban is presently
being violated by large sections of our people need not deter us
from stating what we believe true and desirable. At the present
time the Sabbath is ignored in most other respects by great numbers
of our people. Shall we then appease their attitude and declare the
Sabbath Halachah generally inoperative? Jewish tradition knows
many periods in our history when widespread violation of law was
followed by a new-won respect for it. One thinks of the tribute paid

Rab that prior to his coming Sura was "an unfenced area, but that he fenced it in," making of it a community of Torah observing people. (רב בקעה מצא וגדר בה גדר). We owe it in any case to those who desire to observe the Sabbath and find in it its sanctifying influence, to advise them as to what is sound.

What about travelling on the Sabbath to perform a *mitzvah?* Rabbinic sources, we have noted, allowed travelling under some circumstances to perform a *mitzvah.* But let it be remembered that the cases cited all deal with exceptional situations, or with emergencies. The fixing of the new moon depended on witnesses and the act had to take place at a specified time. In the event of danger of life, as in illness or during war, action at the particular moment might be crucial and a delay perilous. It goes without saying that in some cases today, also, travel on the Sabbath may go on freely to accomplish certain urgent ends. The army of Israel in our own time fought on the Sabbath, and its vehicles moved freely, with the consent of the rabbinic authorities. Travelling to attend services is not in that category. If allowed, it would become regular, continuous. It would then be difficult to distinguish between one kind of travel and another.

It is, moreover, unrealistic to depend on travel for reaching a synagogue on the Sabbath. For many will be the occasions when travel will not be available, surely not for our young children, and then even the willingness to travel will not overcome the barrier of distance. As a normal arrangement a person who cares about religious life must endeavor to live accessibly close to a svnagogue, and accessibly close means within walking distance.

It is fair to add that in many cases the dilemma is not altogether real. People who feel they must travel could and do often walk greater distances on an occasional stroll. Our problem has become acute because, with the prevalence of the automobile, the art of walking has simply disappeared from many people and they use their cars for the shortest distances. It is significant that on the High Holidays many of our people, simply because those days have a greater emotional hold on them, will refuse to travel and insist on walking. That practice itself testifies to the subtle realization on the part of our people that there is something about travel which interferes with the spirit for which these Holidays stand. Intrinsically, of course, there is no distinction, neither in law nor in the values involved, between these Holidays and the Sabbath.

There may be cases where an individual will be unable to live accessibly close to the synagogue. Here we shall be faced with one of the dilemmas confronted by any moral system — a conflict of values. Given a choice between travel on the Sabbath or the total denial of the opportunities of worship on Sabbaths and festivals, we would regard travelling as the less objectionable alternative. On the other hand, there exists no objective standard by which to judge whether these are really the only alternatives we face. The decision rests on subjective factors over which the individual involved alone is sovereign. He, alone, can decide that he had no other alternative as to where to make his home and that the distance involved is his capacity to walk. Jewish tradition recognizes, of course, private prayer at home, on the Sabbath and the Holidays, as on week-days. If he should decide that private prayer at home offers him no adequate religious experience and that he has no alternative but to travel, the rabbi must assure him of his sympathetic understanding of the facts which have led him to his decision.

The Mishnah (Yoma, end) cites the case of an ill person who may eat on the Day of Atonement on the advice of his physician or his own sense of need for food. No authoritarian dictum of the rabbi is needed to suspend the law. It is one of the characteristic marks of Judaism that it trusts the conscience of the Jew who is really zealous for the observance of Torah. We assume that it is toward such Jews that our deliberations are directed. The others will regard our entire problem as unreal. They ride on the Sabbath indiscriminately even as they violate the Sabbath in other respects.

There has been some expression on the part of our colleagues that we ought to remove the sense of guilt from those who under necessity violate the Sabbath law. It is psychologically an impossible demand. Whenever a person breaks a pattern of life which he deems vital to his life, he will feel uncomfortable, he will experience a sense of guilt. That sense of guilt is a divine endowment to maintain that pattern of life and to discourage deviations from it. The sense of guilt Jews feel when they break the Sabbath is an echo of a claim which the Sabbath still has over their souls. Its presence is our opportunity to build toward positive observance. Should even the sense of guilt depart when we break the Sabbath, then will its hold over the emotional life of our people be altogether broken. No, our real problem is not the sense of guilt some of our people feel when they break the law, but the breaking of the law which produces it.

The Sabbath has always been an interference with the free movement of life, but it was an interference in the name of consciously sought values. There is no alternative. The conscious quest for values will always be an interruption of life's "natural" course, an act of its attempted direction and discipline. If we want the Sabbath values for our lives then we must be prepared to surrender a certain measure of freedom, to accept discipline. That discipline will be fully vindicated by what the Sabbath will offer us in the hallowing of life, in giving it serenity and peace. The disabilities that occasionally arise from the elimination of travel is the price for enjoying a Sabbath that is holy unto the Lord.

Section C

THE USE OF ELECTRICITY ON THE SABBATH

By Rabbi Arthur H. Neulander

The great changes that have been effected by technological and scientific inventions and discoveries in our times, force thoughtful Jews to re-examine the Sabbath Halachah, and reinterpret it to the needs of our day.

Electricity has become part of the warp and woof of our life. Our industrial system, our means of transportation and communication, the very conveniences of our home life depend upon electrification. In this paper, we limit ourselves to the legal adjustment required in dealing with the conveniences of home life. Lighting up our homes, telephoning, ringing our door-bells, using the elevator in our apartment houses, listening to the radio, watching television, refrigeration, washing and ironing, using electric razors, controlling our heating systems with thermostats, all involve the use of electricity. Many of these functions we normally direct consciously. Some are quite automatic, but all of these uses of electricity involve the application of Sabbath laws.

The earliest reaction to the problem of the use of electricity on the Sabbath was that of the *maḥmirim*. [23] This is a normal reaction. When studying history we frequently become aware of the fact that many forward steps in human civilization meet with resistance. New thoughts, new methods of procedure, new discoveries and inventions generally meet early disapproval by the conservative minded, particularly in connection with religion which is traditionally conservative in bent; but later these innovations are frequently accepted as the norm.

Thus, the change from the ancient Semitic script to the so-called *K'tav Ashuri* [24] was one that took centuries. Ezra and the prophets

---

[23] Stringent interpreters.

[24] The square Assyrian script.

of his generation are reputed to have brought the new script with them from Babylonia and ordained its use for the Biblical books in the 5th century B. C. E. But the old script continued to be used. The coins of the realm in Macabbean times and in the days of Bar Kochba were embossed in the old script. Even in the second century of the Common Era the Mishna (Yad. IV:5) still contains regulations concerning Biblical books written in the old script. The Samaritans never gave up the use of the old script; but, among us, the progressive forces ultimately prevailed and the *K'tav Ashuri* is the one used today in our Holy Scrolls. Many other illustrations of this process are to be found in human culture.

In the very field of the Sabbath we can actually trace such early opposition against a new invention being broken down by the pressure of social usage. Oil lamps were in Mishnaic times approved for *ner shabbat* (the Sabbath Light). Later, candles were invented. The use of candles for the *mitzvah* of *hadlakat haner* (lighting the Sabbath Light) was at first questioned, then opposed and finally after many generations given grudging approval. Wax candles thus became acceptable. Today, candles for the Sabbath lights are the norm. For Hanukkah there is still a sentimental preference for oil lamps though wax candles are permitted. (Documentation for this development can be found in Rabbi Sanders A. Tofield's "A Study of Sabbath Halakkah on the Use of Light and Transportation.")

The use of electricity is something relatively new in human experience. The question of permitting its use for light on the Sabbath has been debated for the last two or three generations but has not been satisfactorily resolved. No individual opinion has won the approval of Klal Yisrael. The extensive literature on the subject which continues receiving the attention of the scholars of our time testifies to the fact that we are dealing with one of the living issues of the Halachah. Accordingly we may address ourselves to it from our own point of view, and make decisions for the large group of Jews who look to us for spiritual guidance.

We do not pretend in this paper to make an exhaustive presentation of our views on the question of the use of electricity on the Sabbath. But the main line of argumentation is concisely sketched so that a conclusion may be reached and a decision made.

Those who disapprove the use of electricity on the Sabbath base themselves on the Biblical prohibition לא תבערו אש בכל מושבותיכם ביום השבת. They subsume electricity under the category of fire.

We find this identification between electricity and fire to be wrong both on Halachic and on scientific grounds. In order to subsume electricity under the category of fire it would be necessary to prove that electricity has the characteristics which the Halachah ascribes to fire.

According to the Halachah fire is something that is *soref*, i. e., the substance afire is itself consumed in the process of burning and is turned to charcoal or ashes. This characteristic of fire is deduced from the following statement of Samuel (Shab. 42a). מכבין גחלת מתכת ברשות הרבים בשביל שלא יזוקו בה רבים אבל לא גחלת של עץ.[25] Rashi, in reference to כיבוי ביום טוב (Shab. 134a) explains the reason: גחלת של עץ אסור דשייך בה כיבוי לפי שעושה פחם גחלת של מתכת לא שייך בה כיבוי דאינו נעשה פחם.[26] Samuel's statement becomes the basis of the regulation גחלת המונחת במקום שרבים יזוקו בה יכול לכבותה בין אם היא של מתכת בין אם היא של עץ והרמב״ם אוסר של עץ (שלחן ערוך אורח חיים ס׳ של״ד),[27] The Magen Abraham explains this regulation on the grounds that בשל מתכת ליכא כיבוי דאינו שורף.[28] Thus *kibuy* (extinguishing) does not apply to anything that is not *soref*, undergoing the process of combustion or oxidation. Halachically, therefore, anything that is not *soref* is not *esh* (fire).

Another characteristic of fire according to the Halachah is, that is must produce a flame. In a discussion in Pesaḥim 75a on the statement ת״ר חתכו ונתנו על גבי גחלת רבי אומר אומר אני שזה צלי אש the phrase על גבי גחלת in this Baraitha is limited to גחלת של מתכת because it is assumed that אש לאו מתכת של גחלת

---

[25] "We may extinguish a glowing metal coal in the public street so that people should not be injured by it, but not a wooden coal."

[26] Rashi, in commenting on the question of extinguishing coals on a festival, points out that it is forbidden to extinguish a wooden coal because it becomes charcoal i. e. is consumed, but that a metal coal may be extinguished because it is not consumed.

[27] "A glowing coal, lying in a place where people may be injured by it, may be extinguished, whether it is of metal or wood. Maimonides, however, forbids the extinguishing of a wooden coal."

[28] "As regards a metal coal there is no actual extinguishing, because it is not burned or consumed."

היא.²⁹ The assumption is questioned in the Talmud but finally sustained.

In an interesting Halachic discussion of the characteristics of fire in an article on הדלקת החשמל בשבת (Lighting Electricity on the Sabbath) published in the monthly *Sinai*, Vol. 12, No. 3, Rabbi S. Goronchick, chief chaplain of the Israeli Army, categorically states כל מידי שאינו יכול להוציא שלהבת על ידי שרפתו לאו אש היא.³⁰

Similarly another recent authority מהר״ם ח״ב ס׳ רמ״ז states ולא אכחד כי אני חוכך בלבי אם הבערה של הלעקטרי יש בו מלאכה דאורייתא כיון שלא היה. כמוהו במשכן – שהרי אינו אש ממש ואינו שורף חוט הברזל כאש דידן והוא מעין דוגמת אש.³¹

It therefore, follows that by both tests, electricity does not qualify as fire from the standpoint of the Halachah: (a) a filament of an electric light, when it becomes incandescent and gives off light, is undergoing no combustion, and (b) it gives off no flame.

The conclusion we have arrived at on Halachic grounds receives additional force because it is substantiated by science. On purely scientific grounds it is impossible for us to agree that electricity is a form of fire. On the contrary, the scientist considers fire one form of energy and electricity another. It is not necessary for us to belabor this argument. Whoever has studied modern science will not question the conclusion that fire and electricity must be considered two distinct forms of energy.

Let us, furthermore, take into account the mechanical aspect of modern life and consider our dependence on automatic electrical devices, such as the thermostat that controls the heating system in many of our apartments and homes, or the thermostat that controls the cooling apparatus in our electric refrigerators. It becomes necessary even for the *maḥmirim*, who hesitate to distinguish between fire and electricity, to modify their stand on the

---

²⁹ The discussion in *Pesaḥim* quotes the Rabbis as declaring that if a man cut up the paschal lamb and placed it on a glowing coal, then Rabbi Judah regards it as though he had roasted it on fire. A glowing coal, in this context, is regarded as a wooden coal. A metal coal, though glowing, is not considered fire.

³⁰ "Any glowing thing which does not produce a flame when burning is not considered fire."

³¹ "I shall not conceal that I doubt whether lighting electricity can be considered work which is Biblically prohibited, since there was no similar type of burning in the Tabernacle (the criterion used by the Rabbis for defining "work"). For it is not fire and does not consume the filament. It is only like fire."

automatic use of electricity on the Sabbath on Halachic grounds. If they would ban such use of electricity on the Sabbath because of the principle of פסיק רישיה ולא ימות [32] then it would be necessary, strictly speaking, to ban the opening of a window to let in a bit of fresh air, or the opening of a door to enter or leave a house. The room temperature would inevitably be affected and the thermostat would automatically either hasten or delay the working of the heating mechanism. Are we expected, because of the application of the principle of פסיק רישיה, to sit in the cold and confine ourselves to our homes on the Sabbath like Karaites? We may even go further. It is a scientific fact that every bodily movement sets in motion electro-magnetic waves. Some electrical home apparatus is thus inevitably affected by these waves that we ourselves radiate. Are we compelled to resuscitate the literal meaning of the Biblical verse שבו איש תחתיו אל יצא איש ממקומו ביום השביעי [33] which the Halachah reinterpreted centuries ago? Fortunately, loyalty to the Halachah as a living and growing influence does not require such a procedure. The principle of פסיק רישיה is Amoraic and quite unknown in the Mishnah which followed a more liberal attitude on מלאכה שאינו מתכוין. [34]

We must follow the same line of reasoning in the use of electric refrigeration. In opening the door of a refrigerator to take out food, we necessarily raise the temperature within the refrigerator. Although indirectly we automatically hasten the turning on of the cooling apparatus, we must, in order to make life bearable, overlook Abbaye and Rava's principle of פסיק רישיה ולא ימות and follow the older Mishnaic concept of מלאכה שאינו מתכוין. Furthermore, we must utilize the principle of מלאכה שאינו מתכוין and also מלאכה שאינה צריכה לגופה when using such mechanisms as the telephone; for we are not interested in flashing a signal on the switchboard; we are concerned with talking to a friend. [35]

In truth, scientists tell us that we cannot help setting electromagnetic waves in motion at all times. Our very bodies are giving

---

[32] A term which describes a necessary or inevitable result, as e. g. when the head of an animal or a man is cut off, death is an inevitable result.

[33] "Abide ye every man in his place, let no man go out of his place on the seventh day" (Ex. 16:29).

[34] A labor done unintentionally.

[35] See note 12.

off this force and every time we move a muscle these waves are increased. The insight and general responsiveness to life which characterized our sages of old leads us to assume that had they had our scientific knowledge they would not have applied the principle of פסיק רישיה where automatic use of electricity on the Sabbath is involved.

It is, therefore, clear that electricity is not to be regarded as a form of fire either by Halachic definition or from the evidence of science. Its widespread automatic use in modern life underscores the inescapable necessity of reckoning with these facts הלכה למעשה in contemporary civilization.

It is noteworthy that recent authorities, who not having utilized the testimony of science, do not sharply distinguish between electricity and fire, nevertheless are led to various liberalizing decisions in detail.

In a Teshuvah by Rabbi Simcha Levy issued through the Rabbinical Council of America the use of electrity on the Sabbath and Yom Tov for a microphone is permitted in the Synagogue if the electricity has been turned on Erev Shabbos. In the same Teshuvah the statement is made that the use of electricity on the Sabbath for an elevator does not come under the category of fire, even though sparks are produced in the motor. This opinion is given in the name of Rabbi Eliyahu Henkin. We understand that our own Dr. Hyamson, of blessed memory, also permitted the use of an apartment house elevator on the Sabbath. Reference is also made to Rabbi Idelson who states that turning on electric lights is not a מלאכה דאורייתא. All this seems to indicate a tendency to be lenient about the use of electricity on the Sabbath when not used for work prohibited on the Sabbath.

A word is in order on the possible objection that using electricity on the Sabbath means producing something new, נולד which is forbidden. Here the scientific facts clearly disprove the contention. Turning on an electric switch means using something which already exists, not creating anything new. The electricity has been produced through turbines or dynamos at the power stations and is stored in great condensers. It simply flows to us through cables and wires and is tapped by us in much the same way as water brought to us through mains and pipes from the great reservoirs is tapped by us by turning on a faucet.

In conclusion, Halachic consideration coupled with scientific evidence leads us to permit the use of electricity on the Sabbath. It is self evident that this permission applies only to such uses as do not involve work prohibited on the Sabbath. Thus we may permit turning on electric lights, telephoning, refrigeration, using a radio and television. But we cannot countenance the use of electricity for work prohibited on the Sabbath, such as cooking and baking, shaving with an electric razor, using the washing machine or an electric iron. The prohibition is here derived not from the use of electricity but from the nature of the work itself.

It must be clearly understood that whatever use of electric apparatus we permit on the Sabbath, we allow only on condition that use is in consonance with the spirit of the Sabbath. Thus the telephone may be used for conversation to strengthen family ties, to foster friendship and neighborliness, to convey a message of cheer to the sick or for a similar *debar mitzvah*. But the telephone should not be used for shopping purposes, for making a business appointment, much less a business transaction. The first group is in keeping with the holiness of the Sabbath. The second group violates the *menuḥah shelemah* of the Sabbath.

Similarly, in the use of radio or television common sense should dictate that only such programs may be indulged in which are not vulgar and banal and do not desecrate the sanctity of the ideal Sabbath. Only programs of high esthetic taste, of high ethical content, instructive and of social value are in keeping with our concept of a *Shabbat Kodesh* and only such programs should be listened to and seen on the Sabbath day.

We humbly believe that this decision is in conformity with the spirit of the Halachah and not in opposition to its letter. This decision, taking into cognizance the needs of our day, we hope, will promote the goal of Jewish law which has always been to enhance life and add to man's joy in the riches of the world so that he may gratefully acknowledge the goodness of God's providence.

INTRODUCTORY NOTE ON
JEWISH EDUCATION

"If there are no kids, there are no goats;
If there are no goats there are no flocks;
If there is no flock there is no shepherd."

In this allusive way the Talmud undertakes to stress the importance of educating the young in order to assure the survival of Judaism and Jewish life. The proposition would seem to be self-evident and yet it is equally evident that recognition of it has not led to uniform standards of Jewish education in the United States.

The Conservative movement, from its inception, had to face a four-fold problem in relation to Jewish education. In the first place, Jewish education was in many communities the responsibility of the synagogue. At the present time, with the virtual disappearance of the Ḥeder and the Talmud-Torah, Jewish education is almost exclusively in the hands of the congregation and the congregational school. Secondly, the American scene, with its public school system, inevitably made Jewish education peripheral in the thinking of both parents and child. This pattern has become accentuated by the increasing tendency to supplement the child's public school education with instruction in music and the like. Thirdly, there was, and continues to be, a sizeable group in the American Jewish community which regards Sunday School training alone or minimal preparation for Bar Mitzvah as an adequate form of Jewish education. And lastly, there is the undeniable fact that the average Jewish home and the average Jewish parent are increasingly less equipped to provide the child with training in Jewish behavior and worship.

Obviously, no form of Judaism which is minded to preserve Jewish traditional modes of behavior and worship could afford to ignore either the problem of Jewish education or the challenges presented to it in the American scene. In consequence, the Conservative movement has been steadily concerned with attempting to clarify the standards, the goals, the curriculum and the technique for adequate Jewish education in the Conservative congregational school.

409

The two papers printed below are attempts to set forth the thinking on Jewish education which prevails in Conservative Judaism. They overlap to some extent since they deal with the same situation and arrive at closely related conclusions, but there are also different emphases in each. Collectively, they represent what is probably the consensus of the movement.

The first was written by Rabbi Simon Greenberg and reflects some of his experiences in the direction of a large congregational school. The second was written by Rabbi Moshe Davis who is now Provost of the Seminary and was before that Dean of the Teachers Institute of the Seminary. Both papers were delivered to conferences on Jewish education held under the auspices of the Rabbinical Assembly in cooperation with the United Synagogue Commission on Jewish Education and the Teachers Institute.

It should be noted as background and supplement to these papers that the Conservative movement has adopted standards for its congregational schools which call for a minimum of six hours of instruction a week, for the elimination of one-day-a-week instruction and for emphasis upon instruction in Hebrew language and literature. These standards have been widely, though not uniformly, adopted. It should be further noted that the United Synagogue Commission on Jewish Education has steadily increased its publication of text-books and supplementary materials and clarified its curriculum. Moreover, in recent years, the camping and youth programs of the Conservative movement have taken an increasingly significant place as additional means of Jewish education.

BASIC PREMISES OF JEWISH EDUCATION IN AMERICA

By Rabbi Simon Greenberg

I.

A three fold task was enjoined upon us when we entered upon our Rabbinical careers. We were to be Rabbis, Teachers, and Preachers. No one of us can possibly fulfill to his own satisfaction all of the duties associated with these three exalted and exacting offices. Hence, we are constantly subject to the spiritually depressing burden of a sense of inadequacy and failures. We are not the kind of Preachers we would want to be. We are conscious of our shortcomings as Rabbis ministering to the personal needs of our congregation. But the pain of frustration reaches most deeply into our souls when we contemplate our achievements as Teachers in Israel. The most successful amongst us are keenly aware that in the realm of Jewish education the chasm between the goal and the attainment is widest and deepest.

Before a gathering such as this, it surely is not necessary to belabor the fact that failure to increase our efforts and to improve our results substantially in the area of Jewish education will of necessity condemn our movement to spiritual bankruptcy. Instead of helping to lead our people into a new era of Jewish authentic, creative religious and cultural life we will be abetting the progressive spiritual impoverishment now threatening to turn American Israel into an identifiable body without a recognizable mind or soul.

Nor will the success of our activities in other areas of Jewish life compensate for our failure in the educational area. Persuasive, inspiring and erudite preaching can and does influence parents to send their children to our schools. It will not keep them there for an extended period of time. Thoughtful, devoted, wise pastoral guidance can and does forge mighty bonds of attachments to the Rabbi and the congregation. It cannot, however, transmit the knowledge of our heritage prerequisite for intelligent and purposeful Jewish living. As leaders in the ranks of the Zionist movement, philanthropic enterprises and civic causes we unquestionably make invaluable contributions to the welfare of our people and of our faith. Yet, our success or failure as leaders in Israel will be judged historically upon what we as Rabbis do to preserve a knowledge of Torah in its widest sense, amongst our people, and to rouse within our people an abiding love for their heritage and a consuming passion to augment its resources and to transmit it to their children.

We recognize that we are fortunately not alone in carrying the responsibility for the advancement of Jewish education in our communities. Jewish educators are also heroically grappling with this problem. We must acknowledge at the very outset that without their cooperation we would be quite helpless. We have a grave responsibility towards them as well, and we shall return to that somewhat later in this paper. But our role in the educational field, whether we like it or not, is of paramount importance. We cannot shift this responsibility to the shoulders of Jewish educators and piously proclaim "*yadenu lo shafechu*," as we contemplate the desolation now reigning over such vast portions of the field of Jewish education. Jewish elementary and secondary education is centering with increasing tempo around the congregation. The same is true for adult Jewish education. There is every indication to believe that even Jewish higher education may in larger measure come under local or national congregational auspices. Our understanding of the problems involved and our active and courageous leadership in offering and implementing solutions are, therefore, indispensable.

II.

This conference is but one in a series of recent events which indicate our growing awareness of the gravity of the situation and our determination to cope with the challenge it presents to our loyalty, ingenuity and courage. I shall not dwell upon the larger enterprises which testify to the currents of new creative vitality surging through all the branches of our movement beginning with our alma mater, the Jewish Theological Seminary of America and reaching out into the manifold activities of the United Synagogue of America and of our Rabbinical Assembly. There is a new spirit of faith, of devotion, of wide horizons, abroad in our midst, and I believe that all of us are growing increasingly conscious of it and responding to it. I shall, however, refer in some detail to at least three actions recently initiated within our ranks which have a very direct bearing upon the problem of Jewish education. I do so because I believe that with these three actions as background we can better understand the purpose and the scope of this conference.

The first of the more recent educational activities of our movement was directed towards the problem of the Jewish Adult. The creation of the National Academy of Adult Jewish Studies so devotedly and efficiently directed by Rabbi Israel M. Goldman, brought into being in a comparatively short time a considerable body of new literature for adult study circles and institutes. In addition, it stimulated the inauguration of adult institutes in many communities and revitalized the adult study programs in many other congregations. More important perhaps than these immediate tangible results was the fact that through the national conferences sponsored by the National Academy for Adult Jewish Studies and through its propaganda literature it focused attention anew upon the need to reach out for the adult, and that for a double reason. In the first place, it might enable us to make up for the failure of elementary Jewish education to make an impression upon the contemporary Jewish adult while he was a youth. Secondly, it may give us an opportunity to bring Jewish information on an adult level to Jews whose intellectual contact with things Jewish never progressed beyond the elementary level. All of this was altogether in line with the best Jewish tradition which ever viewed the educational process as being essentially life-long. It was also completely in harmony with the new emphasis being placed by all American educators upon the need for making the adult at least in part a student. Educators who had formerly placed their hopes for the future of civilization and democracy upon the public school and high school have since been convinced beyond a reasonable doubt that a literate youth alone will not be capable of coping with the complicated problems of modern civilization. Adult men and women must cope with these problems. They must do so on the basis of the latest completest possible information. We are in need of conclusions reached by minds which are physically and socially mature.

The efforts along the lines of adult Jewish education appear for the time being to have reached a level plane. We are continuing but there is no noticeable spurt forward and upward.

The second significant stirring of an educational nature in our midst was the result of a keen awareness that we had practically no following among the adolescents. We had no high school system worthy of any mention whose curriculum was either of an intensive Hebraic character, or of a rich Jewish content though linguistically English in character. Our adolescents were not thinking of preparing themselves for Jewish religious, educational or recreational leadership. Professor Mordecai M. Kaplan placed that problem with all of its stark consequences vividly before us at one of our recent Rabbinical Assembly conventions. Under his leadership the Leadership Training Fellowship was brought into being. A summer session attracting a promising group of adolescents was held at the Seminary this past year. The seed of what can become one of the most inspiring aspects of our movement has been planted. But it shall require from us great sacrifices and constant vigilance and devotion.

Finally, we turned to the problem of elementary Jewish education. Here is an area in which there is still considerable vitality. A goodly number of boys and girls between the ages of 5 to 13 still come to our schools for one to ten years of instruction. Here we still do not have to go out to draft the members of at least one or two classes. We may not have as high a percentage of our children of school age in our congregational schools as we would like to have. But there is no comparison between the number of adults or adolescents attending a class for Jewish studies and the number of children below the age of 13. But what have we been doing for these boys and girls who do come to us? What kind of a curriculum, what sort of text books, what kind of teachers and supervision have we been offering them? For a number of years the Rabbinical Assembly and the United Synagogue had jointly co-operated through the Joint Commission on Jewish education, seeking thus at least to keep alive within our ranks our sense of duty within that area. A few texts were published and some plans outlined for the future. But the real step forward was taken when Doctor Abraham Millgram accepted our invitation to become the Educational Director of this Education Commission. He has been with us only a little more than a year but his presence is already being felt in the widening circle of our movement.

The first task to which the Education Commission, under Rabbi Millgram's leadership turned its attention, was the formulation of a set of objectives and standards for the afternoon congregational school. The pamphlet containing the results of months of careful deliberating by a group of devoted and thoughtful members of the Assembly has been widely distributed and we hope attentively read by all of you. In the course of the sessions there will surely be some occasion to discuss and examine its contents. But it is important that we understand the frame of mind with which the committee which produced this pamphlet approached its task. The Committee assumed that the afternoon congregational school will continue for a long time to be the predominant factor in Jewish elementary and secondary education. It assumed further that we have thus far failed to take full advantage of the educational opportunities offered by a well organized and well conducted afternoon congregational school. The tragic inadequacies in the realm of Jewish elementary and secondary education are due only *in part* to stumbling blocks inherent in the situation. It may indeed be true that the afternoon supplementary school cannot by its very nature produce the highest type of Jewish *talmid chacham*. It may be true that six hours per week devoted three times weekly to Jewish studies cannot make one sufficiently proficient in the world of Hebrew letters, Biblical, rabbinic, or modern. But it is our contention that far more can be accomplished within those six hours than we have thus far accomplished if only we understand how to utilize them better.

III.

We shall, during this Conference, investigate further ways and means of making our individual congregational school a more effective educational unit. However, our Conference would fail of its true purpose if it were limited only to that area of investigation. We are gathered so that we may encourage one another to a recognition of the fact that even if every congregational school associated with us were functioning at maximum capacity, our problem would yet be far from solved. We are here to stimulate our thinking as individuals and as groups so that we may envisage new educational avenues for us to explore. We have a great fear of becoming a group which in the realm of Jewish education is capable neither of grand vision nor of bold novel action.

Our fear is all the more genuine and justified because outside our ranks there have appeared men and women whose devotion, self-sacrifice and ingenuity have contributed new form and new content to Jewish education. The successful establishment of Camp Massad, the marked growth of Jewish day schools and Yeshivos, the increase in the number of Hebrew Kindergartens all clearly point to the truth that much new territory still remains for us to explore and that the last word has not yet been spoken either in the matter of the structure or the content of American Jewish education.

It is the purpose of this paper to indicate some of the new things we ought to do and some of the old paths we ought to cultivate more assiduously if we are to become more significant forces as Teachers in Israel. There is or there should be at least one basic premise which underlies all of our thinking and all of our action as rabbis and teachers. It concerns our attitude towards the future of Jewish life in America.

We are all Zionists and we believe in the justice of and the need for the establishment in Palestine of a free democratic Jewish commonwealth. But we at the same time affirm our deep conviction that it is both possible and desirable to raise a generation of Jews in America which will have both the knowledge and the will to live in accordance with the teachings of traditional Judaism. We are second to no one in our allegiance to the ideal of *Shivat Zion*. We, nevertheless, must clearly reaffirm our conviction that our Zionist hopes are in no way based upon a negation of the high possibilities of traditional Jewish life in America. It is of considerable importance for us to reiterate this conviction and to hold it clearly in mind, for there is good reason to believe that at least a portion of our neglect of Jewish education is due to an unhealthy pessimism in regarding the possibilities of traditional Judaism in America. Nor is our more hopeful outlook merely a matter of "whistling in the dark." The fact is that we do have encouraging indications of what can be achieved in this land. We do have American born Jewish boys and girls who have acquired in our schools both the knowledge and the will to live traditional Jewish lives. And what can be done for a handful can be done for a larger group.

As Jewish life in Palestine grows and develops, and its influence will begin to be felt more fully here, the basis for our faith in the future of traditional Judaism in America will become steadily wider and deeper. We envision a parallel growth of Jewish life in Palestine and in America. We believe that the two communities are not only historically related but are and must be spiritually and culturally interdependent. The Palestine Jewish community is and must be as greatly in need of a culturally vigorous and creative American Israel, as we are of a spiritually healthy and productive Palestinian Jewry. In the realm of the spirit there is as much room and need for a heroic pioneering spirit within the American Jewish community as there is a need for that spirit in the swamps, the deserts and the stony hillsides of Eretz Yisrael. It is with the hope that we shall be able to do something to call forth from within us some of that pioneering spirit that we are gathered today.

IV.

We start also with the proposition that the afternoon congregational school will continue to be the core of our educational effort as far as we can see into the future. But there is much that we can and should do to improve its effectiveness.

In the first place we must take the initiative to restore to

Jewish education the dignity and the status of an honored and desirable profession. No school can possibly be better than its faculty, and no faculty of standing can ever be recruited as long as teachers' salaries remain on the bare subsistence level or lower. We should not wait until Hebrew teachers organize and make demands for higher salaries and a greater sense of security. It should be our responsibility to establish and to fight for decent wage scales and employment conditions for Hebrew teachers. It is only then that we would be able with clear consciences to urge young Jews and Jewesses to choose Hebrew teaching as a profession. We hesitate even to suggest Hebrew teaching as a career to our own children or to other boys and girls because we know we are today inviting them to a life largely of personal privation and economic insecurity. Hebrew teachers themselves cannot solve this problem. Most of the more enterprising and energetic amongst them simply leave the profession. The more idealistic suffer in silence or in bitterness. The Rabbinical Assembly and lay leaders of the United Synagogue should together work out a scale of salaries and an understanding of employment conditions which would reflect our understanding of the invaluable service which the Hebrew School teacher has to offer to the community. It is only then that we shall have the moral right to demand that the teacher be one who is adequately prepared for his task, and that he continue *to grow* intellectually and spiritually in his work.

We believe that the afternoon school would be much more effective if ways could be found to incorporate within its program some of the activities which usually take children away from it. We all know of the Jewish child who cannot come to Hebrew school in the afternoon because there are dancing lessons, elocution or music lessons to be taken in some studio "downtown." Dancing, music, art, elocution can and should all be within the curricular scope of a congregational school where it is a large enough unit by itself or of a group of congregational schools when they are geographically near enough to cooperate. This would serve a double purpose. It would, on the one hand, eliminate the excuse for failure to attend the Hebrew school. But far more important even than that, it would enable us to put these tremendously valuable forces at the disposal of our Jewish educational purposes. Before a group such as this, one need not elaborate upon the obvious possibilities of using music, the dance, art and elocution to instill in the child a deeper love of things Jewish and a finer understanding of the spirit of Judaism. Some of the things achieved through music and dance in such summer camps as Massad and the Brandeis Institute point the way to what can and should be done all year round as an integral part of an afternoon congregational school. But, as we have said before, even the best possible afternoon congregational school will not solve all of our problems. The afternoon school may remain the core; it dare not remain the whole of our educational effort. Around it we must build a whole network, if you will, of additional educational enterprises.

We might well start with the children of the pre-school age. Hebrew kindergartens for children of pre-school age have yet unexplored possibilities. The parents are happy to send their children to such kindergartens. There is no conflict on that age level either with the public school or with outside non-Jewish interests. Nor does the financing of such schools present too difficult an obstacle. Parents are accustomed to paying substantial tuition fees to privately run kindergartens and they usually prefer to put their children in the care of the congregational school. Between the ages of 4 and 7 some very substantial impressions of a permanent nature can be made upon the child. And once the kindergarten becomes widely accepted in a community its graduates may be sufficiently numerous to continue as a group in the afternoon school.

This matter of kindergartens illustrates vividly the need for courageous cooperative action on our part. There are today many communities ready to start kindergartens but unable to find properly prepared teachers. If we wait until such teachers become available through the ordinary channels of teachers' schools we shall, I am afraid, wait to no avail. There is, therefore, a rather bold project before us. Its details will be fully discussed, I hope, during the course of the day. Under the auspices of the United Synagogue Education Committee and the Teachers Institute plans have been formulated to open a day camp where some 75 children would be under the supervision of trained kindergartners, and where some twelve young people ready to train themselves as kindergarten teachers could receive expert guidance and supervised experience. But this effort will be abortive unless it can have the active cooperation of the members of this Assembly. They must find the candidates ready to assume those studies and pledging to return and to teach in a kindergarten. They must persuade their communities to make the necessary investment of funds both for sending the prospective teacher to the camp-school, and for opening a kindergarten the following year. Few things will breathe new hope and vitality into a congregational school system more readily than a happy group of kindergarten children making their first conscious contact with Jewish life under pleasant circumstances.

We should not, however, limit our use of the summer months merely to the kindergarten level. For decades now we have been conscious of the fact that the summer months hold many blessings for Jewish education, if properly utilized. The field is not totally undeveloped. The Cejwin camps have made an outstanding contribution. Brandeis Institute and Camp Massad have each on different levels indicated how much can be achieved. What can we as a group point to as our achievement in the realm of Jewish education through camping? Unfortunately, nothing. Is it not high time that we have some summer camps for the members of our Young People's groups and for our school children, enough camps at which our boys and girls may live for at least two months out of the year in that type of Jewish environment which will give them by means of actual experiences a conception of the sort of Jewish life we seek to develop in America on a twelve month a year basis. If we do not bestir ourselves soon to do something along those lines we shall, I am afraid, awaken one day within the near future to discover that that whole area of rich Jewish educational experience will have been pre-empted by the Z.O.A., the B'nai B'rith, and other essentially secular Jewish bodies.

V.

Another area we might well investigate as supplementary to our afternoon schools is the area of the Jewish Day School. This at once involves us in a formulation of our attitude towards the public school. Obviously in a paper such as this we cannot present all the manifold aspects of this very delicate and very complicated issue. But we might profitably indicate some lines of thought and leave the rest for further clarification through discussion. We accept as an incontrovertible fact the proposition that the overwhelming majority of Jewish children will always attend the public schools. Their Jewish education will be of a supplementary nature. But we also believe that it is of the utmost importance that a substantial minority of our children should get the benefit of the type of intensive and well rounded Jewish education which only a properly conducted day school can offer. There should be in every Jewish community of any considerable size, at least one school in which children can acquire during their elementary and high school training a thorough grounding in Biblical, Rabbinic and modern Hebrew literature so they might be able if they so desire to continue their Jewish education during their college careers on a high academic level. Such a thorough Jewish training on the elementary and high school level will assure us of adequate resources from which to draw our future well informed lay and professional Jewish leadership. This form of more intensive privately financed religious education is altogether in line with American democratic principles as applied to the realm of education. The public school was not intended to monopolize all educational activity. It was first and foremost to guarantee to every child an education capable of preparing him for useful and happy living as a citizen of a democratic society. If that and more can be achieved in a privately conducted school, American ideals and practices with their emphasis upon individual initiative and individual differences certainly do not oppose it. It is high time that the organization of modern Jewish Day Schools under the auspices of large congregations where such are capable of bearing the burden, or under joint auspices of groups of congregations within one community should become a distinguishing feature of our movement. We will have to do a great deal of thinking on the ideological as well as on the practical aspects of this proposal. We must be clear in our own minds, and make it crystal clear to all others that we are not isolationists, segregationalists, or ghetto minded in our approach. What we shall do along those lines must be done only in the light of the highest interests of our faith and our people and those highest interests can never be in conflict with the highest interests of American and world democracy. In addition, we must grasp and implement more fully than heretofore the implications of the proposition that education is a life-long process and is not limited to the pre-Bar Mitzvah or pre-Confirmation period. Thus far, we have, to some extent, been the victims of a vicious circle. Believing that we cannot have the child in our school for more than an average of 18 months to 2 years we tried to crowd in all possible subject matter into this narrow area of time. The result was inevitable. In our attempt to overfeed the student, he revolted. Starting with the proposition that he probably would not stay longer than two years, the school curriculum was so planned that it well nigh guaranteed that the pupil would not want to stay longer than those two years. Perhaps if we assumed and planned a longer period for the Jewish educational process, we would be able to build a curriculum that would have a better chance than the present one to hold the pupils for a longer time.

But, under any circumstances, the assumption that Jewish systematic education is a life long process would have at least two immediate necessary consequences. 1) It should lead to an assumption on the part of the rabbi that his degree as teacher is not merely an additional ornament on the rabbinic diploma, but an injunction actually to teach. It is not sufficient to organize adult institutes in which invited lecturers hold forth. The rabbi must himself become an effective teacher in the Confirmation class at least, and in Bible classes for adults, which meet at regular intervals in homes or in the synagogue. 2) In addition, we must begin a broad and intensive campaign to the effect that failure on the part of an adult Jew to continue his systematic pursuit of Jewish knowledge in one form or another is as grievous a dereliction in Jewish duty as failure to send a son or daughter to the Hebrew School. The organization of classes for adults then becomes as sacred a duty for the congregation and the rabbi as the organization of the afternoon school. This must become a nation-wide movement and not merely the achievement of a group here and there.

Finally, we must look forward to an immediate implementation of the hope long cherished by all of us that there would be a constant stream of Jewish youth going to Eretz Yisrael for a year of study in the schools of the Yishuv, and of life in the cities and the colonies of the Yishuv. What a tremendous leaven for good it would be for Jews and Judaism everywhere if out of the 300 or more congregations under our leadership some 150 young people annually would be enabled through a congregational grant of $1,500 or $2,000 to spend a year in Eretz Yisrael. The congregations can well afford to grant that money. All that is needed is national leadership for such a movement. Let us work out in detail the conditions under which such grants should be made. Let us present a carefully worked out program to our congregations, and I have no doubt but that they would respond. Let us require of the young men chosen to go abroad for a year that they spend only a month with us in intensive orientation courses so that they may take maximum advantage of their opportunities. Provision might be made too, within the year's study, of a month or so of supervised contact with other Jewish communities abroad. What a challenge that could be to American Jewish Youth, and what a reservoir that youth could become for American Jewish and even for world Jewish leadership.

* * *

My good friends and dear colleagues — These are only a few of the many possibilities that suggested themselves to Rabbi Ira Eisenstein, Rabbi Isaac Klein, Rabbi Davis and to me as we gave thought to these problems together. They are not all realizable at once. Some of them can perhaps never be implemented. But we simply cannot accept with equanimity the status quo in Jewish education. We certainly have no laurels upon which to rest. This is an *et la'asot l'Adonai* עת לעשות לד׳ a time calling for action, and the cry of העפילו — venture forth, challenge the mountain of neglect, indifference, and of failure which has grown up during these past decades — *should give us no rest.*

THE LADDER OF JEWISH
EDUCATION*

A Program for Jewish Education in Conservative Judaism

By Rabbi Moshe Davis

A century ago, the first champions of Historical Judaism in America, under the leadership of Isaac Leeser, issued their call for "a concert of action" in Jewish education. A half-century later Solomon Schechter warned American Israel that higher institutions had been created for the one out of a thousand; but provisions had not been made for the nine hundred and ninety-nine. " . . . As long as we have no proper Talmud Torah, the higher learning will always remain without a basis and never take root on American soil." ("The Problem of Religious Education," in *Seminary Addresses and Other Papers*, Cincinnati, 1915, p. 108).

Now, a hundred years after Leeser's call, we who have assembled at this Second Annual Conference on Jewish Education are still at the very beginning of our educational efforts. The test of a movement is the ability to train its young for future leadership. In these long one hundred years we have not succeeded in training a leadership out of our own congregational ranks. One word describes the history of our educational endeavors — default.

It is no consolation to know that general American education is also in a sad plight. Since 1939, 350,000 school teachers representing one-third of the teachers in America's schools have quit

---

* *Conservative Judaism*, May 1948, vol. IV, no. 3.

the teaching profession. The recently issued first progress report of the President's special Commission on Education admitted that America is wasting its children. These facts are tragic indeed. However, if these reports are ominous for the future of American civilization, their substantiation in American Jewish education spells catastrophe.

Last year, all of the Jewish teacher-training institutions in this country prepared some 50 students who entered the teaching service. Our own Teachers Institute and Seminary College have in the past three years grown from a student body of 28 in the day session and 104 in the evening session (1944–45) to 90 in the morning session and 208 in the evening session (1947–48). We have already reached the peak registration in our thirty-eight years of existence and will graduate 7 teachers this year out of a class of 20 students. According to present standards, we may graduate 13 teachers next year and in 1950, the grand total of 17 teachers.

American Jewry, the people who are now raising, and most necessarily, one quarter of a billion dollars for European Jewry and Eretz Yisrael, the people who now have attained the hegemony of world Israel, that people may produce an estimated 60 class room teachers this year for a community consisting of one-half the Jewish souls in the world. And we, in Conservative Judaism, representing four hundred congregations in Israel, כן ירבו, will give birth to an estimated seven teachers in 1948. To this we must add that an insignificant number of these students come from our own congregational schools. Is not, then, the word default the mildest description one may properly apply to our failure?

We alone of the three religious groupings have not established a system of Jewish schooling which would both meet our needs and satisfy our point of view. The Orthodox sails are now spread wide on the sea of parochial education. Their educational program is consistent with their philosophy of Judaism, and they are extraordinarily active in carrying it through. The Reform are still building Sunday schools and, lately, colleges for Sunday school teachers. That is their program and they are living up to it.

Of the three religious groups we are the only ones who have not declared a national pattern of educational organization. Here and there individual attempts have taken place. But there has

not been a consolidated effort. It is the purpose of this Conference
to make us live up to our promise and to propose a system of
educational practice to be implemented in every congregation
which comes under our influence. The structure of education
herewith presented for your consideration is not revolutionary in
any degree. Rather has it evolved out of our history as a Jewish
religious movement and is in keeping with the American democratic tradition which we espouse and in which we choose to live.

I.

Every design has its underlying principles. The structure of
Jewish education in Conservative Judaism must be motivated by
a philosophy that should embrace and express all aspects of Jewish
life. It cannot be within our province in this single presentation
to give consideration to all these underlying principles. Even more
specific problems in educational philosophy, such as character
education, development of the spiritual being, the role of the
family and society in education, etc., must, however reluctantly,
be put aside in the present discussion.

There are, however, certain questions of Jewish educational
theory which cannot be ignored: the affirmation or negation of
Diaspora Judaism, religion and public school education, the
goals of our Jewish school system, and the time factor in Jewish
education.

A. JUDAISM IN AMERICA

The historic decision to establish a Jewish state in Palestine
has brought into sharper focus the long and much debated question
of relationship between the Jewries of Eretz Yisrael and America.
Too much ink has been uselessly spent on the pros and cons of
Shelilat ha-Golah while the real question has been side-stepped:
Survival or — קיום היהדות באשר היא שם או חיסול היהדות ח״ו באשר היא שם
extinction of Judaism wherever it may now exist.

When the negators of Diaspora living propose *Aliyah* and
Ḥalutziut as the only type of educational theory practicable in
America, they do not mean that religious Judaism and Hebrew
in America are undesirable *per se*. They mean and believe with
all their hearts that it is useless, that time is running out, that it

is an unfortunate investment of energy and funds. For they are convinced, as many classic Zionists predicted, that the Yishuv in *Eretz* Yisrael is to be *K'lal* Yisrael.

It is this very historic prognosis that the editorial writer in the first issue of the newly reorganized bi-weekly *Moznaim* attacks in his review of the two world conferences which took place in Jerusalem in 1946. Although he maintains the supremacy of Palestinian Jewry in the constellation of world affairs — and who will deny this — he counsels against the error of viewing the Yishuv as K'lal Yisrael.

We can have but one refrain against all who would doom intensive Jewish effort in America: קיום היהדות! A healthy and vibrant Yishuv in Eretz Yisrael is an *indispensable part* of that task, not its substitute. It is neither our business to become involved in subjective analyses of pessimism such as Simon Halkin's היהודים והיהדות באמריקה (*Jews and Judaism in America*) nor to walk merrily with our heads in the air because Moshe Kleinman in a series of *Hadoar* articles demonstrates that the flame of Judaism has never been extinguished in any settlement in the Diaspora. Who knows? Who can arrogate to himself the responsibility of condemning a community of five million Jews to oblivion? There is only one historic lesson that our ancient and recent past has taught us: to work for the survival of Judaism in every land, every minute of our lives, with every ounce of our strength. American Jews in this generation have many responsibilities. We must save European Jewry and build Eretz Yisrael without losing America. The Sarahs in Tel Aviv and the Rebekahs in Frankfurt must be helped. Shall the spiritual needs of the Raḥels and the Leahs in Chicago and New York be forgotten? Ephraim in Eretz Yisrael must be guarded; shall not Menasseh, child of America, receive his Sabbath blessing? It is the privilege of each individual Jew to serve the Lord in Jerusalem. For this right, not sufferance, we have struggled and will continue to struggle. But, for those Jews who choose to live in America, this great democratic land is home, and should be made what its history and destiny declare it to be, a strong and firm bedrock in which an inspiring, magnificent and intensive Jewish religious civilization will flourish. Only if such florescence of Judaism is made possible, will the Jewish people in America walk with dignity and serenity.

To this point of view of חיוב היהדות on American soil many of our colleagues may give lip service, yet they do little to translate their views into action, thus frustrating the development of the kind of Jewish living which they claim to desire. Peculiarly enough, the profoundly intensive Jewish activities in this country have been created by individuals who may technically classify themselves as negators of Diaspora living. Camp Massad is a sterling example. The original founding group consisted of some who did not preach the possibilities of Jewish survival in America. Nevertheless, the deed spoke better than their word. In the short span of seven years, Camp Massad has not only developed to the point where it serves five hundred children and has acquired a second site, but it has become the parent idea of similar institutions in many parts of the country, including our own Ramah Camps.

If we in our movement were to bend every effort towards the creation of a spiritual force, an American *Ḥalutziut*, if you will, to strengthen the struggling Jewish communities in this land, then we would contribute not only to the further growth of Judaism in America but to the development of Eretz Yisrael itself.

Has not the time come for those of us who profess to serve American Israel to put to ourselves Elijah's question: "How long halt ye between two opinions?" We come into direct contact with hundreds of thousands of our fellow Jews. As we gaze upon their children and our children in America, we must never forget that every child gained is a horizon gained and that every seedling is a tree.

B. RELIGION AND PUBLIC EDUCATION

When in the early decades of the nineteenth century, Henry Barnard and Horace Mann led the gallant and victorious struggle for the American public school system and its independence from sectarian influence, all Jewish leaders — Isaac Leeser and I. M. Wise, S. M. Isaacs and Max Lilienthal — rallied to their banner. The battle-hymn was the sacred American principle of the separation between Church and State. In the ensuing years the division between religious and public education was rendered *organizationally* complete. However, the written decree of divorce between religion and the public educational system was by no means completely observed, for the religious heritage is the mainspring of American institutions.

Out of the genuine unhappiness of religious groupings with the secular and at best a-religious public school system, many denominations created parochial systems as their independent solution to the integrated and whole education of their children. In turn they have requested public funds for the maintenance of parochial education. On the other hand, various groups sought to convert the public school system into the hand-maid of sectarian education and have made penetrating and, in many cases, successful attempts to achieve their aims. Thus the entire relationship between religious and public education has been subject to upheaval, competitive interest, and confusion. It now needs reexamination.

In this reexamination, we will have to take a well-defined stand based on the best interests of the democratic public school system and Jewish education. It seems clear to me that despite its shortcomings, the present public school sytem is preeminently desirable and superior to all systems now practiced by the West European and Anglo-Saxon (including Canadian) democracies. We must reaffirm the principle of separation of Church and State. Our premise must be that the Jewish school system is complementary to, and not competitive with, public school education. This view is not taken out of a narrow desire for self-protection as a minority religion, but rather out of the deep conviction that democracy and democratic living depend on an integrated as well as upon an enlightened citizenry. It is as important that our children learn to understand and love their fellow Americans — Negro, Chinese, Nisei, Catholic, Protestant and Atheist — as we Jews desire the children of other ethnic, economic or religious groups to understand and love us. The best means to such social integration is a system of common public education, for the public school system is the keystone of our democratic arch.

The continued separation of religious and public education in no wise interferes with the inalienable right of all American citizens of any faith or conviction to establish private secular or private religious schools. Unfortunately, too often, those who would support private secular schools as being part of the American way, because of their desire to offer their children a more adequate academic training, discourage their co-religionists who would in addition seek for their children a more adequate religious training.[1]

Our preference for the common public school need not blind us to the many serious inadequacies and indefensible concomitants of its present curriculum. Public school curricula can be spiritually rooted and religiously motivated without including sectarian teachings. This can indeed be the religious contribution to a spiritual America. The child in the public school can be made to feel that the ethical and moral strivings of mankind as embodied in the religious traditions enhance its personality and make for a better society.

In this respect, however, the public school system has failed. The problem is formulated, with characteristic succinctness, by Professor Kaplan in his article "The Place of Religion in a Democracy."

By eliminating religion from the curriculum of the elementary and secondary schools we inevitably, even if unintentionally, encourage in the growing generation distorted ideas about religion and a negative attitude toward it.

The present solution of having the schools transmit to the child the scientific, literary, social and political aspects of the American heritage, and have the church and home transmit to him their religious heritage is an illusory one. It is an evasion instead of a solution. It carries out in practice a judgment which King Solomon used only as a stratagem to elicit the truth. It, so to speak, cuts up the live body of religion in order to satisfy the rival claims of the different religious denominations.

Those institutions, agencies and policies, on the other hand, when divorced from religion are devoid of what might render them most fruitful of good. To set such religion apart from the day to day vital interests of men and nations is like refusing to gear a dynamo or engine to any kind of vehicle or tool. To expect religion to use up its energy on itself is to

---

[1] There is a special challenge in the further development of Jewish parochial education. We have, of course, always conceived of the day-school as being religiously oriented and based on a curriculum of traditional subjects. Now a new phenomenon has arisen on the scene. The recently established Kinneret Jewish National Day School characterizes itself as "the first secular Jewish school of its kind in the United States." This school promises to be only the first in a series of similar ventures according to plans and discussions on Jewish education in the Yiddish monthly, *Die Zukunft*. In a democracy these Yiddishist secularists have the unquestioned right to establish a Jewish Day School of their own choice, but we cannot endorse such schools.

prevent it from functioning normally. Whether it is possible to overcome this abnormal status without trespassing on the principle of the separation of church and state is the problem . . .

(*The Review of Religion*, Jan. 1948, pp. 180–1)

What is the solution?

Various suggestions have been advanced. A. Victor Murray, President of Chestnut College in Cambridge, England, writing on "The State and Religious Education in England," challenges the view that the complete secularization of education is the only democratic solution of the problem of Church and State. He describes the program of religious teaching under the National Education Act in which trans-denominational and approved religious syllabi are taught in the regular system. (*Christianity and Crisis*, Jan. 10, 1948).

A second suggestion is the development of an anthology of religious literature as a common text along the lines of Florence May Fitch's *One God*. Readings from all the religious faiths could be included. In addition, the customs and ceremonies of the various religious groupings would be demonstrated. In this manner the religious pluralism of America could be taught without demanding uniformity of belief or practice.[2]

The fact that these specific suggestions may not meet the always difficult problem of eating our cake and having it, is no reason to retreat from the quest. This is the challenge. We dare not relinquish the common public school system; we must not desist from filling the religious vacuum in its curriculum. The entire issue must be examined on the highest levels of cooperative thinking, for the alternative to an adequate solution would be the possible crumbling of one of the chief cornerstones of American democratic life.

---

[2] For an exhaustive study of this problem, see *Relation of Religion to Public Education — Basic Principles*, Committee on Religion and Education of the American Council of Education, New York, April 1947. After an inquiry of several years by this highly competent body, further study and experimentation are suggested before any definitive conclusion may be reached as to how to benefit from the blessings of Church and State separation, and yet rid ourselves of the negative features of such a system.

C. THE GOALS OF JEWISH EDUCATION

An affirmative philosophy of American Judaism and a preference for common school education must not lead to a diminution of Jewish experience and educational objectives. Quite the contrary. Full and maximum Jewish schooling is the unqualified prerequisite to the development of a wholesome Jewish personality. What, then, are the objectives of Jewish education in America? Our children should be helped

To acquire the Jewish faith in God;

To apply the Jewish religious ethic as the standard of relations with their fellow-men;

To observe the *Mitzvot Maasiyot* of Judaism in their daily lives;

To feel a sense of kinship and solidarity with the Jewish community the world over so as to desire a share in the common destiny of the people of Israel;

To develop into citizen-builders of America, pervaded by a passion for translating American democratic thought into a world order of peace and justice;

To fulfill the ancient precept of *Yishuv Eretz Yisrael* either as a partner in its re-creation or by regular pilgrimages; to understand the centrality of Eretz Yisrael in the religious and cultural pattern of Judaism;

To gain a deep knowledge of Jewish sources in their original Hebrew; to know the Torah, the Prophets, basic portions of Rabbinic literature, as well as selected post-Rabbinic Hebrew writings;

To read modern Hebrew and Yiddish literature; to appreciate and foster creative expression in all the arts.

The above objectives of Jewish education are not arranged in any priority order and are presented in outline and preliminary fashion for future discussion and consideration.[3] Pedagogic criteria

---

[3] The United Synagogue Commission on Jewish Education recently published a revised statement on *The Objectives and Standards for the Congregational School* which represents the thinking of the official educational body in our movement on this subject.

and specific curricular opportunities alone should determine the accent, age-level and methodology of the particular instruction.

In sum, these objectives should help the child find gratification and joy in Jewish pursuits (the equivalent of the traditional *Simha Shel Mitzvah*) as well as fundamental security and comfort in his Jewishness.

D.   THE   TIME   FACTOR   IN   JEWISH EDUCATION

To attain these objectives, the time factor in Jewish education is of crucial importance, for learning, even in this technical civilization, is a slow and gradual process. The mind is not a machine with absorption press-buttons. No system of Jewish education can hope to be successful if it lacks the primary element of time.

The advocates of parochial education claim as their main contention for the expansion of the day-school that they have solved this vexing problem of time. That claim is obviously justified. Although, in my opinion, the all-day school system is not the best conceivable program for American Jewish education, it cannot be denied, that in comparison with other types of Jewish schools heretofore developed, the day-school is by far the most productive. As parents, many of our colleagues (and I include myself) plan to send our children to all-day schools, for there is no better choice at present to the proper *Jewish* education of our children. Subject to the development of a more effective system of Jewish education within a framework of separate religious and public schools, we should, whenever possible — and particularly in larger cities — establish day-schools under the auspices of our congregations on a community basis.

Having associated ourselves with these endeavors, we must not delude ourselves into believing that we have solved the problem of American Jewish education either ideologically or practically. Let me repeat Schechter's words of caution — remember the nine hundred and ninety-nine! The parochial school is not the answer for the great majority of our American children and it is therefore incumbent upon us to devise a pattern of Jewish education which will make it possible for the children in our congregations to receive an intensive Jewish education while attending the regular public school system.[4]

But time is of the essence. We are between the hammer and the anvil — unless we use the free and leisure time of the student to full advantage. In a recent publication *Education for All American Children* a blueprint for elementary education in an ideal American city of 1958 is presented for twelve-month schools, open six days and some evenings each week, with camping as part of the program. We, too, must cease thinking in curricular and time terms of three decades ago. The pre-school years, summers, winter vacation periods and even daily recreation play could be utilized for Jewish education if we are on the alert.

The following proposed ladder of Jewish education is a structural time scheme which starts with nursery education and continues through childhood, adolescence and college age, and is based on the foregoing considerations.

II.

THE PROPOSED STRUCTURE

Nursery School

The first rung on the proposed ladder of Jewish education is the nursery school. Education should begin at the earliest possible age. The Rabbis had a phrase-concept for it: גירסא דינקותא. The years from three to seven are the pliant years. It is the time when the slow educational process of teaching the child to grow away from, and out of, his complete concern for his own needs to an understanding and an appreciation of the needs of others is no small task. It is not too early to begin learning the art of harmonious group association.[5] In Jewish education, we can use

---

[4] Even the orthodox, the chief architects of the parochial school, recognize the shortcomings of this system as the exclusive solution for Jewish education. See, for example, David Eidelsberg's article in the *Jewish Morning Journal* — די תלמוד תורה'ס א פאזיציע וואס ארטאדאקסיע פארלירט (November 3, 1947), and note the extraordinary efforts which they are expending on the organization of release time classes.

[5] American nursery education has made significant strides during the last two decades, growing from 89 such schools in 1928 to 1,900 in 1945. Jewish education stands to reap rich harvest from this development.

these all-important years, when the child can be made available to us full time, so that he may acquire positive emotional responses to Jewish living, a habit pattern within which Jewish practice is organically integrated, and a Hebrew linguistic background, which will make it possible to teach the language with content materials that are graded to the child's intellectual rather than linguistic growth. This last possibility, of eliminating the late start in the study of Hebrew and the consequent intellectual lag which exists between the child's mother-tongue vocabulary and new-language knowledge, may be a measure that would prevent the high casualty lists in our elementary Hebrew schools. Children whose imagination travels into the stratosphere and whose English vocabularies expand correspondingly, are chained in the Hebrew school to the "boy who sits on the bench" and "the boy who gets off the bench."

Nor can the rare opportunity to attach the child to Jewish habits be underestimated. A generation ago the Jewish school could be content with imparting information, for the home was the central Jewish institution. Now there is a Jewish void and emptiness in the home, and the child too frequently must introduce his father to the blessings at the Torah and his mother to the blessing of the Sabbath candles.

The entire Jewish community is in the everlasting debt of Ivriah which, under the inspiring leadership of Dr. Israel S. Chipkin experimented with the development of bi-cultural education almost two decades ago. Our own Camp Atid experience this past summer under the direction of our gifted and consecrated colleague, Rabbi Abraham E. Millgram, has indicated to us that our congregations can proceed more emphatically in this direction and that through the nursery school we may hurdle some of the major obstacles in our way. For, if at the age of seven, a child will have sufficient linguistic background to begin to study narrative portions of *Ḥumash* and Jewish ethical literature, the first avenues to proper Jewish education will be open to him.

We will, therefore, have to create a nursery school system and train teachers with the greatest speed imaginable, for once we miss the beginning, it is almost impossible to start in the middle.

Afternoon School

The second rung on our educational ladder is the afternoon week-day school. This area of educational endeavor requires complete transformation in keeping with the psychological and social needs of the American child. The suggestion made by Rabbi Ira Eisenstein last year to the planning committee of the first Educational Conference is sound indeed. The afternoon school should be the center where all the extra-curricular activities of the Jewish child may be conducted in addition to his formal and informal Jewish studies. The Jewish school should not be based on the old Jewish center slogan "Invite him to play, he'll stay to pray," but, as indicated, should seek from the very outset to integrate formal curricula into the normal leisure time play and aesthetic studies of the American child. Carpentry and mechanics, dancing and music lessons, are all part of the American child's life, and he should be offered wholesome opportunities to engage in them under completely Jewish auspices. But mechanics and aesthetics (and in rural areas, agriculture) must also be utilized for their remarkable values as pedagogic aids.

Granted that the Hebrew language is basic to our educational system, must it always be taught through grammatical declensions and dictionaries? Dr. Nissan Touroff, in his latest and extremely important volume, הערכות spends much effort in stressing the integral role that the arts can play in the Hebrew-centered curriculum. In the spirit of these proposals, the Hebrew Arts Foundation will shortly embark upon a Hebrew film-of-the-month project. Selected short subjects on Jewish and general themes which will be lip-synchronized in Hebrew will be shown to our children. Students will be able to study the scripts and vocabulary before and after the film. This is but one example, and in one small area, how the pace of study can be quickened and the child-interest motivated. And all this is possible, if we will stop delimiting our own educational opportunities to six formal study hours a week, but rather think of the maximum periods our children can spend in a Jewish atmosphere.

The school-center should be organized on a five-day week basis. At the Inwood Hebrew Congregational School, of which Jacob Radin is rabbi and which is being developed as the demonstration school of the Teachers Institute, the Board of Directors approved our plan to convert the three-day week school into a five-day week school. This at a time when most of our congregations are lopping off hours to meet the so-called competitive demand of other interests. The success was beyond our expectations. More than 90% of the children returned, and the attendance figures for the three month period of September through December were also above 90%. That the children and adults in our congregations are prepared for such radical departures, provided that the new methods are both educationally sound and emotionally intriguing, was demonstrated in the small West Coast community of Stockton, California, of which Ephraim Prombaum is rabbi. Taking seriously the call issued by Dr. Israel M. Goldman at our first Education Conference to liquidate the Sunday school from our educational structure, Rabbi Prombaum abolished all teaching on Sunday morning and established an effective four-day afternoon school to the delight of the children and surprise of the parents.

If it were possible to establish such an afternoon school with all of the suggested ramifications and under the constant guidance, even in the play and informal periods, of properly qualified teachers, then our movement would finally introduce a novel but much needed adjunct of the full educational apparatus.

High School

The high-school years according to the special Educational Supplement of the *Survey Graphic*, are called the "hot-spot" of education. The entire American community has been lacking in imagination in dealing with the educational problems of the adolescent. Dr. John W. Studebaker, Federal Commissioner of Education, reports that four million of the six and one-half million high school children are improperly served. Twenty percent go to college, twenty percent enter semi-professional employment, sixty percent or four million are left floundering in an educational bog. To meet this crisis in the general high-school system, the Commissioner organized a United States Commission on Life Adjustment Education for Youth.

We can do no less. Jewish high-school education is virtually non-existent in our congregational life. It is fantastic how short-sighted we become with this age-level. Congregations are prepared to spend any sum of money for beginners' classes. However, if the original group peters down to a few stalwart students who wish to continue their studies after graduation from the elementary school, the Board suddenly discovers that it does not pay to maintain a teacher for three or four students.

The investment of the first years of study should not be forfeited because "it does not pay." Education is always costly. In larger cities, this problem can be met partially by planning regional schools under joint congregational or bureau auspices. In smaller towns, even where small groups of three or four students may meet, they should not be neglected, for it is in the high school age that we should begin to seek our future lay and professional leadership. These teen-agers will be our immediate successors. Moreover, if we are serious about organizing a *Halutziut* for American Judaism, this is the age group with which to start. The task cannot be effected on a wholesale basis. It is an educational retail job, and must be accomplished by personal letters not a mimeograph machine, by pastoral education not class-room formalism. Corps of trained workers must specialize in this department of education. Every conceivable technique should be developed. One example: where high school students attend afternoon classes, their Jewish studies should be held in the morning hours. The Leaders Training Fellowship is a small step in the right direction. We are only at the beginning of the work and already many opportunities are permitted to slip by for lack of adequate service, teachers and supervising personnel. On the other hand, we wish to gratefully report that many of our men are heeding the behest of the Men of the Great Synagogue to "raise up many disciples." They meet with promising students in limited groups for five to seven hours a week offering these selected individuals personal instruction and inspiration.

On the level of high school age, and preferably at the year of graduation, the South African Palestine Plan should be implemented. This group study program, which has been officially undertaken by the Jewish Agency, calls for a year of work and study in Eretz Yisrael. The students would be sent under the direction of the Leaders Training Fellowship in the company of a faculty member. It is self-evident how fructifying an experience this work-study program can be and how radiating will be the influences in the local congregation when the trainees return to their homes.

Summer Camps

Concurrent with the afternoon week-day school and high school, a chain of study camps, local and country, should be organized. The purposes of Hebrew camping, including formal study, are abundantly clear. On the lower elementary level of the regional country summer camp the prerequisite of admission should be two or three years of study in a congregational school. In the older group we should insist on a reading knowledge of the Hebrew language. Camp Ramah in Wisconsin was an experiment in both directions.[6] We have much to learn, but he who has seen the camp in action can testify that an educational miracle has been wrought. This one single, as yet, baby institution has already raised the standards of all congregational work in the Chicago area, and has set off creative sparks in other parts of the country. Every aspect of our educational objectives can be taught in the twenty-four hour day, nine-week summer program. If the experience is repeated over a period of four or five years the results reproduce geometrically. Of the ninety-eight campers in residence during the 1947 season at Ramah, eighty-six are returning for the coming summer, and there is an important personal reason which explains in each case why these few campers cannot return. They too will continue their Jewish studies.

Thus far we have not experimented on a national scale with the very fruitful suggestion urged by Rabbi Louis Katzoff to create Hebrew summer day-camps for those children in the congregation who, for economic or family reasons, may not be in the position to attend country camps. For the small town congregations, where camping sites are available within a short bus ride, this suggestion has special merit. But even in the cities, where the average congregational school is large, a day-camp could be of inestimable help, particularly for the pre-school and primary school grades. In such an environment, the learning results alone would equal that which the child can achieve during the entire winter season on a supplementary basis.

---

[6] Since this talk was delivered three more Ramah Camps were established: in Pennsylvania, Connecticut and California. [Editor's Note]

The College Campus

The identical pattern outlined for the high school student should be extended to the college years. In large cities, where the students, generally speaking, remain in local colleges, the task is less complicated. Those congregations in smaller communities whose children study away from home must devise some method whereby the educational personnel and the rabbi, perhaps through an expanded Leaders Training Fellowship, will continue to minister even from the home congregation.

In this context, the potential of both the high school and college campuses as centers of Jewish education should become increasingly apparent. The remarkable progress made in New York City through the introduction of Hebrew instruction in twenty-four junior and senior high schools, and five colleges, with a total current registration of about forty-five hundred students, is but advance indication of the new directions which we should pursue throughout the country. The Hillel and local college Foundations offer us extension facilities virtually on every campus in the land. Effective liaison between a National Collegiate Congregational Board, the local rabbi and the Jewish campus head would be a boon to student and congregation.

Adult Education

The dramatic decision of Chancellor Robert M. Hutchins of the University of Chicago to withdraw from active responsibility as head of the University for a period of five years in order to devote himself exclusively to adult education represents a trend in American University life which has been taking definite form in the last decade,— that of expanding unprecedented effort in adult education and community programs.

Chancellor Hutchins was thinking of the major decisions which confront each citizen in the world of the atomic bomb when he expressed his view that, "I regard education of adults as the most urgent business of the day." The nature of the critical questions which confront the individual Jew also require information, reason, and a will to Jewish identity. Similarly, it is our urgent business to supply these needs.

The work of the National Academy for Adult Jewish Studies in our movement is but an excellent introduction to a concentrated program of activity in this seriously neglected field. Dr. Israel Goldman has rendered yeoman service with limited resources. The texts, publications, and syllabi are fine in their place. This is the program which a national agency can undertake. What we need is a vigorous local and home-centered approach to adult Jewish education based on the sad but true appraisal of a detached and Jewishly unhabituated generation of adults. Our generation cannot read elementary Hebrew, cannot recite the *Kiddush*, does not know the form of Jewish prayer. We must teach our people the simplest Jewish habits. They must be reintegrated as adults into our Jewish life pattern just as we would integrate their children into Jewish living. It is on the basis of this introduction into the habit modes of Judaism that history, language and community events can be taught significantly. Rabbi Bernard Mandelbaum has been conducting such an experimental unit during the past few years with as few as three and four couples, meeting in their home and relating the teaching of Judaism to their highly individualized problems. Starting with the approaching festival, unashamedly teaching the Jewish practice on the most elementary level, introducing the newly learned practice in the home, and actually helping the members to conduct their home ceremonies for the first time, he also used the sessions successfully for discussions of the problems of religion, Jewish thought, study of language and the reading of literature. Above all, he has helped these adults arrange for the proper Jewish education of their young. This experience (and similar projects throughout the country) helped redirect the members to the synagogue.

The emphasis on personalized adult education in no way infringes on the conferences, study groups and classes normally conducted by the congregation. They will be necessary. It does remind us, however, that the family is the basic congregational unit. Unless we rebuild the home, there can be no important development of Judaism in America.

Teachers Institute and Seminary College of Jewish Studies

The final rung on our ladder will be a nationally expanded teachers' training school, graduate department and branch colleges of Jewish studies, whose trainees should serve the needs of every age category of Jewish students in our movement, from the pre-school level to the adult. These expanded needs call for new directions in our present schools. Formerly the Teachers Institute and Seminary College were geared to serve the New York community alone. Now they must service, in cooperation with local bureaus, the congregational schools throughout the country.

To begin to serve our congregational needs alone on all the aforementioned levels, the present training schools should be able to accomodate all the students who will come from the hundreds of congregations which are affiliated with us. The Teachers Institute and Seminary College already are beginning to assume this national composition. In our present student body we have twenty out-of-town students and eleven from Canada. The small town of Calgary, Canada, alone has sent us six students. If we are to continue to serve effectively along these lines, we shall have to attract the best minds to the Jewish teaching profession and we shall have to institute stipends and scholarships, a summer-school camp, as well as establish a girls' dormitory in the city.

As one reads and rereads the reports on Higher Education for American Democracy issued by the President's Commission and one becomes aware of the opportunities which will be offered the next teacher-training generation, one prays that these same rights and privileges will be secured for every Jewish student wishing to prepare himself for Jewish service in America.

Colleagues and friends: I submit this plan with one concluding comment. There is much to the cynic's remark that the easiest thing to get is an idea. It is much more difficult to put the good idea into effective motion. Whether the idea presented today is good, bad or mediocre, you will shortly determine. This plan is submitted for your criticisms and modifications. Call it anything you wish, but do not call it impractical. I do not mean to jest, for this plan represents the demonstration of an idea rather than its beginning. First we went out into the field and built. In a more correct sense, this plan represents the collective thinking and efforts of all the educational agencies represented in our movement. For during the past two years we have introduced laboratory workshops, pilot centers, for most of the phases of this proposed ladder of education. As indicated, the experiments have not been controlled in insular fashion; they have been tried in congregations with non-subventioned local resources and have grown on local interest.

Granted an alert and concerned rabbinate, granted fund priorities for Jewish education over mortgages on new buildings, granted a reevaluation of community and national organizational goals, we can yet build our fires. It is appropriate that this very Educational Conference of the Rabbinical Assembly, at which we hope to launch our new ship of Jewish education, is called for the first time in cooperation with the United Synagogue Commission on Jewish Education and the Teachers Institute and College of Jewish Studies of the Seminary. Represented at this very meeting are our rabbinic colleagues, the educator members of the United Synagogue and our Teachers Institute and Seminary College faculty. This union is a happy augury. Perhaps out of this "concert of action" we will make it possible that our children will surpass our own generation in piety, knowledge and devotion. For this is Torah and this its reward — זו תורה וזה שכרה.

INTRODUCTORY NOTE ON THE
JEWISH COMMUNITY

In a period when the Jewish group has become fragmentized religiously and when, in addition, a large number of Jews adhere to varied secular philosophies of Judaism, a Jewish community philosophy is vitally necessary. The relationship between the various religious groups must be defined and the relation between them, individually or collectively, and the Jews who belong in the secular camps must be explored.

On this subject no consistent and over-all point of view has been formulated in Conservative Judaism. At the outset, the Conservative movement seemed to be dedicated to the proposition that, as normative Judaism, it could ultimately bring harmony and unity to American Israel. While it has in some measure achieved this objective, it is questionable that it can go much further in the light of the organizational hardening which has taken place in the Jewish religious groups. A philosophy predicated upon diversity therefore seems necessary, at least for the time being.

The bulk of the thinking in community philosophy in the Conservative movement has come from, or has been inspired by, the Reconstructionist wing. The paper printed below mirrors some of the thinking among Reconstructionists, although its outlook is by no means limited to the members of that group. While it was delivered as an address at a Law Conference of the Rabbinical Assembly some years ago, it employs the problem of law as a spring board for a discussion of a community philosophy.

The paper was written by Dr. Ira Eisenstein, now Rabbi of Congregation Anshe Emet in Chicago and formerly Rabbi of the Society for the Advancement of Judaism. He is a leading figure in the Reconstructionist group, being an editor of The Reconstructionist, *and one of the editors of many of the Reconstructionist publications, including the prayer-books. However, his activity has not been confined to that wing of the Conservative movement. He has been active in every branch of Conservative Judaism, has written both books and articles on Conservative and general Jewish thought and has served as President of the Rabbinical Assembly of America.*

THE NEED FOR LEGISLATION
IN JEWISH LAW

A Community Philosophy

By Rabbi Ira Eisenstein

It has long been recognized that the members of the Rabbinical
Assembly are divided on the subject of Jewish law. The character
of this Law Conference's program is further evidence of that division. My purpose here is to attempt to set forth the major attitudes
of one group within the Assembly whose views are seldom heard
in the deliberations of the Committee on Law, because those views
are basically at variance with the procedures thus far employed
to adjust Jewish law to modern life. How large this group is or
may become has never been established, for the reason that thus
far the Rabbinical Assembly as a whole has not acted upon the
proposal made a year ago by Dr. Mordecai M. Kaplan. His
proposal, you recall, was to recognize formally that there exist
among us several distinct viewpoints within a larger framework
of agreement, and that the Rabbinical Assembly and the United
Synagogue should sanction independent action of each group
within those limited areas in which the groups differ. If and when
the wisdom of such a decision is recognized, we shall know the
relative strengths of the three major groupings. In the meantime,
I content myself with saying that the views expressed by myself
may be said to represent *some others* besides myself.

* * *

Judaism functions in our lives as the expression of group life. The term "Jewish" is a social term. It implies a group. All group life, Jewish included, must be governed by law if it is to retain any semblance of continuity with the past and unity in the present. Law has indeed been a characteristic of Judaism. What has been the characteristic of that law?   1) It has been all-embracing, governing every aspect of life.   2) It has been authoritarian, that is to say, it has been based on a fundamental document whose infallibility was beyond question, and on the interpretation of that document by those qualified to understand its purpose and intent. In those respects, Jewish law was similar to the law of other groups. Whatever differences existed between the content and goals of Jewish law and those of other civilizations, the fact is that the development in Jewish law was subject to the same principle of action and reaction which governed the development of other laws. Jewish law responded to changing conditions of life. This response was translated into law in most instances without the conscious knowledge of the rabbis, who never would have conceded that the Torah should adjust itself to the times. If anything, they would have insisted that the conditions adjust to the law. But somehow they managed to retain their conception of an un-yielding law, and at the same time to make those modifications and innovations which rendered it operative.

The fact that we have come together to discuss the adjustment of Jewish law to life indicates that we do not share the same men-tality as our ancestors. We are consciously attempting to make the law serve our needs. We cannot, therefore, any longer pretend that what we are doing is merely to reaffirm our allegiance to the law. Any changes we suggest will be deliberate and conscious, and in that sense will be democratic in spirit and not authoritarian. The fact that we take our needs into consideration constitutes a psychological revolution. In the new frame of mind we cannot be satisfied until we translate the psychological change into a change of philosophy and procedure.

The many factors responsible for our new frame of mind are too numerous and too involved to warrant discussion at this mo-ment. Suffice it to say, however, that we have been nurtured in the democratic atmosphere. We live in a land which has carried the democratic spirit — not far enough to be sure — but further than any other nation on earth. And we have come to believe that any society, to be free, must be governed by "the consent of the governed"; it must have the power to set up its own constitution and the power to amend it whenever conditions call for amendment. It must choose its representatives and its law makers; it must create instruments for the enforcement of its laws, and courts for the interpretations of those laws.

Many Jewish spokesmen are fervent defenders of democracy in the abstract, or when it is applied elsewhere. But an attempt to apply the criteria of democracy to Jewish law is met with resistance. They, it seems, would like to have their cake and eat it too. They would enjoy the taste of liberalism and at the same time retain the cake of authoritarianism. This is clear from their refusal to acknowledge that Jewish law may be put in the same category as other law. Only one feature of the democratic creed do they accept — and this in an oblique and misleading manner, namely that Jewish law has always represented and must continue to represent the consent of the governed. The concept of "Catholic Israel" with which we are all familiar, maintains that only those values and practices became authoritative law which somehow reflected the will of the people.

The fact is that there is no truly accurate basis for this assumption. That the laws persisted is no proof. The Jewish people certainly accepted them in time. There is no indication that, if presented with alternatives, they might not have chosen otherwise. But even if we assume that the decisions of the rabbis which persisted in Jewish law always reflected the will of the people, is there any reason for assuming further that the will of the people never changes? Setting up tradition as the criterion of what is good is tantamount to asserting that our ancestors never made a mistake. It is hardly seemly in this day and age for us to maintain that Catholic Israel was infallible, that all that future generations can do is to hope, by interpretations here and there, to make such adjustments as are necessary to keep Israel on the correctly chosen path of *halachah*. The defenders of the Catholic Israel concept are frequent critics of Jewish nationalists whose creed, it is said, reeks of chauvinism. Is there, however, any greater chauvinism than that clearly implied in the doctrine that everything which has been is true and good and beautiful, and that all innovations are inherently degenerations?

A curious anomaly is that if the doctrine of the *rightness of the actual* were to be applied to our own generation, we should be shocked to discover what the general will seems to be. Catholic Israel today, by and large, as we come upon it in our daily rounds, spurns the ancient sanctities of our faith, neglects or rejects the time-hallowed standards of Jewish actions and attitudes. Obviously, under no possible interpretation can this composite of ignorance, scorn, and neglect be tolerated as the norm of Jewish life.

Shall we then say that the spirit of Catholic Israel be acceptable only when it coincides with our own? Are we free to choose which period of Jewish history should be the norm and which the abnormal? If we permit ourselves that choice, are we not in reality exercising a personal option? Are we not really setting ourselves and our needs and wants above the law?

These considerations are set forth here merely as commentary upon a basic contention, namely, that if we take the concept of Jewish law seriously, we must transpose it into the key of modern thought. We must have the courage to achieve the democratic revolution. We must face the fact that although kings in their day were, so to speak, *chosen* by the people and hailed as their rulers, we today prefer to ascertain through the ballot who shall serve us in the state. And while our ancestors gladly accepted the yoke of the Torah, Jews today would prefer to have a hand in the fashioning of that yoke. That is the spirit of our time. If the spirit of the next generation is different, I may have to accomodate myself to having my grandchildren revert to authoritarianism.

A not unimportant fact to be considered in this change from pure interpretation of an unalterable law to free and revocable legislation, is the role of the average Jewish citizen in his relation to Jewish life. The elementary law of psychology dictates that responsibility is deeply interwoven with initiative. When a person has a share in the making of a law, he has a stake in it, and is more likely to defend it from abuse or neglect. The average citizen in the state is expected to develop more loyalty to a free nation than to a nation of slaves. Our Jewish laity have had no share in the framing of Jewish law. Under the stress of uncongenial circumstances, they have abandoned it. There remains, however, enough loyalty to Jewish life as a whole as yet so that a sense of responsibility may be rekindled. This can be done, however, only with the spark of initiative. No Jew who believes in the literal truth of supernatural revelation needs that spark, any more than the citizen of any pre-modern nation needed it, who believed sincerely in the divine right of kings.

"How can we permit the average Jew to have a voice in Jewish law? What does he know? He should leave it to the experts." This is the inevitable series of questions and comments that follow. How reminiscent of reaction which does not trust the common man to vote, which fears only the tyranny of the majority, or, when more candid, the tyranny of the mob. Yet, somehow, faith in the common man grows more justified as it is practiced. Responsibility leads to knowledge, since knowledge is then truly motivated. The democratic nations have far to go in this direction, but to turn about now would lead straight to disaster. In reality, the common man does not write the laws himself; experts do that, and legislatures must become expert in many things. But the fact that the legislatures are responsible to an enlightened constituency and dependent upon them for reelection goes a long way toward assuming that the laws they devise correspond to some extent to the popular will.

With the introduction of legislation into Jewish life a similar condition will prevail. We rabbis will be called upon to write the laws — if we are expert enough; expert laity will not be excluded. But those of us will be elected to do the job who satisfy the constituents that we stand upon a general platform which they endorse.

All of this, of course, implies a context. We cannot properly speak of law and legislation and constituencies and law makers, and at the same time avoid a certain dream-like quality, unless we posit the existence of an organized society, in which all these occur and through which they operate. In this country, for the past generation, we have been attempting to function in Jewish life without benefit of community, a strange and unprecedented phenomenon for Jews who wish to live by their Jewish law. We have in a sense grown accustomed to do without the over-arching community structure, and we imagine that we can do without it indefinitely. The fact that Jewish law has been neglected does not seem to gear (in our thinking) into the fact that our community has been liquidated. But the relation exists nevertheless; and our failure to think so does not alter the relation.

In New York, an unsuccessful attempt was made a generation ago to establish a *kehillah*. Whatever may have been the reasons for its demise, one reason must be clearly ruled out, and that is that Jewry did not nor does not stand in need of such a community organization. Strangely enough, events have by their own inexorable character turned the tide in our day, and we are witnessing a return to the communal-mindedness so essential to Jewish life. From fragmentation we are moving in the direction of consolidation. From individualism we are slowly but surely redirecting our steps toward cooperative and communal action. Jews have come around to realizing that they have more in common than they have issues which divide them.

Paradoxically, at this precise moment when American Jewry is retrieving the sense of *Klal Yisrael*, and striving to express that sense in some form of *Keneset Yisrael*, we religious leaders are beating strategic retreats. We are, step by step, narrowing the area over which we retain so tenuous a hold, and interpret religion in very constricting terms. We have surrendered philanthropy. We have had to yield up social service. We have hardly any beachhead in center and recreation work. Defense is out of our hands. Zionism is carried on by others. And even in education, as it becomes more and more the responsibility of the community, our influence wanes. We are left with our prayers, our rituals, and our dubious sway over marital affairs. The *halachah*, as much of it as is still recognized, has ceased to be a broad highway on which Israel travels, but a narrow, unfrequented footpath.

In the meantime, no law governs the relation of a Jew to his synagogue, a Jew to his fellow-Jew within the Jewish community. No law regulates the responsibility of a Jew toward the community, financially and morally. In the meantime, *kashrut* remains the private hunting ground of profit-seeking business men and a drain on the financial resources of the pious. In the meantime, synagogues are run for private profit and Jews bring questions of Jewish life before the civil authorities to bring shame upon themselves and upon all Jews. All our discussions concerning Jewish law, whether the method of interpretation be regarded as adequate, or whether legislation appear necessary, are just so much academic exercise until some contextual framework is established within which the law can function. Much frustration is in store for us unless we mobilize our forces for a reorganization of our entire Jewish life along the lines which, in the *galut* and in *Eretz Yisrael* both, have proved indispensable to our healthy survival and growth. A well organized and democratically conducted community would heal the schism which now separates laity from rabbinate, secular from religious, law from life. It would arouse new interest in the entire problem of Jewish law, and draw in the talents of our legalists among the judges and lawyers who today bestow their gifts upon the general community and leave us deprived.

Need I add that this community would differ in many crucial ways from the *kehillah* of our European ancestors? It would neither seek nor welcome official recognition by our government. It would not in any way affect our status on the American scene. American Jews would be free to affiliate with it or to keep aloof from it. But for those who are within such a community, it would constitute the visible, tangible evidence of our peoplehood and the instruments through which our ethical and spiritual ideals which we persistently profess are realized in life,

Although American Jewry may be said to have begun to come of age, many years must pass before the community organization appropriate to the American scene will emerge. The first faltering steps were taken recently in the formation of the American Jewish Conference. Though it has now transpired that the Conference as constituted was doomed to fail in the purpose some of its adherents set up for it, namely, to become the instrument for American Jewish communal organizations, the experience of the Conference was a healthy and necessary one. It showed how not to establish the American *kehillah*. But until its successor is conceived and brought forth, precious time will have been spent and the condition of Jewish law will have deteriorated perhaps beyond repair. Unless some interim action be taken between now and the devoutly to be wished for establishment of a rational system of Jewish self-government, we shall perhaps have lost our one chance to reclaim for Jewish law the role it must play in our lives.

The alternative to further waiting is action. As rabbis we still can act for and with our congregations. We can apply the principles of democratic legislation in those limited areas where we still exercise some measure of control. Our congregants are clamoring for an end to the present chaos in their Jewish way of life. They are by and large prepared to abide by decisions taken by the Rabbinical Assembly and the United Synagogue. Such decisions, of course, will not bind other groups of religious bodies, nor those Jews who stand outside congregational organizations. It would bind those who share in the making of the decisions.

If this means that even a portion of the Rabbinical Assembly and only some of the United Synagogue congregations are prepared to take the approach here suggested, it would still be necessary for them to proceed alone — and for the rest, if they are unwilling to go along, to give their blessing to those who are determined to go forward. As long as even one segment of the Conservative movement breaks the log jam which has been created over a generation, new hope will be engendered, new confidence will be infused into the entire constituency of our institutions. Action will lead to action. There will be disagreement and perhaps even controversy; but these will be signs of life, wholesome evidences of recovery from the paralysis which has gripped the movement.

We live in an age of rapid change, an age of daring and *halutziut*. New ways are being sought to come to grips with new life situations. In American Israel, too, there is need of vision and courage, of bold and imaginative action. We need the kind of courage and vision which Professor Louis Ginzberg describes in his Introductory Essay on the Palestinian Talmud, and I quote:

> The time was certainly ripe for legislation. Every student of the history of jurisprudence knows that great as are the possibilities of interpretation and commentation, an old code has limits beyond which it cannot be stretched. When the breaking point is reached, legislation comes to the rescue, abrogating obsolete laws and adding new ones which conform to the demands of the age. But how dare one tamper with sacred scripture, in which the Divine Will is revealed? The sages and scholars of that time — about the middle of the Hasmonean era — had the necessary temerity. They took a very important step towards formulating what might be called *de facto* though not *de jure*, a new code; they created the Mishnah.

Let us hope that we shall be worthy in our generation of our great ancestors.

INTRODUCTORY NOTE
ON ZIONISM

The vision of Zion restored has been an integral part of Jewish thought and of religious ritual and liturgy for many centuries. In modern times the Zionist movement has sought to translate this ancient hope into reality. To do so, however, it had to address itself not merely to political work but to the regeneration of the Jewish consciousness, the Jewish people and the Hebrew language and culture.

It was almost inevitable that the Conservative movement which sought many of the same objectives should, from its inception, make Zionism a fundamental part of its program. Alone, among the Jewish religious groupings in America, the Conservative movement has been totally arrayed on the side of Zionism through all the years.

The best statement of what the Zionist movement was and ought to be, as viewed from the standpoint of Conservative Judaism, is the essay published by Dr. Solomon Schechter in 1906 and here reprinted. It remains, after the lapse of time and change of circumstances, a fundamental statement of what Zionism means to the Conservative Jew. It does not, however, stand alone. At convention after convention the Rabbinical Assembly and United Synagogue have issued statements on Zionism and on Israel. These have been elaborated in many statements, books and papers of individuals in the movement.

It is not possible to reflect the variety of pronouncements which have been made on Zionism and the State of Israel in the Conservative movement. However, in the light of the fact that Zionism has, in part, passed from aspiration into the reality of the State of Israel, several excerpts from statements made at conventions and from resolutions are printed below to indicate how this fact has affected the thought and program of the Conservative movement.

ZIONISM: A STATEMENT*

By Rabbi Solomon Schechter

There is a story told of a German Jew of the older generation that when his friends came to him about the beginning of the "eighties" of the last century, and asked what he thought of these *new* attacks on the Jews, he looked rather astonished, and said, "They are not new; they are the old ones." I may say with equal justice that the attacks on Zionism which have come lately from press and pulpit are not new. They have been refuted ever so many times, and have been as often repeated. Lest, however, my ignoring direct challenges would, in accordance with the old rule, "Silence is tantamount to admission," be taken as a proof that I have at last become converted by the arguments of our opponents, I will state here clearly the reasons for my allegiance to Zionism. I wish only to premise that I am no official expounder of Zionism. I am not claiming or aspiring to the role of leadership in this movement. The following remarks have only the value of representing the opinion of one of the rank and file, stating clearly his attitude towards this movement, though he believes that he reflects the views of a great number of fellow Zionists.

Zionism is an ideal, and as such is indefinable. It is thus subject to various interpretations and susceptive of different aspects. It may appear to one as the rebirth of national Jewish consciousness, to another as a religious revival, whilst to a third it may present itself as a path leading to the goal of Jewish culture; and to a fourth it

---

* First published in pamphlet form, December 28, 1906. Also see pp. 100 f. in this volume.

may take the form of the last and only solution of the Jewish problem. By reason of this variety of aspects, Zionism has been able to
unite on its platform the most heterogeneous elements; representing Jews of all countries, and exhibiting almost all the different
types of culture and thought as only a really great and universal
movement could command. That each of its representatives should
emphasize the particular aspect most congenial to his way of thinking, and most suitable for his mode of action, is only natural. On
one point, however, they all agree, namely, that it is not only
desirable, but absolutely necessary, that Palestine, the land of our
fathers, should be recovered with the purpose of forming a home
for at least a portion of the Jews, who would lead there an independent national life. That the language of the leaders was
sometimes ambiguous and not quite definite in the declaration of
this principle is owing to the boldness of the proposition and the
environments in which these leaders were brought up, where everything distinctly Jewish was in need of an apology, rather than to
any doubt about the final aim of Zionism, as conceived in the
minds of the great majority of Zionists. Nor was it strange that
some backslidings should occur, and that in moments of despair,
counsels of despair should prevail, considering the terrible crises
through which we have passed during the last few years. The great
majority of Zionists remain loyal to the great idea of Zion and
Jerusalem, to which history and tradition, and the general Jewish
sentiment, point. It is "God's country" in the fullest and truest
sense of the words. It is the "Promised Land" still maintaining its
place in every Jewish heart, excepting those, perhaps, with whom
Jewish history commences about the year 1830, and Jewish literature is confined to the transactions of the Rabbinical synods of the
last century, and the files of Philippson's *Allgemeine Zeitung des
Judenthums.*

To me personally, after long hesitation and careful watching,
Zionism recommends itself as the great bulwark against assimilation. By assimilation I do not understand what is usually understood by Americanization: namely, that every Jew should do his
best to acquire the English language; that he should study American history and make himself acquainted with the best productions of American literature; that he should be a law-abiding
citizen, thoroughly appreciating the privilege of being a member

of this great commonwealth, and joyfully prepared to discharge the duties of American citizenship. What I understand by assimilation is loss of identity; or that process of disintegration which, passing through various degrees of defiance of all Jewish thought and of disloyalty to Israel's history and its mission, terminates variously in different lands. In Germany, for instance (where the pressure from above in favor of the dominant religion is very strong), it ends in direct and public apostasy; in other countries where this pressure has been removed, it results in the severance of all affiliation with the synagogue, and is followed by a sort of "eclectic religiosity," that coquettes with the various churches, not neglecting even the Christian Science Temple, and is consummated by a final, though imperceptible, absorption in the great majority. This consummation will surely be hastened by the gradual disappearance of social disparity. What this process finally means for Judaism will perhaps be best seen from the following quotation from Wellhausen's *History of Israel*. After giving Spinoza's oft-quoted view regarding the possibilities of the absorption of Israel by its surroundings, the well-known Bible critic remarks: "The persistency of the race may, of course, prove a harder thing to overcome than Spinoza has supposed; but, nevertheless, he will be found to have spoken truly in declaring that the so-called emancipation of the Jews must inevitably lead to the extinction of Judaism wherever the process is extended beyond the political to the social sphere."

The only comfort that Wellhausen leaves us is that "for the accomplishment of this, centuries may be required." We, and the few generations that are to succeed us, are to cheerfully abide in this intermediate condition, and to acquiesce in the tortures of a slow death; or, as the great Alexandrian sage in his description of the punishment awaiting the specially wicked, expresses it, we are "to live continually dying," and to endure an unceasing dissolution until death will have mercy upon us and will give us the last *coup de grace*.

It is this kind of assimilation, with the terrible consequences indicated, that I dread most; even more than pogroms. To this form of assimilation, Zionism in the sense defined will prove, and is already proving a most wholesome check. Whatever faults may be found with its real or self-appointed leaders, Zionism as a whole

forms an opposing force against the conception of the destiny of
Israel and the interpretation of its mission, the leading thought of
which is apparently the well-known epigram, "Whosoever shall
seek to gain his life shall lose it, but whosoever shall lose his life
shall preserve it." Zionism declares boldly to the world that Judaism means to preserve its life by *not* losing its life. It shall be a true
and healthy life, with a policy of its own, a religion wholly its own,
invigorated by sacred memories and sacred environments, and
proving a tower of strength and of unity not only for the remnant
gathered within the borders of the Holy Land, but also for those
who shall, by choice or necessity, prefer what now constitutes the
Galuth.

The term Galuth is here loosely used, expressing, as I have
often heard it, the despair and helplessness felt in the presence of a
great tragedy. And the tragedy is not imaginary. It is real, and it
exists everywhere. It *is* a tragedy to see a great ancient people,
distinguished for its loyalty to its religion, and its devotion to its
sacred law, losing thousands every day by the mere process of attrition. It *is* a tragedy to see sacred institutions as ancient as the
mountains, to maintain which Israel for thousands of years shrank
from no sacrifice, destroyed before our very eyes and exchanged
for corresponding institutions borrowed from hostile religions. It
is a tragedy to see a language held sacred by all the world, in which
Holy Writ was composed, and which served as the depository of
Israel's greatest and best thought, doomed to oblivion and forced
out gradually from the synagogue. It *is* a tragedy to see the descendants of those who revealed revelation to the world and who developed the greatest religious literature in existence, so little familiar
with real Jewish thought, and so utterly wanting in all sympathy
with it, that they have no other interpretation to offer of Israel's
scriptures, Israel's religion, and Israel's ideals and aspirations and
hopes, than those suggested by their natural opponents, slavishly
following their opinions, copying their phrases, repeating their
catchwords, not sparing us even the taunt of tribalism and Orient-
alism. I am not accusing anybody. I am only stating facts that are
the outcome of causes under which we all labor, but for none of
which any party in particular can be made responsible, though it
cannot be denied that some among us rather made too much virtue
of a necessity, and indulged, and are still indulging in experiments

in euthanasia. The economic conditions under which we live; the innate desire for comfort; the inherent tendency towards imitation; the natural desire not to appear peculiar; the accessibility of theological systems, possessing all the seductions of "newness and modernity," patronized by fashion and even by potentates, and taught in ever so many universities, and condensed in dozens of encyclopedias, are sufficient and weighty enough causes to account for our tragedy. But, however natural the causes may be, they do not alter the doom. The effects are bound to be fatal. The fact thus remains that we are helpless spectators in the face of great tragedies, in other words, that we are in Galuth. This may not be the Galuth of the Jews, but it is the Galuth of Judaism, or, as certain mystics expressed it, the Galuth of *Hannephesh*, the Galuth of the Jewish soul wasting away before our very eyes. With a little modification we might repeat here the words of a Jewish Hellenist of the second century who, in his grief, exclaims: "Wherefore is Israel given up as a reproach to the heathen, and for what cause is the people whom Thou best loved given unto ungodly nations, and why is the law of our forefathers brought to naught, and the written covenants come to none effect? And we pass away out of the world as grasshoppers, and our life is astonishment and fear, and we are not worthy to obtain mercy."

The foregoing remarks have made it clear that I belong to that class of Zionists that lay more stress on the religious-national aspects of Zionism than on any other feature peculiar to it. The rebirth of Israel's national consciousness, and the revival of Israel's religion, or, to use a shorter term, the revival of Judaism, are inseparable. When Israel found itself, it found its God. When Israel lost itself, or began to work at its self-effacement, it was sure to deny its God. The selection of Israel, the indestructibility of God's covenant with Israel, the immortality of Israel as a nation, and the final restoration of Israel to Palestine, where the nation will live a holy life on holy ground, with all the wide-reaching consequences of the conversion of humanity and the establishment of the Kingdom of God on earth — all these are the common ideals and the common ideas that permeate the whole of Jewish literature extending over nearly four thousand years, including the largest bulk of the Hellenistic portion of it. The universalistic passages in the Scripture usually paraded by the "prophetic Jew" as implying the final disappearance, or extinction of Israel, are in every case misquotations torn from their context, or ignoring other utterances by the same writer. Indeed, our prophetic Jew

> "Boldly pilfers from the Pentateuch:
> And, undisturbed by conscientious qualms,
> Perverts, the Prophets, and purloins the Psalms."

The interpretations smuggled into the passages are just as false and unscientific as the well-known Christological passages extracted from the Old Testament, and even from the Talmud, to be met with in missionary tracts, composed especially for the benefit of fresh converts.

The reproach that Zionism is unspiritual is meaningless. Indeed, there seems to be a notion abroad that spirituality is a negative quality. Take any ideal, and translate it into action, any sentiment of reverence, and piety, and give it expression through a symbol or ceremony, speak of the human yearning after communion with God, and try to realize it through actual prayer, and you will be at once denounced as unspiritual. However, the imputation is as old as the days when the name Pharisee became a reproach, and it is not to be expected that the Zionists would be spared. In general, it is the antinominian who will tell you that he is the only heir to the rare quality of spirituality, whereas the real saint is in all his actions so spontaneous and so natural that he is entirely unconscious of possessing spirituality, and practically never mentions it.

The Zionists are no saints, but they may fairly claim that few movements are more free from the considerations of convenience and comfort, and less tainted with worldliness and other worldliness than the one which they serve. Nothing was to be gained by joining it. All the powers that be, were, and still are, opposed to it, whether in their capacity as individuals or as wealthy corporations. The Zionists are just beginning to be tolerated, but I remember distinctly the time when adhesion to the cause of Zionism might interfere with the prospects of a man's career, the cry being, "no Zionists need apply." The classes from which the Zionists were recruited were mostly the poorest among the poor. College men and university men, more blessed with enthusiasm and idealism than with the goods of this world, also furnished a fair quota. But this lack of means did not prevent them from responding most generously to every appeal made on behalf of the cause. They taxed themselves to the utmost of their capacity, and beyond. I myself have witnessed cases in which men and women joyfully contributed their last earnings, foregoing their summer vacations, for which they had been saving a whole year.

The activity of Zionism must not be judged by what it has accomplished *in* Zion and Jerusalem — where it has to deal with political problems as yet not ripe for solution — but by what it has thus far achieved *for* Zion and Jerusalem, through the awakening of the national Jewish consciousness, notwithstanding the systematic and ruthless efforts made in the opposite direction during the greater part of the last century. Our synagogues and our homes plainly show the effect. Zion and Jerusalem have not been allowed to stand as a sad, glorious remembrance of a past, as mere objects of pious sentiment. Indeed, the astounding discovery was made that far from being considered as a day of disaster, the Ninth of Ab has to be looked upon as a day of liberation, when Judaism threw off the shackles of nationalism to congeal into a mere Church — with a ritual and a body of doctrines to be promulgated some nineteen hundred years later. Unfortunately, Israel was smitten with blindness, failing to understand its real destiny, and in the perversion of its heart, for eighteen hundred years observed the Ninth of Ab as a day of mourning and weeping, of humiliation and fasting, thus wilfully delaying its redemption. I have always wondered that the Church was not yet enterprising enough to put up a statue in gratitude to its benefactor Titus, the *delectus generis humani*, representing the goddess *Universa*, with a scribe and a priest cowering in chains at her feet.

The work, accordingly, in which Zionism had to engage first, and in which it will have to continue for many years to come, was the work of regeneration. It had to re-create the Jewish consciousness before creating the Jewish state. In this respect, Zionism has already achieved great things. There is hardly a single Jewish community in any part of the globe which is not presented by a larger or smaller number of men and women acknowledging themselves as Zionists and standing out as a living protest against the tendencies just hinted at. It has created a press, and has called into life a host of lecturers and speakers propagating its doctrines and preaching them boldly to Israel all over the world. It has given the world Asher Ginzberg, or, as he is better known, by the pen name of Achad Ha-am, one of our finest intellects and most original thinkers; and he is followed by a whole host of disciples, all of them working under the stimulus of the Jewish national ideal, much as they may differ in the Zionistic aspects they happen to emphasize. It has enriched our literature with a large number of novels and lyrics, and even distinct Zionist melodies are not wanting. It has further called into existence numerous societies, whose aim it is to make the sacred tongue a living language by means of writing and even coversing in it, while in several communities special schools have been established with the same end in view. To better advance this end, a whole series of Hebrew primers, grammars and reading books for the young have been produced. Several translations prepared from German, French and English works bearing on Jewish history and cognate subjects, all of them calculated to strengthen religious-national consciousness, have also appeared under the inspiration of Zionism. Foremost of all, Zionism has succeeded in bringing back into the fold many men and women, both here and in Europe, who otherwise would have been lost to Judaism. It has given them a new interest in the synagogue and everything Jewish, and put before them an ideal worthy of their love and their sacrifice. Cases have come under my notice where Jewish college men, at a comparatively advanced age, began to study the sacred language and to repair to the synagogue, sharing both in its joys and in its griefs, some among them encountering the displeasure and ridicule of their relatives, who were fanatical assimilators and who bring up their children without religious education of any kind. Of course, backslidings and relapses occur; but it is an advantage to Zionism that in its present condition, at least, it is all sacrifice and no gain. It holds out no prospect to the ambitious and to "those who exalt themselves to establish the vision" of a Jewish state without Jewish memories, without historic foundation and without traditional principles. The undesirables and the impatient will thus, under one pretense or another, leave it soon, and indeed are dropping out already, so that its purification of all alloy and discordant elements is only a question of a very short time.

The taunt of retrogression and reaction has no terror for us. To insist on progressing when one has come to the conclusion that a step forward means ruin is sheer obstinacy. Unless we are convinced so deeply of our infallibility that we take every utterance of ours as a divine revelation, and our every action as a precedent and a tradition, there may come a time in our lives when we may have to return. As a fact, Zionism is the natural rebound from an artificial and overstrained condition of things which could no longer last. It is the Declaration of Jewish Independence from all kinds of slavery, whether material or spiritual. It is as natural and instinctive as life itself, and no amount of scolding and abuse will prevent the reassertion of the Jewish soul which in our unconscious Zionism is an actual present-day experience, though the expression given to it takes different shape in different minds. Moreover, Zionism thoroughly believes in progress and development; but it must be progress along Jewish lines, and the goal to be reached must be the Jewish historic ideal.

But, whilst Zionism is constantly winning souls for the present, it is at the same time preparing us for the future, which will be a Jewish future. Only then, when Judaism has found itself, when the Jewish soul has been redeemed from the Galuth, can Judaism hope to resume its mission to the world. Everybody whose view has not been narrowed by the blinkers imposed on him by his little wing or by party considerations, knows well enough that it is not only traditional religion which is on trial. We are on a veritable volcano created by the upheavals of the newest methods of "searching research," which respects as little the new formulae, such as the categoric imperative, conscience, the notion of duty and the concept of morality and ethics, as it does creeds and dogmas. The disruption may come at any moment unless revelation is reasserted. The declaration, *Freedom is our Messiah,* which I have so often heard, may be good Fourth of July oratory, but it is miserably bad theology, and worse philosophy, having in view the terrible woes and complicated problems besetting humanity. Now, what happened once may happen again, and Israel may another time be called upon with its mission to the nations. Under the present conditions, however, we have neither a defined mission, nor does any man take this "mission" seriously, and the talk about it is allowed to be a mere *licencia predicatorum.* But we know that the Bible which influenced humanity so deeply and proved so largely instrumental in the partial conversion of the world, arose in Palestine or in circles which looked on Palestine as their home. Those who wrote the Bible moved and had their whole being in the religious national idea, and lived under the discipline of the Law. History may, and to my belief, will repeat itself, and Israel will be the chosen instrument of God for the new and final mission; but then Israel must first effect its own redemption and live again its own life, and be Israel again, to accomplish its universal mission. The passages in the Bible most distinguished for their universalistic tendency and grandeur are, as is well known, the verses in Isaiah and Micah, and there it is solemnly proclaimed: "Out of Zion shall go forth the law, and the word of the Lord from Jerusalem."

Our sages have themselves given expression to this correspondence between the universalistic and the nationalistic elements in Judaism. A solemn declaration, thus they declare, has the Holy One, blessed be He, registered: "I will not enter the heavenly Jerusalem, until Israel shall come to the earthly Jerusalem." Not in conflict but in consonance with Israel's establishment of the divine institutions in their full integrity in God's own land, will be the triumph in all its glory of the Kingdom of Heaven.

OUR SHARE IN ERETZ YISRAEL*

By Rabbi Moshe Davis

As members of the Conservative Movement we have a special collective commitment to *Eretz Yisrael* which goes beyond the established pattern.

The United Synagogue is exactly what its name says it is: a *union* of synagogues — a religious brotherhood. Our particular commitment to *Eretz Yisrael* must therefore be directed to the religious and educational tasks of Israel's future. We look forward to the day when the young State will be not only a cultural force in the world, but will become once again, as it was in the days of the prophets, a source of spiritual insight and human hope for the family of the world. In the realization of this aspiration, we in the Conservative movement want to have an active share, as part of our own total commitment to the ideals of Judaism . . . .

What, then, is the measure of our own contribution to *Eretz Yisrael*? What does Israel require of us now more than anything else?

The assurance that in American Jewry it has a firm partner in the creative enterprise of the Jewish people and in the transmission of the Jewish Faith.

And what do we require of ourselves in this relationship?

The feeling that we can offer to this partnership not only our material resources but our spiritual strength as well; the assurance

---

* A selection from an address delivered at the United Synagogue Convention, November, 1955.

of our ability to *give* Torah to Israel as well as to receive spiritual guidance from *Eretz Yisrael*.

In order to achieve these ends, the *Eretz Yisrael* program of the Conservative movement must be based on two fundamental propositions.

First, that the greatest contribution we can make to *Eretz Yisrael* is to build an authentic, indigenous and creative Jewish community in America based on the solid foundations of the Tradition. As Dr. Kaplan writes in his *A New Zionism*: "Zionism can emerge from its present crisis strengthened by the experience of challenge and danger. It can lead to the fulfillment of the prophecy that 'from Zion shall go forth Torah,' but before the Torah can go forth from Zion it will have to enter into Zionism." This is the beginning of our task: actually to bring Torah into our lives and into the life of Zionism. Thus, just as Israel has become a vital factor in the recent intensification of Jewish life in America, so will a flourishing and *creative* American Jewry become an important factor in the cultural advancement of the *Yishuv*.

We must not be appalled by the thought that we, too, must bring Torah to *Eretz Yisrael*. In fact, unless this is our ambition, it is inconceivable that we can ever have a full share in the Land. Nor will we be in a position to make a meaningful contribution to the totality of Jewish life. American Jewry is accepted in the council of world Jewry essentially because of its numbers and material strength, but we shall never make a fundamental contribution to the inner life of world Jewry unless we re-orient ourselves about Torah and its teachings . . . .

The second premise on which our program should be based is personal religious commitment. *Aliyah*, that is, settlement in *Eretz Yisrael*, is a word which we avoid out of the fear that any positive affirmation of an American *Aliyah* implies a choice against America.

What is the purpose of *Aliyah*?

Generally, one thinks of *Aliyah* as a program for building Israel. That is obvious! What should be equally obvious is that *Aliyah* is vital to build the American Jewish community, to help create in America an authentic Judaism. A Jewish community that wants to be part of the mainstream of the Jewish tradition should inspire a portion of its numbers to *want* to go up to Jerusalem; otherwise it may not succeed in becoming a *Jewish* community at all. *Yishuv*

Eretz Yisrael, settlement of the Holy Land, is a historic function of all diasporic communities, and the *Aliyah* of select individuals and groups of settlers has always added to the quality of the Jewish community at home, precisely because of the religious significance of *Eretz Yisrael* in Jewish life.

Our religious commitment to *Eretz Yisrael* ought to be that *every* Jew identifies himself with the Land and feels part of it. Those who do not go — for whatever reason — are subject nevertheless to the requirements of Jewish life and discipline. We have been given six hundred and thirteen *mitzvot*. No Jew fulfills all of them. But the Jewish people fulfill all of them as a *people*. Therefore it is a serious mistake to equate any individual's given situation or decision at a particular time with the total experience of the entire Jewish community.

We must look at the decision of *Aliyah* as a collective decision of the American Jewish community. American Jewry collectively should adopt *Aliyah* as a permanent part of its program and its teachings, just as it teaches other *mitzvot*. We do not know who will go, or whose life will be fulfilled by *Aliyah*, but we do know that if part of us will be there, we will be there, America will be there. Fulfilled as a religious ideal, Americans who understand the American tradition, will honor those, who through their *Aliyah*, will pioneer in the furtherance of religious brotherhood and world democracy. And our own American Jewish Community will be spiritually stronger to advance towards its own native program and goals.

A RESOLUTION OF THE UNITED SYNAGOGUE OF AMERICA ON RELATIONS WITH ISRAEL*

WHEREAS, the Conservative movement, while always recognizing that the bonds between American Jewry and the Jews in Israel can and should never be any other than spiritual and religious, has from its very inception been devoted to the ideal of the establishment of a politically independent Jewish community in the Holy Land, and

We of the United Synagogue have in the past given substantial expression to our desire to build such spiritual and religious bonds between the American Jewish Community and our brethren in Israel through the building of the Jeshurun Synagogue in Jerusalem, and

We believe that the continued development of further spiritual and religious bonds between us and them is of the utmost importance to the future of Judaism in the world, and

The recognized leaders of the State of Israel, its President, the Honorable Isaac Ben Zvi, its Prime Minister, the Honorable David Ben Gurion, and others, have expressed a sincere and enthusiastic interest in our United Synagogue Israel Project, and

WHEREAS, the Jewish National Fund has set aside for our purposes a site in the most desirable area of Jerusalem which we must actively begin to occupy no later than August, 1955,

---

* Adopted at the 1953 Convention.

THEREFORE, BE IT RESOLVED THAT

A.   The United Synagogue of America, in convention assembled, greets with enthusiasm the establishment of the Israel Project in co-operation with The Jewish Theological Seminary of America and The Rabbinical Assembly of America.

B.   That we endorse the program of the Project:

1. To build a *Pnimiyah*, a residence hall in Jerusalem where every student of the Rabbinical School and the Teachers Institute may ultimately be able to spend a year of study in Israel.

2. To encourage religious life and thought in Israel.

3. To publish works that could help to bring the best creative thought of one community to the other.

4. To encourage our synagogue members to visit Israel in groups under the auspices of the United Synagogue.

A NEW ZIONISM*

By Rabbi Mordecai M. Kaplan

We need a new kind of Zionism, a Zionism which will vitalize the synagogue, motivate interest in Israel, and make for the growth of a civilization that is religiously Jewish, without being theocratic or clerical.

The new Zionism should have as its purpose the redemption of the Jewish people and the regeneration of its spirit. To achieve these purposes the new Zionism has to be based upon a proper understanding of what has enabled world Jewry to survive to our own day, and a correct diagnosis of the weakening of the will to Jewish survival in recent years.

The reason the Jews, as a people, have succeeded in outliving their most cruel persecutors is that the climate of opinion which prevailed in the past was none other than the one which they, the Jews themselves, had generated through their religious civilization. Their very persecutors, whether Christian or Moslem, derived their entire outlook on life, their ideas of God, the world, human nature and destiny almost entirely from the Jewish tradition. That fact was sufficient to convince the Jews that far from being out of step with reality, they were actually its truest exponents. That alone was enough to keep alive their sense of superiority which brought down the assimilatory potential of their environment to a minimum.

From this position of inner security, regardless of what hap-

---

* Selections from an address delivered before the 1954 Convention of the Rabbinical Assembly of America.

pened without, our people was suddenly catapulted, about a century-and-a-half ago, into a climate of opinion which was entirely alien to it. Ever since then, its self-assurance has been replaced by self-questioning, and its sense of pride by a sense of inferiority. No wonder that the assimilatory potential of the environment has grown by leaps and bounds. The case of the Jewish people has come to be like that of a sea animal suddenly thrust by an earthquake onto the land. Unless it can metamorphose itself, and grow the organs essential to life in the new environment, it cannot survive.

Unless the Jewish people develop attitudes of mind and spirit that can fit it to survive in the contemporary atmosphere of this-worldly scientism, nationalism and socialism, it is bound to succumb. Not yet having achieved those attitudes of mind and spirit, Jews suspect that the Jewish people has become an anachronism. This self-doubt, which at times degenerates into self-hate, is undermining the will to Jewish survival.

The metamorphosis we Jews have to undergo involves the reconstruction of Jewish peoplehood, the reclamation of Eretz Yisrael, and the replenishment of Torah. These must, henceforth, become the main objectives of the new Zionism. While these objectives must have their roots in historic Judaism they have to be made relevant to the social, cultural and intellectual realities of the world we live in, even if it be to challenge or modify them in accordance with the dictates of faith, reason and experience.

THE RECONSTRUCTION OF JEWISH PEOPLEHOOD

Without some formal act to reconstitute world Jewry into a self-accepting as well as publicly recognized societal unit, Jews are nothing more than a disbanded nation. The Jewish nation began to break up when its members were admitted as citizens of the Western nations. To be sure, they are still treated as a societal unit by non-Jews who cannot free themselves from their religious tradition, in which Jews figure as a people accursed. Thus the larger portion of the force which sustains the *House* of Israel comes from without rather than from within. That abnormal condition must no longer be permitted to continue. On the other hand, to assume that Jewish nationhood can be reconstituted in Israel is to delude ourselves. Israel as a modern democratic state, must foster *Israeli* nationhood, in which Diaspora Jews can have no part. Their bond of unity is only with the *Jewish community in Israel*. All this makes it evident how imperative it is for Jews throughout the world to reaffirm their unity as a people, which is the bearer of a moral and spiritual tradition. The Jew needs that tradition in order to validate his faith in the God-given capacity to attain salvation and to motivate him in striving to achieve it.

"The group to which an individual belongs is the ground on which he stands," writes Kurt Lewin. "The firmness or weakness of this ground might not be consciously perceived just as the firmness of the physical ground on which we tread is not always thought of. Dynamically, however, the firmness and clearness of this ground determine what the individual wishes to do, what he can do, and how he will do it. This is equally true of the social ground as of the physical."

"Without a sensed reality of a Jewish people," writes Rabbi Theodore Friedman, "my own being as a Jew dissolves into meaninglessness." The individualistic approach to Judaism has given rise to what Ernst Simon aptly calls the "Protestant" point of view. As a matter of fact, it has gone almost all the way of placing itself within the climate of opinion which recent existentialist, neo-orthodox Christianity is trying to generate, and differs from the latter only by a few *sancta*. That approach looks to personal piety as a solution of the present crisis in Jewish religion. It is not, however, as Simon himself admits "a legitimate construction of Judaism as such. When a forest is on fire, is not the time to prune the trees. When a house is about to collapse, as a result of an earthquake, is not the time to discuss with the decorator what kind of draperies to use for the living room. Now that the House of Israel is in danger of collapse is not the time to concentrate on theological or ritual problems to the exclusion of problems affecting the very survival of world Jewry as an identifiable group, to say nothing of surviving as a creative group in the better world that is struggling to be born.

The new Zionism has to find a new designation, or give a new meaning to an old designation, by which to identify the Jews throughout the world as a societal unit. That designation should embrace within its scope the majority of Jews who cannot, or will not, migrate to the State of Israel. It will have to acquire a religious significance, even at the cost of redefining the term religion. Perhaps the old term *people* is best suited for that purpose. World Jewry will have to constitute henceforth a permanent international religio-cultural society known as "a people," with the Jewish community in Israel — but not with the State of Israel — as its most creative nucleus.

Recognizing that need, the Zionist World Congress should appoint a commission to make a thorough study of the problem of group status, with the view of issuing a formal declaration concerning the status of world Jewry and the role of Jewish unity.

THE RECLAMATION OF ERETZ YISRAEL

The second objective of the new Zionism should be the reclamation of Eretz Yisrael. The consolidation of the State of Israel should be treated only as a means, though an absolutely indispensable one, to the actual settlement of Jews in Eretz Yisrael and building there a civilization that is animated by the highest prophetic idealism.

The new Zionism will have to interpret this particular objective in a spirit that reckons with the current climate of opinion with its scientism, nationalism and socialism, by having Eretz Yisrael become the seat of moral and spiritual values which are as superior to these current doctrines as ethical monotheism is superior to various idolatries.

Judaism, by resuming its career in Eretz Yisrael, the land that embodies its highest aspirations, will demonstrate the validity of a highly important principle that is implicit in its tradition. The principle in question is the following: Religion, or the striving for salvation, should normally consist in utilizing as a means to salvation the day-to-day experiences arising from the entire gamut of interaction which a common land makes necessary for those who live in it. This conception of religion gives the Jewish people a high vocation, something to live for, both in the Diaspora and in Israel.

Given that vocation, Jews who live in the Diaspora are likely to act as a brake on the chauvinistic tendencies that the Israeli struggle for suvival is only too apt to arouse in the Jews of Israel. On the other hand, they are also likely to share the experience of the Jews in Eretz Yisrael, together with the moral and spiritual values which those experiences would yield. We need only recall how closely the average American Jew still follows the daily events in Israel and how sensitive he is to what goes on there. "The bond with the Jewish people wherever they may live," recently declared Moshe Sharett, "is the solid foundation of our life, just as the spiritual attachment to the State of Israel is the central fact in the life of the Jewish people." Sharett speaks advisedly of our attachment to the State of Israel as "spiritual." That attachment should exercise a vitalizing and spiritualizing influence on American Jewish life.

If Jews will reconstitute themselves as a people functioning through nationhood in Eretz Yisrael and through religion everywhere, they will place themselves in the vanguard of all peoples that will learn to look to their own national civlizations as sources of personal salvation, but they will, at the same time, realize that they must integrate those civilizations within an international framework. Otherwise, mankind will revert to the national idolatry, with all its nationalist excesses, from which the historical religions if awake to their responsibility, might still save mankind.

Thus, by treating the reclamation of Eretz Yisrael as part of a modern messianic or religious movement, Jews are in a unique position of being able to serve mankind by fostering a method of group-life whereby this-worldly salvation will have to be achieved. That will justify the age-old refusal of the Jewish people to renounce its claim on Eretz Yisrael.

The method of living which is implied in the attachment of the Jewish people to Eretz Yisrael is now in need of being made explicit. That method of living consists of utilizing for self-fulfilment as human beings that wide range of interactivity which is possible only among those who are rooted in a common land. The earthy interests to which this interactivity gives rise should constitute the stuff out of which human beings might mold their destiny. That is the Jewish contribution to the method of salvation of which God is the source and guarantor.